Swarm Intelligence Optimization

Scrivener Publishing
100 Cummings Center, Suite 541J
Beverly, MA 01915-6106

Publishers at Scrivener
Martin Scrivener (martin@scrivenerpublishing.com)
Phillip Carmical (pcarmical@scrivenerpublishing.com)

Swarm Intelligence Optimization

Algorithms and Applications

Edited by

Abhishek Kumar,
Pramod Singh Rathore, Vicente Garcia Diaz

and

Rashmi Agrawal

Scrivener
Publishing

WILEY

This edition first published 2021 by John Wiley & Sons, Inc., 111 River Street, Hoboken, NJ 07030, USA and Scrivener Publishing LLC, 100 Cummings Center, Suite 541J, Beverly, MA 01915, USA
© 2021 Scrivener Publishing LLC
For more information about Scrivener publications please visit www.scrivenerpublishing.com.

Wiley Global Headquarters
111 River Street, Hoboken, NJ 07030, USA

For details of our global editorial offices, customer services, and more information about Wiley products visit us at www.wiley.com.

Limit of Liability/Disclaimer of Warranty

Library of Congress Cataloging-in-Publication Data

ISBN 978-1-119-77874-5

Cover image: Pixabay.Com
Cover design by Russell Richardson

Set in size of 11pt and Minion Pro by Manila Typesetting Company, Makati, Philippines

Contents

Preface

Resource optimization has always been a thrust area of research, and as the Internet of Things (IoT) is the most talked about topic of the current era of technology, it has become the need of the hour. Therefore, the idea behind this book was to simplify the journey of those who aspire to understand resource optimization in the IoT. To this end, included in this book are various real-time/offline applications and algorithms/case studies in the fields of engineering, computer science, information security, and cloud computing, along with the modern tools and various technologies used in systems, leaving the reader with a high level of understanding of various techniques and algorithms used in resource optimization.

Nearly all aspects of resource optimization using the IoT are covered in the 18 chapters of this book. Chapter 1 basically describes what the IoT is, and how electronic devices are connected to the Internet in order to start thinking about and generating the data which can be very beneficial for mankind. The objective of Chapter 2 on the perspectives and foundations of swarm intelligence (SI) is to discuss some biomimicry algorithms and their applications. Along with the basics of SI, ant colony optimization (ACO), bee-inspired algorithms, particle swarm optimization (PSO), bacterial foraging optimization, firefly algorithms, fish swarm optimization, and many more SI algorithms are presented.

Industrial IoT (IIoT)–enhanced energy management systems are created to help advance changes in undertakings. Among the topics covered in Chapter 3 on energy management in IoT are the ability of systems to increment the straightforwardness of vitality utilization insights, improve the workforce consciousness of vitality misfortunes, and give prescient investigation instruments for determining potential modern mishaps and future vitality requests. The main focus of Chapter 4 on healthcare data analytics using SI is on some foundation principles that help to find solutions in optimistic form. This chapter also discusses SI techniques like PSO, ACO, and the use of swarm AI in healthcare; along with the issues and challenges of SI healthcare systems.

Chapter 5 discusses SI for group objects in wireless sensor networks (WSNs), which are utilized in different places as alert finders and sensors. Quantities of grouping calculations have been created to improve the vitality parity of the WSNs on the grounds that vitality is the fundamental part of the WSN during information transmission. These calculations are chiefly utilized for expanding the lifetime of these sensor systems. The support vector machine (SVM) using PSO in various healthcare domains is reviewed in Chapter 6. The PSO is motivated by the social conduct of winged animal rushing and fish tutoring. It is a stochastic optimization algorithm in which each key is regarded as a "particle" and each particle has a fitness value calculated by a function called the "objective function."

In Chapter 7, different bird and insect swarm–based algorithms are studied. Complex problems with incomplete information and dynamic properties are used to resolve different

SI algorithms. In Chapter 8, a design based on an artificial neural network is proposed for automatic detection of epileptic signals from an electroencephalogram dataset obtained from the University of Bonn, Germany, which contains observations from healthy and epileptic brains. Electroencephalogram signals are nonstationary and nonlinear in nature, so it becomes quite difficult for medical doctors to interpret details about the significant data. Therefore, it is important to design a smart system by combining the IoT-based network with artificial intelligence to sense the disease conditions with more accuracy.

The main purpose of Chapter 9 is to present some biological motivations and basic SI concepts using two models: ACO and PSO. These are probabilistic techniques which help to solve computational problems by finding optimistic solutions. Chapter 10 on data management and mining technologies to manage and analyze data in IOT presents a layered reference model for IoT information on the dashboard. IoT has become a functioning zone of research, since it guarantees, among other things, the improvement of the nature and security of smart cities, making assets flexible, and ensuring executives are progressively effective. Also reviewed are advanced traffic management systems applications, including grouping, bunching, affiliation investigation, and time arrangement examination, along with the most recent application cases.

In Chapter 11, the authors supply an orderly technique to audit the mining of facts in order to know the device view and alertness, including characterization, bunching, affiliation examination, time association research, and exception investigation. Furthermore, the most current software instances are likewise overviewed. As an ever-increasing number of gadgets are associated with IoT, a huge amount of records must be dissected and the maximum recent calculations have to be altered to use facts. Authors evaluate these calculations and highlight open research problems associated with them. Finally, an endorsed significant records mining framework is proposed. Chapter 12 answers the frequently asked questions of what, why, how, and where SI can be applied so as to optimize network energy utilization. The chapter covers almost 60+ SI algorithm applications in brief. Furthermore, various issues of WSN clustering and WSN services are presented for the sake of completeness. A major contribution of this chapter is the survey of various SI techniques applied for WSN, in particular for cluster formation and CH selection.

Chapter 13 discusses SI for clustering in WSNs. The term "swarm" refers to a group of flying objects/insects which cooperatively work to achieve a common goal. The concept of "swarm intelligence" means "collective intelligence" inhibited by the group of units involved in a given network. SI owes its roots to the life of social insects (i.e., wasps, ants, bees, and termites), which are known for their organization and for having an efficient communication and warning system, maintaining an army and dividing labor.

System lifetime, discussed in Chapter 14, is a standout among the most critical measurements in wireless body area networks (WBANs). The authors propose a healthcare monitoring system based on IoT which monitors the sensor's data/information to analyze the patient's condition in a mobile WBAN (MWBAN). For this, the implementation of a transfer for determining harmful acts is proposed under the topology which defines a heuristic approach to enhance the network lifetime. Chapter 15 reviews the effectiveness of SI for handling fault-tolerant routing problems in the IoT. The SI algorithms are most effective for handling routing problems in the IoT. Swarm is an optimization algorithm so this chapter presents an in-depth discussion of how the drawbacks present in IoT can be compensated for using SI. The places where IoT is used, its benefits, as well as the use of swarm in different fields are elaborated.

Cluster nodes play a precious role in preserving energy. Clustering perspective targets resolves the collision of data, resulting in useful information being broadcast. In Chapter 16, the authors define some modern adequate clustering approaches for power system control to enhance the life of sensing networks.

Data mining faces challenges in the case of dynamic nodes. These dynamic nodes are a part of smart systems called the IoT and work together with certain techniques to create intelligence. Since SI is one such area that helps to manage data when the nodes are moving and sharing data in a distributed network, Chapter 17 discusses SI models inspired by nature, examines them, and finds implementable models using this technology. Finally, Chapter 18 presents a fundamental overview of different algorithms and performance optimization for SI.

In conclusion, we would like to thank all those who contributed to this book and hope that readers will not only enjoy reading it but also benefit from its contents.

Editorial Team
August 2020

A Fundamental Overview of Different Algorithms and Performance Optimization for Swarm Intelligence

Manju Payal[1]*, Abhishek Kumar[2]† and Vicente García Díaz[3]

Software Developer, Academic Hub, Ajmer, India
Chitkara University Institute of Engineering and Technology, Chitkara University, Rajpura, Punjab, India
Department of Computer Science, Universidad de Oviedo, Asturias, Spain

Abstract

Swarm Intelligence (SI), normally, is based on the problem-solving ability. It solves the problem using the interaction of simple information processing units. It contains some types of the terminologies which are the distribution, multiplicity, messiness, stochasticity, and randomness. The problem-solving approach is based on three terminologies which are suggested by the SI. These terminologies are the creativity, cognition capabilities, and learning. It contains some types of the methods which depend on the optimization techniques. These methods are the ABC, ACO, and PSO. Here, ABC is referred as the Artificial Bees Colony, ACO is referred as the Ant Colony Optimization, and PSO is referred as the Particle Swarm Optimization. It also depends on the scheduling optimization. It is the massive number of homogenous. These methods have grown as, of late, with a bunch of population-based algorithms, nature-driven equipped to quick, deliver least effort, and robust answers to few composite issues. Optimization is the term of the chosen best solution of the problems. It is chosen as the best solution from the set of the solutions. This solution is based on some types of features which are the highest achievable performance, cost effectiveness, and so on.

Keywords: Swarm intelligence, ant colony optimization, artificial bee colony, machine Learning, partical swarm optimization, population algorithms, agents, artificial intelligence

1.1 Introduction

SI is an essential section of the AI. Here, SI is referred as the Swarm Intelligence and AI is referred as the Artificial Intelligence. It is the bio-inspired computation [1]. Now, it has been recognized as a developing field. It was developed by the two professors. These professors are Gerardo Beni and Jing Wang. It was developed since 1989. It is the based on the cellular robotic systems. It consists of many types of algorithms. These algorithms depend on the bio-inspired

Corresponding author: manjupayal771@gmail.com
†*Corresponding author:* abhishek.kumar@chitkara.edu.in

Abhishek Kumar, Pramod Singh Rathore, Vicente Garrcia Diaz and Rashmi Agrawal (eds.) Swarm Intelligence Optimization: Algorithms and Applications, (1–20) © 2021 Scrivener Publishing LLC. ISBN 978-1-119-77874-5

computation. Now, it has the most growing popularity because it consists many types of the SI algorithms. These algorithms consist of many types of the features such as versatility and flexibility. It consists of two most important features which are adaptability and self-learning capability [2]. This features the performance by the SI algorithms. It has identified different types of the application areas. Lately, SI has developed in prevalence with the expanding prominence quality of NP-hard issues where the discovery of a global ideals turns out to be practically inconceivable continuously situation [3]. The quantity of potential arrangements which may exist in such issues frequently will, in general, be unending. In such circumstances, finding a work capable arrangement inside time constraints gets significant. SI discovers its utility in taking care of nonlinear structure issues with real-based applications, thinking about practically all zones of sciences, designing and enterprises, from information mining to enhancement, computational insight, commercial arranging, in bioinformatics, and commercial modern applications. Some top applications contain incorporate route control, planetary motion sensing, interferometry, malignant tumor detection, micro-robot control, micro-robot control, and control [4].

There are some types of instances available in the SI which are the flock of birds, ant colonies, bacterial growth, schools of fish, and so on. It does not contain any type of the centralized control. It depends on the collection of the behavior in the nature [5].

The fundamental objective of the SI is to enhance the performance of the complex problems. It also enhances the solution of the complex problems. The incredible accomplishment of natural swarm systems has led many researchers to find out how to solve complex problems by the swarms in nature [6]. There are three types of the SI algorithms available, which provide the best solutions with the optimal issues. These algorithms are the BA, BCO, and ACO. Here, BA is referred as the Bat algorithms, BCO is referred as the Bee Colony Optimization, and ACO is referred as the Ant Colony Optimization [7].

SI, normally, is based on the problem-solving ability. It solves the problem using the interaction of simple information processing units [8]. It contains some types of the terminologies which are the distribution, multiplicity, messiness, stochasticity, and randomness. The problem-solving approach is based on three terminologies which are suggested by the SI. These terminologies are the creativity, cognition capabilities, and learning. It contains some types of the methods which depend on the optimization techniques. These methods are the ABC, ACO, and PSO. Here, ABC is referred as the Artificial Bees Colony, ACO is referred as the Ant Colony Optimization, and PSO is referred as the Particle Swarm Optimization. It also depends on the scheduling optimization [9].

It is the massive number of homogenous. These methods have grown, as of late, with a bunch of population-based algorithms, nature-driven equipped to quick, deliver least effort, and robust answers to few composite issues [10]. Optimization is the term of the chosen best solution of the problems. It is chosen as the best solution from the set of the solutions. This solution is based on some types of the features which are the highest achievable performance, cost effectiveness, and so on [11]. Finding an option with the most practical or most noteworthy feasible execution under the given requirements is by augmenting wanted factors and limiting undesired ones. In correlation, amplification implies attempting to achieve the most noteworthy or greatest outcome or result regardless of cost [12].

This term can be characterized as the joined mindset of decentralized or self-sifted through structures in normal or reproduced [13]. The inspiration begins from commonly natural structure. SI is a trademark computation since it is created by following the evolution and task behavior of basic animals and dreadful little creatures. The instance of the swarm of birds is the flock of birds. The second instance of the SI is the bee swarming. It is based on the agents that are bees. In case we are about watch a single insect or a bumble bee, we will appreciate that they are not all that sharp, yet, rather their settlements are. Multitude information can help individuals to understand complex systems, from truck controlling to military robots. A settlement can illuminate any issue, for instance, ACO calculation is utilized for finding the most limited way in the system directing issue, and Particle Swarm Intelligence is utilized in optical system improvement [14]. As an individual, the multitude might be little fakers; yet, as provinces, they respond quickly and enough to their condition. There are two kinds of social associations among swarm people, to be specific, direct communication and round-about collaboration [15]. Direct collaborations are the undeniable cooperation through visual or sound contact, for instance, winged creatures communicate with one another with sound. Roundabout communication is known as the Stigmergy [16], where operators collaborate with the earth. A pheromone trail of ants is a case of backhanded association.

SI, an essential part in the field of AI, is continuously retrieving conspicuousness, as increasingly more high multifaceted nature issues require arrangements, which might be imperfect, yet feasible inside a sensible timeframe. For the most part motivated by natural frameworks, swarm knowledge embraces the aggregate conduct of a composed gathering of creatures, as they endeavor to endure [17]. This investigation plans to examine the overseeing thought, distinguish the potential application territories, and present a nitty gritty review of eight SI calculations [18]. The recently evolved calculations examined in the examination are the creepy crawly–based calculations and creature-based calculations in minute detail. All the more explicitly, we center around the calculations roused by ants, honey bees, fireflies, sparkle worms, bats, monkeys, lions, and wolves [19]. The motivation examinations on these calculations feature the manner in which these calculations work [20]. Variations of these calculations have been presented after the motivation examination. Explicit territories for the utilization of such calculations have likewise been featured for analysts inspired by the space. The investigation endeavors to give an underlying comprehension to the investigation of the specialized parts of the calculations and their future extension by the scholarly world and practice [20].

Moreover, SI is not just purposely utilized in multitudes of specialized gadgets. Additionally, in the plan of (advancement) calculations, swarm insight can be applied by taking motivation from multitudes of creatures. In numerous real-world optimization issues, the real target method is not known. For example, if numerous sets of 2D medical pictures, one from CT and one from MRT, must be enlisted, i.e., be adjusted so as to make their structures overlay in an important manner, the pictures must be changed to streamline a closeness metric. The genuine target work relies upon the pictures and cannot be productively streamlined by exceptionally planned calculations. So, this is a run of the mill case, where purported metaheuristics are applied, i.e., techniques that get the target work f as a black box and are looking for an information x* that upgrades f.

1.2 Methodology of SI Framework

It has no any centralized management. It is a decentralized system. Mostly, it contains two advantages which are as follows:

1. Agents

2. Self-Organization

Agents are the collection of the possible solution to a given problem. It is not centralized on the particular agents.

Adding to this are, without a doubt, the SI focal points. Multitude does not have any outside administration; however, every specialist in the multitude controls their conduct self-sufficiently. Specialist for this situation speaks to a potential answer for a given issue. In view of that, we can reason the subsequent bit of leeway, which is self-association. The insight does not concentrate on the individual operator however rises in the multitude itself. Along these lines, the arrangements (operators) of the issue are not known ahead of time, yet change themselves at the hour of the running programming. The self-association assumes a significant job in versatility. The last is recognizable in changing situations where operators react well to the referenced changes, adjust their conduct, and adjust to them self-sufficiently. Furthermore, because there is no focal coordination, the multitude is powerful, as there is no single purpose of disappointment. Besides, the multitude empowers excess in which two different focal points stow away. The first is adaptability, implying that the multitude can comprise of a couple to up to a great many specialists and, in any case, the control design continues as before. In addition, in light of the fact that there is no single operator fundamental for the multitude, the SI advantage adaptability is completely fulfilled.

SI contains four primary stages which are as follows:

1. First stage is to set population.
2. Second stage is to calculate fitness function.
3. Third stage is to define terminated condition.
4. Fourth stage is to update and remove solution and find another solution.
5. Fifth stage is to return the best global solution.
6. Sixth stage is to terminate condition.

1. Set Population:
It is the first stage of the SI algorithm. It contains six types of methods that are used. The first method is to set the population. It contains collection of the features. It is also called as the backward selection. The second method is to assign the population. In the second method, the collection of the features is not assigned. The second method is called add the forward selection. The third method is to the randomly generate swarm population. In this method, the features are randomly selected.

The fourth method is the derivatives. In this method, the collection of the features is selected using the derivations. The fifth method is to collect the few features with the second method that is limited. The sixth method is to collect massive number of the features using the first method with the limitation selected features.

In the SI, some types of the method are used to assign the population of agents with the floating point.

2. Calculate Fitness Function:
For every solution, $\sim Z_i = [z_{i1}, z_{i2}, z_{i3}, z_{i4}................, z_{id}]$. Here, I and d represents the collections of the solutions. The SI method gets the best solution using the fitness function

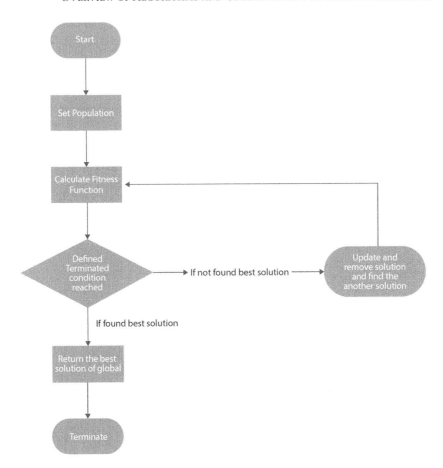

f($\sim$Zi). Here, $\sim$Zi is denoted as the fitness function. The given solutions are compared with the search agents.

For instances: In the RIO, search agent is the cockroach. In the PSO, the search agent is the particle. In the GSO, the search agent is the glowworm.

In the ABC method, the collection of solution is the food resources.

This function is mostly considered as classification accuracy. One method is used to develop solutions. This method is considered as the classifier method. This method is known as the SVMs. In this method, the introduced fitness is the average of the classification error rate. There are three types of the classifiers used to obtain classification error rate. These classifiers are the C-SVM, u-SVM, and LS-SVM in the SI algorithm.

One method also evaluated frequently using the classification. This method is known as the KNN. At the first time, every ant is evaluated in ASO using this method. It also evaluated every ant using the MSE. Here, MSE is referred as the Mean Square Error. In the binary ABC algorithm, the classification performance was also applied with this method.

Some researchers introduced this function where every solution is calculated with the OCA. Here, OCA is referred as the Overall Classification Accuracy. It considers some types of the method which are the KNN, 1NN, and WKNN. The value of k is modified, which randomly depends on loop of the method. Here, KNN is referred as the K-Nearest Neighbor, 1NN is referred as the 1-Nearest Neighbor, WKNN is referred as the Weighted Nearest Neighbor.

The GWO used one function, which is known as the composed weighted fitness. This function is used for the comparison between an error rate. This function also compared the number of selected features. There are some types of algorithms that are also used to compare the classification accuracy. In the BA algorithm, this function is used to compare classification accuracy of OPF. Here, OPF is referred as the Optimum Path Forest.

In the FA algorithm, this function is used to compare classification accuracy of the RMSE. Here, RMSE is referred as the Root Mean Squared Error. In ABC algorithm, this function is used for the clustering using the GRASP. Here, GRASP is referred as the Greedy Randomized Adaptive Search Procedure.

In the RIO and ACO algorithms, this function is used to compare the classification accuracy using the BPNN. Here, BPNN is referred as the Back Propagation Neural Network.

3. Define Terminated Condition:

Terminate condition is considered as the parameter. This condition is used to terminate the execution of a method. In the SI methods, there are three types of terminate condition. First, terminate condition is considered as one condition. The second terminate condition is the collection of two conditions. The third condition is to consider different conditions. The most normally terminate condition is the obtained measures of the loop. It is also known as the generations. There are some researchers that used the measures of the loop. Some researchers considered the minimum number of the loop like 200, 100, 500, 25, 50, and 70. When the method is considered as the composed terminate conditions, then it is always consider as the collection of the number of the loop. Sometimes, terminate conditions are considered the threshold value, the target function is equal to 0, and optimal solution is reached.

4. Update and remove solution and find another solution:

It is the fourth stage of the SI framework. If the terminate condition is not reached, then go to this step and update the solution or remove the solution. Now, find another solution. Then, go to the fitness function. The fitness function selects another solution and then goes to terminate condition. If the given solution reached the best solution, then return the global best solution. If the solution of the given problem is not the best, then go to the update and remove solution condition and so on.

5. Return the Best Global Solution:

It is the fifth stage of the SI method. This stage explained the social behavior of the swarm. This stage is used to give the best target function between the positions have been visited by all particles in the multitude. When a molecule arrives at a place that has a superior target work than the past best target work for entire multitude, the global best position is likewise refreshed.

6. Terminate Condition:

It is the last stage of the SI algorithm. If the best solution of the given problem has gotten, then execution of the program is terminate.

1.3   Composing With SI

SI is the branch of CI. Here, SI is referred as the Swarm Intelligence. CI is referred as the Computational Intelligence. It is the collection of the behavior of the swarm. It is the most important feature of the SI algorithms. The SI algorithm also considers another feature which is the self-organizing. SI has not contained any type of centralized control. It has only agent that manages. It is motivated through the observation of the combined behavior in societies in nature, for example, movement of fish and birds.

The aggregate conduct of such biological systems and their counterfeit partner of SI is not encoded inside the arrangement of decision that decides the development of each detached specialist; yet, it rises through the connection of numerous operators. Albeit a few varieties that have been proposed in the writing, the key arrangement of rules utilized for music piece depends on the "boids". These principles characterize the development of every operator by altering its speeding up inside brief timeframe spans as indicated by certain conditions in the condition that it sees. In particular, these standards fuse the accompanying rules for the development of every specialist:

1. Shoaling: It is the first rule. This rule is followed by the agents. Push toward the focal point of mass of the operators that you see.
2. Collision avoidance: It is the second rule of the SI algorithm. This rule is followed by the agents. Move away from the operators that are excessively near you.
3. Schooling: It is the third rule. This rule is followed by the agents. Push toward adjusting your speed to the mean speed of the specialists that you see.

For these standards to be applied, a few constants must be foreordained, for example, the sweep of operator observation, i.e., at which separation does a specialist see an article in its condition, and the range of crash shirking. These standards characterize the conduct of every specialist, which starts framing composed gatherings known as the "swarms," which presents aggregate conduct (joined intelligent as though they were a solitary life form).

1.4   Algorithms of the SI

SI, an essential part in the field of AI, is continuously retrieving conspicuousness, as increasingly more high multifaceted nature issues require arrangements which might be imperfect, yet feasible inside a sensible timeframe. For the most part motivated by natural frameworks, swarm knowledge embraces the aggregate conduct of a composed gathering of creatures, as they endeavor to endure. This investigation plans to examine the overseeing thought, distinguish the potential application territories, and present a nitty gritty review of eight SI calculations. The recently evolved calculations examined in the examination are the creepy crawly–based calculations and creature-based calculations in minute detail. All the more explicitly, we center around the calculations roused by ants, honey bees, fireflies, sparkle worms, bats, monkeys, lions, and wolves. The motivation examinations on these calculations feature the manner in which these calculations work. Variations of these calculations have been presented after the motivation examination. Explicit territories for the utilization of such calculations have likewise been featured for analysts inspired by the space.

The investigation endeavors to give an underlying comprehension to the investigation of the specialized parts of the calculations and their future extension by the scholarly world and practice.

SI, normally, is based on the problem-solving ability. It solves the problem using the interaction of simple information processing units. It contains some types of the terminologies which are the distribution, multiplicity, messiness, stochasticity and randomness. The problem-solving approach is based on three terminologies which are suggested by the SI. These terminologies are the creativity, cognition capabilities, and learning. It contains some types of the methods which depend on the optimization techniques. This method is the ABC, ACO, and PSO. Here, ABC is referred as the Artificial Bees Colony, ACO is referred as the Ant Colony Optimization, and PSO is referred as the Particle Swarm Optimization. It also depends on the scheduling optimization.

1. FFA:

It is referred as the Firefly Algorithm. It is the algorithm of the SI. It is the insect-based method. It is the type of the luminous. It is the metaheuristic method. This algorithm is evaluated by the Xin She Yang. It was evaluated since 2008. It was evaluated through got knowledge about the behavior of the fireflies and the flashing patterns.

Metaheuristic is one of the algorithms. This algorithm is used to obtain optimal solutions of the given problem. It is used several engineering branches. There are four types of the algorithms available which are used in the metaheuristic algorithm. The first is the evolutionary algorithm. The second algorithm is the swarm-based methods. The third algorithm is the physical-based methods. The last and fourth algorithm is the human-based methods. This algorithm is the most important algorithm in the SI. In the SI, it generates optimal result of the given problem. It is to return the global optimum solution.

In this algorithm, there are some types of the hybrid and modified variants available which are as follows:

1. Binary Represented Firefly Algorithm: In this algorithm, the problem is solved through the binary representation. It depends on the flashing conduct of fireflies. It generates a modified brightness that depends on position among the fireflies. The existing position is identified through the modified value of the previous position of the firefly, yet the measurement of the existing position is an actual number. This problem is reduced by the binary function. It is the comparison between the binarization and random number generated. It consists of the two values which are the 0 and the 1.

2. Elitist Firefly algorithm: It is the part of the FA. FA is used as the elitist firefly method to enhance the convergence speed. This method depends on the random selection. This method can lead the firefly to actual direction.

3. LFA: It is the referred as the Lagrangian firefly algorithm. It is the variant of the FA. It is introduced by Rampriya *et al.* It is used to solve problem related to the power system.

4. DFA: It is referred as the Discrete firefly algorithm. This algorithm was evaluated by Sayadi *et al.* It is used to solve NP-hard scheduling issues. It is the variant of the FA.

It is the population-dependent method. The target function of a define optimization problem depends on variance in light intensity. It encourages the fireflies to move toward more brilliant and increasingly appealing areas so as to get ideal function. Whole fireflies classified according to their light intensity. The light intensity is related to the target method. Every firefly is in its alternative position of the loop. It contains three types of principles which are as follows:

1. The first principle is related to the unisex. Whole fireflies are the unisex. Whole fireflies will move toward more brighter and attractive ones.
2. The second principle is related to the attractiveness. It is comparative to the brightness. It reduces the distance from another firefly enhance. When there is no any available type of the attractive firefly, then it moves dynamically.
3. The third principle is related to the brightness of a firefly. This brightness is obtained by the value of the target function. If the problem is the greater, then the brightness is comparative to the value of the target function.

Pseudo code of the Firefly algorithm: Here, pseudo code is available for the Firefly algorithm, which is as follows:

1. The first step is to declare the variable for the Firefly algorithm:
   - $\beta 0$, γ, α,
   - Total fireflies available: it is denoted by one variable which is the "n".
   - Define maximum value of the loop. The loop is denoting to the "ii" and the maximum value of the loop is denoting to the MaxGen.
2. The second step is to initialize the target function Z(j). Here, j contains the collection of values which is the j to n times like ji = j1, j2, j3.....................jn. ji is denoted as the assign the value of population. jn is the total solutions of the given problems. It finds the solution using the light intensity of firefly. The ji is retrieved using the target function. The target function is denoted by the Z(j).
3. The third step is to execute the while loop. First, take the variable, then initialize the variable with 1. This variable is the "k". This loop is terminated when the value of the k is equal to the MaxGen.

   K = 1;
   While (k ≤ MaxGen)(k=1:MaxGen), Then
       For j = 1:jn// Whole fireflies is denoted by the jn.
         For mm = 1:jn
           If(Imm > Ij), then
             Firefly j is replaced to the mm firefly.
           End if condition when get the attractiveness distance.
         If the not get best solution then search the new solution and then modified light intensity.

End for mm
End For j
If the get best global solution the while loop is terminated. If the given condition is give the false, then the while loop is terminated.
4. The fourth step is to return the best global solution.
5. The last step is to finish the execution of the program.

When the population of the Firefly method is set, then go to the iteration. This iteration denotes the maximum number of the MaxGen. MaxGen is the number of the generation. Every generation is considered the firefly. It also considers the maximum light intensity. It finds the worst value of the target function. It selects the value of target function. This value has been potential optimal solution. This method is considered as the parallel execution idea.

The in are the collections of solution which is find out using the loops.

SSO:

Here, SSO is referred as the Simplified Swarm Intelligence. It is the method of the SI. Here, SI is referred as the Swarm Intelligence. It is related to the spiders' behavior. In the biological term, the spiders are classified into two clustering. These spiders depend on the behavior. The first cluster is the solitary spider. The second cluster is the social spider. This first cluster does not consider any another spiders. It has a minimum chance to contact another spider. It is living in their own web. The second cluster lives in their colonies which is called the social spiders. This cluster is also known as the communal web. This type of spider spatially contacts with the nearest spider. This algorithm is mostly construct on social spider. Both male and female creepy crawlies exist together in the mutual web with females dwarfing guys by around about 70%. It is seen that prevailing guys mate with their female neighbors situated inside a specific scope of separation and non-predominant guys stay in a position near different guys of web and rely on the last for nourishment. Aside from mating, creepy crawlies connect with one another by methods for vibrations, and the force of the vibrations is reliant upon two huge components—weight of the bug and the separation between the imparting insects.

This algorithm was introduced by the Cuevas. It depends on the metaheuristic algorithm. Metaheuristic is one of the algorithms. This algorithm used to obtain optimal solutions of the given problem. It used several engineering branches. There are four types of the algorithms available which are used in the metaheuristic algorithm. The first is the evolutionary algorithms. The second algorithm is the swarm-based methods. The third algorithm is the physical-based methods. The last and fourth algorithm is the human-based methods. This algorithm is the most important algorithm in the SI. In the SI, it generates optimal result of the given problem. It is to return the global optimum solution.

This algorithm also depends on the spiders' behavior.

Pseudo code for the Simplified Swarm Intelligence:

1. In the first step, declare the variables which are I, Niter, and N.
   Here, I is the initial position of the male and female spider.
   N is denoted as the total number of spider members. There are two types of the spiders which is the total count of the female spider and second is the total count of male spiders.
   Niter is the total count of the loops.
2. The second step is the process. Now, consider the while, which is used to measure of radius of mating for spider members.

While jj ≤ Niter.

If the best global solution is gotten, then terminate while loop.
3. The third step is the output. In this step, the best global solution of the given problem is obtained. It is also obtain the fitness value of target function.
4. The fourth step is related to the update solution. If the obtain solution is not best, then update the solution and remove the solution. Then, go to the first step.
5. The fifth step is to terminate the execution of the program.

ACO:
Here, ACO is referred as the Ant Colony Optimization. This algorithm was introduced by the Dorigo *et al*. It depends on the population heuristic method. Metaheuristic is one of the algorithms. This algorithm is used to obtain optimal solutions of the given problem. It used several engineering branches. There are four types of the algorithms available which used the metaheuristic algorithm. First are the evolutionary algorithms. Second algorithm is the swarm-based methods. Third algorithm is the physical based methods. Last and fourth algorithm is the human-based methods. This algorithm is the most important algorithm in the SI. In the SI, it generates optimal result of the given problem. It is to return the global optimum solution. This algorithm depends on the behavior of the ant. The ant has a different behavior for searching the food resources. Every ant of the colony creates a best path for the searching the food resources. In such manner, the ants discharge flagging pheromone to stamp their own way for the source. This is the fundamental quality of this methodology and the devotee ants want to go on the way with more grounded pheromone so that the change on the thickness of the pheromone level determines the choosing possibility of every way.

It is used to the same method for solving combinatorial optimization issues using the ACO. ACO referred as the Ant Colony Algorithm. Artificial ants are initially from an underlying inquiry point (home) and assemble the parts of another potential arrangement individually. For every segment, a probabilistic choice is made among choices. This method is evaluated by detecting the food finding exertions of ant groups. For finding the food sources by the ant colony, the smart and organized method is used.

The subtleties of the procedure are displayed with scientific apparatuses, and afterward, the methodology is changed into an enhancement issue structure to use for designing issues, for example, the inquiry zone is characterized as chart and the specialists (ants) are depicted as moving point on this diagram. As the specialists proceed onward the chart, a reenactment variant of pheromone discharging model is acknowledged with a stochastic way to deal with mark the most mainstream ways through the source. Every insect begins to move from arbitrarily chosen focuses on the diagram. The association line from the beginning stage to the objective portrays a way, and every way is sorted with pheromone level and corresponding heuristic worth so that higher of these parameters for a way offers ascend to higher the likelihood an insect inclines toward this shorter way through the source.

The remainder of the ants utilize the pheromone saved on the way for looking through additionally encouraging course through the food target. At that point, this iterative system goes on until every one of the ants completes their movement for the food, and pheromone level is refreshed on every way visited by the ants. Therefore, every insect gives an answer and, in any event, one way among the arrangements ought to satisfy the end rule to complete the all technique. As the principle normal for this method relies upon the pheromone level on the course through the food source, the higher the keeping phero-mone load, the higher optimality an answer is arranged. This calculation comprises of four fundamental parts (subterranean insect, pheromone, daemon activity, and decentralized control) that add to the general framework. Ants are fanciful specialists that are utilized so as to mirror the investigation and abuse of the inquiry space. In actuality, pheromone is a substance material spread by ants over the way they travel and its force changes after some time because of vanishing. In ACO, the ants drop pheromones when going in the hunt space and the amounts of these pheromones demonstrate the power of the path. The ants pick the bearing dependent on way set apart by the high power of the path. The power of the path can be considered as a global memory of the framework. Daemon activities are utilized to accumulate global data which is impossible by a solitary subterranean insect and utilized the data to decide if it is important to add additional pheromone so as to support the intermingling. The decentralized control is utilized so as to make the calculation hearty and adaptable inside a unique situation. The significance of having a decentralized frame-work in ACO is expected to coming about adaptability even with insect lost or subterranean insect disappointment offered by such a framework. These essential parts add to a helpful connection that prompts the development of briefest ways that portray the underlying stage, mid-go status of any framework, and the ultimate results of the ACO calculation separately.

Ants live in provinces and are "practically visually impaired", and they lay pheromone in travel from the home when they go searching for food source. On accomplishing the food point, the subterranean insect accumulates the food and returns a comparable way the com-pound pheromone is laid. This course is pulled in by the different ants. More ants follow-ing end up being all the more engaging for different ants. ACO is the primary calculation charmed by the search for ideal way through the pheromone correspondence considering the direct of ants to locate the briefest course in examining the food. This technique is called as Stigmergy. Rummaging conduct of ants is the best case for explaining the limit of sub-terranean insect provinces. Scavenging conduct of ants is according to the accompanying:

1. Singular ants go searching for food; they meander dynamically around states searching for food basis.
2. In this algorithm, the agents do not particularly communicate with another agent. Here, the agent is the ant. In this algorithm, indirect communication between the agents is established. This process is known as the Stigmergy.
3. Right when the ants discover their food source, they instantly return near the home on its way back and they leave a substance called as pheromone. These pheromones are capricious in nature and they keep disseminating. They use pheromone system to guarantee no subterranean insect surpass another. Along these lines, they never have car influxes or chance upon each.
4. Ants are fit for distinguishing this pheromone, and the progress is pulled in by various ants; they continue ahead a comparative track. Likewise, every insect leaves their substances and thickness the track so that in the event that some different ants are in the source, at that point, they can follow the pher-omone thickness and find their food source.
5. If other insect has found most concise ways for a comparable food source, at that point, that briefest way can be trailed by numerous different ants and this course ends up being all the more engaging as addition in the union of pheromone.

6. Their speed stays consistent. Regardless of what number of ants are on the path.

If there is any impediment in the course, then it will move self-assertively to begin with regardless, later they will find the briefest way.

It contains many types of the variation which are as follows:

1. First variation is the AS.
2. Second variation is the ACS.
3. Third variation is the EAS.

1. AS:

Here, it is the referred as the ant system. It is the first method of the ACO. In this method, the value of pheromone is modified through the whole ants. In the ACO, there are three types of the versions available, which are introduced by the Maniezzo V, Colorni A, and Dorigo M. This method was introduced since 1991. This version is the ant cycle, ant quantity, and ant density. It is mostly used in the WDSD, QAP, VRP, and TSP.

Here, WDSD is referred as the Water Distribution System Design.

QAP is referred as the Assignment Problem.

VRP is referred as the Vehicle Routing Problem.

2. ACS:

It is referred as the Ant colony system. State Transition Rule provides an immediate method to adjust between investigation of new edges and misuse of from the earlier and gathered information about the issue. Global Updating Rule is applied uniquely to edges which have a place with the best insect visit. Local Pheromone updates the rule, while ants build an answer, and a nearby pheromone refreshing standard is applied. It is mostly used in the, VRP, TSP, WDSD.

3. EAS:

It is referred as the Elite Ant System. In EAS, alongside different ants, the worldwide best arrangement (the best subterranean insect) stores pheromone at each cycle. Individual ants do not naturally leave pheromone. Thus, the hunt is significantly progressively concentrated around the worldwide best arrangement. It is used in the Post-Enrolment Course Timetabling Problem.

Pseudo code for ACO Algorithm:

1. First step is to declare variables:

t: This variable is denoted as the total number of the loop.

$P(t)$: This variable is denoted as the tth generation.

$P_{heromone}$: This variable is denoted as the pheromone matrix of the tth generation.

P_{rior}: This variable id denoted as the prior knowledge of information matrix.

2. Second step is to assign the value of variables.

t = 0;

p(t) = assignPheromone(P());

Devlop(P(t));

$P_{heromone}(t) = assignPheromone(P(t));$
$P_{rior} = assignPriorKnowledge();$

3. Third step is to start the while loop:
While(Terminate criteria unsatisfied)
$(p + t) = SearchWay(p(t)), P_{heromone}(t), P_{rior);}$
Devlop(P(t + 1));
$P_{heromone}(t + 1) = ModifiedPheromone(P(t + 1)), P_{heromone}(t), P_{rior)}$
$t = t + 1;$
End While Loop

4. After searching the best path, then terminate the execution of program.

In this pseudo code, take the two function which is the SearchWay() and ModifiedPhermonoe(). These functions are used for the search the best path using the dynamic pheromones and static prior knowledge.

4. ABC:

It is referred as the Artificial Bee Colony. It is the algorithm of the SI. This algorithm was introduced by the Karaboga. This algorithm was developed since 2005. This algorithm is motivated through behavior of honey bee. This algorithm is used for solving many types of issues. Like other stochastic method, this algorithm faces up some trying issues. For instance, ABC shows moderate combination speed during the hunt procedure. Because of the unique pursuit example of honey bees, another user solved is created by modified an arbitrary measurement vector of its parent solution. In this manner, the posterity (novel user solution) is like its parent, and the union speed turns out to be moderate. In addition, ABC effectively falls into neighborhood minima when taking care of complex multimodal issues. The pursuit example of honey bees is acceptable at investigation yet poor at misuse. In any case, a decent improvement method should adjust investigation and misuse during the hunt procedure.

This method is an, as of late, introduced improvement procedure which recreates the intelligent scavenging conduct of honey bees. A lot of honey bees are known as swarm which can effectively achieve assignments through social participation. In this method, there are three kinds of honey bees:

1. First, honey bee is the employee bees.
2. Second, honey bee is the scout bees.
3. Third, honey bee is the onlooker bees.

The utilized honey bees search food around the food source in their memory; in the interim, they share the data of these food sources to the onlooker honey bees. The third type of honey bees will, in general, select great food sources from those found by the first type of honey bees. The food source that has more excellent (wellness) will have a huge opportunity to be chosen by the onlooker honey bees than the one of lower quality. The scout honey bees are deciphered from a couple of first type of honey bees, which desert their food sources and search new ones.

In this algorithm, the main portion of the multitude comprises of employee honey bees, and the subsequent half establishes the onlooker honey bees. The quantity of employed honey bees or the onlooker honey bees is equivalent to the quantity of arrangements in the multitude.

It is obvious from the above clarification that there are four control boundaries utilized in the ABC: The quantity of food sources which is equivalent to the quantity of utilized or spectator honey bees (SN), the estimation of breaking point, MCN. MCN is referred as the Maximum Cycle Number. Point-by-point pseudo-code of the ABC calculation is given beneath:

Step 1: First, take the variables:

$$Z_i, k, \text{cycle}, SN, \text{and } D.$$

Step 2: Assign the population of solutions.

$$I = 1 \ldots\ldots\ldots SN;$$

$$K = 1 \ldots\ldots\ldots D;$$

$$\text{cycle} = 1;$$

Step 3: Develop population function.
Step 4 Repeat.
Step 5. Generate novel solutions hi. Here, k is denoted as the employed bees and develop them.
Step 6. Implement the greedy selections execution.
Step 7. Estimate the Pi. This Pi is used for the solution of Zi.k by step 2.
Step 8. Generate the novel solution for problems which is indicated by the hi. Here, k is used for the third type of honey bee from the solutions Zi. K value is based on the Pi and implemented them.
Step 9. In this step, implement the greedy selection process ABC optimization method.
Step 10. Recognize the uncontrolled solution for the second type of honey bee. When this exists, supplant it with another haphazardly created solution Zi.
Step 11. In this step, remember the greatest solution reached so far.
Step 12. In this step, the value of cycle is increase by 1.
Step 13. All step terminated which the cycle is equal to the MCN. Here, MCN is referred as the Maximum Cycle Number.
Step 14 Stop.

5. PSO:
It is referred as the Particle Swarm Optimization. It is a heuristic global optimization algorithm. Metaheuristic is one of the algorithms. This algorithm is used to obtain optimal solutions of the given problem. It is used several engineering branches. There are four types of the algorithms available which used the metaheuristic algorithm. First are the evolutionary algorithms. Second algorithm is the swarm-based methods. Third algorithm is the

physical-based methods. Last and fourth algorithm is the human-based methods. This algorithm is the most important algorithm in the SI. In the swarm intelligence, it generates optimal result of the given problem. It is to return the global optimum solution.

This method was introduced by the Kennedy and Eberhart. This method was introduced since 1995. This method is the mostly general optimization method for used [4]. On one hand, there are some advanced PSO available which is the bare-bones PSO, fuzzy PSO, chaotic PSO, and quantum-behaved PSO, and so on. It also includes the hybridization. It is used with the simulated annealing, genetic method, artificial immune system, Tabu search, biogeography-based optimization, harmonic search, ABC, ant colony method, and another serval type of the evolution. It also includes the population topology which is the ring, non-annealing, fully connected, random, and so on. It also includes the extensions which is the binary optimization, constrained, mutiobjective, and so on. It also includes the parallel implementation which is the CPU, Multicore, Multiprocessor, and cloud computing forms. It also includes the theoretical analysis which is the convergence analysis, tuning, and parameter selection. There are eight types of the field available which used the PSO. This field is the automation control systems, electronic engineering, electrical engineering, operations research, communication theory, medicine, fuel, biology, energy, and chemistry.

The improvement of molecule swarm streamlining depends on ideas and decisions that administer socially composed populaces in nature, for example, flying creature runs, fish schools, and creature groups. Dissimilar to the subterranean insect province approach, where Stigmergy is the fundamental correspondence component among people through their condition, in such frameworks, correspondence is somewhat immediate without modifying the earth.

In specialized words, PSO, is a populace-based stochastic inquiry in which every molecule speaks to a potential competitor answer for the issue. Components of every molecule are, in reality, the boundaries of the issue. This method imparts numerous likenesses to other transformative registering procedures like Genetic Algorithms (GA). First, the number of inhabitants in particles are introduced by arbitrary boundary esteems, and these boundary esteems are refreshed in every emphasis (age), until a stop standard has been met or the calculation is combined to some optima. Be that as it may, this procedure does exclude exceptional administrators like change or hybrid. In PSO, the particles "fly" over the inquiry space by following the current ideal particles. A definitive reason for any enhancement method is to appraise the backward of the Hessian network (estimation of the second subsidiary of the capacity) of the capacity and ascertain a function's form guide to locate the worldwide optima. Anyway, strategies like PSO (populace-based techniques when all is said in done) just as our strategy are free from the angle of the capacity and use "instinct" and social conduct of the people to accomplish the worldwide ideal of the capacity.

Pseudo code for PSO:
Step 1. Define the size of multitude, measurement of search space, most extreme number of emphases, and the PSO constants. Characterize the arbitrary numbers. Discover the current wellness of every molecule in the populace.
Step 2. Initialize the particles with some irregular introductory positions and speeds. Set the counter for cycle to zero. For the underlying populace, nearby

best fitness of every molecule is its own fitness worth, and neighborhood best situation of every molecule is its own present position that is, the current best solution for given problem.

Step 3. The global best fitness esteem is determined by The position comparing to global best fitness is the global best position.

Step 4. Modify the molecule speed and molecule position for next cycle.

Step 5. Through setting, increase the emphasis counter. Discover the current wellness of every molecule. In the event that current fitness < nearby best fitness.

Step 6. In the wake of computing, the neighborhood best fitness of every molecule, the current global best readiness for the kth cycle is resolved by if current global best fitness < global best fitness, then the position comparing to global best fitness.

6. BCO:

It is referred as the Bee Colony Optimization. Honey Bee Colony Optimization (BCO) is one of the primary calculations that use essential gauges of total bumble bee knowledge for managing combinatorial enhancement issues. It is a metaheuristic enlivened by the scrounging conduct of bumble bees. The fundamental idea behind BCO is to build the multi-administrator system which prepared to explain diverse combinatorial improvement issues. The bumble bee framework is a standard instance of created cooperation, particularly arranged affiliation, coordination, work division, simultaneous undertaking execution, explicit individuals, and well-weave correspondence.

Counterfeit honey bee province for the most part comprises of few people. They examine through the quest space searching for the possible arrangements. In order to find the most ideal arrangements, self-sufficient counterfeit honey bees cooperate and trade data. Using aggregate information and data sharing, reenacted bumble bees center around all the more reassuring extents and progressively give up courses of action from the less promising ones. Bit by bit, counterfeit honey bees out and out produce and improve their answers. The BCO search is running in emphases until some predefined halting basis is satisfied.

Each and every reproduced bumble bee is arranged in the hive close to the beginning of the pursuit system. In the midst of the inquiry methodology, bumble bees impart straight-forwardly. Each fake honey bee makes a movement of close by moves and thusly gradually builds up an answer of the issue. Bumble bees are adding arrangement segments to the present midway plan until the point that they make in any event at least one possible arrangement. When flying through space, fake honey bees perform forward development or, in turn, around advance. In the midst of a forward development, bumble bees make different incomplete arrangements. They do this by methods for a mix of individual examination and total comprehension from an earlier time. Starting now and into the foreseeable future, they play out a regressive development, for example, they return to the hive. In the hive, every single bumble bee checks out an essential initiative procedure. The pursuit procedure is made out of emphases. Each accentuation closes when at least one practical arrangement is made.

In 2005, Karaboga D. analyzed the scavenging conduct of bumble bee swarm and proposed another method reenacting this conduct for understanding multi-dimensional and multi-modular enhancement issues, called ABC. In the model, there are three gatherings of honey bees. These are utilized honey bees, spectators, and scouts. In the ABC calculation, the primary bit of the settlement includes the used bumble bees and the subsequent half consolidates the spectators. The method is taken a stab at three unquestionably comprehended test limits. From the reenactment results, it is gathered that the introduced method can be used for explaining unimodal and multi-modular numerical streamlining issues. During the time of 2001 to 2003, Lucic and Teodorovic tried the Bee Colony Optimization approach on account of Traveling Salesman Problem (TSP).

1.5   Conclusion

Adding to this are, without a doubt, the SI focal points. Multitude does not have any outside administration; however, every specialist in the multitude controls their conduct self-sufficiently. Specialist for this situation speaks to a potential answer for a given issue. In view of that, we can reason the subsequent bit of leeway, which is self-association. The insight does not concentrate on the individual operator however rises in the multitude itself. Along these lines, the arrangements (operators) of the issue are not known ahead of time, yet change themselves at the hour of the running programming. The self-association assumes a significant job in versatility. The last is recognizable in changing situations where operators react well to the referenced changes, adjust their conduct, and adjust to them self-sufficiently. Furthermore, because there is no focal coordination, the multitude is powerful, as there is no single purpose of disappointment. Besides, the multitude empowers excess in which two different focal points stow away. The first is adaptability, implying that the multitude can comprise of a couple to up to a great many specialists and, in any case, the control design continues as before. In addition, in light of the fact that there is no single operator fundamental for the multitude, the SI advantage adaptability is completely fulfilled.

The fundamental objective of the SI is to enhance the performance of the complex problems. It is also enhance the solution of the complex problems. The incredible accomplishment of natural swarm systems has led many researchers to find out how to solve complex problems by the swarms in nature. There are three types of the SI algorithms available which provide the best solutions with the optimal issues. These algorithms are the BA, BCO, and ACO. Here, BA is referred as the Bat algorithms, BCO is referred as the Bee Colony Optimization, and ACO referred as the Ant Colony Optimization.

References

1. Baldominos, A., Saez, Y., Isasi, P., Hybridizing evolutionary computation and deep neural networks: an approach to handwriting recognition using committees and transfer learning. *Complexity*, 2019, Article ID 2952304, 16 pp. 2019.
2. Chang, Y. and Yu, G., Multi-Sub-Swarm PSO Classifier Design and Rule Extraction. *Int. Work. Cloud Computing Information Security*, pp. 104–107, 2013.
3. Cheng, C., Yang, Z., Xing, L., Tan, Y., An improved genetic algorithm with local search for order acceptance and scheduling problems. *IEEE Workshop on Computational Intelligence in Production and Logistics Systems (CIPLS)*, pp. 115–122, 2013.
4. Siqueira, H., Figueiredo, E., Macedo, M., Santana, C.J., Bastos-Filho, C.J., Gokhale, A.A., Boolean binary cat swarm optimization algorithm, in: *Proceedings of the 2018 IEEE Latin*

American Conference on Computational Intelligence (LA-CCI), November, IEEE, Guadalajara, Mexico, pp. 1–6, 2018.

5. Hamdi, M. and Zaied, M., Resource allocation based on hybrid genetic algorithm and particle swarm optimization for D2D multicast communications. Appl. Soft Comput., 83, 105605, 2019.

6. Faraji, I., Bargabadi, A.Z., Hejrati, Z., Application of Binary Cat Swarm Optimization Algorithm for Unit Commitment problem, in: The First National Conference on Meta-Heuristic Algorithms and Their Applications in Engineering and Science, Fereydunkenar, Iran, August, 2014.

7. Hadi, I. and Sabah, M., Improvement cat swarm optimization for efficient motion estimation. Int. J. Hybrid Inf. Technol., 8, 1, 279–294, 2015.

8. Guo, L., Meng, Z., Sun, Y., Wang, L., A modified cat swarm optimization based maximum power point tracking method for photovoltaic system under partially shaded condition. Energy, 144, 501–514, 2018.

9. Pappula, L. and Ghosh, D., Cat swarm optimization with normal mutation for fast convergence of multimodal functions. Appl. Soft Comput., 66, 473–491, 2018.

10. Orouskhani, M., Mansouri, M., Orouskhani, Y., Teshnehlab, M., A hybrid method of modified cat swarm optimization and gradient descent algorithm for training ANFIS. Int. J. Comput. Intell. Appl., 12, 2, Article ID 1350007, 2013.

11. Orouskhani, M., Orouskhani, Y., Mansouri, M., Teshnehlab, M., A novel cat swarm optimiza- tion algorithm for unconstrained optimization problems. Int. J. Inf. Technol. Comput. Sci., 5, 11, 32–41, 2013.

12. Zhao, M., A novel compact cat swarm optimization based on differential method. Enterp. Inf. Syst., 2018, 1–25, 2018.

13. Pan, Q., Ni, Q., Du, H., Yao, Y., Lv, Q., An improved energy-aware cluster heads selection method for wireless sensor networks based on k-means and binary particle swarm optimiza- tion, in: International Conference in Swarm Intelligence, October, Springer, Cham, Switzerland, pp. 125–134, 2014.

14. Qiu, T., Li, B., Zhou, X., Song, H., Lee, I., Ioret, J.L.A., Novel Shortcut Addition Algorithm with Particle Swarm for Multi-sink Internet of Things. IEEE Trans. Ind. Informat., 16, 3566–3577, 2020.

15. Arora, S. and Singh, S., Butterfly optimization algorithm: A novel approach for global optimi- zation. Soft Comput., 23, 3, 715–734, 2019.

16. Shakhatreh, H., Khreishah, A., Alsarhan, A., Khalil, I., Sawalmeh, A., Othman, N.S., Efficient 3D placement of a UAV using particle swarm optimization, in: Proceedings of the 2017 8th International Conference on Information and Communication Systems (ICICS), Irbid, Jordan, 4–6 April, pp. 258–263, 2017.

17. Kumar, Y. and Sahoo, G., An improved cat swarm optimization algorithm based on opposition- based learning and Cauchy operator for clustering. J. Inf. Process. Syst., 13, 4, 1000–1013, 2017.

18. Kumar, Y. and Singh, P.K., Improved cat swarm optimization algorithm for solving global opti- mization problems and its application to clustering. Appl. Intell., 48, 9, 2681–2697, 2017.

19. Sharafi, Y., Khanesar, M.A., Teshnehlab, M., Discrete binary cat swarm optimization algorithm, in: Proceedings of the 2013 3rd International Conference on Computer, Control & Communication (IC4), September, IEEE, Karachi, Pakistan, pp. 1–6, 2013.

20. Yan, X., Wu, Q., Liu, H., Huang, W., An Improved Particle Swarm Optimization Algorithm and Its Application. Int. J. Comput. Sci., 1, 316–324, 2013.

2

Introduction to IoT With Swarm Intelligence

Anant Mishra* and Jafar Tahir

EEE Department, ASET, Amity University, Noida, India

Abstract

This paper tells us about what is basically Internet of Things (IoT), how the electronic devices are been connected with the Internet, and start thinking and generating the data which can be very beneficial for the mankind. IoT is not only the thing which has electronic portion; it has a wider area under software part which includes technologies like Artificial Intelligence, Machine Learning, Hadoop, Data Security, Cloud Computing, and Fog Computing. This paper explains each and every concept related to IoT and the interlinked technologies in a very elaborative manner which will be easy for the reader to understand and get a brief insight overview of the text and will gain the knowledge of the technologies along with the current market situation as many industry-related examples are mention along with the text. At the end, there is also a part which includes swarm intelligence and its relation with the IoT. All the efforts are applied to keep the text free from any kind of grammatical and scientific error.

Keywords: IoT, Hadoop, cloud computing, fog computing, haze computing, AL, ML

2.1 Introduction

The Internet of Things (IoT) is a developing theme of specialized, social, and financial hugeness. Purchaser items, strong products, vehicles and trucks, modern and utility parts, sensors, and other regular articles are being joined with the Internet network and amazing information diagnostic abilities that guarantee to change the manner in which we work, live, and play. Projections for the effect of IoT on the Internet and economy are great, with some envisioning upward of 100 billion associated IoT gadgets and a worldwide monetary effect of more than $11 trillion by 2025 [1].

In the meantime, in any case, the IoT raises critical difficulties that could obstruct understanding its potential advantages. Eye catching features about the hacking of Internet-associated gadgets, observation concerns, and security fears, as of now, have caught open consideration. Specialized difficulties remain and new approach, and legitimate and advancement difficulties are rising [2].

Corresponding author: Anant1999mishra@gmail.com

Abhishek Kumar, Pramod Singh Rathore, Vicente Garrcia Diaz and Rashmi Agrawal (eds.) Swarm Intelligence Optimization: Algorithms and Applications, (21–40) © 2021 Scrivener Publishing LLC. ISBN 978-1-119-77874-5

2.1.1 Literature Overview

Here, it has been demonstrated that this innovation is extremely useful, lessening human endeavors to most extreme endeavors; however, next to each other, we need to make different game plans additionally, as legitimate stockpiling innovation such as IoT gadgets produces information, likewise giving adequate security to that information. So, we can say that IoT with itself offers creations to new advances; yet additionally, it is delicate to the point that a solitary bug can result to time utilization and superfluous human endeavors. A more advancement is required which will be fulfilled by full and honest dedication of researchers and students and along with their hones efforts. IoT has the potential of changing the course of this world, and that time will surely come very soon when a micro device will be connected via Internet and each single step of the human will be analyzed at large scale.

2.2 Programming

2.2.1 Basic Programming

There are two basic sorts of PC programming: framework programming and application programming. Application programming projects are made to achieve a specific undertaking or gathering of errands. For instance, Cisco Packet Tracer is a system recreation program that enables clients to show complex systems and ask "imagine a scenario in which" inquiries concerning system conduct. Framework programming works between the PC equipment and the application program.

It is the framework programming that controls the PC equipment and permits the application projects to work. Regular instances of framework programming incorporate Linux, Apple OSX, and Microsoft Windows. Both framework programming and application programming are made utilizing a programming language. A programming language is a formal language intended to make programs that convey directions to PC equipment. These projects actualize calculations which are independent and well-ordered arrangements of activities to be performed. Some programming languages incorporate their projects into a lot of machine-language directions. C++ [3] is a case of an incorporated scripting language.

Others translate these guidelines straightforwardly without first incorporating them into machine language. Python is a case of a deciphered programming language [3].

At the point when the programming language is resolved and the procedure is diagrammed in a flowchart, program creation can start. Most programming languages utilize comparable program structures.

2.2.2 Prototyping

What is Prototyping?
Prototyping is the way toward making a simple working model of an item or framework. For prototyping in the IoT, it has structure abilities, electrical aptitudes, physical/mechanical aptitudes (work with your hands to assemble things), programming aptitudes, and to see how TCP/IP works. Be that as it may, you should not be a specialist in any of these regions. Actually, prototyping encourages you to refine these abilities.

Since the IoT is as yet creating, there are as yet obscure assignments to find. This is an incredible time to develop something that is a piece of the IoT. Since the IoT consolidates individuals, procedure, information, and things, there is no closure to the developments that the IoT can help make and afterward fuse.

From Ehere Should We Get a Prototype?

Discretionary Lab - Setting up Prototyping Lab App (PL-App) with the Raspberry Pi [4] Cisco Prototyping Lab is a lot of equipment and programming parts that empower the fast prototyping and displaying of different IoT digitization and information investigation arrangements. The equipment segments are a piece of the Prototyping Lab Kit (PL-Kit). The PL-Kit depends on Open HW prototyping sheets, for example, Raspberry Pi and Arduino. The PL-Kit incorporates extra sensors, actuators, and electronic segments. The PL-Kit can be utilized to assemble complex models of start-to-finish IoT frameworks that can detect and activate the genuine physical world, examine and process the information, and associate with system and cloud frameworks. The essential programming segment of the Prototyping Lab is the PL-App.

Network Inventor and Entrepreneurship Workshops
Along these lines, maybe you have quite recently made something extremely incredible. What now? There are various spots where you can get help uncovering your thought or model to other people. Research what is accessible in your locale. Check with your nearby government, schools, and council of business for data about workshops, classes, and master counsel.

2.3   Data Generation

2.3.1   From Where the Data Comes?

Information will be data that originates from an assortment of sources, for example, individuals, pictures, content, sensors, and sites. Information likewise originates from innovation gadgets like mobile phones, PCs, stands, tablets, and money registers. Most as of late, there has been a spike in the volume of information produced by sensors. Sensors are currently introduced in a regularly developing number of areas and items. These incorporate surveillance cameras, traffic lights, smart vehicles, thermometers, and even grape vines.

Enormous Data is a great deal of information; however, what is a ton? Nobody has a definite number that says when information from an association is considered "Enormous Data." Here are three attributes that show an association might manage Big Data.

They have a lot of information that undeniably requires more extra room (volume). They have a measure of information that is developing exponentially quick (speed). They have information that is created in various arrangements (assortment).

What amount of information do sensors gather? Here are some oassessed models:

- Sensors in one independent vehicle can produce 4,000 gigabits (Gb) of information every day.
- An Airbus A380 Engine produces 1 petabyte (PB) of information on a departure from London to Singapore.

- Security sensors in mining tasks can produce up to 2.4 terabits (TB) of information consistently. Sensors in a single shrewd associated home can create as much as 1 gigabyte (GB) of data 7 days. While Big Data creates difficulties for associations as far as capacity and examination, it can likewise give significant data to adjust activities and improve consumer loyalty.

2.3.2 Challenges of Excess Data

IBM's Big Data appraisals reason that "every day we make 2.5 quintillion bytes of information". To place this into setting, each moment of consistently:

1. We transfer more than 300 hours of YouTube video.
2. We send over 3.5 million instant messages.
3. We stream more than 86 thousand hours of Netflix video.
4. We like more than 4 million Facebook posts.
5. We demand more than 14 million figures from The Weather Channel [5].

The quick development of information can be a preferred position or an impediment with regard to accomplishing business objectives. To be effective, ventures must most likely effectively get to and deal with their information resources.

With this gigantic measure of information being always made, customary innovations and information distribution centers cannot stay aware of capacity needs. Indeed, even with the distributed storage offices that are accessible from organizations like Amazon, Google, Microsoft, and numerous others, the security of put away information turns into a major issue. Huge Data arrangements must be secure, have a high adaptation to internal failure, and use replication to guarantee that information does not get lost. Huge Data stockpiling is not just about putting away information, it is likewise about overseeing and verifying it.

2.3.3 Where We Store Generated Data?

Huge information is regularly put away on numerous servers, as a rule housed inside server farms. For security, availability, and repetition, the information is typically appropriated or potentially repeated on a wide range of servers in a wide range of server farms.

Haze Computing [6]
Haze registering is a design that uses end-client customers or "edge" gadgets to complete a generous measure of the pre-handling and capacity required by an association. Mist figuring was intended to keep the information closer to the hotspot for pre-preparing. Sensor information, specifically, can be pre-handled nearer to where it was gathered. The data picked up from that pre-prepared examination can be encouraged once more into the organizations' frameworks to change forms whenever required. Since the sensor information is pre-handled by end gadgets inside the organization framework, interchanges to and from the servers and gadgets would be faster. This requires less data transmission than always going out to the cloud.

After the information has been pre-handled, it is frequently delivered off for longer term stockpiling, reinforcement, or more profound examination inside the cloud.

2.3.4   Cloud Computing and Fog Computing

As referenced previously, the cloud [7] is an accumulation of server farms or gatherings of associated servers. Access to programming, stockpiling, and administrations accessible on the servers is gotten through the Internet by means of a program interface. Cloud administrations are given by numerous huge organizations, for example, Google, Microsoft, and Apple. Distributed storage administrations are given by various merchants, for example, Google Drive, Apple iCloud, Microsoft OneDrive, and Dropbox.

From a person's viewpoint, utilizing the cloud administrations permits you:

1. To store the majority of your information, for example, pictures, music, motion pictures, and messages, opening up nearby hard drive space.
2. To get to numerous applications as opposed to downloading them onto your nearby gadget.
3. To get to your information and applications anyplace, whenever, and on any gadget.
4. One of the burdens of utilizing the cloud is that your information could fall into the off-base hands. Your information is helpless before the security strength of your picked cloud supplier.
5. From the point of view of a venture, cloud administrations, and registering bolster an assortment of information the executives' issues.
6. It empowers access to hierarchical information anyplace and whenever.
7. It streamlines the IT tasks of an association by buying in just to require administrations.
8. It wipes out or diminishes the requirement for on location IT hardware, upkeep, and the board.
9. It decreases the expense of hardware, vitality, physical plant necessities, and faculty preparing needs.
10. It empowers quick reactions to expanding information volume prerequisites.

Distributed Processing
From an information, the executives' point of view, examination was basic when just people made information. The measure of information was sensible and moderately simple to filter through. Be that as it may, with the blast of business mechanization frameworks and the exponential development of web applications and machine-produced information, investigation is winding up progressively increasingly hard overseeing. Truth be told, 90% of information that exists today has been produced in simply the most recent 2 years. This expanded volume inside a brief timeframe is a property of exponential development. This high volume of information is hard to process and investigate inside a sensible measure of time [8].

Instead of huge databases being prepared by enormous and incredible centralized server PCs and put away in monster circle clusters (vertical scaling), appropriate information handling takes the huge volume of information and breaks it into littler pieces. These littler information volumes are appropriated in numerous areas to be prepared by numerous PCs with littler processors. Every PC in the disseminated engineering dissects its piece of the Big Data picture (level scaling).

Most dispersed record frameworks are intended to be imperceptible to customer programs. The conveyed record framework finds documents and moves information; however, the clients have no chance to get of realizing that the records are appropriated among a wide range of servers or hubs. The clients get to these records as though they were nearby to their very own PCs. All clients see a similar perspective on the record framework and can get to information simultaneously with different clients. Hadoop was made to manage these Big Data volumes. The Hadoop task began with two features: The Hadoop Distributed File System (HDFS) is a conveyed flaw tolerant document framework, and MapReduce, which is a disseminated approach to process information. Hadoop has now developed into a complete biological system of programming for Big Data, the board.

Hadoop is open-source programming empowering the dispersed preparing of huge informational indexes that can be terabytes in size and that are put away in bunches of PCs. Hadoop is intended to scale up from single servers to a large number of machines, each offering nearby calculation and capacity. To make it progressively effective, Hadoop can be introduced and keep running on numerous VMs. These VMs would all be able to cooperate in parallel to process and store the information.

Hadoop has two principles, which include that have made it the business standard for dealing with Big Data:

Versatility: Larger group sizes improve execution and give higher information handling capacities. With Hadoop, group size can undoubtedly scale from a 5-hub bunch to a 1000-hub group without unnecessarily expanding the regulatory weight.

Adaptation to Internal Failure: Hadoop consequently imitates information crosswise over bunches to guarantee information would not be lost. In the event that a plate, hub, or an entire rack comes up short, the information is protected.

Generated Data's Role in Business: In business, it is very important that strategy should be appropriate, as that will decide the percentage of profit in future. So, the data generated due to IoT devices, sometimes, helps to analyze the previous situation, the scenario, and also the market situation; so, by analyzing this data, business firms prepare their strategy, implement it, and try to increase their profit margins. Hence, IoT provides advantage not only to technological sector but also to the business and corporate world.

2.4   Automation

2.4.1   What is Automation?

Automation means when a machine starts doing the work by itself, but in the start, some human interventions are required. Automation is a part of Machine Learning (ML); basically, it deals with computer since (core), where the algorithm is designed as such that the software starts doing thing by its own, when ML is linked with mechanical engineering, we get a new thing, called mechatronics [9]; here, software takes the shape of hardware, and machines completely replace humans.

2.4.2   How Automation is Being Used?

At home level: For some, the home condition has turned into a progressively mechanized condition. Gadgets, for example, the Apple Homekit, Amazon Alexa and Echo, and Google

Assistant, enable us to give voice directions to control such things as lights, locks, entryways, indoor regulators, plugs, switches, caution frameworks, window covers, sprinkler framework sensors, and that is only the tip of the iceberg. Indeed, even kitchen machines and pet consideration capacities are being robotized. Organizations are creating new items consistently to work with these home computerization frameworks.

Automation in entire house: Enterprises of all types are using smart technology to automate building processes [10]. Smart buildings deploy many of the same technologies as smart homes. These processes provide efficient lighting, energy, heating, air conditioning, and security. For example, a smart building can reduce energy costs using sensors that detect how many occupants are in a room and adjust the heating or cooling appropriately.

Mechatronics and automated devices in industries: The Industrial IoT (IIoT) unites machines, progressed examination, and individuals. It is a system of assembling gadgets and sensors associated by secure and fast interchanges advances [11]. This outcomes in frameworks that can screen forms; gather, trade, and investigate information; and utilize that data to persistently modify the assembling procedure. We are, as of now, in the fourth mechanical upset, or what is called Industry 4.0. This depicts a domain where hardware and gear can improve forms through computerization and self-streamlining. Industry 4.0 stretches out past the assembling procedure and into capacities like arranging, inventory network coordinations, and item advancement.

Automated technology in cars [12]: The vast majority of the present new engine vehicles have incorporated innovation that helps drivers to be more secure out and about. Innovation exists that keeps drivers from floating into contiguous paths or making hazardous path changes. Frameworks naturally apply the brakes if a vehicle in front of them stops or moderates all of a sudden. These well-being innovations utilize a mix of equipment and programming to recognize dangers and to make a move to keep away from an accident. The proceeding with advancement of these advances have offered ascend to Automated Driving Systems (ADSs) that can deal with the entire errand of driving when we would prefer not to or cannot do it without anyone else's help. Self-driving vehicles would now be able to work completely self-sufficiently, without the mediation of a driver.

Self-flying planes: Planes today are worked to fly themselves. A mind-boggling accumulation of frameworks robotizes a plane's tasks. After a flight way is entered, the autopilot framework gathers data about the course, area, velocity, elevation, and motor push. It makes acclimations to keep the plane securely on the proposed way. Repetition in framework configuration guarantees that a disappointment in any one framework would not risk traveler security.

Intelligent towns: What do Hamburg, Barcelona, Kansas City, Jaipur, Copenhagen, and Manchester share for all intents and purpose? They are all "keen urban areas" that utilization computerized innovation to make their city a superior spot to live. A portion of these urban areas use innovation to diminish carbon discharges or screen CO_2 levels [13]. Others use innovation to give free city-wide Wi-Fi to improve open security or improve transportation choices [13, 14].

IoT in mobile application: Errands that were once done by individuals are presently progressively being finished by machines. Drive-through eateries are setting up self-serve booths for request passage, banks are progressively going to robotized teller machines or applications that are intended to keep running on advanced mobile phone, and markets and retail chains have introduced self-serve checkouts [15].

Artificial Intelligence and Machine Learning

Artificial Intelligence (AI) is the insight exhibited by machines. This is as opposed to characteristic insight which is the knowledge shown by living beings. Man-made intelligence utilizes clever operators that can see their condition and settle on choices that amplify the likelihood of getting a particular objective or target. Man-made intelligence alludes to frameworks that copy intellectual capacities regularly connected with human personalities, for example, learning and critical thinking.

A portion of the undertakings that, at present, are regarded to require a level of AI are self-ruling vehicles, astute steering in substance conveyance systems, vital game playing, and military reenactments. As innovation creates, huge numbers of the assignments that, at one time, required AI have turned out to be standard. A significant number of these assignments have relocated from AI to ML.

ML is a subset of AI that utilizations factual methods to enable PCs to "learn" from their condition [16]. This empowers PCs to enhance a specific undertaking without being explicitly modified for that task.

This is particularly helpful when structuring and programming explicit calculations is troublesome or infeasible. Instances of such undertakings in software engineering incorporate noxious code location, organize interloper discovery, optical character acknowledgment, PC discourse acknowledgment, and PC vision.

One target of learning is to have the option to sum up dependent on experience. For machines, this includes the capacity to perform precisely on new, beforehand inconspicuous undertakings in the wake of picking up involvement with a learning informational index. The preparation informational collection must originate from information that is illustrative of the bigger information pool. This information pool empowers the machine to fabricate a general model about this information, which would enable it to make exact expectations.

Application of ML in IoT

One of the highlights of the IoT is that it empowers the gathering of incredibly huge pools of information that can "educate" programs how to react in specific conditions [17]. A portion of the more typical employments of ML innovation includes the following:

- Discourse Recognition: Many various organizations currently offer advanced collaborators which enable you to utilize discourse to speak with a PC framework. Apple, Microsoft, Google, and Amazon all offer this administration. These organizations enable directions to be given verbally, yet offer discourse to content capacities.
- Item Recommendation: Systems develop a client profile and prescribe items or administrations dependent on past examples. Clients of Amazon and eBay get suggestions on items. Associations, for example, LinkedIn, Facebook, and GooglePlus prescribe clients you may wish to interface with.

- Shape Recognition: Programs exist that permit rough hand-attracted graphs and notes to be changed over to increasingly formal charts and content. This permits the shapes and lines of hand writing to be changed over to increasingly formal content which would then be able to be looked and investigated.
- Visa Fraud Detection: A profile is developed about the buying examples of a customer. Any deviation from these examples triggers a caution and the framework consequently makes a move. This activity ranges from denying the exchange to informing the experts. A portion of the occasions that are recognized and could demonstrate a fake exchange incorporate obtaining items not ordinarily acquired, buys in an alternate geographic region, quickly buying a wide range of items, and buying huge ticket things.
- Facial Recognition: Security cameras are all over the place, from stores and avenues to airplane terminals and transportation centers. These cameras consistently examine the groups, regularly looking for hazardous or unlawful exercises; yet, they can likewise be utilized to distinguish and follow people. The framework fabricates an example of explicit facial highlights and afterward looks for a match to these facial examples setting off some activity [18].

Intent-Based Networking [19]

For a business to endure, it must be light-footed and react rapidly to the necessities and requests of its clients. Organizations are progressively subject to their computerized assets to satisfy client needs; so, the basic IT system should likewise be responsive enough to rapidly adjust to these necessities. This ordinarily includes acclimations to numerous frameworks and procedures. These modifications may incorporate changes to security strategies and techniques, business administrations and applications, and operational arrangements. With customary systems, a wide range of segments must be physically acclimated to meet regularly changing business prerequisites. This requires various professionals and architects to guarantee that the frameworks are changed in a way that enables them to cooperate to achieve their objective. This occasionally brings about mistakes and delays and, frequently, in imperfect system execution.

The new business system should flawlessly and safely coordinate IoT gadgets, cloud-based administrations, and remote workplaces in a dexterous, responsive, and business-applicable way. Also, the system must verify these new advanced activities from the regularly changing danger scene.

To address this need, the IT business has started a push to make a methodical way to deal with bind framework the board to business purpose. This methodology is known as aim-based systems administration. With this new worldview, business needs are naturally and constantly converted into IT foundation execution.

How IBM, AI, and ML are connected to each other? Intent-Based Networking administration outfits the intensity of computerization, AI, and ML to control the capacity of a system to achieve a particular reason, or plan.

Goal-based systems administration permits the IT group to indicate, in plain language, precisely what they need the system to achieve and the system gets it going. The system can make an interpretation of the plan into approaches and after that utilization mechanization to convey the fitting setups required over the system.

The aim-based system utilizes AI and ML to guarantee that any administrations that are conveyed meet the required administration level. In the event that they do not meet the administration level, the purpose-based system can make alarms and give proposals to progress. At times, the expectation-based system can consequently reconfigure the system to agree to the administration levels. The expectation-based systems administration model comprises of three key components. Confirmation: The affirmation component is start-to-finish check of system wide conduct. It predicts the after effects of any changes, tracks consistence with the first purpose, and makes proposals or alterations when there is a mis-alignment between the expectation and the result. This stage depends vigorously on AI and ML. Frameworks are a piece of a shut circle that consistently screens execution and security of the system, and reconfigures the system to guarantee consistence. Interpretation: The interpretation component is the capacity to apply business aim to organize setup. The plan is the thing that you wish to achieve, not how it is practiced. This purpose is indicated in plain language and utilized by the framework to make approaches over the framework. For instance, a purpose may be to section visitor traffic from corporate traffic or to empower access for remote clients [20]. Enactment: The actuation component happens after the goal has been determined and the approaches made. This is when individual gadgets are pro-visioned to coordinate the expectation-based arrangements. This can be a mechanized or semi-robotized mode that permits the system group to check arrangement before the gad-gets are conveyed. An expectation-based system makes a deft, responsive system that scales effectively and adjusts to meet business prerequisites. It utilizes profoundly gifted assets and enables man and machine to cooperate to upgrade the client experience. Furthermore, plan-based systems administration gives a progressively secure advanced involvement via mechanizing tedious or confounded procedures. This makes conveying security approaches a lot simpler [21].

Current technology based on IBN: Intent-Based Networking administration enables the organization to concentrate on business objectives. It gives a mechanized framework that comprehends what the association needs and afterward gets it going.

The Cisco Digital Network Architecture (Cisco DNA) is a case of an aim based system. It is an open, extensible, and programming-driven design. It quickens and improves under-taking system activities, while bringing down expenses and diminishing dangers. Cisco DNA computerization and confirmation are based on a product characterized organizing (SDN) controller, rich logical investigation, arrange virtualization, and the boundless ver-satility of the cloud.

2.5 Security of the Generated Data

2.5.1 Why We Need Security in Our Data?

As the generated data has the records of past activity, if this data goes to wrong hands, the results will not be fruitful to the firm. Since this data has the complete image of current scenario, strategy, personnel policies, and all the record the firm, it will give benefit to the rival firm. So, it is really important for the organization that if the data is being generated, then there must be proper security.

2.5.2   What Types of Data is Being Generated?

Has information truly changed? Well in fact no, information produced by PCs and computerized gadgets is still gatherings of 0's. That has not changed. What have changed are the amount, volume, assortment, and quickness of the created information. Generally, organizations would approach our data accumulated from structures, spreadsheets, applications, charge card buys, and different kinds of records. A significant part of the data was put away and broke down sometime in the future. Touchy information was as yet gathered, put away, and broke down, yet, truly, programmers were progressively keen on hacking into frameworks to acquire corporate or government insider facts [22].

Today, assembled information is taking on new qualities. The digitized world has opened the conduits for information gathering. IoT sensor-empowered gadgets are gathering an ever increasing number of information of an individual sort. Wearable wellness trackers, home checking frameworks, surveillance cameras, and platinum card exchanges are on the whole gathering individual information just as business and natural information. Information is regularly consolidated from various sources and clients might be ignorant of this. Joining wellness observing information with house checking information could create information focuses to help map the developments or area of a property holder. This changing sort of information accumulation and total can be utilized for good purposes to support the earth. It likewise expands the likelihood of attack of our protection, fraud, and corporate surveillance.

By and by, recognizable data (PII) or delicate individual data (SPI) is any information identifying with a living person that can be utilized without anyone else or with other data to distinguish, contact, or find a particular person. The information assembled by organizations and government establishments can likewise contain touchy data concerning corporate insider facts, new item licenses, or national security. Since we are assembling and putting away exponential amounts of both delicate and enlightening information, it has expanded the requirement for additional security to shield this data from catastrophic events, programmers, and abuse.

Which people can steal our data?
Real organizations have an understanding set up that gives them consent to utilize the gathered information about you for motivations behind improving their business. Keep in mind those "Terms and Conditions" or "Terms of Service and Agreements" records that we express yes to yet do not typically peruse. Whenever that you are given one, set aside the effort to peruse it. The substance may shock you.

Other genuine clients of our information would be organizations that utilization sensors all alone gadgets or vehicles. Governments that have natural sensors and urban areas who have introduced sensors on trains, transports or traffic lights likewise reserve an option to the information they produce.

A few programmers, called white cap programmers, are paid by authentic organizations and governments to test the security of a gadget or framework. Their objective is not to take or adjust information yet to secure it.

The Bad Guys
Different programmers, called dark cap programmers, need access to gathered information for some loathsome reasons:

- To offer the data to an outsider.
- To change the information or handicap usefulness on a gadget.
- To get to gadgets, website pages, and information to make political distress or to own a political expression.
- To get to client IDs and passwords to take personalities.
- To get to information to carry out a wrongdoing.
- To hack into frameworks to demonstrate that they can do it.

2.5.3 Protecting Different Sector Working on the Principle of IoT

Private sector: Verifying the system includes the majority of the conventions, advancements, gadgets, instruments, and methods that protected information and alleviate dangers. System security is generally determined by the push to remain one stage in front of poorly intentioned programmers. Similarly, as restorative specialists endeavor to avert new ailments while treating existing issues, organized security experts endeavor to avoid potential assaults while limiting the impacts of continuous assaults. Systems are routinely enduring an onslaught. It is not unexpected to peruse in the news about one more system that has been undermined.

Security arrangements, methods, and guidelines must be followed in the plan of all parts of the whole system. This ought to incorporate the links, information in travel, put away information, organizing gadgets, and end gadgets.

Remote systems are mainstream in numerous kinds and sizes of organizations since they are anything but difficult to set up and advantageous to utilize. For workers and visitors, the organization needs to convey a remote encounter that empowers versatility and security. On the off chance that a remote system is not appropriately verified, programmers inside range can get to it and invade the system.

Similarly, firms can do things like installing a proper firewall software to their router and networking systems, like internet explorer, routers, etc., on the same side they should install a well reputed antivirus software to their systems, so that if the virus comes, they do not face much damage. Also, all the Wi-Fi should have proper security type, so that they cannot be hacked easily. All the systems should have proper and strong passwords [23]. Household level: Keen home innovation has turned out to be prominent and its notoriety is expanding each year as the innovation advances. Who does not think that it is engaging turn your home indoor regulator up or down while you are grinding away, or to have your cooler request staple goods to be conveyed when you return home? How cool is it to keep an eye on the pooch or to confirm that your young people are getting their work done after school by enacting your home surveillance cameras?

As we introduce an ever increasing number of shrewd sensors into our homes, we do build the potential for security issues. Frequently, the sensors are associated with a similar system as our home or independent company gadgets so a rupture of one gadget can emanate outward to influence every single associated gadget. The sensors could likewise give an approach to programmers to get into our home system and access any PCs and information that are associated with it.

Indeed, even menial helpers, for example, Apple SIRI, Amazon Echo, or Google Home, can be security dangers. Individuals utilize these gadgets to turn on music, modify room temperatures, request items online, and get headings for where they are going. Would this be able to bring about any mischief? It is conceivable that individual data, for example, passwords or Visa data could be spilled.

Luckily, huge numbers of the security blemishes of the early keen innovation sensors have just been found. Engineers are attempting to address the blemishes and improve safety efforts to shield their frameworks from assault. Before obtaining home security frameworks, it is imperative to look into the designer and the security and encryption conventions that are set up for its items.

Some more ways to increase security: When you are far from home, an open Wi-Fi problem area enables you to get to your online data and surf the Internet. Normal exercises on open Wi-Fi incorporate signing into an individual email account, entering by and by recognizable data, signing into internet based life, and getting to bank or budgetary data. The majority of this data could be stolen if the Wi-Fi association is unbound.

Security principles to pursue in the event that you are utilizing an open or unbound Wi-Fi hotspot:

Try not to get to or send any delicate individual data over an open remote system.

Confirm whether your PC is arranged with record and media sharing, and that it requires client confirmation with encryption.

Utilize scrambled virtual private system (VPN) passages and administrations. The VPN administration gives you secure access to the Internet, with a scrambled association between your PC and the VPN specialist co-op's VPN server. With a scrambled VPN burrow, regardless of whether an information transmission is captured, it is not understandable.

Numerous cell phones, for example, cell phones and tablets, accompany the Bluetooth remote convention. This ability permits Bluetooth-empowered gadgets to associate with one another and share data. Shockingly, Bluetooth can be abused by programmers to spy on certain gadgets, set up remote access controls, appropriate malware, and channel batteries. To dodge these issues, keep Bluetooth killed when you are not utilizing it.

2.6   Swarm Intelligence

2.6.1   What is Swarm Intelligence?

Swarm intelligence is the subject that deals with natural and artificial structures composed of many people that coordinate the usage of decentralized manage and self-organization [24]. In particular, the discipline specializes in the collective behaviors that end result from the local interactions of the people with each different and with their environment. Examples of structures studied by using swarm intelligence are colonies of ants and termites, colleges of fish, flocks of birds, and herds of land animals. Some human artifacts also fall into the domain of swarm intelligence, significantly some multi-robot systems, and additionally sure computer packages which can be written to tackle optimization and facts analysis problems.

2.6.2   Classification of Swarm Intelligence

Swarm intelligence has a marked multidisciplinary person on the grounds that structures with the above stated traits can be discovered in a diffusion of domain names. Research in swarm intelligence may be categorized in step with different standards.

Natural vs. Artificial: It is commonplace to divide swarm intelligence studies into two areas in keeping with the character of the systems below evaluation. We speak therefore of herbal swarm intelligence studies, in which organic systems are studied, and of synthetic swarm intelligence, wherein human artifacts are studied.

Scientific vs. Engineering: An opportunity and come what may greater informative category of swarm intelligence research can be given based on the goals which are pursued: we are able to perceive a scientific and an engineering circulate. The goal of the medical stream is to model swarm intelligence systems and to single out and apprehend the mechanisms that permit a system as an entire to behave in a coordinated manner because of local man or woman-person and character-environment interactions. On the other hand, the purpose of the engineering movement is to take advantage of the expertise advanced through the clinical circulate to be able to layout systems which might be capable of clear up issues of sensible relevance.

The two dichotomies natural/synthetic and scientific/engineering are orthogonal: despite the fact that the everyday medical research issues, natural systems, and the everyday engineering utility concerns the improvement of an artificial gadget, some of swarm intelligence studies had been done with swarms of robots for validating mathematical fashions of organic structures. These researches are of a merely speculative nature and honestly belong inside the scientific move of swarm intelligence. On the other hand, one may want to have an impact on or adjust the behavior of the people in a biological swarm so that a brand new swarm-degree behavior emerges this is come what may functional to the answer of a few project of practical interest.

2.6.3   Properties of a Swarm Intelligence System

The common swarm intelligence system has the following homes:

- It is far composed of many people.
- The individuals are tremendously homogeneous (i.e., they're both all identical or they belong to three typologies).
- The interactions of some of the people are based totally on simple behavioral guidelines that take advantage of simplest nearby statistics that the individuals exchange immediately or thru the surroundings (stigmergy).
- The overall behavior of the gadget outcomes from the interactions of people with every different and with their environment, that is, the organization behavior self-organizes.

The characterizing belonging of a swarm intelligence device is its ability to behave in a coordinated way without the presence of a coordinator or of an outside controller. Many examples can be observed in nature of swarms that perform a few collective behaviors without any character controlling the group, or being privy to the general organization behavior. Notwithstanding the shortage of individuals in rate of the organization, the swarm as an entire can display a sensible conduct. This is the end result of the interaction of spatially neighboring people that act on the idea of easy policies.

Most often, the behavior of every man or woman of the swarm is defined in probabilistic terms: Each individual has a stochastic behavior that relies upon on his local belief of the neighborhood.

Because of the above houses, it is possible to layout swarm intelligence gadget which are scalable, parallel, and fault tolerant.

- Scalability way that a machine can keep its feature while growing its length without the want to redefine the way its parts interact. Because in a swarm intelligence gadget interactions involve most effective neighboring individuals, the number of interactions has a tendency not to develop with the overall quantity of individuals within the swarm: each person's conduct is simplest loosely stimulated by using the swarm size. In synthetic structures, scalability is interesting due to the fact a scalable gadget can boom its performance via clearly increasing its length, without the need for any reprogramming.
- Parallel motion is feasible in swarm intelligence systems due to the fact individuals composing the swarm can perform exceptional actions in distinct locations on the identical time. In artificial systems, parallel motion is suited due to the fact it may assist to make the device greater bendy, that is, successful to self-prepare in teams that take care concurrently of different aspects of a complex project.
- Fault tolerance is an inherent assets of swarm intelligence systems due to the decentralized, self-organized nature in their manage structures. Because the gadget is composed of many interchangeable individuals and none of them is in rate of controlling the overall device behavior, a failing individual may be without difficulty disregarded and substituted by means of some other one that is absolutely functioning.

Interrelation of Swarm Intelligence and IoT

As we realize, the IoT is basically a method of established order of connectivity between the one of a kind gadgets, especially electronic components from small length to big length, with the assist of net and gathering the facts, that has been generated via the ones devices and with the assist of that statistics, we make future strategies, plans, or any other execution primarily based on the existing information for the future effects. Now, swarm intelligence is the generation via which we can enable those gadgets to work in a collective manner without any outside controller just like birds fly in herds and many others. So, if the algorithms of swarm intelligence are blended with the software program part of IoT devices, then a global of complete automation can be formed.

In present time, a full stack of IoT primarily based structure requires a superior to deal with any immediately hassle or to deal with the facts on the frequently foundation, but if the combine IoT with the newly rising technologies like ML, AI, deep learning, and yes the but apparent swarm intelligence in which the OPTIMIZATION is the key feature so the need or requirement of that advanced can be eliminated, so that you can in reality consequences in reduction of cost and labor which may be a monetary advantage to the IoT or IT-based totally firms.

Just as an instance, currently, the absolutely computerized houses are in fashion which definitely rely on IoT components; there is a wider scope of swarm intelligence, because it has been visible in among the Hollywood movies, that a residence is self-sufficient of executing any characteristic with none human
Intervention

So, at remaining, it may be concluded that with the emerging technology, our mankind is heading in the direction of a brief witted lifestyles and the way of life of the destiny generation will exchange completely.

2.7 Scope in Educational and Professional Sector

The most recent couple of years have given us upgrades in the speed and accessibility of Internet administrations, just as advances in distributed computing and sensor innovation. These specialized additions, together with ongoing improvements in robotization and computerized reasoning, have made a profoundly digitized world. Digitization as of now impacts each part of our day by day lives. Digitization keeps on giving new chances to experts who are prepared to create and bolster the innovation that is utilized to convey the IoT. The IoT gives an immense measure of data that is promptly accessible for utilization. This data can be immediately broke down and used to mechanize numerous procedures that were recently viewed as difficult to go over to machines. For instance, only a couple of years back self-driving vehicles existed uniquely in our minds and now they are a reality. Consider what else has changed in your life as a result of the IoT.

The IoT is additionally liberating people from the drudgery of standard and redundant errands, for example, restocking racks and request satisfaction. We may now possess more energy for higher scholarly interests and the opportunity to investigate all the IoT brings to the table. We are at a point in time wherein openings are constrained distinctly by our creative mind. We currently can grasp the majority of the advantages that the IoT brings to the table and to help shape what is to come [25].

Increasing percentage of employment: The IoT is changing the activity advertise. Conventional occupations are being supplanted with employments that are intended to grasp this new world and all it offers.

In IT, openings might be explicit to mist registering, growing new procedures, or a specialization in a control that has not yet been figured it out. These employments reflect aptitudes traversing different orders that incorporate software engineering, PC designing (a mix of software engineering and electrical building), and programming building in the accompanying zones:

- Man-made reasoning
- Application development
- IoT Program developer
- IoT security specialist
- Joint effort
- Endeavor networks
- Server farm and virtualization

Not all occupations made by the IoT are IT-related. The IoT ought to be viewed as an empowering innovation which has applications over all businesses and parts of our everyday lives. For instance, a city organizer utilizes the information gathered by IoT-empowered gadgets to plan out new city administrations. Sales reps use IoT innovation to upgrade the business involvement with the client, and stores use IoT innovation to keep up appropriate stock levels to coordinate client request.

The IoT has made a wealth of employments inside its circle. These employments exist crosswise over different ranges of the structure, advancement and empowering of the IoT. There are general classifications that condense the openings for work that exist in the advancing digitized world:

- Enablers: These employments create and actualize the basic innovation.
- Engagers: These employments configuration, make, incorporate, and convey IoT administrations to clients.
- Enhancers: These employments devise their own worth including administrations, over the administrations given by Engagers, which are one of a kind to the IoT.

Making people independent: The IoT is additionally making an interest for another sort of IT master. These are people with the information and ranges of abilities to grow new IoT empowered items and procedure the information they gather.

A pioneering workforce is required that has practical experience in both data science and programming or PC designing. This helps in startups and decrease unemployment.

2.8   Conclusion

So here we go, as we came to know about what is IoT, what literally means IoT. It is just a method of connecting different small or large components with the help of Internet. So now, the beginning step in IoT is programming, the basic language that is widely used is Python, C++ is also used sometimes. So, the moment a device gets connected to the internet, it starts generating data, on small as well as on large scale and this data is very useful for future plans, strategies, etc. Now, if the data is generated, it needs to be stored. So, for that we have different technologies like haze computing, cloud computing, fog computing, Distributed Processing, and, finally, the latest one which is in trend, i.e., Hadoop. These types of technologies are not only used for storing data which is been generated by IoT devices, but they are also used by different IT firms like TCS, WIPRO, ACCENTURE, CAPGEMINI, etc., for storing their millions of terabytes.

There comes the different technology which gives a different level of height to IoT. As the word Automation is very common now a day, so when Automation gets combined with the IoT, a new era may be generated in future. Automation has pillars like AI, ML, and deep learning, which have a wider scope in future and may retain for a longer time. So, when the algorithms of such technologies get combined with code stuffs of IoT devices, they can behave like human minds which can transform the life style of common public. Intent-Based Networking is also discussed here. Now, when the data is generated, it gets stored, then we also need to protect that time from technical flaws as well as from external elements which are known as hackers. Hackers are mainly of two types: the white collar and the black collar. White collars are our friends, but not the black collars. Many companies try to protect their data and get the data of their rivals in order to improvise their strategy to be a step ahead in the market. So, data security is one of the most important elements.

At last, we discussed about the swarm intelligence; this technology has its grass roots in the nature as it is evolved after observing natural phenomenon like formation of a group of birds while flying and how ants move in a group. So, basically IoT with swarm intelligence is a huge step toward the lightening fast technology and changing the life of mankind.

At the end, we find that will all these technologies, our education sector will defiantly grow and new job opportunities will rise, which will definitely contributes in the economic development of the world.

References

1. http://www.scholarpedia.org/article/Swarm_intelligence
2. Baldi, Autoencoders, unsupervised learning, and deep architectures. *ICML unsupervised and transfer learning*, vol. 27, no. 37–50, p. 1, 2012.
3. Becker, Indoor positioning solely based on user's sight, in: *International Conference on Information Science and Applications*, Springer, pp. 76–83, 2017.
4. Bengio, *et al.*, Learning deep architectures for AI. *Found. Trends R Mach. Learn.*, 2, 1, 1–127, 2009.
5. Borkowski, Schulte, S., Hochreiner, C., Predicting cloud resource utilization, in: *Proceedings of the 9th International Conference on Utility and Cloud Computing*, ACM, pp. 37–42, 2016, http://www.justscience.in/articles/applications-of-mechatronics/2017/07/11.
6. Bottou, Large-scale machine learning with stochastic gradient descent, in: *Proceedings of COMPSTAT'2010*, Springer, pp. 177–186, 2010.
7. Chauvin, and Rumelhart, D.E., *Backpropagation: theory, architectures, and applications*, Psychology Press, USA. 1995.
8. Chung, Gulcehre, C., Cho, K., Bengio, Y., Empirical evaluation of gated recurrent neural networks on sequence modeling, arXiv preprint arXiv:1412.3555v1 [cs.NE], *Variational Encoder* 1, 1, 2014.
9. Dai, Fidler, S., Urtasun, R., Lin, D., Towards Diverse and Natural Image Descriptions *via a* Conditional GAN, in: *Proceedings of the IEEE Conference on Computer Vision and Pattern Recognition*, pp. 2970–2979, 2017, https://en.wikipedia.org/wiki/Vehicular_automation.
10. Deng, A tutorial survey of architectures, algorithms, and applications for deep learning, in: *APSIPA Transactions on Signal and Information Processing*, vol. 3, pp. 1–29, 2014, https://expertsystem.com/machine-learning-definition/.
11. Doersch, Tutorial on variational autoencoders, arXiv preprint arXiv:1606.05908v2 [stat.ML], *Variational Encoder* 1, 3, 2016.
12. Kahou, E., Bouthillier, X., Lamblin, P., Gulcehre, C., Michalski, V., Konda, K., Jean, S., Froumenty, P., Dauphin, Y., BoulangerLewandowski, N. *et al.*, Emonets: Multimodal deep learning approaches for emotion recognition in video. *J. Multimodal User Interfaces*, 10, 2, 99–111, 2016, https://www.networkworld.com/article/3202699/what-is-intent-based-networking.html.
13. Rumelhart, E., Hinton, G.E., Williams, R.J., Learning representations by back-propagating errors. *Nature*, 323, 6088, 533, 1986.
14. https://iottip.com/lab-setting-up-pl-app-with-a-raspberry-pi/
15. https://www.amazon.in/Core-Python-Programming-Dr-Nageswara-ebook/dp/B075QGJ5NQ
16. https://www.apache.org/
17. https://www.coursera.org/lecture/iot/lecture-2-3-python-vs-c-c-43qlg)
18. https://www.educba.com/cloud-computing-vs-fog-computing/
19. https://www.linkedin.com/pulse/cloud-computing-fog-haze-oliver-meili

20. https://www.mtu.edu/mechatronics/what-is/
21. https://www.netacad.com/
22. https://www.webopedia.com/TERM/D/distributed_processing.html
23. www.cisconetworking.com
24. www.google.com
25. www.wikipedia.com

3

Perspectives and Foundations of Swarm Intelligence and its Application

Rashmi Agrawal

Manav Rachna International Institute of Research and Studies, Faridabad, India

Abstract

Swarm intelligence (SI) is the cooperative behavior of self-organized, decentralized systems which may be natural or artificial. Examples of SI include the nest-building of social insects, cooperative transportation, group foraging of social insects, and collective cataloging and grouping. Ant colony optimization, bee-inspired algorithms, particle swarm optimization, bacterial foraging optimization, firefly algorithms, fish swarm optimization, and many more are SI algorithms.

Optimization methods have grown over the time to unravel many engineering problems of variable complexity. Hence, this is an emerging area of scientific research. Optimization using SI is used to solve many engineering problems now days. Optimization tools are exploited to assist optimal decision-making in the development, strategy, and operation of major systems. Primarily, optimization encompasses systematically selecting solutions from permissible set of decision variables for maximizing the repayment and minimizing the fatalities. The objective of this chapter is to discuss some bio-mimicry algorithms and their applications.

Keywords: Swarm intelligence, bee foraging, ABC algorithm, MBO algorithm, GSO algorithm

3.1 Introduction

We, at all times, need innovative computing techniques because the digital revolution has changed the cultures in terms of industrial production, transportation, communication, technological advances, administration, and many more other fields [1]. All the solutions to these problems cannot be provided by the available hardware and software because of the drawback of the traditional techniques. The computing tasks/devices must be:

- fairly predictable;
- well defined;
- quantifiable in realistic time with serial computers.

Email: drrashmiagrawal78@gmail.com

Abhishek Kumar, Pramod Singh Rathore, Vicente Garrcia Diaz and Rashmi Agrawal (eds.) Swarm Intelligence Optimization: Algorithms and Applications, (41–48) © 2021 Scrivener Publishing LLC. ISBN 978-1-119-77874-5

Swarm intelligence (SI) is a key concept in artificial intelligence with evolving properties. The critical inspiration of SI algorithms is to utilize numerous effortless agents applying roughly no rule which leads to an evolving inclusive behavior. In general terms, SI can be considered as the collective behavior evolved from social insects working over very few set of laws in which self-organization is the primary component. Several illustrious examples of SI come from the world of animals, such as fish school, birds flock, and bugs swarm [2]. The social relations among individuals facilitate them to acclimatize to the surroundings more proficiently since more information is gathered from the whole swarm. In 1994, Millonas gave five principles which should be satisfied by a swarm in order to exhibit smart behavior. These are the following:

1) Proximity Principle: It is the ability to accomplish simple time and space computation.
2) Quality Principle: Able to retort to factors (quality) present in the atmosphere.
3) Diverse Response Principle: Ability to allocate resources into many nodes.
4) Principle of Stability: Stable behavior of swarm in fluctuating environment.
5) Principle of Adaptability: Adaptable behavior whenever needed.

Conduct of swarm with the above features has been modeled by various researchers [3, 4]. The motivation in this area emerged around 1990 by the work of [4] on ant colony optimization and by [4, 5] on bird flocking and fish schooling.

3.2 Behavioral Phenomena of Living Beings and Inspired Algorithms

In this section, we present the natural phenomena of some living beings which motivated problem solving of computational models.

3.2.1 Bee Foraging

Foraging is a significant assignment in hive as many social insects spend most of their life in only food foraging. Besides the eminence of food and direction, the bee can calculate approximately the distance of food source and the hive location along with the idea of energy consumption in this. They immediately share this information with other bees through a particular type of dance, known as waggle dance and also through the direct contact (trophallaxis). Two types of bees are found—scout bees which decide the foraging and other bees which are involved in waggle dance. The information related to quality of food source is shared through waggle dance and contacts through antennae (Reinhard and Srinivasan, 2009). Dance intensity and antennae contact is directly dependent on the food quality. Better the quality of food, intense dance, and contact, more accurate information related to source is found.

After deliverance of food, the bee can exhibit three types of behavior—involve in waggle dance to attract more bees, return to food source, or abandon the old food source and find new food source.

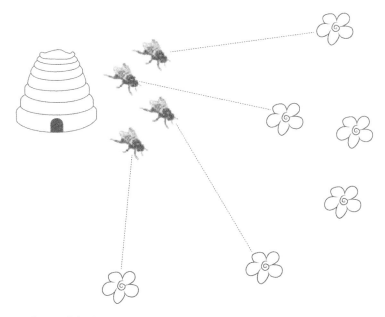

Figure 3.1 Bee foraging behavior.

Such behavior inspired to have algorithms for optimization problems. Some of the interesting algorithms found in literature based on fee foraging behavior (as shown in Figure 3.1) are honey bee algorithm given by [7], bees swarm optimization proposed by [8], virtual bee algorithm by [8, 9], and artificial bee colony algorithm popularly known as ABC [9]. In this chapter, we present the algorithm—artificial bee colony (ABC).

3.2.2 ABC Algorithm

The ABC algorithm simulates the bee foraging behavior for solving the computational problems. This algorithm is generally preferred over other optimization algorithms owing to its flexibility, robustness, and simplicity. It is also easy to implement in terms of the relational and logical form. The algorithm uses three forms of the scout bees, onlookers, and employed bees [10].

During the initial phase, the colony is divided into two types of bees: 50 % of bees are employed bees and rest is onlookers. A random initial candidate solution is generated for the employed bees. A fitness value of the novel result is calculated and if fitness of new candidate solution is better, it is replaced with the previous. The process is repeated for all employed bees so that the colony have the best employed bees. The ABC algorithm has been shown in Figure 3.2.

This algorithm is applied to solve the complex problems like graph coloring, traveling salesman, bioinformatics, and other benchmarking optimization problems.

3.2.3 Mating and Marriage

In the colony of honey bee, only the queen is the reproductive female and this mating happens during a mating flight when several male bees (drones) follow a high fly behind the

```
Initialization: Generate the initial population zᵢ = 1, 2,..., SN
Evaluate the fitness (fᵢ) of the population
cycle = 1;
REPEAT
  FOR each employed bee {
    Produce new solution
    Calculate the value fᵢ
    Apply greedy selection process }
    Calculate the probability values pᵢ for the solutions zᵢ
  FOR each onlooker bee {
      Select a solution zᵢ depending on pᵢ
      Produce new solution
      Calculate fᵢ
      Apply greedy selection }
    IF an abandoned solution for the scout exists,
    THEN replace it with a new solution at random
  Memorize the best solution so far
  cycle++;
UNTIL cycle = MCN
```

Figure 3.2 ABC Algorithm.

queen bee. The mating between drone and queen happens in the air. The queen's abdomen stores the sperms of the drones and uses them to fertilize eggs in its complete lifecycle.

The computational model is imitated grounded on the fact that the queen is best in the colony and a drone is selected probabilistically from a group. Various optimization algorithms based on bee mating are given by [11]. In this section, we discuss the MBO algorithm.

3.2.4   MBO Algorithm

Marriage in (MBO) honey bee optimization is the initial algorithm given by Abbas (2001a) which is based on mating of honey bee. We can summarize it in the following steps:

First Step: Mating flight where a queen selects a drone randomly.

Second Step: Creation of new broods (trial solution) by applying crossover genotypes of drones and queen.

Third Step: Utilize workers (which is heuristics in computational model) to perform local search on broods (trial solutions).

Fourth Step: Adjustment of workers' appropriateness which is based on the amount of enhancement achieved on broods.

Final Step: Finally, weaker queens are substituted by fitter broods.

3.2.5   Coakroach Behavior

There is a novel version of the PSO algorithm which is called Roach Infestation Optimization (RIO). This algorithm is motivated by current findings in the social behavior of cockroaches. Practically, cockroaches not only have a version for the light, but the corporation of groups is also enjoyed by them.

It is clear from the recent research that social behavior of cockroaches is more adaptable as compare to the human being. There is a complexity in the social conduct of cockroaches. Aggregates or groups can also be formed by the cockroaches [12].

3.3   Roach Infestation Optimization

On the basis of cockroach behavior, we can define three simple behavior of cockroach agents:

In the search space, cockroaches always search for the darkest location.

Cockroaches enjoy the company of friends and socialize with nearby cockroaches.

After a particular time period, there is a feeling of hunger in the cockroaches and for this they can leave the comfort of darkness or friendship to search for food.

The RIO is a cockroach-inspired. Find_Darkness behavior and a portion of the velocity update equation in the particle swarm optimization can be modeled together.

Find_Friends behavior is an important element in the RIO algorithm. It is assumed that all cockroach agents initiate themselves as individuals and their Find_Darkness behavior is used to govern them. Every cockroach has its own radius of moving area. If any cockroach agent found within another cockroach agent's detection radius, then there is a probability that these roaches will socialize or they will form a group. When two cockroach agents meet, there is always a probability of communication between them in regard of their knowledge of the search space to each other.

Find_Food behavior in RIO algorithm arises when a cockroach agent becomes hungry and it searches for food. This can be imitated with the help of defining a hunger counter with the specified threshold value and the same can be used to count the level of hunger for each agent. After reaching at the defined threshold limit by the counter, random food location can be guided to each cockroach agent. Initially, these food locations are randomly initialized within the specified limit in the search space. A piece of food can be placed randomly at different locations after eaten by a hungry cockroach agent. In this way, there is always a probability of presence of food in the search space as shown in Figures 3.3 and 3.4.

3.3.1   Lampyridae Bioluminescence

Lampyridae is a family of insects that are gifted to turn out natural light to catch the attention of a mate or a prey. They are generally known as fireflies or lightning bugs. Whenever the firefly looks for a mate or is hungry, it glows its light to catch the attention of the opposite. The

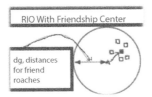

Figure 3.3 RIO.

```
initialize n roaches to random positions
loop tMax times
  compute distances between all roaches
  compute median distance
  for-each roach
    compute number neighbors
    exchange data with neighbors
    if not hungry
      compute new velocity
      compute new position
      check if new best position
    else if hungry
      relocate to new position
    end-if
  end-for
end loop
return best position found
```

Figure 3.4 Algorithm: Roach Infestation Optimization (RIO) (source: https://docs.microsoft.com/en-us/ archive/msdn-magazine/2016/february/test-run-roach-infestation-optimization).

brightness intensity is dependent on the pigment luciferin [13]. Two main algorithm in this category are glow-worm swarm optimization (GSO) algorithm and firefly algorithm (FA).

3.3.2   GSO Algorithm

Considering as usage to cooperative robotics of the GSO algorithm [14], the actions are constructed only on limited information and discriminating neighbor interactions. This empowers the swarm to split into separate subcategories that can congregate to numerous optima of a given multimodal function. Flowchart of GSO algorithm is shown in Figure 3.5, as given below.
   Applications of GSO:

- Solving nonlinear equation systems.
- Localization and neutralizing of hostile sensors or transmitters.
- Spotting various causes of a general nutrient profile, disseminated on a two-dimensional workspace, using multiple robots.
- To solve multi-constrained (QoS) multicast routing problem (MQMR) problem [15].

3.4   Conclusion

We performed a literature review to find the applications of SI in the algorithms mentioned above. Although this is not extensive, we have covered the major important algorithms which are used in swarm optimization in different domains. The community of computer science has understood the significance of swarm behavior for solving the complex problems. Knowledge about the communal behavior of living beings is able to provide motivating and constructive swarm-based meta-heuristics. In fact, there is no best approach;

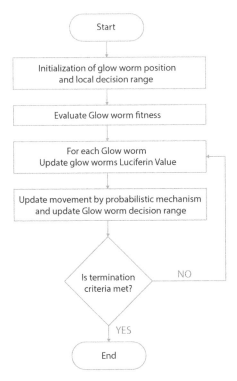

Figure 3.5 Flowchart of GSO algorithm.

more work is required in this area to implement these swarm-based meta-heuristic to get improved solutions. Future research may be done in the mathematical modeling of discrete optimization, continuous optimization, or for the multi-objective optimization.

References

1. Abbass, H.A., Marriage in honey bees optimisation: A haplometrosis polygynous swarming approach, in: *The congress on evolutionary computation, CEC2001*, Seoul, Korea, vol. 1, pp. 207–214, 2001a.
2. Abbass, H.A., A monogenous mbo approach to satisfiability, in: *International conference on computational intelligence for modelling, control and automation, CIMCA2001*, 2001b.
3. Abbass, H.A., A single queen single worker honey bees approach to 3-sat, in: *The genetic and evolutionary computation conference, GECCO2001*, San Francisco, USA, 2001c.
4. Abbass, H.A. and Teo, J., A true annealing approach to the marriage in honey-bees optimization algorithm. *Int. J. Comput. Intell. Appl.*, 3, 199–211, 2003.
5. Dorigo, M., Maniezzo, V., Colorni, A., Positive feedback as a search strategy. Technical Report 91-016, Politecnico di Milano, Italy, 1991.

6. Drias, H., Sadeg, S., Yahi, S., Cooperative bees swarm for solving the maximum weighted satisfiability problem, in: *IWAAN International Work Conference on Artificial and Natural Neural Networks*, pp. 318–325, 2005.

7. Grosan, C. and Abraham, A., Stigmergic optimization: inspiration, technologies and perspectives, in: *Stig-mergic optimization. Studies in computational intelligence*, vol. 31, pp. 1–24, Springer-Verlag Berlin Heidelberg, Berlin, 2006.

8. Karaboga, D., An idea based on honey bee swarm for numerical optimization. Technical report, Erciyes University, Engineering Faculty, Computer Engineering Department, Turkey, 2005.

9. Kennedy, J. and Eberhart, R., Particle swarm optimization, in: *IEEE international conference on neural networks*, Piscataway, NJ, pp. 1942–1948, 1995.

10. Krishnanand, K. and Ghose, D., Detection of multiple source locations using a glowworm metaphor with applications to collective robotics, in: *Proceedings of the IEEE Swarm Intelligence Symposium*, pp. 84–91, 2005.

11. Millonas, M.M., Swarms, phase transitions, and collective intelligence, in: *Artificial life III*, pp. 417–445, Addison-Wesley, Reading, New York, 1994.

12. Nakrani, S. and Tovey, C., On honey bees and dynamic allocation in an internet server colony, in: *Proceedings of 2nd International Workshop on the Mathematics and Algorithms of Social Insects*, 2003.

13. Reinhard, J. and Srinivasan, S., The role of scents in honey bee foraging and recruitment, in: *Food Exploitation by Social Insects: Ecological, Behavioral, and Theoretical Approaches*, 1st ed., pp. 165–182, CRC Press, Florida, 2009.

14. Sousa, T., Silva, A., Neves, A., Particle swarm based data mining algorithmsfor classification tasks. *Parallel Comput.*, 30, 767–783.26, 2004.

15. Stützle, T. and Hoo, H.H., MAX-MIN ant system. *Future Gener. Comput. Syst.*, 16, 889–914.27, 2000.

4

Implication of IoT Components and Energy Management Monitoring

Shweta Sharma[1]*, Praveen Kumar Kotturu[2†] and Prafful Chandra Narooka[3‡]

[1]MDSU Ajmer, Ajmer, India
[2]Big Data & Analytics, KPMG, India
[3]Agarwal College Merta Cityr, Rajasthan, India

Abstract

The Internet of Things (IoT) gives chances to control interconnected shrewd gadgets by means of pre-structured situations with little or no human association. Because of the requirement for efficient improvement of mechanical vitality productivity and the importance of IoT-based vitality, the board frameworks (EMS) are continually expanding. Mechanical IoT (IIoT)–improved EMS are made to help the advanced change of undertakings. They increment the straightforwardness of vitality utilization insights, improve the work force consciousness of vitality misfortunes, and give prescient investigation instruments to determining potential modern mishaps and future vitality request.

Keywords: (IoT) components, energy management, smart energy management system, intelligent energy management in buildings, smart home for energy management using IoT

4.1 Introduction

Internet of Things (IoT):

The ascent of the Internet of Things (IoT) in all likelihood is the most significant single improvement in the long advancement of vitality management. The reason of vitality of the executives is controlling components at a central and granular level. The more significant and the more firmly is the control, the better. In a world that is soaked in IoT gadgets, that control will be very profound. The billions—and necessarily trillions—and various sensors of gadgets will make a work that will stimulate centrality of the authorities and administrations and an approach that would have been incomprehensible generally.

The IoT is the continuous movement in media transmission will be prepared, wherein the devices for customary day-to-day survival will be outfitted with microcontrollers, handsets for cutting edge correspondence, and acceptable, which show that it will set them up

---

Corresponding author: sharmashweta671@gmail.com
†*Corresponding author:* kotturu@me.com
‡*Corresponding author:* narooka.prafull@gmail.com

Abhishek Kumar, Pramod Singh Rathore, Vicente Garrcia Diaz and Rashmi Agrawal (eds.) Swarm Intelligence Optimization: Algorithms and Applications, (49–66) © 2021 Scrivener Publishing LLC. ISBN 978-1-119-77874-5

Figure 4.1 Internet of Things (IoT).

to chat with each other and with the customers, changing into an imperative piece of the internet. The opinion in IoT web of things focuses in making the Internet progressively reliable and unpreventable. In this way, by allowing basic access and communication with a wide sequence of contraptions, for example, home devices, recognition cameras, checking sensors, actuators, grandstands, vehicles, and etc. The IoT will help in the improvement of specific operations that will utilize the possibly immense aggregate and collection of knowledge created through such information to give new organizations to inhabitants, associations, and open associations (Figure 4.1) [1].

Figure 4.2 displays the different inclinations of the network of things like the various techniques for interfacing our gadgets and mechanical that get together to the web from wherever in this world and incorporating this network with our home and the related gadgets. IoT advancement is the relationship of different frameworks in installed contraptions utilized in the customary day-by-day presence integrated into the Internet. It intends to computerize the activity of various spaces, for example, home machines, human services frameworks, security and observation frameworks, mechanical frameworks, transportation frameworks, military frameworks, electrical frameworks, and numerous others. So as to accomplish a completely mechanized procedure, gadgets in the various spaces must be furnished with miniaturized scale controllers, handsets, and conventions to encourage and institutionalize their correspondence with one another and with outside substances. Sensors, Global Positioning Systems (GPS), cameras, and Radio Frequency Identification Devices (RFIDs) are instances of gadgets that endure at acknowledgement layer.

Figure 4.2 Relation with different phases.

IoT structures utilize a mixture of Internet and short-go systems, subject to the passed on the social events. Short-expand correspondence developments, for instances, Bluetooth and Zigbee, are used to give the data from acumen gadgets to a near to entry. Various advances, for instances, Wireless Fidelity, 2G, 3G, and 4G, are pass on the data for long partitions, subject to the application. These structures and machines consolidate sensors and actuators that screen nature and assign perception information to a control unit at home. The control unit empowers the homeowner to interminably screen and totally control the electrical machines. It, furthermore, utilizes the observation data to foresee future enterprise to be set up ahead of schedule for a progressively strong, pleasing, secure, and convincing living condition. Different usages about the brilliant network idea continue in human services, overseeing common assets, and empowering bolster person to person communication. The idea of a shrewd network is stretched out to build up a savvy city. This trouble has incited the development of various and real proposal for the reasonable confirmation of IoT structures. In this manner, from the frameworks, it can be seen that the imitation of an IoT composition, together with the required back end that manages organizations gadgets, still comes up the mark on a developed best practice because of its peculiarity and multifaceted nature. Despite the specific difficulties, the gathering of the IoT perspective is like a manner obstructed by the nonappearance of a sensible and large recognized strategy that can pull in dares to propel the sending of these advancements. Here, in unpredictable circumstance, the utilization of the IoT to an urban setting is very convincing, as it reacts to the information of various national governments to grasp Information and Communication Technology (ICT) courses of action in the organization of open issues, thus understanding the alleged Smart City thought. Regardless of the way that there is not yet a formal and for the most part recognized significance of "Wise City," the last point is to use the open resources, extending the possibility of the organizations that allow the inhabitants, although diminishing the operational expenses of the open affiliations. Within explanation should be possible through the execution of an IoT that will be essential and straightforward to different foundation of open organizations. A staggered IoT may convey different preferences to the organization and improve the standard open organizations, for instances, transportation and halting, lighting, observation and upkeep of open districts, defending of social legacy, waste combination, centers, and academy. Besides, the accessibility of various sorts of information, assembled through Arduino with IoT, may moreover be mishandled to build the straightforwardness and advance the activities of the cognizance of individuals about the status of their home, brace the dynamic enthusiasm for the association of criticalness use, what's more vitalize the formation of new associations upon those gave by the IoT [2].

The most significant features about IoT is to coordinate man-made intellectual competence, web, sensors, dynamic commitment, and little device use. The features are given below.

- Artificial Intelligence: IoT, in essentially every practical sense, all intents all "savvy", which means it improves any piece of presence with the depth of data assortment, man-made awareness estimations, and frameworks. This can mean something as immediate as upgrading your cooler and cabinets to admit when milk and your favored grain come up short and to then place in a solicitation with your favored sustenance seller.
- Availability: New empowering advancements for systems association and specifically IoT that are analyze through mean structures are never again simply associated with basic suppliers. Systems can exist on a considerably smaller and increasingly reasonable scale while as, of not long ago, being pragmatic. IoT generates these little systems between its structure apparatus.
- Sensors: IoT loses its differentiation without sensors. They go about as portraying instruments which modify IoT from a standard inert arrangement of gadgets into a working framework that organizes to do veritable joining.
- Dynamic Engagement: Much of the present assistance with identification of development happens through uninvolved responsibility. IoT presents another perspective for dynamic substance, component, or organization responsibility.
- Small Devices: Devices, as externalize, have reduced, more affordable, and significantly all the more common after some time. IoT exploits the logic that assembled little application to pass on its precision, versatility, and adaptability [3].

Focal Points
- The upsides of IoT have length over every area of lifestyle and business. Here is a once-over of a segment of the central focuses that IoT brings to the table.
- IoT Enhanced Customer Engagement: Present assessment experiences the corrupt effects of defenseless sides and flaws that are critical imperfections in precision; and as noted, authority remains confine. IoT perfectly changes this to conclude progressively excessive and frequently ground-breaking duty for swarms.
- Innovation Development: Comparable advances and data which improve the client experience additionally improve gadget use and help in continuously astonishing moves up to improvement. IoT opens an immense breadth of fundamental sensible and handle information.
- Reduced Waste: IoT gains regions of ground clear. Current assessment gives us shallow mindfulness, yet IoT gives genuine information that is continuously viable association of advantages.
- Enhanced Information Collection: Modern data assortment experiences its obstructions and its arrangement for detached use. IoT breaks it out of those spaces and places it decisively where people truly need to go to analyze our world. It allows a precise picture of everything [4].

4.2   IoT Components

We present an idea that will help in describing the sections recommended for IoT from a raised level viewpoint. Focal points of all part can be discovered somewhere else. There are three IoT parts which connect steady capability. 1) Hardware: These contain sensors, actuators, and implanted correspondence framework. 2) Middleware: These limit and figure devices for information examination. 3) Presentation: This has depiction and explanation programming, which can be found a workable pace arrangements and can be expected for various applications. Here, we talk about the advancement of a certain class that the three sections communicated already [5].

The ArduinoMega 2560 R3

ATmega2560 belongs in an umbrella of microcontrollers.Atmega2560, commonly found in the Arduino Mega 2560 as its main microcontrolle. The Arduino Mega 2560 is an ATmega2560 microcontroller board. It has 54 computerized information/yield sticks in which 14 Pulse Width Modulation (PWM) yield pins, 4 Universal Asynchronous Receiver/Transmitter (UART), a 16-MHz gem oscillator, 16 information basic, a USB association, a force jack, an In Circuit Serial Programming (ICSP) header, and a reset catch. It has everything that is expected to help the ATmega2560 microcontroller. It might be an essentially interface with a PC with a USB interface. The can't avoid being the pictorial depiction of the ATmega2560. The Arduino Mega 2560 is an ATmega2560 microcontroller board. It has 54 mechanized information/yield sticks in which 14 PWM yield pins, 16 data basic, 4 UART, a 16-MHz pearl oscillator, a USB affiliation, a power jack, an ICSP header, and a reset catch. It has all that is expected to help the ATmega2560 microcontroller. It may be essentially interfaced with a PC with a USB interface, and it will, in general, be topped off by an Ac-to-Dc connector or battery. It will be largely topped up through an Ac-to-Dc connector or battery (Figure 4.3) [6].

"Espressif Module" ESP8266

Figure 4.4 addresses the picture of infrared (IR) sensor. IR sensor works through utilizing unequivocal light source as a medium to recognize light wavelength in the IR range.

Figure 4.3 The Arduino Mega 2560 R3.

Figure 4.4 The ESP8266.

Utilizing Light Emitting Diode (LED) makes light at same wavelength which the sensor is looking. At the point when moving toward the sensor, the light from the LED ricochets off from the thing and within the light sensor. This outcomes in an enormous bounce of the force, that will be recognized utilizing an edge signal [7].

RFID

Radio Frequency Identification is the most recent model in correspondence which utilizes outstandingly arranged microchips by remote information correspondence. They support in customized recognizing confirmation of anything they are joined to going about as an electronic institutionalized distinguishing proof.

Figure 4.5 addresses to the uninvolved RFID marks, which is not battery controlled, and they utilize the force of the perusers questioning sign to confer the Id through the RFID peruser. This has achieved various functions particularly in trade and stock framework of the board. The functions can be established in transportation and, moreover, entry control operations. The uninvolved marks are correct currently utilized in many bank cards and street cost names which are among the essential overall plans. Effective RFID names have their own inbuilt battery supply and can be without quite a bit of a stretch impart. Of the couple of uses, the key use of effective RFID marks is in port compartments for confirming load [8].

Temperature and humidity sensor DHT11

Figure 4.6 speaks to the DHT11 sensor. This DHT11 is a Temperature and Humidity Sensor with an aligned computerized yield with the temperature and moistness perusing. This innovation guarantees the high unwavering quality and a long haul ease of use. It has an eight-piece microcontroller. This sensor incorporates a resistive component and a feeling of wet NTC temperature estimating gadgets. It has magnificent quality, quick reaction, hostile to obstruction capacity, and significant expense execution preferences.

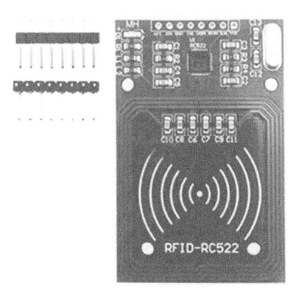

Figure 4.5 RFID wireless component.

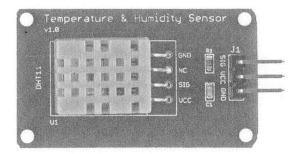

Figure 4.6 DHT11 sensor.

All DHT11sensors have an exact adjustment for stickiness chamber. The alignment coefficients put away in the OTP program memory, inward sensors identify flags all the while, and we should call these adjustment coefficients. The sequential interface framework is incorporated to turn out to be speedy and simple. Little size, low force, and sign can be transmitted up to 20 meters, making it an assortment of utilizations and even the most requesting applications. This has four-pin single-line pin. The association has extraordinary variations that can be given by clients' need [8, 9].

Gas Sensor

Figure 4.7 shows the gas sensor. A gas sensor is a gadget that recognizes the closeness of gas in a particular zone. This sensor works together including a gas utilizing manufactured substances into evaluate its obsession. All gas admits an intriguing breakdown voltage

Figure 4.7 Gas sensor.

sensor that perceives gases by evaluating these voltages. The centralization of the gas can be directed through assessing the present release in the gadget. The mq5 gas sensor perceives the proximity of different gases, for instances, carbon monoxide, hydrogen, methane, and liquefied petroleum gas (LPG) going from 100 to 3,000 ppm. While a gas teams up by the manufactured mixes in the sensor, it is first inside constituents and is then adsorbed by the recognizing elements. At the time, in this methodology, the potential differences are given through the pins. The gas sensor component has a steel body under which an identifying part is housed. This distinguishing element is presented to current through interfacing leads. The gases moving toward the recognizing elements get inside and are devoured by the distinguishing part. This moves the resistance of distinguishing elements, which changes the current going out [9].

4.3   IoT Energy Management

IoT empowers process robotization and operational effectiveness in fundamentally every industry—medicinal services, retail, fabricating, vitality, and coordination. IoT applications in the vitality segment develop unique consideration from shoppers, management, and even governments. Aside from various advantages to the electric force store network, IoT vitality of the board frameworks offers approach to new more brilliant lattices which guarantee remarkable reserve funds, improved security, and upgraded productivity [10].

"Vitality investment funds are acknowledged through improved perceivability. Information perceivability drives fitting vitality sparing activities, along these lines accomplishing hierarchical goals."

Our savvy vitality of the administration framework is intended to upgrade vitality utilization along these lines, improving use, diminishing costs, anticipating upkeep needs, and expanding the unwavering quality of vitality resources. It carefully procures vitality information, which can empower ventures to delineate powerful execution against characterized focuses to recognize deviations. This, thus, will guarantee very much oversaw and controlled activity to convey the most vitality and emanation proficient degree of efficiency [11].

Essentialness is one of the critical resources for any business. Rising essentialness costs, expanding request, and severe requirement of government arrangements are a portion of the impelling elements that have driven various associations to discover shrewd ways for observing, controlling, and sparing vitality. Examining essentialness use over your whole affiliation is a staggering endeavor and routinely ends up in a plenitude of data. In the present related world, the future of essentialness will be relentlessly associated with IoT. The vital need is a shrewd Energy Management System (EnMS) that can add to diminishing the costs, improving profitability, and fulfilling your imperativeness needs.

IoT Energy Management Solution is the answer for clients' hardships and an empowering influence of computerized change. Our answer can be used to more readily deal with your vitality utilization designs in business and mechanical parts by assuming total responsibility for your vitality information at a major and granular level [12].

4.4   Implication of Energy Measurement for Monitoring

Estimation can extend from just utility meters for little associations up to finish observing and estimation frameworks associated with a product application fit for combining

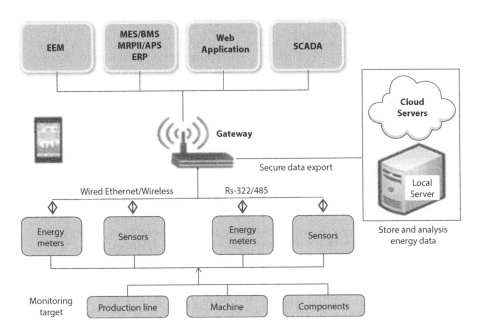

Figure 4.8 Energy management (IoT).

information and conveying programmed examination. It is dependent upon the association to decide the methods and strategies for estimation (Figure 4.8) [13].

Estimating vitality information is a key segment for executing the vitality of the board plan. To be done successfully, a director needs to:

- Establish a vitality information estimation framework;
- Designate staff responsible for checking vitality use;
- Ensure appropriate utilization of vitality estimating instruments and guarantee well-being of meters; and
- Provide vitality information in a total and convenient way.

Assigning staff individuals to actualize vitality estimation is significant in making a powerful framework. Setting up a report that the organization estimates vitality in subtle ways is fundamental.

Despite the fact that estimating vitality information just reflect "by and large utilization" instead of vitality productivity, it is as yet major in assessing vitality effectiveness and vitality sparing chances.

Organizations should gauge vitality utilization by considering:

- Overall vitality utilization;
- Utilization of energy in electrical cables and offices;
- Utilization of energy in office and creation gear.

4.5   Execution of Industrial Energy Monitoring

Vitality effectiveness checking and benchmarking are significant for vitality of the executives, as they empower leaders to distinguish improvement openings and to monitor the impacts of their choices on vitality use. Checking and examining machines' vitality utilization and

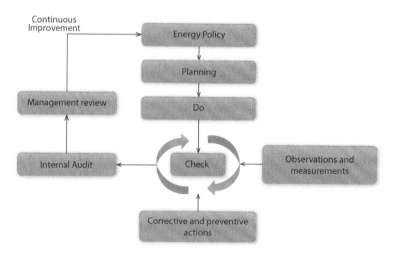

Figure 4.9 Energy monitoring.

backing and assembling forms are the initial move toward expanding vitality productivity. Inadequate checking may bring about organizations not monitoring their potential for productive vitality ventures. Also, observing of vitality utilization of the venture underpins the judgment with respect to whether foreseen vitality investment funds could be accomplished or not. Observing additionally recognizes the most serious procedures of vitality. In this segment, all parts of vitality checking, for example, information assortment, examination, introduction, and proportions of execution will be secured. This segment likewise dissects existing procedures for information assortment, examination, show, and execution measures [14].

4.6 Information Collection

Gathering information with standard strategies is significant. One of the ongoing principles for an information trade gadget is ELB-REV4, which was utilized to screen vitality utilization. Vitality utilization information can be assembled, utilizing measurable information, vitality reviews, and vitality asset reports and polls. All enormous industry organizations and vitality suppliers are gathering verifiable vitality utilization for factual information. Essentialness audit joins examination and examination of imperativeness streams for essentialness assurance in a system, method, or structure to diminish the proportion of essentialness commitment to the system without conflictingly affecting the output(s), perceiving the wellsprings of essentialness use and the coordinated efforts with atmosphere, inhabitance, and working timetables. Information assortment uses the vitality asset reports, where it shows the pertinent vitality information and yield and separate vitality utilized in different procedures to distinguish the "vitality focuses," which may then be broke down for vitality sparing potential [15].

4.7 Vitality Profiles Analysis

Commonly, machines comprise of some vitality devouring parts that create a particular vitality profile while delivering. Examination of vitality profiles from various worldly creation levels gives point-by-point data about vitality utilization and distinguishes issues and possibilities for vitality proficiency improvement [16].

Wise Power and Energy Management utilizing IoT
A path for the corporate and private grounds structures to proficiently oversee power utilization.

The IoT—an innovation where the edge gadgets are coordinated and trade information by means of the web—offers critical open doors for organizations to settle on more brilliant and increasingly educated choices to improve their center business activities with negligible manual mediation [17].

IoT, as far as force and vitality of the board, empowers the business to successfully comprehend their vitality utilization and expenses continuously at every hub, in this way, giving significant bits of knowledge that can lessen the working expenses and increment proficiency in the use of power. A constant test and the arrangement that Daemon Software with its ability in IoT gets to determine the issue.

Think about a structure in an instructive organization. There are number of floors with each floor having numerous rooms and it is not essentially practical to physically screen each room's capacity utilization and control the wastage of power continuous when detainees are nowhere to be found. Basic zones which need not bother with electric lights cannot be turned off remotely dependent on a particular arrangement of rules.

The above issue was completely investigated in various situations, and a powerful IoT arrangement was given. Daemon's IoT group has given a versatile arrangement NABTO IO stage with a two-advance methodology that settled the above challenge. A viable method for utilizing the force in the structure was executed with the Daemon Electro-POD gadget [18].

- Monitor the force utilization on explicit interims and gather use designs for analytics.
- Real-time control of the force utilization at the edge dependent on Business Intelligence (BI) activating computerized rules to oversee utilization (Figure 4.10) [19].

Screen and Analyze
- With remote observing capacities, the framework would have the option to gather information on use in every unit to comprehend use examples and pinnacle use.
- The framework can help outline use rules dependent on the information gathered.
- Monitoring cautions are sent dependent on use design special cases.
- Regular use information can be accounted for to the upkeep staff for mediation.

Control
- The power supply for the individual unit can be turned on/off, remotely utilizing the IoT application during non-top hours or when the detainees are not utilizing the unit.
- The power supply for a whole floor can be controlled where every one of the rooms/units in a specific floor is turned on/off, remotely utilizing IoT application during non-top hours.
- Rules can be set to turn-off force in like manner territories according to typical utilization designs.

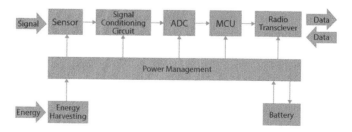

Figure 4.10 Power management in IoT.

- A manual abrogate alternative can be utilized if the IoT gadget neglects to work/react and client can supersede control for special cases.

Force the Executives' Experiences

The information is gathered through IoT gadget and sent to the unified server where the reports can be created to realize the utilization example of each room/unit and floors and find a way to oversee power utilization and lessen the expense [20].

4.8 IoT-Based Smart Energy Management System

Introduction

Vitality is a significant angle for any family unit, enterprises, and, thus, farming. Dealing with the vitality proficiently and saving it cleverly for machines are particularly significant. The vitality use is legitimately influenced by coal, oil, and, thus toward, power age. Toward this, there has been piece of analysis task did in working up few keen lighting framework relating to homeroom for moderating the vitality. In other research, analysts have created Android-established Smart home framework for checking the utilization of capacity to stay away from each sort of inconsistency [21].

4.9 Smart Energy Management System

The flow smart home and power administration controlling the framework have looked more toward the gear, just overseeing instability for electrical deficiencies. In none of the examination, framework is to be made into imperativeness, safeguarding through normal conditions, was checking and should be controlling the hardware use in like manner. So, with the best in class of machine to machine correspondence called IoT, we have to help an IoT arranged energy management system where basic sensors like warmth and light force sensor utilized and breakdown distinguished are sent to Arduino Microcontroller. Considering recognized examination, the Arduino microcontroller is changed to control the machine usage as necessities will be. Regardless of controlling the machine use, the extent of current drawn by each device is figured using hall sensor which is sent remotely using Wi-Fi element to Raspberry Pi3 where full-scale power use of any mechanical get together is PC unpredictably and same plotted as framework. The graphical information on power use versus time for every mechanical gathering with differentiating trademark situation is moved in cloud server. The structure plan of IoT-based energy management system is showed up in Figure 4.11. Figure 4.12 shows the data flow diagram and use case outline of our structure.

The light force sensor BH1750 is used to check the power of light from lux and send it to the Arduino. The heat and soddenness from the DHT11 sensor accomplish the code runs by Arduino. The Arduino though controls fan and light that are subject to the heat, humidity, and light power. Considering the information got, the Arduino will comparatively control the voltage that should have been sent to the machine with the assistance of transistor. The hall sensor will check the proportion of current sent to the mechanical assembly and deliver it to the Arduino. The Arduino will by then send the current used to the Raspberry Pi [22]. The pi gets the current expended and figure the force devoured and a brief timeframe later

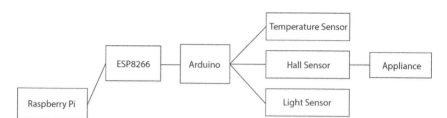

Figure 4.11 Smart energy management system.

trade it to a page and, moreover, will plot a chart dependent on the proportion of current devoured [22, 23].

4.10 IoT-Based System for Intelligent Energy Management in Buildings

The vitality segment is firmly interconnected with the structure division and coordinated ICT that answers for successful vitality of the board, supporting basic leadership at building, region, and city level that are key essential components for making a smart city. The accessible frameworks are planned and expected solely for a predefined number of cases and structures without taking into consideration development and interoperability with different applications that is, in part, because of the absence of semantics [24]. A propelled IoT-based system for clever vitality of the executives in structures. A semantic structure is displayed, focusing on the brought together and institutionalized demonstrating of the substances that establish the structure condition. Appropriate guidelines are framed, focusing on the keen vitality of the executives and the general usual way of doing things of Smart Building. In this specific circumstance, an IoT-based system was executed, which overhauls the instinct of the structures' imperativeness and the officials' structures [25].

4.11 Smart Home for Energy Management Using IoT

Figure 4.13 shows the square outline of smart home importance the board structures utilizing IoT. There are different kinds of sensors are such as gas sensor, fire sensor, passive IT sensor (PIR sensor), temperature sensor, and IR sensor for different purposes, and all these are connected with the Arduino mega microcontroller, and the stores are connected with the microcontroller through the hand-off circuit. This entire model is controlled by sun arranged noteworthiness and a 12v dc battery. The standard perfect circumstance of this structure is that it is connected with the web so the entire strategy can be controlled from wherever on the planet at whatever point related with the web. Adroit home robotization and criticalness the authorities frameworks got together with IoT is a work which accentuation on the more sagacious world [26]. The reason for the work is to build up a sharp home which can be controlled over web from remote spots. The usage of IoT gives the client to check his own location over the web by utilizing mobiles and PCs [27].

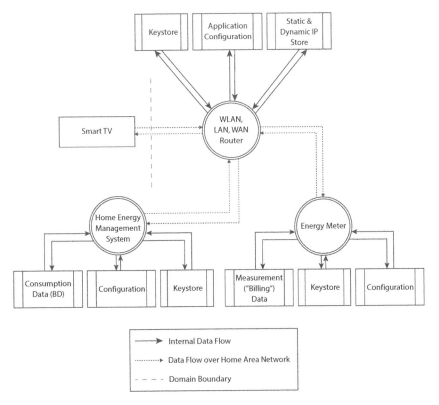

Figure 4.12 Data flow diagram (DFD).

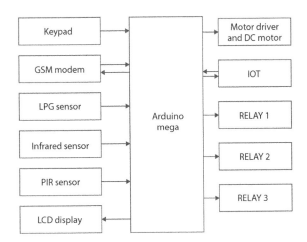

Figure 4.13 Block diagram of smart home energy management systems using IoT.

References

1. Balakrishnan, B. and Balachandran, S., FLECH: fuzzy logic based energy efficient clustering hierarchy for nonuniform wireless sensor networks. *Wireless Commun. Mobile Comput.*, 3, 1–13, 2017.

2. Karaboga, D., An idea based on honey bee swarm for numerical optimization, Technical Report TR06, Erciyes University, Engineering Faculty, Computer Engineering Department, 52, 53, 2005.

3. Darougaran, L., Shahinzadeh, H., Ghotb, H., Ramezanpour, L., Simulated annealing algorithm for data aggregation trees in wireless sensor networks and comparison with genetic algorithm. *Int. J. Electron. Electr. Eng.*, 62, 59–62, 2012.

4. Dhasian, H.R. and Balasubramanian, P., Survey of data aggregation techniques using soft computing in wireless sensor networks. *IET Inform. Secur.*, 7, 4, 336–342, 2013.

5. Yang, E., Ahmet, T., Arslan, T., Barton, N., An Improved Particle Swarm Optimization Algorithm for Power-Efficient Wireless Sensor Networks, IEEE, 0-7695-2919-4/07, 2007.

6. Tan, H.Ö. and Körpeoğlu, İ., Power efficient data gathering and aggregation in wireless sensor networks. *ACM SIGMOD Rec.*, 32, 4, 66–71, Dec. 2003.

7. HevinRajesh, D. and Paramasivan, B., Fuzzy based secure data aggregation technique in wireless sensor networks. *J. Comput. Sci.*, 8, 6, 899–907, 2012.

8. Islam, O., Hussain, S., Zhang, H., Genetic algorithm for data aggregation trees in wireless sensor networks, in: *3rd international conference on Intelligent Environment*, IEEE, pp. 312–316, 2007.

9. Kennedy, J. and Eberhart, R., Particle Swarm Optimization. *IEEE International Conference on Neural Networks*, 1995.

10. Shanbehzadeh, J., Mehrjoo, S., Sarrafzadeh, A., An intelligent energy efficient clustering in wireless sensor networks. *Lecture Notes in Engineering and Computer Science: Proc. of The International Multi Conference of Engineers and Computer Scientists 2011*, 16-18 March, 2011, IMECS, Hong Kong, 2011, pp.

11. Ferentinos, K., Tsiligiridis, T., Arvanitis, K., Energy optimization of wireless sensor networks for environmental measurements, in: *Proc. of the International Conference on Computational Intelligence for Measurement Systems and Applications*, 2005.

12. Kim, J.Y., Sharma, T., Kumar, B., Tomar, G.S., Berry, K., Lee, W.H., Intercluster ant colony optimization algorithm for wireless sensor network in dense environment. *Int. J. Distrib. Sens. Netw.*, 10, 4, 1–10, 2014.

13. Kulkarni, R.V. and Venayagamoorthy, G.K., Particle swarm optimization in wireless-sensor networks: A brief survey. *IEEE Trans. Syst. Man Cybern. Part C (Appl. Rev.)*, 41, 2, 262–267, 2011.

14. Kumar, H. and Singh, P.K., Analyzing Data Aggregation in Wireless Sensor Networks. *4th International Conference on Computing for Sustainable Global Development INDIACom*, IEEE, pp. 4024–4029, 2017.

15. Kumar, H. and Singh, P.K., Node Energy Based Approach to Improve Network Lifetime and Throughput in Wireless Sensor Networks. *J. Telecommun. Electron. Comput. Eng. (JTEC)*, 9, 3–6, 79–88, 2017.

16. Lu, Y., Comsa, I.S., Kuonen, P., Hirsbrunner, B., Probabilistic Data Aggregation Protocol Based on ACO-GA Hybrid Approach in Wireless Sensor Networks, in: *IFIP Wireless and Mobile Networking Conference (WMNC)*, pp. 235–238, 2015, October.

17. Lu, Y., Comsa, I.S., Kuonen, P., Hirsbrunner, B., Probabilistic Data Aggregation Protocol Based on ACO-GA Hybrid Approach in Wireless Sensor Networks, in: *IFIP Wireless and Mobile Networking Conference (WMNC)*, pp. 235–238, 2015, October.

18. Misra, R. and Mandal, C., Ant-aggregation: ant colony algorithm for optimal data aggregation in wireless sensor networks, in: *IFIP International Conference on Wireless and Optical Communications Networks*, pp. 1–5, 2006, April.

19. Mohsenifard, E. and Ghaffari, A., Data aggregation tree structure in wireless sensor networks using cuckoo optimization algorithm. *J. Inf. Syst. Telecommun. (JIST)*, 4, 3, 182–190, 2016.

20. Mohsenifard, E. and Ghaffari, A., Data aggregation tree structure in wireless sensor networks using cuckoo optimization algorithm. *J. Inf. Syst. Telecommun. (JIST)*, 4, 3, 182–190, 2016.

21. Nayak, P. and Vathasavai, B., Energy Efficient Clustering Algorithm for Multi-Hop Wireless Sensor Network Using Type-2 Fuzzy Logic. *IEEE Sens. J.*, 17, 14, 4492–4499, 2017.

22. Nayak, P. and Vathasavai, B., Energy Efficient Clustering Algorithm for Multi-Hop Wireless Sensor Network Using Type-2 Fuzzy Logic. *IEEE Sens. J.*, 17, 14, 4492–4499, 2017.

23. Neamatollahi, P., Naghibzadeh, M., Abrishami, S., Fuzzy-Based Clustering-Task Scheduling for Lifetime Enhancement in Wireless Sensor Networks. *IEEE Sens. J.*, 17, 20, 6837–6844, 2017.

24. Ni, Q., Pan, Q., Du, H., Cao, C., Zhai, Y., A novel cluster head selection algorithm based on fuzzy clustering and particle swarm optimization. *IEEE/ACM Trans. Comput. Biol. Bioinf.*, 14, 1, 76–84, 2017.

25. Norouzi, A., Babamir, F.S., Orman, Z., A tree based data aggregation scheme for wireless sensor networks using GA. *Wireless Sens. Netw.*, 4, 08, 191–196, 2012.

26. RejinaParvin, J. and Vasanthanayaki, C., Particle swarm optimization-based clustering by preventing residual nodes in wireless sensor networks. *IEEE Sens. J.*, 15, 8, 4264–4274, 2015.

27. Jin, S., Zhou, M., Wu, A., Sensor network optimization using a genetic algorithm, in: *Proc. of the 7th World Multiconference on Systemics, Cybernetics and Informatics*, 2003.

28. Lindsey, S. and Raghavendra, C.S., Pegasis: Power-efficient gathering in sensor information systems, in: *Proc. IEEE Conf. Aerosp*, Big Sky, MT, Mar, vol. 3, pp. 1125–1130, 2002.

29. Singh, S.P. and Sharma, S.C., A Particle Swarm Optimization Approach for Energy Efficient Clustering in Wireless Sensor Networks. *Int. J. Intell. Syst. Appl.*, 9, 6, 66–74, 2017.

30. Sudarmani, R. and Kumar, K.S., Particle swarm optimization-based routing protocol for clustered heterogeneous sensor networks with mobile sink. *Am. J. Appl. Sci.*, 10, 3, 259–269, 2013.

31. Sun, Y., Dong, W., Chen, Y., An improved routing algorithm based on ant colony optimization in wireless sensor networks. *IEEE Commun. Lett.*, 21, 6, 1317–1320, 2017.

32. Heinzelman, W.B., Chandrakasan, A.P., Balakrishnan, H., An application specific protocol architecture for wireless microsensor networks. *IEEE Trans. Wireless Commun.*, 1, 4, 660–670, 2002.

33. Heinzelman, W., Chandrakasan, A., Balakrishnan, H., Energy efficient communication protocol for wireless micro sensor networks, in: *Proc. of the Hawaii International Conference on System Sciences*, 2000.

34. Wang, X., Li, X., Leung, V.C., Artificial intelligence-based techniques for emerging heterogeneous network: State of the arts, opportunities, and challenges. *IEEE Access*, 3, 1379–1391, 2015.

35. Xie, M. and Shi, H., Ant-colony optimization based in-network data aggregation in wireless sensor networks, in: *Pervasive Systems, 12th International Symposium on Algorithms and Networks (ISPAN)*, pp. 77–83, 2012, December.

36. Zhou, Y., Wang, N., Xiang, W., Clustering hierarchy protocol in wireless sensor networks using an improved PSO algorithm. *IEEE Access*, 5, 2241–2253, 2017.

5

Distinct Algorithms for Swarm Intelligence in IoT

Trapty Agarwal*, Gurjot Singh†, Subham Pradhan‡ and Vikash Verma§

Maharishi University of Information Technology, Sector 110, Noida, India

Abstract

As the technologies are advancing (such as wireless telecommunication, data analysis, and machine-to-machine interactions), Internet of Things (IoT) aims at connecting different systems for communication and sharing of information. Since systems that are based on IoT are a combination of dynamic and complex entities, it usually lacks the decentralized control. Swarm Intelligence (SI) provides a possibility to decentralize and self-organize algorithms. Complex problems with incomplete information and dynamic properties are used to be resolved by different SI algorithms. In this chapter, we will study different Swarm Bird–based Algorithm and Swarm Insect–based Algorithm.

Keywords: Particle swarm optimization, cuckoo search algorithm, bat algorithm, ant colony optimization, artificial bee colony, honey-bee mating optimization, firefly algorithm, glowworm swarm optimization

5.1 Introduction

There are many creatures (such as birds, bees, and fish) in nature which possess group behaviors. The abilities for such creatures have a strong vitality in a whole group as compared to their individual abilities. These strong group behaviors are the simple aggregation of the individual abilities. But, it also reflects the adjustment made by individuals through cooperation and exchange of information, which finally reflects as group intelligence. To simulate this biological group intelligence, a simulation method is used that is known as Swarm Intelligence (SI) algorithm. The SI algorithms have the capability and possibility of solving complex problems with robustness, search ability, and self-adaptability [1].

---

*Corresponding author: trapty@gmail.com
†Corresponding author: gs130899@gmail.com
‡Corresponding author: pccshubham@gmail.com
§ Corresponding author: vvikash073@gmail.com

Abhishek Kumar, Pramod Singh Rathore, Vicente Garrcia Diaz and Rashmi Agrawal (eds.) Swarm Intelligence Optimization: Algorithms and Applications, (67–82) © 2021 Scrivener Publishing LLC. ISBN 978-1-119-77874-5

5.2   Swarm Bird–Based Algorithms for IoT

5.2.1   Particle Swarm Optimization (PSO)

When we talk about the behavior of animals in a group, a good example is a flock of birds. Birds fly in a big group, but they never collide with each other. They move in a smooth coordination as if controlled but it is never about only one bird leading the flock [2]. A SI could be considered as the flock of birds. Hence, the birds of the flock have to follow certain rules.

The following are the rules for every bird of the flock:

Every bird

1. Avoids collision with one another;
2. Moves in the same direction of the neighboring bird or the closest bird;
3. Moves equidistant with each other;
4. Information is shared with the neighboring bird.

5.2.1.1   Statistical Analysis

Elements are the agents in the optimized task parameter of space in PSO. Each element has two vectors: velocity and position. For every position of the element, its corresponding function value is calculated due to certain rules as the position and velocity changes constantly. It is a statistical probability optimization method. It operates with one uniform sample whose members constantly adjusts on receiving information about the search space rather than updating existing populations.

5.2.1.2   Algorithm

1. Begin the algorithm
2. Initialize agents
3. Find best_in_current
4. Set best_in_global = best_in_current
5. FOR x= 0 : number of iterations
6. Calculate the velocity of the element
7. Change the velocity of the element
8. Update the positions of the element
9. Based on the selection strategy, new agents are selected accordingly
10. IF best_in_current good than best_in_global
11. SET best_in_global to best_in_current
12. End of IF statement
13. End of FOR loop
14. save best_in_global
15. End the algorithm

5.2.1.3   Applications

1. In a traditional power grid, there is a one-way communication: Generation of electricity to consumption of electricity. On the other hand, a smart grid provides communication between the utilities and the consumer. This two-way interaction leads to exchange of information and electricity. There is a complex architecture where all the devices interact with each other. A smart grid is made up of complex architecture which deals with the optimization of generation, distribution, and consumption of the product or electricity. PSO is one of the best optimized algorithms. Such types of issues are handled in an efficient manner by implementing PSO algorithm.

2. It is the requirement to provide the mobile coverage to the areas of any building. It is definitely desired at minimum cost of power and equipment. The requirement is fulfilled by In-Building or Indoor Distributed Antennas System (I-DAS). A central base supplies power to different floors with the help of cables. The cables have been routed through each floor via telephone room. The incoming signals are split into multiple output ports or antennas through passive splitters. The cables are connected to these passive splitters. It works as a tree form where signals are distributed from a base station to different floors. An optimization is required for such flow of signals further involving cost. The optimal connection can be achieved efficiently by incorporating PSO model using Prüfer code for mapping [3].

5.2.2   Cuckoo Search Algorithm

Some cuckoo species possess some breeding strategies. Cuckoo Search Algorithm (CSA), new optimization algorithm, is based on the same.

5.2.2.1   Statistical Analysis

Each egg, which is in the nest, represents a solution in the CSA algorithm. Each newly laid cuckoo's egg is considered as new solution. This algorithm aims to replace the less good solutions with the best solutions in nests. The simplest case is having one egg in every nest [4].

The following rules need to be followed for the algorithm:

1. Choosing a nest randomly and each cuckoo has to lay one egg at a time.
2. Each nest having high-quality eggs is considered as best nests and moves in to a next generation.
3. The nest owner can find the nest where the cuckoo has laid the egg with $\xi a \in$ (0,1) probability and thereby remove the egg from those nests.

Description of CSA algorithm scheme could be done in the following form:

1. The sample population is initialized as P = {si, i $\in$ [1:|P}]} from |P| foreign nests and a cuckoo, i.e., the initial values of the vector fields is defined as Yi, i $\in$ [:|P|]} and the initial position vector is defined as YC;

2. The search space is updated with the number of random moves of cuckoo's by executing Lévy flights and the new cuckoo's position YC is selected;
3. A new point Pi, i ∈ [1:|P|] is picked randomly and if f(YC) > f(Yi), then substitution of an egg is done in this nest to the cuckoo's egg, i.e., Yi = YC;
4. The worst nests are chosen randomly and are removed with the probability ξa from sample population and the equivalent number of new nests are created which is in line with the rules specified above;
5. Proceed further to 2nd step unless and until end conditions are satisfied.

5.2.2.2   Algorithm

1. Begin the algorithm
2.   Generation of the initial population of k nests P_b, (b = 1, 2,..., k)
3.   Repeat the steps (steps 4 to 10)
4.   Placement of a cuckoo to point P_a by performing Lévy flights randomly
5.   Random selection of nest b among k nests
6.   IF $Q_a < Q_b$
7.   Replacement of P_b on finding a new solution
8.   End if statement
9.   Deletion of worst nests from the population nests with probability Pa and creation of the equivalent number of new nests
10.   Set the best nest (solution)
11.   Until stop criteria is fulfilled
12.   Post processing of results and visualization of data
13. End the algorithm

5.2.2.3   Applications

1. IoT-based devices have made Smart City a famous concept in urban areas. It is used to effectively manage services, resources, and assets. One of the major concerns in urban area is waste management. There have been many techniques for machine learning which have been applied on data collection based on IoT for waste. But, these techniques are flawed with lower predictive accuracy, thereby reducing efficiency of the entire process of waste recycling and management. The Cuckoo Search Optimized Long Short-Term Neural Networks (CLSTRNNs) increase the accuracy of waste material classification, increase the truck size and bin overflow prediction, and reduce errors in bin overflow and waste material analyses [5].
2. The main ingredient of Internet of Things (IoT) is sensors. To achieve sensor precision, the great significance is error correction. Building a dynamic measurement error model is one of the basic methods, which uses current error series to help predict future error values. A learning technique, support vector machine (SVM), a new regression method based on the structural risk minimization principle with good generalization ability. It needs only few samples, nonlinear data, etc., to solve the problems. The selection of the appropriate parameters

is an important aspect in learning, performance, and generalization ability of SVM. The precision of the model predictions are in direct relation with the parameters selected. The SVM model on the Cuckoo-based Search Algorithm achieves better accurate prediction and is much effective in predicting dynamic measurement errors for sensors than the other models because CSA effectively avoids the "overfitting" or "underfitting" characteristics of SVM [5, 6].

5.2.3   Bat Algorithm

Bats have the echolocation ability. The Bat Algorithm (BA) is based on the same ability of bats. The echolocation ability of bats helps them to see in the darkness enabling them to differentiate between different types of insects and even enabling them to detect their food and preys. This involves the fundamentals of sound reflection. A loud sound is emitted by the bats and they further listen to the echo from the surrounding objects, which is created by the reflection of the sound. Bats emit sounds of various properties depending on the different strategies they use for hunting.

Every sound emitted by bats has a frequency range between 25 and 150 kHz along with impulse rate from 8 to 10 ms. During any hunt, the bat can emit around 200 signals [7].

5.2.3.1   *Statistical Analysis*

The following principles are followed in BA:

1. The echolocation ability of the bat is being used to estimate the distance and calculate the distance between an obstacle and its food or prey.
2. Let the bats fly randomly in position Xi emitting wavelength λ, with a velocity of Vi, frequency Fmin, and loudness Ao while searching a prey or food. The wavelength is variable and frequency is fixed. The frequency (or wavelength) is adjusted by them automatically while emitting sound impulse and level of emission is r ∈ [0, 1]. The level of emission depends on the victim's proximity.
3. There are different ways to change the volume. The assumption is that the loudness varies in range [Ao, Amin]. Another assumption and approximation is that the frequency f lies in range [fmin, fmax] which results in corresponding wavelength range [λmin, λmax].

5.2.3.2   *Algorithm*

1. Begin the algorithm
2. The target function will be g(p), p = $(p_1,..., p_m)$T
3. The bat population can be initialized as p_a (a = 1, 2,..., n) and u_a
4. The frequency of the pulse $freq_a$ is defined at p_a
5. The pulse rates rt_a is initialized and the loudness L_a is initialized
6.   While loop count < max number of iterations
7.   New solutions are generated by updating velocities, adjusting frequency and locations or solutions
8.   IF random > rt_a

9.   A best solution is shortlisted out of many solutions
10.   A local solution is generated around the best solutions that have been selected
11.   End of If statement
12.   A new solution is generated or created by flying randomly
13.   IF random $< L_a$ AND $g(p_a) < g(p^*)$
14.   Acceptance of the new solutions
15.   Increase rt_a and reduce L_a
16.   End of IF statement
17.   The bats ranking will be done and the current best solution p* is selected
18. End of While loop
19. The post processing of results and further result visualization

5.2.3.3 Applications

1. The on-spot big data analytics services is provided by a big data sensing system (BDSS) that is based on the fully connected sensors, that can be considered as a component of IoT, which is further used for diverse applications. A very well-known algorithm, low energy adaptive clustering hierarchy protocol (LEACH), is used to reduce the cost of energy. Selection of the cluster head nodes are done randomly that are located away from the base station. The solution of this problem lies in the enhanced BA that includes the weighted harmonic centroid strategy. The local search capability is increased that enhances its performance [8].

2. When a network of little devices (sensor nodes) is distributed partially, it is define as the Wireless Sensor Network (WSN). It is used to communicate the information effectively which is collected by observing the fields via wireless links. They are the key enablers of the IoT environment. The lifetime energy and the network stability can be increased effectively using a mutated BA [9].

5.3 Swarm Insect–Based Algorithm for IoT

5.3.1 Ant Colony Optimization

Ant colony optimization (ACO) algorithm is based on population and uses probabilistic technique to solve problems. The computation problems can be optimized to search best paths using different graphical methods [9, 10].

A good solution is searched for the given optimization problem using ACO algorithm. Artificial ants act as software agents who look for the best solution. A weighted graph is used to find the best path, and to obtain this, the optimization problem is transformed into the same. The ACO algorithm is thus applied. The solution is further build incrementally by the artificial ants by moving on the weighted graphs. The values of the components of the graph (nodes and edges) can be modified by the ants at runtime. This type of solution is known as stochastic process and this solution is biased by pheromone mode [11].

ACO is a group of optimization algorithms that are modeled on the movements of an ant colony. A parameter space represents all the possible solutions of an optimization problem.

The simulation agents (in this case, artificial ants) move through the parameter space to figure out the optimal solutions. Pheromones are laid by the real ants where they direct one another during the exploration of the environment. The positions and solutions of real ants are recorded by the artificial ants or simulated ants. This record is further used during the simulation iteration to figure out better solutions [12].

5.3.1.1   Flowchart

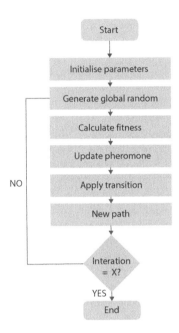

5.3.1.2   Applications

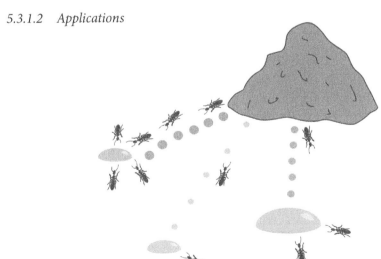

Knapsack problem: The ants prefer the smaller drop of honey over the more abundant, but less nutritious, sugar

ACO algorithms are applied to quadratic assignments, combinatorial optimization problems, derived methods, stochastic problems, etc. It can be used in finding solutions to routing vehicles, multi-targets, parallel implementations, and dynamic problems in real variables. ACO algorithm can be used to produce optimal solutions for the salesman who is traveling. Since the weighted graph changes dynamically as ACO adapts to the real time change continuously, it can be used in network routing and transportation scenarios [13].

5.3.2   Artificial Bee Colony

An intelligent swarm of bees has employed a technique to identify their food source. A meta-heuristics method that adopts this technique can be named as the "Artificial Bee Colony" algorithm. The study is done on the nature of bees which is based on their communication skills, task allocation skills, reproduction skills, selection skills of nest location, dancing skills, mating skills, movement skills. All these skills are subsequently modified in the form of algorithm to meet the requirement of the problem. The ABC algorithm searches for the solution iteratively which fits best among a large data and thus performs optimization while solving the critical problems. There are three categories, i.e., the scouts, the onlooker, and the employed, in which the members of bee swarm are differentiated. The job of scout bees is to search the resources of fresh food. Once the food source is identified (let us consider it as one of the candidate solutions), it is assigned with a fitness parameter. In further steps, the employed bees are supposed to look for the food resources. If they locate the fresh food resource with a higher quality of fitness, that food resource is selected otherwise it is rejected. The database of the employed bees is constantly updated with the data or information on the latest and the better food resources. In this process, it keeps on discarding the older data. The quality is thereby transferred to the onlooker bees in the hives. The onlooker bees will finally select the best location of food or the finest solution by calculating the frequency of the food present. The frequency can be obtained as a ratio of the fitness value of the food source to the sum of fitness values of other food sources. If the quality of the source of the food is not improved by the bees, the solutions are not taken into account. The solution is nullified [14, 15].

5.3.2.1   Flowchart

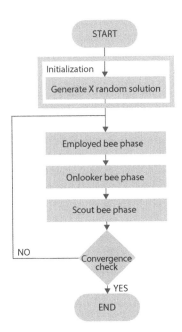

5.3.2.2   Applications

The numerical value optimizer for single-objective parameter uses the ABC algorithm. This algorithm is used in solving the problems which include the ask allocation, searching, multi-level thresholding, assignment, routing, minimization, and maximization. A collective decision-making which involves multi-criteria selection problems also makes use of the ABC algorithm. The ABC algorithm can be used in domains which are characterized by the computation requirements with differential change and scalability of high level within the potential solutions. This algorithm can be used for both constrained optimization and unconstrained optimization domains. The usage of this algorithm can also be in different domains of continuous and discrete optimization problems, multidimensional numeric problems, differential evolution, and multiple-objective optimization problems.

Fraudulent activity detection and mobile e-commerce environment in marketing also find the usage of ABC algorithm in customer segmentation. The expert systems that are focused on agriculture also make use of ABC algorithm [16].

5.3.3   Honey-Bee Mating Optimization

The Honey-Bee Mating Optimization (HBMO) algorithm is based upon the technique the actual honey bee uses for mating. It is one of the traditional algorithms to achieve optimization solution using swarm techniques. The outcomes of well-developed genetic algorithms are being evaluated based on its overall performance [17].

5.3.3.1   *Flowchart*

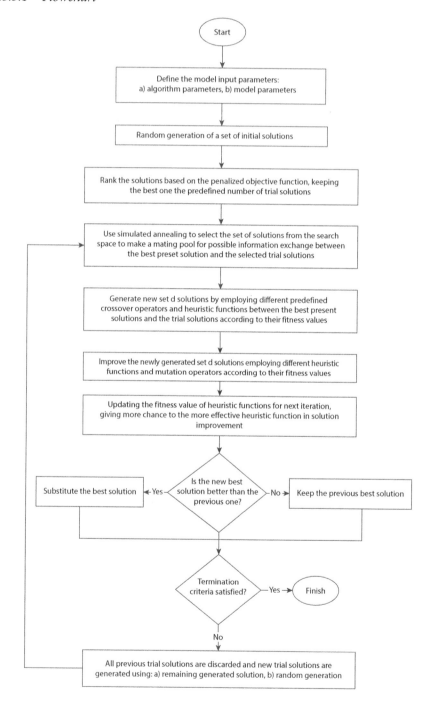

5.3.3.2   Application

It is additionally utilized in the operation of one reservoir with 60 intervals where the goal is diminishing the whole square deviation from the goal demands. Results received are promising and evaluate nicely with the outcomes of some other different ordinary heuristic approaches

The overall enactment of the algorithm is kind of evaluating the outcomes of the developed genetic algorithm.

5.3.4   Firefly Algorithm

Firefly algorithm (FFA) works in the difficult scenarios where troubles have two criteria based on equality and inequality. FFA also takes care of multimodal features which have higher efficiency. FFA also follows the population-based random search like bee-based and ant-based algorithms. It gains the knowledge from the members of the crew with diverse options and uses the most error-free and convergence outcome. Flashing indicators are used for different fireflies which are in turn herbal use of the conduct of fireflies to find their food or preys, mates, or for communication only. The fireflies have the ability and the capability of self-organizing and they can also decentralize their decision-making capabilities. These traits make them comparable with the swarm brain. Flashing intensity can be considered as the fitness indicator for the male firefly. However, all fireflies get attracted together in the traditional algorithms, all fireflies are regarded to be one single sex, and hence, all fireflies are regarded to be attracted together in a comparable manner [18]. The opulence of the firefly is immediately proportional to the mild depth (flashing) that acts as a qualification of fitness in flip for a workable "candidate solution".

There are many algorithms based on FFA that are used in many areas and domains of engineering, communication, science, etc.

The list of few popular algorithms is as follows:

- Adaptive Firefly Algorithm (AFA)
- Discrete Firefly Algorithm (DFA)—to clear problems related to NP-hard scheduling, photo segmentation
- Multi-Objective FA (MOFA)—to fix the problems related to dispatch of multi-objective load
- Lagrangian FA (LFA)—to sort out problems related to machine optimization
- Chaotic FA (CFA)
- Hybrid FA (HFA)
- FA-based Memetic Algorithm (FAMA)—to forecast electrical load

5.3.4.1   Flowchart

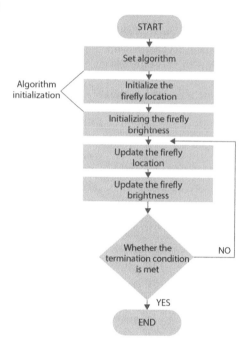

5.3.4.2   Application

There are bunch of applications which are based on FFAs. The FFA is best known for the constrained and multi-modal feature optimization in statistical probability algorithms and statistical probability optimization. These algorithms are further used in eagle-based Lévy flight systems and to find solutions for the dispatch problems of non-convex monetary. The literature assessment with the aid of additionally aids in imparting higher perception involving the algorithm, for forecasting the correct momentary load, for grayscale photo watermarking, for clearing problems related to capacitate facility area, and for prediction of sickness related to the coronary heart and the introduction of primary FFAs based on oppositional and dimensional statistics.

The FFA is also used for finding solutions for NP-hard problems that includes complicated classification, equality or inequality-driven constraints, discrete area domains, and combinatorial and parallel optimization domains.

The FFA can be used in coordination with many different techniques like multi-valued good judgment (e.g., tough set theory), cell mastering automata, and the application in artificial neural networks to strengthen the defined hybrid approaches. These algorithms are further used to resolve problems related to load dispatch, forecast the charge of inventory market, photo compression, and format the mobile phone, schedule the job store, and strength conservation.

5.3.5   Glowworm Swarm Optimization

The Glowworm Swarm Optimization (GSO) is the algorithm which is based on the ability of insect glowworms to glow specific part of the body. It is further optimized for multimodal functions that are developed by sinking the behavior of the insect glowworms in artificial intelligent systems.

Luciferin is a chemical that is emitted by glowworms and they also have the capability to change the emitted intensity levels of this chemical that let the glowworms glow at different intensities. The capability of glowing is used by the glowworms to communicate with each other. The glowworms use the intensity of glowing to attract the mates during the reproduction process.

The more the emission of chemical Luciferin is, the more the male glowworms look attractive to female glowworms or to the prey. The attraction is better with brighter intensity of the glow. This behavior of the glowworms is the basis of the artificial glowworm swarm optimization algorithm.

5.3.5.1   *Statistical Analysis*

The communication among glowworms happens among each other by glowing. Each artificial glowworm in the crowd has two values: a function associated and a value of chemical, Luciferin intensity which is based on its present position. While traveling, the comparison between the intensity level with the neighboring glowworm is done by every glowworm in the crowd. The path of travel is changed when the glowworm with more intensity of Luciferin is found. This whole process is followed in loop until there is most of the high-intensity convergence and the best suited solution candidate is reached.

5.3.5.2   *Flowchart*

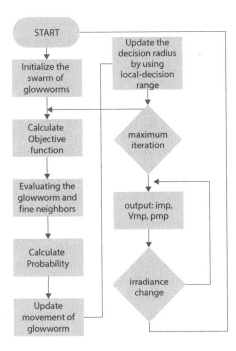

5.3.5.3   Application

In GSO, objective function definition space is distributed by each and every glowworm. These glowworms respectively carry the chemical Luciferin on their own, and it has its own decision range called local decision which is based on its respective field of vision scope. The brightness of the glowworm is concerned with the position of the function value associated with each worm of the swarm. Glowworm glow brighter and have a good target value when they are positioned correctly. Glowworm adjusts it's brightness which in turn attracts the glow towards it's traverse and also sets local decided range with neighbor.

The flight direction changes each time, and the direction changes along with the choice neighbor. The direction of flight changes every time, and the directions are changed along with the chosen neighbor glow warm.

Local size of glow range is decided by the density of neighboring glowworms. When low in density, glowworms enlarges radius. The need for more neighbor reduces.

At the end, the majority of glowworms returns and gathers at the multiple optima of the given function which is associated with each glowworm.

References

1. Abedin, Z.U., Shahid, U., Mahmood, A., Qasim, U., Khan, Z.A., Javaid, N., Application of PSO for HEMS and ED in Smart Grid, 2015 Ninth International Conference on Complex, Intelligent, and Software Intensive Systems, Blumenau, 2015, pp. 260–266.
2. Alqahtani, F., Al-Makhadmeh, Z., Tolba, A., Said, W., Internet of things-based urban waste management system for smart cities using a Cuckoo Search Algorithm. *Cluster Comput.*, 2020, 10.1007/s10586-020-03126-x.
3. Chakraborty, A. and Kar, A.K., Swarm Intelligence: A Review of Algorithms. In: Patnaik S., Yang XS., Nakamatsu K. (eds) Nature-Inspired Computing and Optimization. Modeling and Optimization in Science and Technologies, vol 10. Springer, Cham. https://doi.org/10.1007/978-3-319-50920-4_19
4. Cui, Z., Cao, Y., Cai, X., Cai, J., Chen, J., Optimal LEACH protocol with modified bat algorithm for big data sensing systems in Internet of Things. *J. Parallel Distrib. Comput.*, 132, 217–229, 2018, 10.1016/j.jpdc.2017.12.014.
5. Hildmann, H., Atia, D.Y., Ruta, D., Poon, K., Isakovic, A.F., *Nature-Inspired? Optimization in the Era of IoT: Particle Swarm Optimization (PSO) Applied to Indoor-Distributed Antenna Systems (I-DAS). In: Elfadel I., Ismail M. (eds) The IoT Physical Layer. Springer, Cham*, 2019. https://doi.org/10.1007/978-3-319-93100-5_11
6. https://github.com/SISDevelop/SwarmPackagePy#bat-algorithm
7. https://github.com/SISDevelop/SwarmPackagePy#cuckoo-search-optimization
8. https://github.com/SISDevelop/SwarmPackagePy#particle-swarm-optimization
9. https://www.ijitee.org/wp-content/uploads/papers/v8i11/K24840981119.pdf
10. Javed, M.Y., Mirza, A., Hasan, Rizvi, H., Ling, Q., Gulzar, Safder, Mansoor, M., A Comprehensive Review on a PV Based System to Harvest Maximum Power. *Electronics*, 8, 1480, 2019, 10.3390/electronics8121480.
11. Jiang, M., Luo, J., Jiang, D., Xiong, J., Song, H., Shen, J., A Cuckoo Search-Support Vector Machine Model for Predicting Dynamic Measurement Errors of Sensors. *IEEE Access*, 4, 5030–5037, 2016.

12. Krishnanand, K.N. and Ghose, D., Glowworm swarm optimization for simultaneous capture of multiple local optima of multimodal functions. *Swarm Intell*, 3, 87–124. 2009, https://doi.org/10.1007/s11721-008-0021-5

13. Kumar, R., Talukdar, F., Dey, N., Balas, V., Quality Factor Optimization of Spiral Inductor using Firefly Algorithm and its Application in Amplifier. *Int. J. Adv. Intell. Paradig.*, 11, 299–314, 2016.

14. Okonta, C.I., Kemp, A.H., Edokpia, R.O., Monyei, G.C., Okelue, E.D., A heuristic based ant colony optimization algorithm for energy efficient smart homes. Paper presented at: 5th International Conference & Exhibition on Clean Energy. 2016: pp. 1–12.

15. Bozorg Haddad, O., Mariño, M.A., Dynamic penalty function as a strategy in solving water resources combinatorial optimization problems with honey-bee mating optimization (HBMO) algorithm. Journal of Hydroinformatics 1 July 2007, 9, 3, 233–250. https://doi.org/10.2166/hydro.2007.025

16. Randazzo, A., Swarm Optimization Methods in Microwave Imaging, International Journal of Microwave Science and Technology, vol. 2012, Article ID 491713, 12 pages, 2012. https://doi.org/10.1155/2012/491713

17. Safari, A., Ahmadian, A., Aliakbar Golkar, M., Controller Design of STATCOM for Power System Stability Improvement Using Honey Bee Mating Optimization. *J. Appl. Res. Technol.*, 11, 144–155, 2013.

18. Sun, W., Tang, M., Zhang, L., Huo, Z., Shu, L., A Survey of Using Swarm Intelligence Algorithms in IoT. *Sensors.* 20, 1420, 2020.

6

Swarm Intelligence for Data Management and Mining Technologies to Manage and Analyze Data in IoT

Kashinath Chandelkar

CSIR-Central Electronics Engineering Research Institute, CEERI Pilani, Rajasthan, India

Abstract

Content management is important because of increasing data volume, variety, and velocity in which data are collected for further processing. Managing and analyzing such a huge unstructured data is constrained due to traditional architecture, design, and implementation of policies. The recent trends demand real-time data collected from different sensors. The data are stored, managed, and analyzed across the distributed network.

Data management needs special skills. The use of techniques and technologies together using swarm intelligence produces better results in comparison with available standards. Swarm intelligence is a motivation and approach to solve a problem. The chapter is a gamete that initiates a swarm-based problem-solving approach having vast application areas in the upcoming digital world.

Keywords: Content management, data volume, data velocity, data variety, unstructured data, traditional architecture swarm based problem solving, swarm intelligence

6.1 Introduction

Data management [1] has always remained a challenge for an individual and database administrators. The data has evolved from its various forms like text, image, audio, video, and its permutations; together we term it as content. The system that manages this diverse unidirectional, unstructured data is called Content Management System [2] or CMS.

Data management consists of data storage, retrieval, searching, and indexing in a data warehouse. Different data management and mining techniques [3] are utilized to extract information for knowledge mining and efficient decision making.

Data mining faces challenges in case of dynamic nodes. These dynamic nodes are a part of smart systems called Internet of Things [4, 5] or IoT. These dynamic nodes work together with certain techniques creating intelligence. Swarm Intelligence [6] is one such area that helps to manage data when the nodes are moving and sharing data in a distributed network. Swarm Intelligence being inspired from natural consciousness, observing and finding implementable models using technology, is initiated in this chapter.

Email: kashinath45@gmail.com

Abhishek Kumar, Pramod Singh Rathore, Vicente Garrcia Diaz and Rashmi Agrawal (eds.) Swarm Intelligence Optimization: Algorithms and Applications, (83–100) © 2021 Scrivener Publishing LLC. ISBN 978-1-119-77874-5

6.2   Content Management System

CMSs are broadly categorized into proprietary and open source softwares [7]. An organization retains copyrights, permission, and license so that business and profit can be generated. An individual has to purchase developer license after paying necessary fees. Alteration to the code is not possible. In case of open source CMS, no licensing cost is needed and the code is made available for modification free of cost under open licensing. Citing an original author gives credibility and motivation to contribute for society. Many templates and Open Source Softwares are made available by the Open Source Community for end users.

CMS includes apparatus, software, and methods for organizing content from variety of sources. The content is presented in a unified manner. The content is created by content creators like photographer, specialized artist, and others. Internet-based system [9] helps to deliver this content across the channel and to required user. Content is made available in the form of text, image, audio, video, and its permutations.

The content is created and designed by its owner using content creation tools [10]. The created content is stored and retrieved from the repository when needed. The content creator like web master provides content management as a service to its users across the globe. The services [11] are independent of platform and its device location. Website management is shown in Figure 6.1, which is an example of CMS. Widely used CMSs [8] are listed below.

Web Content Management System (WCMS): Organizations that deliver most of their content to the internet. It may include manual and reports in suitable file format.

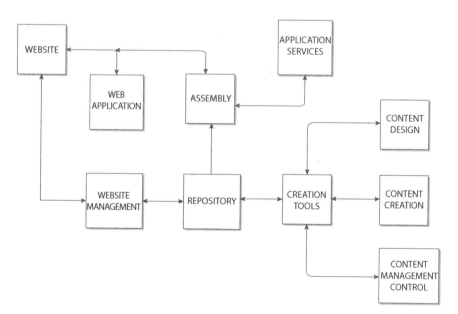

Figure 6.1 Content management system.

Digital Asset Management System (DAMS): This content management software is dedicated to graphic and multimedia management—not text.

Document Management System (DMS): A DMS is a document manager. Instead of focusing on content's details, it concentrates on content at the file level (e.g., Word or PDF documents). A DMS, for example, tracks who modifies documents, but it controls who can access and update a document.

Enterprise Content Management System (ECMS): This type of CMS takes a global approach to managing content. It can handle your emails, documents, instant messaging, and other electronic files. Corporations and large organizations rely on ECMS to consolidate their content and improve their productivity for producing new internal documents, as well as materials for their customers.

Component Content Management System (CCMS): Unlike a DMS, CCMS focuses on your content's details rather than the files themselves. Components include conceptual topics, procedures, sensitive information (cautions and warnings), product descriptions, and many others. Duplicate contents, such as your company's copyright disclaimer, are saved as a single component. Content security can be managed at a lower level than in other types of CMS, giving greater flexibility for content ownership and updates.

Mobile CMS: Due to exponential growth in mobile devices like smart phone and Personal Digital Assistant, content management has become a need of an hour. The aim was to deliver content with respect to Business to Consumer (B2C) needs. It was extended for Business to Employee (B2E) and Business to Business (B2B) consumers. The type of content managed over the secure channel comprises of movies, music, games, text messages, and location-based services like news. The information is shared in useful, effective, and efficient manner between business and corporation.

Traditionally, designed content is deployed onto the traditional CMS architecture. It consists of limited storage, processing capacity, and data transmission bandwidth. Application designed using waterfall model does not suit the cloud architecture because of its platform dependencies; hence, both application design and deployment process need to be revised. Data loss, slow searching, and data redundancy are some of the challenges [12] faced during information retrieval. The cloud-based technology provides infrastructure, platform, and software as services on pay per use basis.

6.3   Data Management and Mining

Data mining [13] is a process of extracting useful information and patterns from enormous data. Data mining includes extraction, collection, analysis, and visualization of data. It is also known as the knowledge discovery process [14]. Once the required information and patterns are found, they are used to make decisions. The competent decision creates business opportunities. Data life cycle is a basic unit of data science that is used to manage data on large scale. Let us understand how the cycle works.

6.3.1 Data Life Cycle

We can implement the data life cycle [15] for many applications like server management and data warehouse management. Smart irrigation system was one of the application area tested across the state. The generic data life cycle, as shown in Figure 6.2, was used only during IoT implementation. It consists of following stages. Some of the stages can be ignored based on the project implementation process.

Plan: A village farmer was identified having minimum requirements in a state where rainfall and ground water is very less. The intention was to have improved crop with controlled water supply. A team comprising of subject matter specialist, technical fellows, and identified farmer has planned to implement smart irrigation system at the dedicated site.

Collect: The collection includes seed, ready site with water source nearby, smart IoT system, and trained human resource that forms part of a system.

Assure: The project being onsite it is assured and assisted by the farmer and his team. The assurance also includes how to make use of grown seeds for the benefit of nearby farmers in the long run.

Describe: This includes a stage wise implementation plan in the identified field under cultivation. Each IoT component was placed in the field with initial training to the concerned in charge. These components were connected via smart sensors. The information like humidity, temperature, pH, and water level was collected and sent to android-based application. The application is currently running using traditional architecture. We are planning to migrate it on to the private cloud infrastructure.

Preserve: The collected information from the different sensors is preserved for further analysis and necessary action. The current data is stored at in charge terminal and at centralized server.

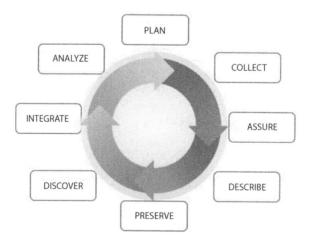

Figure 6.2 Generic data life cycle.

Discover: The discovery in this case refers to locating the sensors using designed technology. This helps us to trace back the nodes for re-calibration if needed to retain the quality of data collected in the process.

Integrate: The integration is done at sensor level and at centralized server. Each sensor sends data from the identified filed to a dedicated terminal. These so called in charge terminals placed in the different identified fields sends data to the main server. This helps to keep atrack of particular state or district for efficient planning and resource deployment on site as an when needed.

Analyze: The collected data at centralized server are analyzed and placed in front of concerned authorities to make and implement policies based on available data across the states.

6.3.2   Knowledge Discovery in Database

Knowledge Discovery in Database (KDD) [16] is the process of discovering useful knowledge from a collection of data. This widely used data mining technique is a process that includes data preparation and selection, data cleansing, incorporating prior knowledge on datasets, and interpreting accurate solutions from the observed results. Major KDD application areas include marketing, fraud detection, telecommunication, and manufacturing. The basic terminologies used in the process of data mining and knowledge discovery are listed below.

- *Data*: Raw, bidirectional, unprocessed content ready for processing.
- *Information*: processed unidirectional data that makes meaning.
- *Knowledge*: processed information based on facts and experience.
- *Wisdom*: processed information ready for efficient decision making.

The definition is true for all cases. They also stand true in case of smart irrigation system. For example:

- *Data*: A green land.
- *Information*: An acre of land at one of the district in Rajasthan is identified for smart irrigation system project.
- *Knowledge*: The crop yields in identified areas have increased in last 5 years with controlled humidity. The selected crop has performed as expected.
- *Wisdom*: Based on the last 15 years of experience, observation, and from the collected information three seeds are identified that retained profit. The crop is under testing to new identified locations in other states.

In case of smart irrigation system, centralized nodes are responsible for handling KDD process. A target data like seed quality, surrounding temperature, humidity, pH, soil nutrients, and area under cultivation with its location is identified. Since the data is saved in warehouse, preprocessing and transformation becomes essential as shown in Figure 6.3. Preprocessing includes data cleaning using traditional algorithms. Retaining a common file format is also important to avoid data conflicts if any.

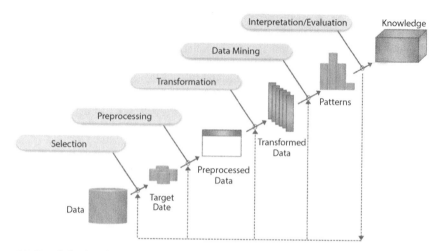

Figure 6.3 Knowledge data discovery.

Streamlining data as per available mining technologies is considered as data transformation. The required results can be obtained and displayed using graphical patterns. An android-based platform can be designed to fulfill requirements. The obtained knowledge is further used for efficient decision making and creating standard policies, to be implemented across the nation.

6.3.3   Data Mining vs. Data Warehousing

Data mining and warehousing [17] are two different entities. Mining refers to process used on the data using technology. Data warehouse is a place to park data. The way in which it is done may differ.

Data mining is a process of analyzing unknown patterns of data. Data warehouse, on the other hand, is designed for analytical work instead of transactional work. Right patterns are found using data mining methods. Data warehousing is data centralization method from different sources into one common repository. Mining is done by business users but warehousing needs to be done before any data mining can take place. Mining is considered as a process for extracting data while warehousing is pooling all relevant data together. Mining allows easily detection and identification of errors. Warehousing is an ability to upgrade consistently. Mining suggests patterns from important factors, warehousing differs by adding extra value to the business.

6.3.4   Data Mining Techniques

Data mining refers to finding the hidden details from the dataset so that efficient decisions can be made. We have used COVID-19 pandemic dataset (India, 2020) published by Government of India as on 15 May 2020. It comprises of total confirmed cases, people who are cured/discharged/migrated, and total deaths in a given state. Figure 6.4 only highlights confirmed cases. Using data mining techniques [25], let us understand the impact of Coronavirus across the nation.

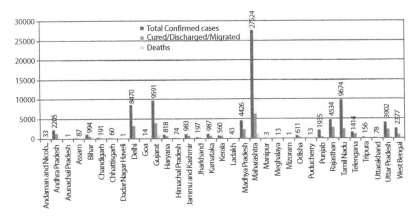

Figure 6.4 COVID-19 impact in India until 15 May 2020.

Data mining techniques [18] begin with data cleaning. This may include arranging the data and files in a similar format that are widely accepted. It also includes finding values that are empty or not in proper format. After obtaining a clean dataset, the following data mining techniques are implemented.

a) Statistical Techniques: Professor Maurice Kendall in 1943 said "Statistics is the branch of scientific method which deals with the data obtained by counting or measuring the properties of populations of natural phenomena. In this definition 'natural phenomena' includes all the happenings of the external world, whether human or not".

Descriptive statistics, as shown in Figure 6.5, gives you a general idea about trends in your data including mean, median, and range. Tests like T test and Chi-squire test are part of this method. Obtained results using statistical technique (Babatunde, 2018) only depicts minimum, maximum, and an average values.

b) Association Rules Mining: These rules are used to find the association between the variables. Market base analysis is similar to Association Rule Mining (ARM). Using

Name		Type	Missing	Statistics	Filter (4 / 4 attributes):	Search for Attribut
∨ **Name of State / UT**		Polynominal	0	Least West Bengal (1)	Most Andaman [...] lands (1)	Values Andaman [...] r Islands
∨ **Total Confirmed cases**		Integer	0	Min 1	Max 27524	Average 2483.939
∨ **Cured/Discharged/Mi...**		Integer	0	Min 0	Max 6059	Average 846.061
∨ **Deaths**		Integer	0	Min 0	Max 1019	Average 80.273

Figure 6.5 Results using statistical methods.

COVID-19 pandemic database, we observed a relation between person found to be COVID-19–positive and need of an immediate treatment. The treatment is expected as per the guidelines issued by the World Health Organization (WHO).

A Total of seven association rules as shown in Figure 6.6 are created. Confidence is an indication how often the rule has been found to be true. From the pandemic dataset, it is observed that person may die if he is confirmed to be COVID-19–positive patient and proper treatment is not given. The person may lead to death if he is migrated and not treated within a time frame. A person maybe discharged after treatment if found negative from the identified confirmed cases. Even if a person is discharged, chances are he may become infected later and may lead to death.

c) Classification Technique: Classification can be performed on both structured and unstructured data. The method classifies data into number of classes. The main objective of the technique is to identify a class in which new data will fall. Among the classification techniques [19] like binary, multi-class and multi-label, K Nearest Neighbor (KNN) is used for classification and regression. It is more simple to use and very useful for non-linear data. It has relatively high accuracy compared to other classification algorithms. It is computationally more expensive as it stores all the training data. Predictions are slow in case of large N values. We observed 100% accuracy with our dataset. The stream graph for deaths and predicted deaths are shown in Figure 6.7.

New dataset can be tested on the five new models that were created in the process. Beyond accuracy, the technique can be evaluated using the following factors.

- *Precision*: It is a ratio of number of relevant records retrieved from the total number of irrelevant and relevant records retrieved. It can be given as

$$\text{Precision} = \text{True Positive}/(\text{True Positive} + \text{False Positive}) \tag{6.1}$$

- *Recall*: It is a ratio of relevant records retrieved from the total number of relevant records in the database.

Association Rules

[Total Confirmed cases] → [Cured/Discharged/Migrated] (Confidence 0.970)

[Cured/Discharged/Migrated] → [Total Confirmed Cases] (Confidence 1.000)

[Deaths] → [Total Confirmed Cases] (Confidence 1.000)

[Deaths] → [Cured/Discharged/Migrated] (Confidence 1.000)

[Deaths] → [Total Confirmed Cases, Cured/Discharged/Migrated] (Confidence 1.000)

[Total Confirmed Cases, Deaths] → [Cured/Discharged/Migrated] (Confidence 1.000)

[Cured/Discharged/Migrated, Deaths] → [Total Confirmed Cases] (Confidence 1.000)

Figure 6.6 Association rules.

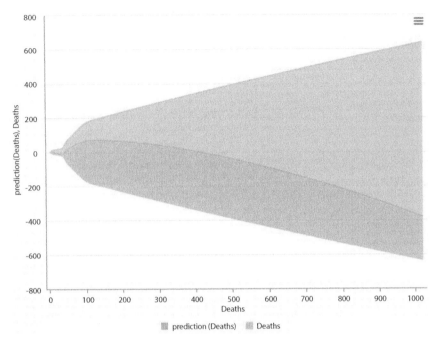

Figure 6.7 Stream graph for deaths and predicted deaths.

$$\text{Recall} = \text{True Positive}/(\text{True Positive} + \text{False Negative}) \qquad (6.2)$$

d) Clustering Technique: Cluster [20] is a set of data divided into groups. This group or cluster may be meaningful, useful, or both. The cluster provides abstraction for individual data objects. Various approaches are used to divide data into clusters. The data objects within a group may be similar to one another and different from objects from other groups. The greater the similarity within group and greater the difference between groups are, more distinct the clusters are. The technique used to divide data objects into groups is called clustering technique. The clusters may be well separated, prototype based, graph based, and density based. One may observe conceptual cluster in certain scenarios. The following cluster types may be useful while managing the big data scenarios.

- *Hierarchical versus partitioned clustering*: If the data objects are nested, then it is called hierarchical cluster (Chen *et al.*, 2016). If the objects are not nested, then the cluster is called partitioned. If a cluster has subclusters, then it belongs to hierarchical cluster. In case of partitioned cluster, division of dataset is into non-overlapping subsets.
- *Exclusive versus overlapping versus fuzzy*: The cluster is said to be exclusive if each data object is assigned to a single cluster. If an object is simultaneously

Table 6.1 Clustering using K Means.

Attribute	cluster_0	cluster_1	cluster_2	cluster_3	cluster_4
Name of State/UT	16	17.125	15.444	20	26
Total Confirmed cases	9245	1464.125	118.667	27524	4287.333
Cured/Discharged/ Migrated	3012.667	616	59.556	6059	2274.333

belongs to more than one group, then it is called overlapping or non-exclusive clustering. In case of fuzzy cluster [21], every object belongs to every cluster with membership weight that is belongs to 0 (absolutely doesn't belong) and 1 (absolutely belong). It does not address true multi-class situation.

- *Complete versus partial clustering*: If every data object is assigned to cluster, then it is termed as complete clustering; if not, it becomes partial cluster.

From Table 6.1, we can observe that pandemic dataset has created five clusters. Cluster 0 has least number of states with 9,245 confirmed cases. Total recovered persons are about 3012.67. Cluster 3 has highest confirmed cases of about 27,524. Total cured cases on a given day are 6,059. Other details are self-explanatory from Table 6.1.

6.3.5 Data Mining Technologies

Many technologies are available that helps in understanding data science. The word cloud in Figure 6.8 shows some of the widely accepted technologies. They are grouped based on the following characteristics.

Structured vs. Unstructured Data: Oracle and MySQL are the examples that holds structured or traditional data. The data is presented in the form of tables, having rows and column. These tables are linked during information retrieval based on the relations having some key. Technologies like Hadoop Ecosystem [22], Apache spark, and mangoDB hold unstructured data.

Open Source vs. Close Source: Weka and Rapid Miner Studio are the applications available for free download. The source code is freely available for modification and upgradation. The upgraded application is validated by open source community and is made available under Global Public License (GPL). The applications like Microsoft Azure is available for public use, but the organization does not give access to code. No modification is possible except developer in such a system as and when required.

Traditional Deployment vs. Cloud Service: File server, application server, and proxy servers are some of the applications deployed on the traditional architecture [23] within an organization. The organization needs skilled labor, physical infrastructure, and cost as a part of management. Most of

Figure 6.8 Word cloud portraying data mining technologies.

the technologies can be made available as infrastructure, platform, and software as a service. These services are used on pay per use basis. No extra cost, management, and physical infrastructure is needed. Google Cloud and IBM Modular are examples of cloud technology.

6.3.6   Issues in Data Mining

Mining issues [24] are broadly classified (as ahown in Figure 6.9) under three heads. Issues begin if the collected data is noisy or incomplete. Multiple levels of abstraction can be used by the system in-charge that creates abstraction layers. Data abstraction refers to hiding irrelevant data from the user. Control abstraction is implemented whenever the mining process needs to be protected from the user. Negligence may lead to data loss putting data privacy and security on priority. An experienced professional is needed to understand mined data visualized and presented using different tools.

Data mining is possible using traditional algorithms. The performance of an algorithm increases if revised to meet the latest trends. Parallel processing in a distributed environment increases overall efficiency. Hadoop and mangoDB are designed that have a potential to handle unstructured data. Multiple data types like TXT, CSV, and JPEG are supported at the same time.

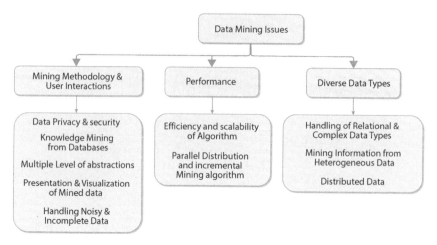

Figure 6.9 Data mining issues.

6.4   Introduction to Internet of Things

IoT is a subset of Internet of Everything (IoE). Each of them is defined as under:

> *Internet of Thing (IoT) is a networking of physical objects that contains electronics, embedded within their architecture in order to communicate and sense interactions among each other or with respect to external environment.*
> *Internet of Everything (IoE) refers to billions of devices and consumer products connected to the internet in an intelligent networked environment, with expanded digital features.*

The IoT devices [26] are important because they consume less power and are supported by cloud technologies. The cloud enables system to handle big data. Physical and virtual networks are the core components through which each virtual machine [27] or device is connected. The system is widely used because it gives real time data for intelligent action. Sensors like RFID, sensors, nanotechnology, and smart network together makes an intelligent system. Some of the application areas are smart agriculture, e-governance, smart study, and green energy.

6.5   Swarm Intelligence Techniques

> *Beli and Wang, in 1989 defined Swarm Intelligence (SI) as "A type of Artificial Intelligence based on the collective behavior of decentralized, self-organized system."*

We use computing techniques for communication, transportation, industrial production, entertainment, and technical advancements. We observed that some problems cannot be solved using traditional hardware and software due to its limitations. To overcome these challenges, DNA-based computing (chemical based), quantum computing (quantum and physical), and bio computing (biological mechanism) are suitable alternatives.

Swarm Intelligence [6] can be designed using three simple steps. First, identify analogies between swarm and technology. Second, understand computer modeling with realistic swarm biology. Third, model engineering using latest trends and technology. The following Swarm Intelligence Algorithms [28] can be used because of their cluster intelligence and biological performance characters.

6.5.1   Ant Colony Optimization

Ant Colony Optimization (ACO) is inspired from the behavior of real ant colonies. The study is implemented for Traveling Salesman Problem (TSP). Ants create pheromone while traveling from nest to food and vice versa to find the shortest path, as shown in Figure 6.10. Ants are forced to decide the direction of movement by placing an obstacle in the path. The decision made by ants is random to reach food. The pheromone accumulated on the path decides the shortest path that is traced by the next ant until the food is moved to the nest. The pseudo code is given below.

```
Pseudo Code: Ant Colony Optimization
Begin:
    Initialize the pheromone trail and parameters
        Generate population of m solutions (ants)
        For each individual ant p ∈ m; Calculate fitness (p)m; Calculate fitness(p)
        For each ant determine its best position
        Determine the best Global ant Update the Pheromone Trail
    Check if termination = True
End
```

6.5.2   Particle Swarm Optimization

Particle Swarm Optimization (PSO) is a population-based optimization technique developed by Dr. Kennedy and Dr. Eberhart in 1995. It was inspired by social behavior of birds flocking. The system begins with population of random solution and search for optima by updating generations. The potential solution called particles flies through problem space by following current optimum particle. Data fitness value is calculated for each particle

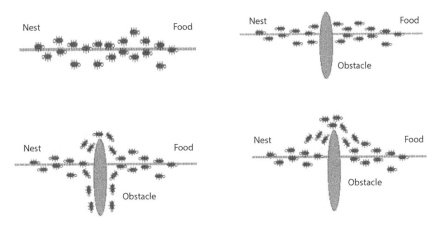

Figure 6.10 Ant colony optimization to find food.

called particle Best or pBest. If the current fitness value is better, then it is replaced with pBest. In other terms, if the bird in search of food moving in the right direction where food is expected, then it is pBest as it is closest to the food at that moment. If another bird or particle overtakes the leading bird using minimum distance traveled, then it holds new best value called gBest or Global best. The swarm continues to travel until the destination is reached. Pseudo code elaborates the details.

Pseudo Code: Particle Swam Optimization
Begin:
    For each particle
      Initialize
      particle
    Do until maximum iterations or minimum error criteria
    For each particle
      Calculate Data fitness value
      If the fitness value is better than pBest
        Set pBest = Current fitness value
      If pBest is better than gBest
        Set pBest = gBest
    For each particles
      Calculate particle velocity
      Use gBest and velocity to update particle data
End

6.5.3   Differential Evolution

Pseudo Code: Differential Evolution
Begin:
    Initialize Population Evaluation
    Repeat
    Mutation Recombination Evaluation Selection
    Until requirements are met
End

Differential Evolution (DE) [29] is a population-based algorithm using operators like mutation, cross-over, and selection. It is based on difference in randomly sampled pair of solution in the population. The algorithm uses mutation operation as a search mechanism and selection operation to direct the search toward the prospective regions in the search space. The algorithm also uses a non-uniform crossover that take child vector parameters from one parent more often than it does from others. Each new solution produced competes with a mutant vector and the better one wins the competition. The pseudo code is given above for further development.

6.5.4   Standard Firefly Algorithm

The Standard Firely Algorithm (SFA) [28] is inspired by the flashing behavior of firefly insects. The fireflies use flashing behavior to attract other fireflies for sending signals.

It is assumed that fireflies are unisex and attracted to each other. The brightest firefly moves randomly as no other firefly is there to attract. The brightness depends on the fitness of the firefly. The distance between the two fireflies is called a Euclidean distance. The pseudo code for the algorithm is given below.

Pseudo Code: Standard Firefly Algorithm
Begin:
    Objective function f(x), x = $(x_1, ..., x_d)^T$
    Generate initial population of fireflies X_i (I = 1,2,..., n)
    Light intensity I_i, at X_i is determined by $f(X_i)$
    Define light absorption coefficient γ
    while (t < maxgeneration)
      For I = 1:n
      For j = 1: n
        If $(I_j > I_i)$
          Move firefly i towards j
      Evaluate new solution and update light intensity
     Rank the fireflies and find the current best
      Process and visualize results
End

6.5.5   Artificial Bee Colony

Artificial Bee Colony (ABC) [30] is motivated by the intelligent behavior of honey bees. It uses parameters such as colony size and maximum cycle number. In ABC system, artificial bees fly around in a multidimensional search space and some (employed and onlooker bees) choose food sources depending on the experience of themselves and their nest mates. Some bees (scouts) fly and choose the food sources randomly without using experience. If the nectar amount of a new source is higher than that of the previous one in their memory, they memorize the new position and forget the previous one. Thus, ABC system combines local search methods, carried out by employed and onlooker bees, with global search methods, managed by onlookers and scouts, attempting to balance exploration and exploitation process. The pseudo code is given below.

Pseudo Code: Artificial Bee Colony
Begin:
    Initialize population
    While remaining iterations do
      select sites for local search
      Recruit bees for the selected sites and to evaluate fitness
      select the bee with the best fitness
      Assign the remaining bees for random search
      Evaluate the fitness of remaining bees
      Update Optimum
    Return best solution
End

6.6   Chapter Summary

Internet of Things is an important data dimension that needs special attention while managing unstructured data. The chapter elaborates about need of data management in Internet of Things platforms. This real time data collected from the diverse sensors and platforms can be managed using techniques and technologies as discussed in this chapter to avoid data loss. The chapter speaks about problem solving approach using swarm intelligence. The approach is motivated from the ants, birds, and similar lives, as discussed in this chapter.

References

1. Kelly, L., The Information Retrieval Challenge of Human Digital Memories. *BCS IRSG Symp.*, Fdia, 2007.
2. P. Examiner and D.D. Mizrahi, content management system, US 6,356,903 B1, 2002.
3. Zhang, W., Feng, S., Li, H., Research and implementation of predictive modeling based on logistic regression modeling about possibility of customer to buy a Tablet PC. *Proc. 2012 5th Int. Jt. Conf. Comput. Sci. Optim. CSO 2012*, pp. 639–642, 2012.
4. Mukherjee, M. *et al.*, Security and Privacy in Fog Computing: Challenges. *IEEE Access*, 5, 19293–19304, 2017.
5. Abu-Elkheir, M., Hayajneh, M., Ali, N.A., Data management for the Internet of Things: Design primitives and solution. *Sensors (Switzerland)*, 13, 11, 15582–15612, 2013.
6. Kopyszka, I., Zbiory Rozmyte I Skierowane Liczby Rozmyte. *Artif. Intell. Rev.*, 31, 1–4, 1599–1622, 2009, [Online]. Available: http://link.springer.com/10.1007/s10462-009-9127-4.
7. Alouneh, S., Hababeh, I., Al-hawari, F., Alajrami, T., Innovative Methodology for Elevating Big Data Analysis and Security, in: *2016 2nd International Conference on Open Source Software Computing (OSSCOM)*, pp. 1–5, 2016.
8. Zuccon, G. *et al.*, CSE598i - Web 2. 0 Security Zend Framework Tutorial The tutorial source code is available at. *IEEE Trans. Cloud Comput.*, 2, 1, 1–1, Apr. 2014.
9. Thu, P., Khine, T., Pa, H., Win, P., New, K., Tun, N., Indexing Relational Databases for Efficient Keyword Search. *Int. J. Sci. Eng. Res.*, 2, 10, 1–5, 2011.
10. Wijesundara, M.B.J. and Azevedo, R., System Integration, in: *Silicon Carbide Microsystems Harsh Environ.*, vol. 22, no. May, pp. 189–230, 2001.
11. Elmisery, A.M., Rho, S., Botvich, D., A fog based middleware for automated compliance with OECD privacy principles in internet of healthcare things. *IEEE Access*, 4, no. Idc, pp. 8418–8441, 2016.
12. Lease, M. and Yilmaz, E., Crowdsourcing for information retrieval. *ACM SIGIR Forum*, vol. 45, no. 2, p. 66, 2012.
13. Bendersky, M., Metzler, D., Croft, W.B., Rey, M., Croft, B.W., Effective query formulation with multiple information sources. *Proc. fifth ACM Int. Conf. Web search data Min. - WSDM '12*, 2012.
14. Sunil, T. and Suvarchala, K., A Study : Web Data Mining Challenges and Application for Information Extraction. *IOSR J. Comput. Sci.*, 7, 3, 24–29, 2012.
15. Whyte, A. and Jonathan, T., Making the Case for Research Data Management. *A Digit. Curation Cent. Brief. Pap.*, no. September, pp. 1–8, 2011.
16. Bendersky, M., Wang, X., Metzler, D., Najork, M., Learning from User Interactions in Personal Search *via* Attribute Parameterization. *Proc. Tenth ACM Int. Conf. Web Search Data Min. - WSDM '17*, pp. 791–799, 2017.

17. Haug, F.S., Bad Big Data Science, in: *2016 IEEE International Conference on Big Data (Big Data)*, pp. 2863–2871, 2016.
18. Qin, X., Luo, Y., Tang, N., Li, G., DeepEye: An automatic big data visualization framework. *Big Data Min. Anal.*, 1, 1, 75–82, 2018.
19. Chen, X., Vorvoreanu, M., Madhavan, K.P.C., Mining social media data for understanding students' learning experiences. *IEEE Trans. Learn. Technol.*, 7, 3, 246–259, 2014.
20. Dutt, A., Ismail, M.A., Herawan, T., A Systematic Review on Educational Data Mining. *IEEE Access*, 5, 15991–16005, 2017.
21. Frigui, H., Clustering: Algorithms and applications. *2008 1st Int. Work. Image Process. Theory, Tools Appl. IPTA 2008*, 2008.
22. Salem, A.M., Facebook Distributed System Case Study For Distributed System Inside Facebook Datacenters. *International Journal of Technology Enhancements and Emerging Engineering Research*, 2, 7, 152–160, 2014.
23. Sahoo, J., Salahuddin, M., Glitho, R., Elbiaze, H., Ajib, W., A {Survey} on {Replica} {Server} {Placement} {Algorithms} for {Content} {Delivery} {Networks}. *IEEE Commun. Surv. Tutorials*, 99, 1, 2016.
24. Harish, B.S., Guru, D.S., Manjunath, S., Representation and classification of text documents: A brief review. *IJCA, Spec. Issue Recent Trends Image Process. Pattern Recognit.*, no. 2, pp. 110–119, 2010, [Online]. Available: http://scholar.google.com/scholar?hl=en&btnG=Search &q=intitle:Representation+and+classification +of +text+documents:+A+brief+review#0.
25. Bharadwaj, D., Text Mining Technique using Genetic Algorithm. *Int. Conf. Adv. Comput. Appl.*, pp. 7–10, 2013.
26. Nauman, A., Qadri, Y.A., Amjad, M., Bin Zikria, Y., Afzal, M.K., Kim, S.W., Multimedia internet of things: A comprehensive survey. *IEEE Access*, 8, 8202–8250, 2020.
27. Fukai, T., Shinagawa, T., Kato, K., Live Migration in Bare-metal Clouds. *IEEE Trans. Cloud Comput.*, vol. PP, no. c, p. 1, 2018.
28. Gong, X., Liu, L., Fong, S., Xu, Q., Wen, T., Liu, Z., Comparative research of swam intelligence clustering algorithms for analyzing medical data. *IEEE Access*, 7, 137560–137569, 2019.
29. Zhan, Z.-H., Wang, Z.-J., Jin, H., Zhang, J., Adaptive Distributed Differential Evolution. *IEEE Trans. Cybern.*, 1–15, 2019.
30. T. Erciyes University, *Artificial Bees Colony Algorithm*, Intelligent system research group, Intelligent Systems Research Group, Department of Computer Engineering, Erciyes University, Turkiye, 2020, https://abc.erciyes.edu.tr/ (accessed May 23, 2020).

7

Healthcare Data Analytics Using Swarm Intelligence

Palvadi Srinivas Kumar[1], Pooja Dixit[2*] and N. Gayathri[3]

*[1]Department of Computer Science Engineering, University of Madras,
Chennai, Tamilnadu, India*
[2]Lecturer, Sophia Girls College Autonomous Ajmer
*[3]School of Computing Science and Engineering, Galgotias University, Greater Noida,
Uttar Pradesh, India*

Abstract

In present scenario, healthcare system procreates a huge amount of heterogeneous data. So, AI healthcare system is an interactive or intelligent system that managed that data in a meaningful way. It gives various techniques to optimize the data. Basically, SI is a rising technique of AI that is based on the behavioral model of social insects. SI is a problem-resolving technique that comes from the information processing category. SI theory depends on the multiplicity, dispensation, haphazardness, and untidiness. This technique solves problems, which relies on learning, creativity, and perception ability. The main focus of the chapter is to produce some principle foundation that helps to find the solutions in optimistic form. This paper also discusses the SI techniques like Particle Swarm Optimization (PSO) and Ant Colony Optimization (ACO), use of Swarm AI in healthcare, and issues and challenges of SI healthcare system.

Keywords: Swarm intelligence, data mining, artificial intelligence, iot, ant colony optimization, practical swarm optimization

7.1 Introduction

Artificial Intelligence (AI) is a domain where the devices play a role like a human intelligence and knowledge. It is the research area where this name presently roaming in all the subjects of engineering and sciences. Major competitors of this domain such as ImageNet which is a multi-scaled domain where they are offering human to computer interaction mechanisms. AI also has the special properties such as speech recognition as well as natural language processing (NLP). By seeing all the features regarding how this domain is possibly working in medical field or how it is helpful for taking the human decisions regarding healthcare [1]. Till date, two powerful research papers were published regarding healthcare using AI with small examples. The main advantage of AI is the information that we have

---

*Corresponding author: poojadixit565@gmail.com

Abhishek Kumar, Pramod Singh Rathore, Vicente Garrcia Diaz and Rashmi Agrawal (eds.) Swarm Intelligence Optimization: Algorithms and Applications, (101–122) © 2021 Scrivener Publishing LLC. ISBN 978-1-119-77874-5

in the database will be only the relevant data. In healthcare domain, we have lot of data. Even though, the accessing of the data and with the data privileges to the specific users became a greatest challenge in the United States. On one side, the user's health data is a very challenging task in collecting and providing privacy to the data while the data is sharing among users by comparing with other types of the data. Furthermore, we can say that it is very difficult to collect the health information and making the collected data more secure because of guaranteed service providers. Furthermore, using of the data from the software is a simple task, but for that, it needs the mechanism to handling the software and providing privacy of the data. If the data is leaked by extracting the data in the improper way, there may be a chance of leaking any one user's data so, here, we are missing the confidentiality issues. At present stage, there are multiple startups for the providing the privacy of users data; this range value increased more in the year of 2016 which we can observe in Figure 7.1. US 106 startup companies in different parts of the world such as UAE, Germany, France etc., came with their ideas in securing the data in their own way of that 76 companies were accepted. Two of the most popular topics like taking medical data in image forms, problem identification, calculating risk of the particular disease of that particular person were the concepts said in this report. Finally, the other major targets on the situation that gives attention to situations which are going to happen in the activity were shown [2].

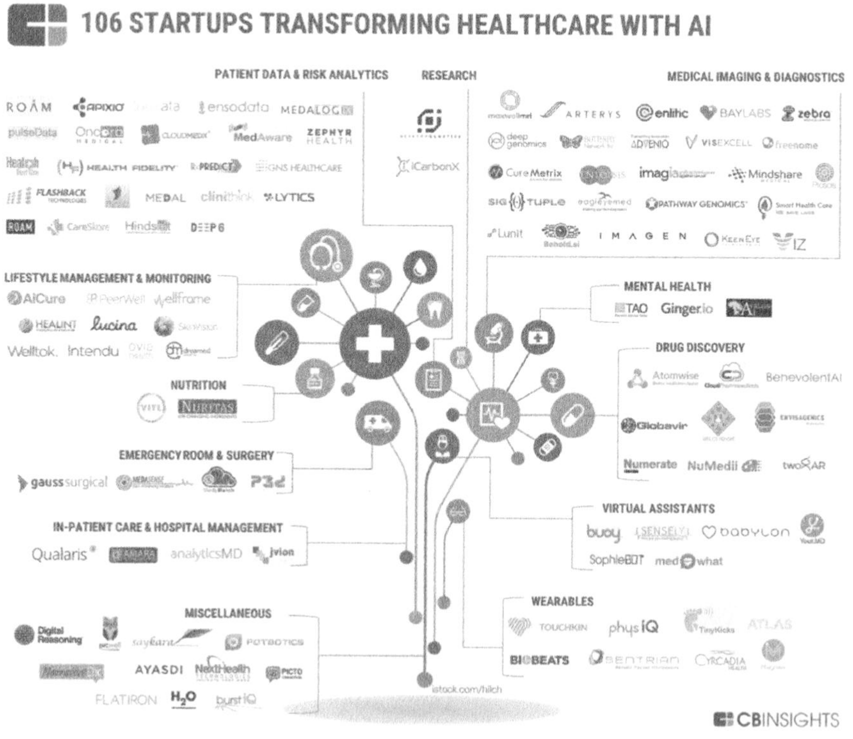

Figure 7.1 AI in healthcare startups. From CB Insights (2016).

Is it a time for AI?

AI is the research area where the concept is making a tremendous history and by some of the challenges left behind. Completely developing of computing technology with the algorithm designing has created the hype in the market. The research in this concept was ebbed along flowed. JASON 2017 survey concludes regarding the background and comments regarding the concept of AI:

"At beginning in the year of 2010. Concept regarding AI was designed by the board along the unseen faiths of the particular, generations of previous technologies: multiple neural networks (NNs). This stage provides in energizing the domains of AI which shows the resultant in the development of AI. The development of AI is done in 2 stages namely:

(i) Faster hardware Graphics Processor Units (GPUs) which provide to train up the devices data in more bigger terms specially in depth manner along (ii) High valued information Such as photos, online questions, social marketing and so. On which can be used for the triangular data beds. By combining all these gives value for data driven mechanism in Deep Learning (DL) at Deep Neural Networks (DNN's), specially by the help of methodology named as Convolution Neural Networks (CNNs)."

7.1.1 Definition

AI over the healthcare domain gives the usage of using difficult pseudo codes in estimating human cognition in the analysis over complicated medical information. Especially, AI has the capability to code the algorithm by which we can get the conclusions based on the human input.

The main theme of AI is to work and perform like as humans. Three types of devices act as "intelligent agents". If our main agenda in developing the devices which require system coding, casually, the AI is defined as "it is a field of sciences which is linked with the device understanding regarding what is intelligence behavior" along also defining an intelligent third party generally treated as intelligent behavior, along by defining the intelligent agents which shows "behaving nature". In simple terms, AI is defined as "the device estimating human capabilities", further improving the human talent by computer devices which make computers like things think same as what humans do [3]. In the more detailed manner, we can say that "the scientific knowledge in making intelligent devices" [4].

7.2   Intelligent Agent

AI concept was known by the help of intelligent agent concept. For the development of AI, skills same as a human to machines are needed. So, here, we require an intelligent third party which has the tolerance of taking actions and achieving goals. Here, the agent will take the decisions based on human actions over the device. Some of the major issues led into the action which can be taken by observations regarding the environment, having the knowledge of environment, previous knowledge, past knowledge, needed for the achieving the environment. This agent provides with sensors as well as by the help of effectors. When the computer is linked with hardware devices or sensors that act by the effecting manner and when the hardware part is performing action with software part, this mechanism is called as "robot". When the third party is performing action purely based on online mode, it is an "infobot" along when the certain suggestions are giving by a system which is linked with a human knowledge such mechanisms are called as "decision support systems" [5].

7.3 Background and Usage of AI Over Healthcare Domain

In the present days, many of the latest use of the medical advancements came into the existence. We can clearly say that it performs same as the human brain; in other terms, we can also say as a replica of human brain. When the time period of 1970, William B Schwartz, one specialist, tried to use computing mechanism over the medicine and some research and published the article at *New England Journal of Medicine* with title "*Medicine and the computer: the promise and problems of change*". In this article, the author made the argument "computer science is a domain which is going to affect all the domains in coming days". At the time over 1970s, there is a large problem in solving the several computing techniques that were not fixed in solving the computing problems. A progressively complex computing mechanism which fixes the reenacted human intellectual procedures is the AI methods, which are needed for medical critical thinking. Previous endeavors were there in producing AI methodology in medication comprised in fixing rules-based frameworks in helping therapeutic thinking. Be that as it may, genuine clinical issues are too mind boggling to even consider lending them to basic principle–based critical thinking procedures. Deep thinking regarding medication particularly in the designing of PC projects is dependent on models of ailments. It is not simply in the domain at general prescription that AI concept was deeply enquired regarding the concept of deep learning, the concept of an intelligent agent is describe in Figure 7.2. In 1976, the Scottish specialist Gunn used computerization analysis for analyzing intense stomach torment. This method was done by various reviews in which the analysis where different case studies were done by the help of PCs, whereby finding through this course demonstrated nearly 10% more exact compared to regular course. By the 1980s, AI examines different networks settled all round the world; yet, by pointedly, the learning method comes up in US. The overall development made more helpful extension in using the relevant and inventive AI methods in dealing with

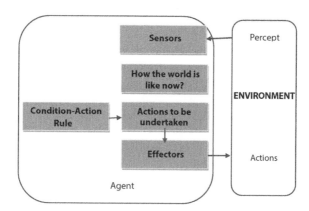

Figure 7.2 Concept of an intelligent agent.

clinical judgments. Quite a bit of this push was on the grounds that prescription was a perfect proving ground for these AI applications. Countless AI methods in the clinical domain in this stage have depended on main architecture. At the end of 1990s, investigation at medicinal AI technology began in using at the systems like AI as well as counterfeit neural devices in helping clinical basic leadership. The following segment investigates current utilization of AI in different parts of human services [6].

7.4   Application of AI Techniques in Healthcare

1.   The accurate acknowledgment regarding AI at social insurance identifies with the complexities of present day medication, which includes securing and investigation of the overflowing measure of data and the restriction over the clinical in addressing necessities by simply human insight. Restorative AI mechanisms with the propelled processing capacity are defeating this constraint and are utilizing a few methods to help clinicians in therapeutic consideration.

AI is being utilized for all the three old style restorative errands: conclusion, anticipation, and treatment, yet for the most part in the region of therapeutic determination. For the most part, the medicinal analysis cycle as shown in Figure 7.3 includes perception and assessment of the patient, accumulation of patient information, elucidation of the information utilizing the medical learning as well as experience afterward definition regarding conclusion, a remedial arrangement with the help of doctor. In the event that we can contrast the restorative analytic cycle, as in Figure 7.3, with the idea of an insightful specialist framework, the doctor is the wise operator, and the patient information was the information along finding that is the yield. Here, the few strategies, where AI frameworks which duplicate the demonstrative phases along, help hospitals by the help of restorative finding. One of such kind is a utilization of expert devices. Master frameworks depend on rules plainly illustrating the means engaged

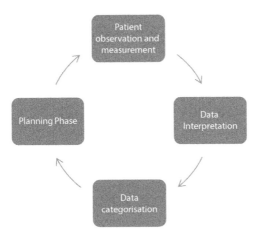

Figure 7.3 Medical diagnostic-therapeutic cycle.

with advancing from contributions to yields. The movement happens through the development of various IF-THEN type rules. All those principles were developed by assistance regarding specialists such as clinical domains that have intrigue as well as involvement at specific space. Achievement of the master framework depends over unequivocal portrayal at information territory as standards. The center of the master framework is the induction motor, which changes the contributions to noteworthy yields. Ordinarily, the use of the master framework approach in therapeutic programming writing computer programs is seen in Clinical Decision Support Systems (CDSS). Basically, CDSS was the programmed programs that empower clinicians to settle on clinician choices. CDSS gives altered evaluation or exhortation dependent on examination of patient informational indexes. Before, the form of CDSS was a type of MYCIN programmed thing which created during the 1970s. MYCIN was a CDSS concentrating regarding administration over irresistible sickness patients. Irresistible illness information was spoken to as creation rules, which are restrictive proclamations, concerning how perceptions can be construed properly. Nonetheless, MYCIN has low accentuation in finding along large amounts of tasks on administration at people by irresistible infections. Further part of assessment regarding MYCIN framework which is discovered it contrasted positively and the counsel gave by irresistible ailment specialists. MYCIN made ready for the advancement of learning-based frameworks and the commercialization of guideline base methodologies in medication and different fields. Another CDSS that was at first created around a similar timeframe as MYCIN however keeps on being utilized is the QMR framework. The QMR framework uses a tweaked calculation demonstrated on the clinical thinking of one single University of Pittsburgh internist. Henceforth, the framework was, at first, called INTERNIST-I. In keeping a view of the chronicled as well as hardware discoveries, QMR framework produces different types of finding of things. Using huge server which arranges ailment discoveries into "bringing out qualities", "significance", and "frequencies" areas, the framework produces the differential finding. Heuristic principles drove the framework to deliver a rundown of positioned analyses established on infection learning spaces in manufactured into the framework. Where the framework was not able to make a decided finding, it tested the client that gave exhortation regarding upcoming tasks of an assurance in which the terms were made. By the time MYCIN as well as QMR frameworks gave demonstrative help, different types of CDSS can give alarms and updates and exhortation about patient treatment and the executives. These frameworks work by making prescient type and multi-dimensional patient view by extracting the from different sources including learning and patient server. The treatment what's more, the executives of maladies have developed, CDSS design is currently using multi-operator frameworks. Every one of the numerous specialists performs particular assignments and tasks in different limits or various areas however transmit information to a focal storehouse so totaled information can be utilized for learning revelation [7].

7.5 Benefits of Artificial Intelligence

There are more advantages in the AI compared to other things are from past few decades. The improvement in AI is done in great manner; the AI cannot operate by them only. Here, the user will instruct the tasks. Moreover, we have to understand all the tasks compared to real world.

• Fast and Accurate Diagnostics

For some type of diseases, we need fast and easy methods for curing. As of our luck, AI devices can extract the knowledge from previous historical data and store the data based on the requirement it analyze the data, from all over where it is stored around the globe [8]. By doing few researches or case studies on artificial neural networks, the research expert in this domain says that the AI is technically proven that is solved many of the problems and it identified in a fast and accurate manner which includes the problems like eye problems, heart problems, etc. [9].

• Reduce Human Errors

By AI technique, we can avoid human made mistakes. Moreover, the people are mixed with emotional and sentiments; in this case, any type of emotional problem or any type of stress is identified from the side of doctor, the AI will be the best assistant and also have the ability to monitor complete method, as well as it also reduces the stressful things.

• Cost Reduction

By trending technologies such as AI, the person can consult doctor by visiting or by not visiting to hospital that gives rise to cross cutting. AI gives guidelines in using online method and helps patient in adding there information such as medical reports to their portal, etc.

• Virtual Presence

This innovation is otherwise known as TeleMedicine; it is a process which will be helpful for their patients who live in rural locations. By identifying the rural places, robots were introduced which connect to their patients as well as to their employees at the time of emergency clinics. These are only portion of the advantages known to us until further notice. As AI advances, we are well on the way to continue seeing numerous new leaps forward in science and drug.

7.6   Swarm Intelligence Model

A swarm is a mechanism where the multiple things can interact by themselves local in a same location along their location, without extending any type of behavior to extent globally. Swarm-based pseudo codes were recently developed for nature-inspired population-based mechanisms which help in producing with lower costs, with speed, along with good secured solutions for several critical problems. Swarm Intelligence (SI) is further more termed as a latest domain of AI which helped for social swarms that occur naturally, like ant colonies, honey bees, as well as bird flocks. Even though, these agents (such as insects else swarm) were in not a good manner and having limited opportunities and having different behaviors for their own survival purpose. The social communication among the swarm devices may be in direct manner or indirect manner, for example, they will communicate by the help of facial expressions or by eye contacts like waggle dance of honey bees. Aberrant transfers take place among to only one person because it changes from user to user based on condition. In the situation the ant trails are stored in different origins. The backhanded sort in association was allocated to stigmergy, which basically implies correspondence through the earth [10]. The domain of research presented in this significance paper revolves around SI. Even more expressly, this paper discusses two of the most standard models of swarm learning inspired by ants' stigmergic lead and flying animals' running behavior. In the earlier decades, scientists and normal analysts have been focusing on the acts of social frightening little creatures because of the astounding efficiency of these trademark swarm systems. In the late 80s, PC analysts proposed the coherent bits of information of these basic swarm structures to the field of AI. In 1989, the enunciation "Swarm Intelligence" was first introduced by G. Beni and J. Wang in the overall improvement structure as a lot of estimations for controlling the mechanical swarm. In 1991, Ant Colony Optimization (ACO) was exhibited by M. Dorigo and accomplices as a novel nature-impelled metaheuristic for the game plan of hard combinatorial improvement (CO) issues. In 1995, particle swarm improvement was introduced by J. Kennedy *et al.* and was first gotten ready for reenacting the flying animal running social directly. By the late 1990s, these two most standard swarm information computations started to go past an unadulterated consistent interest and to enter the space of genuine applications. It is, perhaps, worth referencing here that different years afterward, correctly in 2005, Artificial Bee Colony Algorithm was proposed by D. Karabago as another person from the gathering of swarm learning computations. Since the computational showing of swarms was proposed, there has been a tireless addition in the number of research papers itemizing the successful utilization of three SI counts in a couple of improvement assignments and research issues. SI principles have been successfully applied in an arrangement of issue spaces including limit progression issues, finding perfect courses, arranging, assistant streamlining, and pictures, and data assessment. Computational showing of swarms has been furthermore applied to a wide extent of various territories, including AI, bioinformatics and therapeutic informatics, dynamical systems, and exercises investigation; they have been even applied in reserve and business.

7.7   Swarm Intelligence Capabilities

Key capabilities for swarm intelligence is shown in Figure 7.4

1) Scheduling/Load Balancing: The accentuation is on the general situation of the activity instead of its immediate antecedent or its immediate successor in the calendar and summation assessment rule/worldwide pheromone assessment principle is pursued.
2) Clustering: Clustering mechanism is defined as a collection of similar type of data into one group.

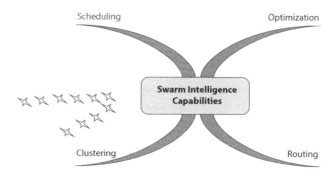

Figure 7.4 Key capabilities of Swarm Intelligence.

3) Optimization: Optimization can be defined as the identifying the best solution of a particular problem.

4) Routing: This depends on the rule that retrogressive ants use the helpful data assembled by the forward ants on their excursion from source to goal.

7.8 How the Swarm AI Technology Works

Swarm insight is a developing field of organically enlivened man-made brainpower dependent at conduct mechanisms over social bugs, for example, ants, honey bees, wasps, termites, and so forth. As per technicality about the articles to until last statement, this article brings the concept to the bottom level where the research should bring to SI. This is a kind of design of a huge number of people which picked one over unity on a shared objective. This method is simply the complex collective, organized, coordinated, flexible, and robust behavior in gathering adhering to straightforward principles.

The innovation called Swarm AI permits a "little gathering of specialists to be associated by knowledge calculations that empower them to cooperate as a hive mind". Swarm AI permits "organized gatherings to consolidate their individual experiences continuously, utilizing AI calculations to merge on ideal arrangements". Here are the five primary principles of SI.

1. Each member must know their surroundings along abilities.
2. Every member should operate by themselves independently (not as slave).
3. Whenever the work was completed, then every member should automatically find and migrate to the new work.
4. Here, the devices were increased dynamically where as members were statically arranged.
5. When members come out of task if a problem happens to the device, the system should have a capability to identify the problem and restore the problem and should come back to the normal state.

A utilization of swarm standards to robots is called swarm apply autonomy. Essentially, swarm standards have been utilized with regard to anticipating issues. The different inquires about and examinations going on in this field have produced some significant applications. US military is researching swarm systems for controlling unarmed vehicles. Likewise, robots with swarm insight empowered them to imitate the sorted out conduct of creepy crawlies. NASA has additionally been contributing about planetary mapping. In the field of medicinal science, it is utilized to find and execute malignant growth tumors. In the media transmission division and activity explore, insect-based directing is performed utilizing rule of swarm. It is called ACO calculation. Constant methods bring out gathering among people to which was bring nearby in making average value which makes elements for making forecasts, giving solutions for bringing out assessments. These all intensify human knowledge. Likewise, swarm innovation is especially appealing on the grounds that it is modest, powerful, and straightforward.

In spite of the fact that this attribute is found wherever in nature, analysts have, as of late, started utilizing it to change different fields, for example, mechanical technology, informa- tion mining, military, media transmission, and so forth. It would not be long that people tackle its adequacy [10].

7.9   Swarm Algorithm

Swarm insight methods were eluded by the computing mechanisms enlivened for charac- teristic frameworks. Until this point, a few swarm insight models are dependent on various characteristic swarm frameworks which were brought out for writing, as well as effectively applies for some genuine methods. Instances in swarm knowledge methodologies were ACO, Particle Swarm Optimization (PSO), Artificial Bee Colony, Bacterial Foraging, Cat Swarm Optimization, Artificial Immune System, and Glowworm Swarm Optimization. In this context, we basically concentrate on the major two prevalent swarm insight methods, to be specific, ACO along PSO [11].

7.10   Ant Colony Optimization Algorithm

In the primary position, the principal case of a fruitful swarm insight mechanism is ACO that is presented by M. Dorigo *et al.*, as well as this method initially helps in taking care of discrete streamlining issues at the time of 1980s. ACO shows motivation by the society in conducting of insect states. It was the characteristic perception by a gathering "practically visually impaired" ants totally together make sense of the briefest course between their nourishment and their home with no visual data. The accompanying segment introduces a few insights regarding behavior of ants along and it also says how these generally sim- ple creepy crawlies agreeably cooperate with each other in doing mutual understandings assignments that are essential to their endurance [12]. Figure 7.5 show the Navigation of ants through ants colony algorithm.

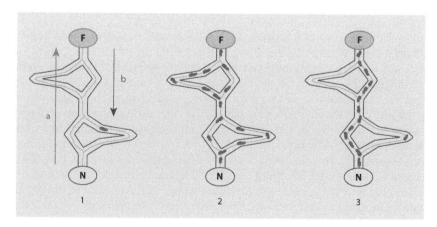

Figure 7.5 Navigation of ants through ants colony algorithm.

1. Strategy: The main theme is to improvise the historical data, i.e., pheromone-based and heuristic data to develop up-and-comer arrangements each in a probabilistic advance savvy way and overlap the data gained from building arrangements over history. Probability in choosing part is determine with the help of heuristic commitment over segment to general expense in arrangement, and nature for arrangement along background was refreshed relatively over nature regarding the well-known arrangement ACO mechanism that is used for various problems such as for clustering and classification. Figure 7.6 is a pictorial representation concept using ACO. ACO mechanism is used to solve many logic problems and also helps in solving the address in the form of one node on top of other node. This procedure was the part in ant colony. ACO mechanism was used in a lot of optimization problems, expanding by the quadratic task to protein collapsing which gives resultant techniques that were concerned for the dynamic problems at genuine factors, stochastic issues, multi-targets, as well as parallel activities [13].

ACO is a sort of heuristic technique by worldwide enhancement that incorporates dispersed figuring along positive input strategies which are having excellencies: 1. More grounded heartiness: ACO can transplant different issues, particularly a wide range of amassed advanced issues. 2. More prominent capacity to locate the better result: The calculation embraces the positive input guideline, which animates the advancement preparing and does not caught in neighborhood optima. 3. Disseminating parallelism computing: ACO is an advancement calculation dependent on subterranean insect provinces and has

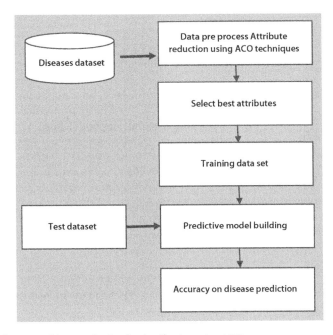

Figure 7.6 Architecture of feature selection for classification using ACO.

parallelism base on them. The individual ants can proceed to trade and move the data (pheromone), which can prompt a superior outcome. 4. It is anything but difficult to join ACO with different techniques: The calculation can incorporate other illuminated strategies to improve the presentation of the calculation [14].

7.11   Particle Swarm Optimization

The secondary reality of swarm mechanism was PSO. PSO is a heuristic global mechanism. This kind was first found and portrayed by James Kennedy and Russell C. Eberhart in 1995. This method was proposed from the investigation of swarm insight. Swarm or a gathering of herds when they scan for nourishment, the sort of knowledge they use in associating with their companion swarms is the primary guideline behind the starting point of this procedure. At the point when a gathering of swarms goes looking for nourishment, it is possible that they go together or in the gathering until they discover a spot where nourishment can be found [15]. One of the winged animals among them looks through the best nourishment called the ideal search. Presently, every flying creature is moving with some speed to look through the nourishment. Presently, the strategy which this winged animal receives to pass on the message of the best nourishment to every single other fledgling and the group goes to that spot is utilized in PSO. It was believed that this collaboration among flying creatures can be proficiently used in finding the ideal arrangement. These feathered creatures or swarms are said to be particles in molecule swarm streamlining. Presently, in PSO, each molecule is moving with some speed and when the ideal arrangement is found by one molecule, there is a memory which aides in passing on the message to every single other molecule [16].

This paper depicted a somewhat basic calculation (and time has seen no compelling reason to change its clear essentials), referring to Craig Reynolds' task was inspired by flying creature runs [17]. Essential thought was joining the accompanying two types of ideas: (i) conduct for group in winged animals roaming around 3D space regarding few objectives, and (ii) a swarm answers for the enhancement issue, traveling by multi-dimensional pursuit space by the great arrangements. In this way, we liken a "molecule" with an applicant answer for a streamlining issue. Such a molecule has both a position and a speed. Its position is, truth be told, accurately the up-and-comer arrangement it presently speaks to. Its speed was dislodging task at the pursuit space, by that (trusts) will move among the productive modification on its situation at the following cycle. Core at great PSO calculation over the progression that computes another situation for the molecule is dependent in three impacts. Motivation from Reynolds (1987) was clear, yet subtleties were very unique as well as obviously, abuse way in which molecule was transferring at the pursuit location along it able to gauge the "fitness" in any type of angle. Impacts—segments which makes position to refreshed place—are as follows:

- Current velocity: the particle presents velocity (obviously).
- Personal best: the molecule identifies best fit of the item which was found, termed as the personal best. The component is defined as the distance from that node to the nearest node.

- Global Best: Each molecule at swarm knows about the position at the molecule was to found (for example, the best of the individual bests). Last segment in speed update, transferred among all particles, was vector toward path by the present situation to all inclusive well known angles.

2. Strategy: The main theme of the algorithm is to identify the place over the multi-dimensional space; firstly, it is given to random position as well as random velocity, slowly by improving toward local optima by usage in explorating along spreading of good, well known locations at space.

PSO Rules:

1) Separation: should not move against flockmates.
2) Alignment: everyone keeps a separate route for their own data packets.
3) Cohesion: forward among the average plots of neighbors.
4) Desire factor per bird for roosting areas: it is mandatory in swarming that gets harder when a termed roosting where ever is needed.

7.12   Concepts for Swarm Intelligence Algorithms

At the point where we take into effect of swarm knowledge over software engineering, two groups in calculations unmistakably hanged on as far as measure in task distributed, level for the present tasks as well as general effect at the industry. One of the kind was propelled legitimately with the help of pheromone-trail that follows the conduct of subterranean insect species, along this field is known as ACO. Figure 7.7 describe the pictorial representation of Ant Colony Optimization. Another kind of family was propelled in rushing along swarming conduct, and along fundamental model calculation family is treated as PSO. Here, in this family, there are calculations dependent at bacteria scavenging, along a portion at calculations that depend at honey bee rummaging; the offers with PSO, the expansive manner by which the characteristic wonder is mapped onto the idea of search inside a scene. In this section, we talk about these two calculations that are PSO and ACO [18].

Algorithm steps:

1) Start the process.
2) Begin the particles.
3) Calculate capacity level of each and every particle.
4) If the present value of particle is good compared to pbest, then give the new pbest value.
5) If the present value of particle is less when compared to pbest value, keep the previous pbest value.
6) At this stage, give the pbest resultant term to the gbest term.
7) Now, start the crossover method.
8) Now, begin mutation.
9) If estimation is found correct, then we move toward to the final value.
10) End of algorithm.

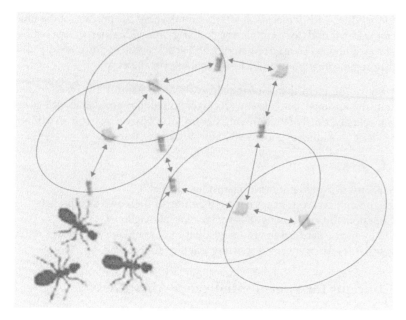

Figure 7.7 Ant colony optimization.

7.13 How Swarm AI is Useful in Healthcare

Swarm mechanism gives a large response to the patients' safety by providing on time action along improving organization safety procedure. A research by Stanford University School of Medicine and Unanimous AI has identified the swarm method can make more accurate treatment when compared to the doctor alone or MI algorithm too alone. Designed with the help of unanimous AI, the swarm technique can gather the group of doctors' talent with AI; these mechanisms combine to the real-world scenario to get the more desired output. In the research, the scholars measured the correctness in diagnosing pneumonia by the help of chest X-rays, the casual mechanism at the US. The probability of the swarm diagnosing pneumonia in a patient is stated in Figure 7.8. The experts' team in the group said that AI mechanism which helps in the interconnected tasks and bundle of tasks in a real-time manner detecting the way in which bird flock, fish school, along bees swarm to detect the animals' knowledge. "The technology having the 'hive mind' of networked participants, designed by AI techniques, for aggregating the group information, wisdom, insights, along intuition over the concise result". Regarding the concept of hive, Rosenberg defined: "Animals uses same procedure they've have been from many years by feedback loops which converge on an optimal combination of insights". It is found that diagnoses by the help of Swarm AI devices lead to a 33% decrement over the average misfield rate, compared with traditional approached of individual.

Safwan Halabi, a clinical associate professor at Stanford University School of Medicine "has improved a mechanism in generating exact along by increasing the perfection of all devices

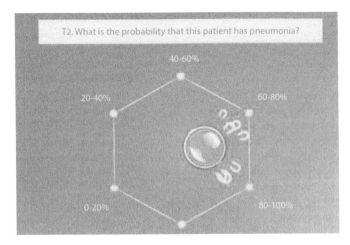

Figure 7.8 The probability of the swarm diagnosing pneumonia in a patient. Credit: PRNewsfoto/ Unanimous AI.

in training over medical datasets." Unanimous said its Swarm AI mechanism having the potential in generating more potential results "ground truth" datasets for training algorithmic systems such as CheXNet that can bring consequences to break through. Ground Truth is a keyword used in ML and AI which helps in checking results of machine learning on perfection compared to real world.

7.14   Benefits of Swarm AI

Swarm Artificial knowledge in medicinal services is an exceptional idea that can essentially improve constant pro correspondence and social protection specialists. Maybe the best bit of leeway of AI, especially in development, is that it overhauls the capacity to process and store a great deal of data. This technique is a mainstreamed and organized way and makes an elucidation of that information into utilitarian instruments. Man-made cognizance is imperative in social protection. It can assemble data after some time, get to data set away in various PCs, go over data made on the web, online books, and research notes in just seconds, and choose a decent decision relying upon all of the data it has been done.

When completing new development as a system in our preparation, various things can turn out seriously as a result of the nonattendance of learning or human misstep during the execution time of the advancement. As much as AI is new development that can be of preferred position to social protection providers, it can, in like manner, show to be inconvenient later down the line generally as a result of human screw up previously. Before we get any new system or development, it is basic to totally fathom it to stay away from basic or even lethal mistakes.

The continuous development of data innovation is joined by a no less striking increment in correspondence supporting therapeutic basic leadership. With the assistance of current instruments, we can impart quicker, on numerous levels, autonomous of area. With the assistance of data innovation, the therapeutic network is turning into a dynamic, discussing aggregate with the highlights of a swarm.

The medicinal network, with its exponentially developing collaborations, is continuously picking up characteristics of swarms with intrinsic knowledge characterized as the average in conducting the average unique-composed methods, normal else fake. Another advancement or change by and by is imparted from individuals from the swarm, for example, doctors, emergency clinics, and medicinal social orders, casually and quickly, rendering the swarm ready to pursue improved methods.

Despite the fact that there is no formalized regular system of a network, endeavors are being made to recognize basic approaches (e.g., with examples of care and ponders). They give significant input on what's going on and assist us with perceiving patterns [19].

7.15   Impact of Swarm-Based Medicine

People, furnished with Internet innovation, practice swarm knowledge in different circles of social connection going from anticipating races to the organization the board. The web-based connection may bring about various results, for example, improved reaction ability and basic leadership quality.

The immediate correlation of swarm-based drug with proof or greatness based is intriguing; however, these ideas ought to be seen as supplementing one another and working autonomously of one another. Ideal basic leadership relies upon a parity of individual learning and swarms knowledge, considering the nature of each, with their weight in choices being adjusted likewise. The probability of adjusting disputable angles and accomplishing worthy ends for most of members has been a significant errand of logical and medicinal meetings since the Age of Enlightenment in the seventeenth and eighteenth hundreds of years. Our swarm proceeds with this interconnecting synchronization at a remarkable speed and is, on account of votes, Internet gatherings, and so forth, more receptive than any time in recent memory. Quicker alters in our course of development, similar to a school of fish, are getting to be conceivable. Data spreads starting with one individual then onto the next. It is oblivious, yet with our own move, we impact the remainder of the apiary.

Inside a situation, singular conduct decides the conduct of the group and the other way around. Web innovation has significantly changed the earth we act in. Customarily, medicinal data was given to patients just as to doctors by specialists. This intermediation was portrayed by a specialist remaining between the wellsprings of data and the client. Right now, and likely significantly more so later on, Web 2.0 and proper calculations empower clients to depend on the direction or conduct of their friends in choosing and devouring data. This is one of the numerous procedures encouraged by medication 2.0 and is depicted as "apomediation". Apomediation, regardless of whether certain or unequivocal, expands the impact of people on others. For a person to adjust its conduct inside a swarm, different people should be seen and their activities responded upon. Through apomediation, more people participate in the swarm.

Our patients are better educated; second conclusions can be looked for through the Internet inside hours. Our individual conduct is affected by online assets just as advanced correspondence with our partners. This adjustment in singular conduct impacts the manner in which we find, comprehend, and receive rules. Social orders speaking to bigger gatherings inside the swarms utilize this innovation to make proposals. This procedure is affected by people and past activities of the network; these then consequently impact singular conduct. Data innovation majorly affects the lifecycle of rules and proposals. There is no section and leave point for IT in such a manner. With an expanding effect on singular conduct, its impact on aggregate conduct increments, affecting the other bearings to a similar degree.

Dynamic changes in the development of the swarm and inside the swarm may prompt people leaving the crowd. These may impact the crowd to move toward the anomalies. Simultaneously, an individual leaving a herd or swarm is uncovered. Doctors, just as clinical focuses, uncover themselves when they leave the gathering for advancement. Negative outcomes and disappointment may prompt a lawful presentation should medicines fall flat.

The view of swarm conduct itself changes the manner in which we approach rules. At the point when a few rules are distributed, monitoring them because of association expands our familiarity with the predisposition. Significant deviations from different suggestions warrant investigation. The view of swarm conduct and grasping the learning of the swarm may prompt an enhanced utilization of assets. Data that has just been acquired might be fused straightforwardly by specialists, empowering them to expand on this and set up new information—as social learning operators [20].

7.16   SI Limitations

The Limitations of Swarm Intelligence: The swarm approach gives a rich wellspring of motivation and its standards are straightforwardly relevant to PC frameworks. Be that as it may, despite the fact that it accentuates auto-setup, auto-association, and versatility abilities, the swarm-type approach stays valuable of a non-defined terms including multiple redundancies for similar situation over a generally huge territory, for example, finding the briefest way or gathering rock tests on Mars [21]. Without a doubt, the swarm-type approach manages the participation of enormous quantities of homogeneous specialists. Such methodologies ordinarily depend on scientific intermingling results (for example, the irregular walk) that arrive at the ideal result over an adequately significant stretch of time. Notice that, what's more, the operators included are homogeneous.

- The ability of swarm learning is in reality rapidly creating and clearing. It offers another alternative, an untraditional strategy for organizing complex structures that neither requires concentrated control nor wide pre-programming. That being communicated, SI structures still have two or three imprisonments, for example, Time-Critical Applications: Because the pathways to game plans in SI systems are neither predefined nor pre-modified, however rather creating, SI structures are not suitable for time-essential applications that require (i) online control of systems, (ii) time-fundamental decisions, and (iii) great courses of action inside restrictive time designations, for instance, the lift controller and the nuclear reactor temperature controller.

It remains to be useful, regardless, for non-time fundamental applications that incorporate different redundancies of a comparable development [22].

- Parameter Tuning: Tuning the parameters of SI-breathed life into progress systems is one of the general detriments of swarm understanding, as in most stochastic upgrade methods, and not at all like deterministic headway techniques. As a matter of fact, in any case, since various parameters of SI structures are issue subordinate, they are often either precisely pre-picked by the issue characteristics in an experimentation way, or shockingly better adaptively adjusted on run time (as in the flexible ACO and the cushy adaptable PSO [23].

- Stagnation: Because of the nonappearance of central coordination, SI structures could encounter the evil impacts of a stagnation condition or an unfavorable intermixing to a close by perfect (e.g., an ACO), stagnation happens when all of the ants, over the long haul, seek after the comparable flawed way and build up a comparable visit. This requirement, in any case, can be obliged by means of mindfully setting figuring parameters, e.g., the parameter in ACO, or the parameter ω in PSO. Different assortments of ACO and PSO computations could further diminish the probability of that requirement (e.g., by unequivocally or unquestionably confining the proportion of pheromone primers), as proposed in Max-Min AS or Ant Colony Systems, similarly as by contrasting dormancy weight, ω, exponentially (rather than straightly), starting late proposed in a continuous PSO assortment called Exponential PSO [24].

7.17   Future of Swarm AI

The best opportunity of next few upcoming years is using AI with hybrid models, where the hospitals are used in diagnosis, planning the way of treatment along analyzing the risk factors, even though it guarantees for patients' health with efficiency. Figure 7.9 shows the benifits of AI in health. By this research, many were adopted this technique by perceived risk, along the beginning to give the scalable improvements of the patient outcomes along operational efficiency at scale. This new technique is making a great revolution in many ways. By starting to drug development until clinical research, AI mechanism helped to improve patient health and saved lot of man power and money. Besides, the introduction of this concept over healthcare which gives easy access, affordability, as well as effectiveness of the capacity of AI that is to use the most suited methodologies along to adopt the new challenges from the large amount of data is truly we can have managing skills. By the help of AI mechanisms, insights for assisting clinical practice can be obtained. AI concept was included by the self-learning and rectifying capacity which makes device for better correctness for the data it gives, whereas it comes better with time. The AI mechanism is helpful for physicians in several ways. Since they are having lot of data with them, they can help in giving the better decisions and assistance in the clinical domain. Additionally, analytic mistakes and remedial blunders can be minimized. Besides, AI frameworks approach enormous volumes of information; they can make expectations about by separating helpful data.

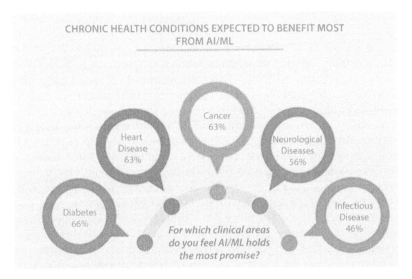

Figure 7.9 AI benefits in health.

Constant well-being conditions are relied upon to profit the most from AI frameworks. Malignant growth, diabetes, and heart infections are enormous open doors for human services patterns, for example, popular culture and accuracy drugs.

7.18 Issues and Challenges

On the off chance that AI mechanisms are to progress past which gives explicit patient problem and altogether empower more extensive well-being and human services exercises, there are noteworthy difficulties to be tended to. The main source is this certain suspicion which was capacities of AI that naturally beat issues by huge mind boggling along flawed well-being information. The hazards of this presumption and the related need to address it with methodical ways to deal with the two information the executives and straightforwardness in calculation improvement are examined in this segment. A stunning case of the problem which should tend to referred to by Ching *et al.* "A propelling model ... that will be identified where the mechanism prepared to anticipate probability regarding loss of life the treatment is allowed below hazard to people who is suffering from asthma, yet simply that's the reason those kind of people were treated with special care which are needed by the emergency clinic. With regard to profound picking up, by agreeing premise for model's yield was especially significant, which is profound learning mechanisms are curiously defenseless to antagonistic models that can yield certainty range certainly upto 99.999% tests which look like unadulterated clamor."

The more extensive condition is the "anticipated result of identifying is done was an altogether variety of thing" compared to the "anticipated result when standard framework accomplishes the typical thing." Two types can be helpful yet confound each and every method as the savage mix-up.

By the time of usage of AI in the transport in human administrations having a reassuring capacity, it defeats two types of particular along good presence. Recreated knowledge research is, as it were, driven and driven by PC scientists without restorative getting ready, and it has been commented this has incited a precisely drawn in and issue arranged system in the use of AI in human administration transport. Contemporary therapeutic administrations transport mechanisms are dependent upon human reasoning, tireless clinician correspondence along working up a capable relationship by the help of patients to make sure regarding consistency. The perspectives were some type of AI that cannot override adequately. The usage of computerized relates in restorative administrations was shown up the problems regarding the mechanization over powerless conditions where as people association along the identification were likely all the additionally captivating. There is, in like manner, the aversion at medical domain at accepting AI developments which envision that, at last, merge them. In any case, there is nothing question in utilizing progress which robotize along quicken look into office decisive system. This has provoked some proposing a model of staying together. Such type of mechanism which suits AI as well as human segments at social protection movement along imagines inevitable automatization for gigantic pieces for restorative systems by the time of sparing people pieces at clinical domains which thought such as correspondence, process along essential initiative.

7.19 Conclusion

Swarm conduct may encourage the age and appropriation of information. Swarm conduct may likewise be negative. A few advancements might be upset as they may be seen as exceptions. Be that as it may, this negative impact may likewise be halfway balanced by a cognizant impression of the swarming part of our conduct. The measure of the gathered information is expanding exponentially and information mining and recommender frameworks are improving in parallel. These new instruments will give us data on our aggregate conduct, which was not available as of not long ago. Similarly, with valuable sources, it would be very engrossing to see how they would be used by the scholarly community and industry.

This data should not be delivered; it lies before us and all we have to do winds up mindful of it. Instructions to coordinate swarm-based prescription into training are left to the individual doctor; however, even this choice will be impacted by the swarm.

References

1. Asir Antony Gnana Singh, D., Surenther, P., Jebamalar Leavline, E., Ant Colony Optimization Based Attribute Reduction for Disease Diagnostic System. *Int. J. Appl. Eng. Res.,* 10, 55, 2015.
2. Dhingra, P., Gayathri, N., Kumar, S.R., Singanamalla, V., Ramesh, C., Balamurugan, B., Internet of Things–based pharmaceutics data analysis, in: *Emergence of Pharmaceutical Industry Growth with Industrial IoT Approach*, pp. 85–131, Academic Press, 2020.

3. Ahmed, H. and Glasgow, J., *Swarm Intelligence: Concept, Models and Applications*. School of Computing Queen's University Kingston, Ontario, Canada K7L3N6, 2012.

4. http://www.techferry.com/articles/swarm-intelligence.html

5. https://ekare.ai/artificial-intelligence-benefits-applications-healthcare/

6. https://www.medicaldevice-network.com/news/swarm-ai-system/

7. https://www.chthealthcare.com/blog/artificial-intelligence-in-healthcare

8. https://www.healtheuropa.eu/how-artificial-intelligence-can-revolutionise-healthcare/92824/

9. https://www.internationalsos.com/client-magazines/in-this-issue-3/how-ai-is-transforming-the-future-of-healthcare.

10. https://www.medicaldevice-network.com/news/swarm-ai-system/

11. Bansal, J.C., Sharma, H., Deep, K., Das, K.N., Nagar, A., Special issue on swarm intelligence and its applications to engineering. *Int. J. Syst. Assur. Eng. Manag.*, 9, 739–740, 2018. https://doi.org/10.1007/s13198-018-0742-9

12. JASON The Mitre Corporation, *Artificial Intelligence for Health and Health Care*, December 2017.

13. Miley, J., This Start-Up Uses Human Swarm Intelligence to Develop AI That Can Predict the Future, *J. Med. Internet Res.*, 15, 9.March 27th, 2018.

14. Kumar, S.R., Gayathri, N., Muthuramalingam, S., Balamurugan, B., Ramesh, C., Nallakaruppan, M.K., Medical Big Data Mining and Processing in e-Healthcare, in: *Internet of Things in Biomedical Engineering*, pp. 323–339, Academic Press, India, 2019.

15. Kennedy, L.P., *How Artificial Intelligence Helps in Health Care*, https://www.webmd.com/a-to-z-guides/features/artificial-intelligence-helps-health-care#1.

16. Zajmi, L., Ahmad, F.Y.H., Jaharadak, A.A., Concepts, Methods, and Performances of Particle Swarm Optimization, Backpropagation, and Neural Networks, Applied Computational Intelligence and Soft Computing, vol. 2018, Article ID 9547212, 7 pages, 2018. https://doi.org/10.1155/2018/9547212

17. Sun, L., Song, X., Chen, T., An Improved Convergence Particle Swarm Optimization Algorithm with Random Sampling of Control Parameters". *J. Control Sci. Eng.*, vol. 2019, Article ID 2019, 7478498, 11, 2019. https://doi.org/10.1155/2019/7478498

18. Nagasubramanian, G., Sakthivel, R.K., Patan, R., Gandomi, A.H., Sankayya, M., Balusamy, B., Securing e-health records using keyless signature infrastructure blockchain technology in the cloud. *Neural Comput. Appl.*, 1–9, 2018.

19. Putora, P.M. and Oldenburg, J., Swarm-Based Medicine, *J. Med. Internet Res.*, 15, 9, 2013, Sep 19.

20. Budhathoki, P., *Swarm Intelligence*, Dec 7, 2018.

21. Reddy, S., *Use of Artificial Intelligence in Healthcare Delivery*, eHealth - Making Health Care Smarter, Thomas F. Heston, IntechOpen, Available from: https://www.intechopen.com/books/ehealth-making-health-care-smarter/use-of-artificial-intelligence-in-healthcare-delivery

22. Maji, S., Study of Swarm Intelligence Technology, Its Principals, Capabilitiesand Concepts for Algorithms REVIEWED. 04, 04, July-September 2017.

23. Olariu, S. and Zomaya, A.Y., *Handbook of Bioinspired Algorithms and Applications*, 29 September 2005.

24. Sharma, S. and Singh, S., Heart Disease Diagnosis using Genetic and Particle Swarm Optimization. *International Journal of Engineering Research & Technology (IJERT)*, 3, 8, 1499–1503, August - 2014.

8

Swarm Intelligence for Group Objects in Wireless Sensor Networks

Kapil Chauhan[1]* and Pramod Singh Rathore[2]

[1]Aryabhatta College of Engineering and Research Center, Ajmer India
[2]Aryabhatta Engineering College, Ajmer, India

Abstract

Wireless sensor networks are utilized at different places as alert finders and sensors. Quantities of grouping calculations have been created to improve the vitality parity of the WSNs on the grounds that vitality is the fundamental part of WSNs during information transmission. These calculations are chiefly utilized for expanding the lifetime of these sensor systems. Vitality proficient calculations and burden adjusting are utilized during the grouping calculations. This paper recommends a calculation that is dependent on Particle Swarm Optimization (PSO) system for improving system life time. It helps in shaping the bunches just as the Cluster Head (CH) choice. The proposed calculation is broadly tested, and after that, the consequences of this calculation are contrasted and the recently proposed calculations, for example, LEACH, and so on.

In recent WSN, information accumulation system is the difficult region for analysts from extended time period. Quantities of scientists have proposed neural system and fluffy rationale-based information collection techniques in wireless environment. The primary target of this paper is to break down the current work on Artificial Intelligence (AI)–based information accumulation systems in WSNs.

Keywords: Particle swarm optimization, data aggregation, wireless sensor network, ant colony optimization

8.1 Introduction

Wireless sensor network (WSN) allows to gather scattered sensors that are set in an enormous territory and essentially help in checking, identifying, and analyzing the physical or the natural states of that specific spot. Such types of physical situation for the most part incorporate temperature, sound, wind, and so forth. It is portrayed as accumulation of hubs that are set haphazardly in sensor field. These hubs are associated with one another through a remote channel to such an extent that the information transmission can occur between them. Vitality productive calculations are required as the sensor hubs are battery worked.

---

*Corresponding author: kapilajmer86@gmail.com

Abhishek Kumar, Pramod Singh Rathore, Vicente Garrcia Diaz and Rashmi Agrawal (eds.) Swarm Intelligence Optimization: Algorithms and Applications, (123–142) © 2021 Scrivener Publishing LLC. ISBN 978-1-119-77874-5

To display the wide practices emerged from a swarm, we present a few general standards for swarm insight.

Vicinity rule: The fundamental units of a swarm ought to be fit for straightforward calculation identified with its encompassing condition. Here, calculation is viewed as a direct conduct reaction to natural change, for example, those activated by cooperation among operators. Contingent upon the intricacy of specialists included, reactions may differ enormously. In any case, some crucial practices are shared, for example, living-asset looking and home structure.

Quality rule: Apart from essential calculation capacity, a swarm ought to have the option to reaction to quality elements, for example, nourishment and security.

Guideline of different reaction: Resources ought not to be moved in restricted area. The conveyance ought to be planned with the goal that every operator will be maximally secured confronting ecological variances.

Winged animal running and fish tutoring are the motivations from nature behind molecule swarm streamlining calculations. It was first proposed by Eberhart and Kennedy. Mirroring physical amounts, for example, speed and position in fledgling rushing, fake particles are developed to "fly" inside the hunt space of improvement issues [1].

In any case, not quite the same as the past two calculations utilizing pheromone or input as apparatuses to dispose of undesired arrangements, molecule swarm streamlining calculations refresh the present arrangement straightforwardly. As should be obvious from the accompanying portrayal of the edge work of PSO calculations, with less parameter, PSO calculations are anything but difficult to execute and accomplish worldwide ideal arrangements with high likelihood.

At first, a populace of particles is conveyed consistently in the multi-measurement search space of the target capacity of the streamlining issue.

Be that as it may, not the same as the past two calculations utilizing pheromone or criticism as devices to dispose of undesired arrangements, molecule swarm advancement calculations refresh the present arrangement legitimately. As should be obvious from the accompanying depiction of the edge work of PSO calculations, with less parameter, PSO calculations are anything but difficult to execute and accomplish worldwide ideal arrangements with high likelihood. At first, a populace of particles is circulated consistently in the multi-measurement search space of the target capacity of the improvement issue.

Artificial Intelligence (AI) incorporates number of methods like Particle Swarm Optimization (PSO), Neural Networks (NNs), Genetics Algorithms (GAs), Ant Colony Optimization (ACO), and so forth. Computerized reasoning–based methods help in progress of system lifetime and throughput. ACO might be utilized for the better steering to remote sensor systems and PSO is great answer for grouping to choose the best bunch head in the system. These methodologies might be utilized in remote sensor systems at various stages. Essentially, there are four vitality scattering courses in remote sensor systems. First one is retransmitting the information, second one is catching that signifies "when a specific hub get undesirable information", third one is inactive tuning in, and fourth one is overhead of the information. At the point when information accumulation activity performed in WSN, information clashing emerges in the systems. Information transmission is beyond the realm of imagination over the system, at whatever point hub is vitality insufficient. Bunching is one such method which is utilized to improve the lifetime of these hubs. Various leveled steering conventions isolate the system in to bunches with one group head and part hubs. The Cluster Head (CH) hubs gather the information from residual hubs in the group and after that send the information to a base station (BS). In any case, this is conceivable just until the system is alive. System life time is straightforwardly identified with the battery. In this manner, real worry in WSN is to spare hub vitality. Vitality is required in arrangement of bunches just as in deter- mination of CHs. CHs exhaust their vitality in accepting the information from sensor hubs, in information collection and in transmission of information to the sink. Along these lines, CHs must be vitality proficient hubs due to the transmission and gathering duty. In the event that CH hubs kick the bucket rapidly, the individual bunch disengaged from the system and significant occasions might be passed up a great opportunity. In this examination, we have concentrated on accomplishing vitality productivity through ideal choice of group head.

Bunching implies the demonstration of dividing an unlabeled dataset into gatherings of comparative items. Each gathering, called a "bunch", comprises of items that are compa- rable among themselves and not at all like objects of different gatherings. In the previous couple of decades, bunch examination has assumed a focal job in an assortment of fields going from designing (AI, man-made reasoning, design acknowledgment, mechanical building, and electrical building), PC sciences (web mining, spatial database investigation, literary record accumulation, and picture division), life and restorative sciences (hereditary qualities, science, microbiology, fossil science, psychiatry, and pathology), to earth sciences (topography and remote detecting).

Information mining is an amazing new innovation, which goes for the extraction of concealed prescient data from huge databases. Information mining instruments antic- ipate future patterns and practices, enabling organizations to make proactive, learning driven choices. The procedure of information disclosure from databases requires quick and

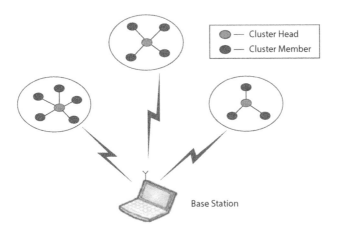

Figure 8.1 The clustering phenomena [2].

programmed bunching of exceptionally enormous datasets with a few qualities of various sorts. This represents an extreme test before the old style grouping systems. As of late, a group of nature roused calculations, known as Swarm Intelligence (SI), has pulled in a few specialists from the field of example acknowledgment and bunching. Bunching strategies that are dependent on the SI devices have allegedly outflanked numerous old style techniques for parceling an intricate genuine world dataset.

SI is a moderately new interdisciplinary field of research, which has increased enormous fame in nowadays. Calculations having a place with the area, draw motivation from the aggregate insight rising up out of the conduct of a gathering of social creepy crawlies (like honey bees, termites, and wasps). When going about as a network, these bugs even with very constrained individual ability can mutually (helpfully) perform numerous intricate errands important for their survival. Issues like finding and putting away nourishments and choosing and getting materials for future utilization require a point by point arranging and are settled by creepy crawly states with no sort of director or controller. A case of especially effective research bearing in swarm insight is ACO (Dorigo *et al.*, 1996, Dorigo and Gambardella, 1997), which spotlights on discrete streamlining issues and has been connected effectively to countless NP hard discrete advancement issues including the voyaging sales representative, the quadratic task, booking, vehicle directing, and so on, just as to steering in media transmission systems (Figure 8.1) [2].

PSO is a meta-heuristic inquiry calculation that assumes a significant job in expanding the life expectancy of the remote sensor systems. This calculation gets quicker and less expensive outcomes contrasted and different strategies. Molecule swarm enhancement (PSO) is impacted by conduct of winged creatures or fish in a gathering. They generally travel in gathering looking for nourishment without impacting and henceforth decrease their own individual exertion while scanning for sustenance, water, and asylum. Different examinations and calculations have been created utilizing the PSO calculation in WSNs. This paper gives a careful clarification of various recently proposed calculations and their highlights at various stages. PSO has assumed a noteworthy job in expanding the effectiveness of the remote sensor systems.

Wireless sensor systems (WSNs) comprise of different sensor hubs, which have the ability to detect, process, register, and impart. An enormous number of sensor hubs and their various applications incite different blocks during usage in sensor systems. Other than execution, certain territories, to be specific, getting to of data, information accumulation, and capacity are as yet a situation. Different determinations of sensor hubs like their size, computational capacity, cost, equipment requirement, vitality productivity, and other plan parameters make the execution of the sensor arrange a troublesome assignment. In present situation, advancement issues become increasingly repetitive. A vitality particular of sensor systems winds up horrendous in an immense domain which thusly requests a worry identified with different streamlining parameters. That is the reason why we figured to evaluate the power of different developmental calculations to improve the system life expectancy with vitality as an imperative properly focusing on the different transmission techniques. For several years, various developmental calculations have been used for assessment of issues that get the most ideal outcome from the different arrangements. A large number of the proposed calculations focus on the standard of the populace-based heuristic hunt strategies, for taking care

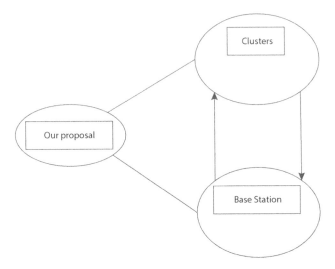

Figure 8.2 Centralized clustering algorithm [6].

of general advancement issues. A swarm astute calculation deals with the rule conduct of flying feathered creatures so as to get to the assets being actualized in Low-Energy Adaptive Clustering Hierarchy (LEACH) convention. In these conventions, the swarm insightful calculation is actualized to shape different groups which thus help in characterizing their separate CHs while structuring a WSN with indistinguishable conditions from progressively arrange. The swarm-based calculation produces attractive outcomes. System life expectancy can be additionally improved by actualizing different most ideal course identification strategies. Counterfeit honey bee state calculation is another up and coming methodology whose working thoroughly takes after that of swarm-based advancement procedures while checking the groups in WSN [3].

8.2 Algorithm

1. Introduce the hub of the swarm.
2. Figure the hub with the best position and dole out it Gbest.
3. Figure the particular hub's close to home palatable Pbest.
4. Start the emphasis:

   - As the position and condition of the hub update, update them into the cushions.
   - Calculate the wellness work for the hub where
        Fitness = W1*MaxDist + W2*MaxHops
   - Set Pbest = Pi

5. End cycle.

6. Start cycle:

- If the present wellness of the hub is not exactly the hub best, at that point set Pbest = Pi.

7. End cycle.

In concentrated bunching system, if focal hub bombs, the whole system will go down, in this manner, unwavering quality is not ensured. Henceforth, rather than incorporated bunching system, the circulated instrument is utilized for a couple of explicit reasons like hub disappointment/focal hub reinforcement drawback, data total, and so on. As there is no focal hub, the system must act naturally sorted out. Also, it limits the detected excess data sending because of self-sorted out system. In distributed bunching system, group heads are not fixed; however, the determination depends on some reassigned parameters. Drain and Hybrid Energy-Efficient Distributed (HEED) are the two most prominent circulated bunching calculations for remote sensor systems. Bunches are framed utilizing distinctive group arrangement calculations. In a developed PSO, masses are based absolutely on stochastic advancement technique animated through social conduct of feathered creature running or fish tutoring. In PSO, the usefulness arrangements, known as particles, fly through the problem area by means of following the contemporary awesome molecule. Every molecule proceeds with melody of its directions in the issue territory, which may be related with the quality answer (wellness); it has performed up to now (the wellness cost is likewise put away). This cost is alluded to as pbest. For some other "best" costs, this is followed; the guide of the molecule swarm streamlining agent is the charming expense and got to this point through any molecule inside the neighbors of the molecule. This region is alluded to as lbest. At the point when a molecule accepts all the populace as its topological neighbors, the tasteful expense is a worldwide incredible and is called gbest. There are just a couple of parameters with slight variety functions admirably while working with PSO for some applications. In have effectively done a decent arrangement of work in this field and present Linear/Nonlinear Programming (LP/NLP). Two calculations proposed are dependent on PSO: the directing calculation and the bunch development calculation. Multi-objective wellness capacity and molecule encoding plan utilized in the steering calculation while burden adjusting utilized in grouping calculation for preservation of vitality. The proposed calculation contrasted and existing calculation as far as vitality utilization, organize lifetime, number of live hubs, and throughput. In a given review of different bunching calculations like heuristic plans that connected grouping, most astounding availability groupings are MAXMIN D bunching and weighted plans weighted bunching; various leveled plans are LEACH, TLLEACH, EECS, and HEED lattice plans—PEGASIS, so as to decrease the vitality utilization and thought about their quality and constraints. In a given study, some, oftentimes, utilized dispersed bunching calculations like LEACH, HEED, EEHC, LCA, CLUBS, FLOC, ACE, and DWEHC, expressing their favorable circumstances and drawbacks and made a relative examination of the different introduced calculations in the condition of research. Filter is additionally improved in and proposed a convention to lessen the vitality utilization in each round. Results demonstrate noteworthy vitality protection contrasted with LEACH. It has been demonstrated that a sensor hub may not reacts to the promotions gotten by the nearest CH yet join a most distant CH for better vitality proficiency and longer lifetime [4].

The LEACH calculation straightforwardly or by implication affected the past research on effective grouping calculations for remote sensor systems. Drain was a profoundly powerful model during the 1990s yet neglected to satisfy its notoriety in true situations. This started the improvement of many LEACH subordinates, for example, Advanced LEACH (Ad-LEACH), LEACH-C, TL-LEACH, and HEED chain of command. Later on, the center was moved to different as well as ever advancement calculations, for example, Genetic Algorithm and PSO. Adopting a comparable strategy, we began our exploration by examining the effectively archived procedures for sensor system bunching. The main method that we examined was Ad-LEACH. Advertisement LEACH is a method, which developed the old style LEACH convention by considering two unmistakable sorts of sensor hubs in the system, common hubs, and propelled hubs where the propelled hubs are at a default vitality level higher than that of standard hubs. The model, along these lines, considered the factor that few hubs might be at various vitality levels at first a point, which the old style LEACH overlooks. Despite the fact that the outcomes were superior to anything what we got from the old style LEACH calculation, it was, all the while, missing the mark in numerous regions. Following this, we forayed into the domain of streamlining calculations where we examined the working of the PSO method. The PSO procedure is a flexible advancement calculation having establishes in the manner gatherings of creatures in nature scan for nourishment. PSO has been utilized to take care of an assortment of issue, in particular those in Digital Image Processing. The adaptable idea of the PSO system settled on it an appealing decision. Its capacity to deal with crossover information models in two-dimensional and three-dimensional space joined with paired, discrete, and combinatorial informational collections roused trust in this strategy [5].

The issue of productive grouping in WSNs is certifiably not another one. It has spread over long stretches of research and has included old style just as heuristic and meta-heuristic approaches. In a two-level WSN; sensor hubs are gathered to shape bunches, henceforth a few number of groups in a system. Each bunch has its very own CH. Sensor hubs send the collected information to the leader of the group. CH sends the information

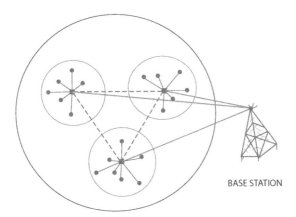

Figure 8.3 Schematic diagram of clustering mechanism [12].

to the BS straightforwardly or through different CHs or in a solitary bounces relying upon the scope of the sensors. The issue here emerges that sensors are battery worked and, in this manner, power compelled. To keep a system ready for action for the greatest conceivable time, it is imperative to broaden the lifetime of its hubs. As separation is the significant wellspring of vitality scattering, by lessening the separation we can guarantee increasingly proficient transmission. However, because of the time basic nature of WSN activity, we can't, in any way, shape or form such a large number of jumps to arrive at the BS. Subsequently, we have to limit the quantity of jumps to the BS to improve proficiency. Consequently, while structuring steering calculations, we have to fuse an exchange off between transmission separation and number of advances as they present two clashing targets.

The instruments depicted in these calculations moderately increment the usage of the efficiency in parcel transmission and extend scope of the sensor systems. This proposed work actualizes the PSO in grouping and for ideal determination of bunch head to upgrade the improvement in the leftover vitality of hub by sending an information bundle to the bunch head which is found very closest to the BT [6].

PSO is an advancement system wherein normal species social practices are considered with the end goal of calculation. It is a swarm knowledge procedure which depends on populace that performs improvement process with the goal of advancing a wellness work. This methodology utilizes a swarm with the end goal of inquiry on each molecule and records the wellness estimation of every molecule. At that point, the particles are connected with their coordinating speed. It will assist the molecule with making a transition to an appropriate area by considering the advanced wellness capacity's expense. From every one of the particles of insight neighborhood, better place upgrades the worldwide best position to recognize the group head position so as to limit the general vitality utilization. PSO calculation has more productivity and results when contrasted and other numerical and informed technique [7].

8.3 Mechanism and Rationale of the Work

To upgrade the system lifetime properly, many steering conventions and bunch-based calculations are utilized to satisfy the application prerequisites in WSN. From existing exploration techniques, upgrading vitality dispersal for correspondence turns out to be exceptionally basic. For expanding lifetime of the WSN, some portion of a vitality utilization of every sensor hub has a significant job while imparting among other sensor hubs.

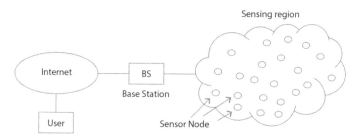

Figure 8.4 Architecture of WSN [20].

This examination work centers around vitality preservation in every sensor hub by utilizing PSO-based grouping and bunch head choice vitality streamlining calculation. The group head is chosen utilizing PSO, in view of the good ways from the bunch part hub to sink hub (BT) and the leftover vitality in that hub [8].

8.3.1   Related Work

WSNs have large research difficulties and system aspect when conveying the sensor hubs to screen the physical world. Various leveled steering conventions are proper for sorting out the hubs to build the adaptability of the WSNs. The conventional bunching calculation LEACH uses randomized pivot with uniform grouping of nearby bunch heads to build the versatility and system execution. The lifetime of the system has stretched out by using a HEED bunching convention; this shaped the grouping and bunch head determination that are dependent on the lingering vitality of sensor hubs and the expense of correspondence from source to goal. This paper proposed Energy-Efficient Hierarchical Clustering (EEHC) that expands the lifetime of the sensor arrangement. Be that as it may, progressive grouping made over-burden in bunch heads and diminishes its capacity sooner than different hubs. This paper proposed a conveyance plan of group heads to lessen vitality dispersal by staying away from superfluous repetition and contrasted existing LEACH; it draws out system lifetime. This paper proposed vitality effective versatile multipath steering system to diminish directing overhead and proficiently uses the vitality accessibility. It chooses the last head among the aggressive competitors that are dependent on their outstanding vitality and rivalry radio range length. This calculation structures bunches in little size close to the finite sink hub that causes the head hub to be nearer to the BS and expends lower vitality during information assembling among the groups. For executing singular sensor hubs in WSN, the better advancement scopes which essential sensible memory space and assets to create better outcomes. One of the prominent enhancement methods is called PSO that has the benefit of arrangements with better quality, higher proficiency in calculation, simple usage, and rapid of combination. PSO bunching in took care of NP hard improvement issue effectively by utilizing grouping that is dependent on a group which lies in a close by neighborhood and picking the sensor hub closer to BS moves toward becoming header for that specific group. PSO-C calculation considers accessible vitality and separation between the hubs concerning their bunch heads. The creators have demonstrated that PSO outflanks both LEACH and LEACH-C as far as the system length and the general throughput. The creator proposed diagram hypothesis for directing and PSO for multihop sensor organize. For each ith round, the bunch head is chosen with the assistance of a weighted capacity indicated as (i), which will be figured in an iterative way. In light of the separation taken by the information bundle to arrive at a goal hub from the source hub and remaining vitality, directing of parcels is advanced with the wellness work. The recreation results are assessed with the focused grouping approach of choosing bunch heads and appeared as positive outcomes. With the objective of boosting the system inclusion in versatile sensor arranges, the creator in connected PSO to streamline the sensor sending technique. It is executed in a brought together way which builds the weight of the BS. To diminish the intra group separation, the creators of the paper proposed PSO-based bunch head choice way to deal with recognizing the best territory for head hubs with an expectation to confine the focal point of group thickness. Reenactment results are coordinated with the current LEACHC and PSO-C, and an enhancement in system lifetime and sparing vitality is appeared. The recluster development made system overhead and extra control utilization for conveying bunching data from BS to the sensor hubs. In this paper, an improved bunching calculation utilizing PSO strategy is proposed for vitality protection [9].

8.4 Network Energy Model

The advance work reproduces the WSN comprising of "n" number of sensor hubs conveyed for temperature calculating applications. A few presumptions are considered seeing the sending of hubs as given in the accompanying:

a) All selected hubs are considered as static after arrangement.
b) Two sorts of hubs are as per the following: one is sensor hub for detecting temperature observing condition and another kind of hub is sink or BS fixed in the focal point of the sensor arrange.
c) Sensor hubs are allocated with a particular distinguishing proof (ID) and comparative primer vitality.
d) Vertex (node) is permitted to utilize propagation control by various levels which are linked to the remoteness to the objective hub.
e) The BT every so often sends a solicitation message as far as the bundle to the group head for getting examining information from sensors [10].
f) Connections are similar.

8.4.1 Network Model

The hubs can utilize power control to change transmission control that is subject to the separation to the recipient.

- The sensor hubs are stationary.
- For every hub, a one of a kind character is allotted.
- The hubs know about self-position (by means of GPS).
- The hubs are homogeneous system; it implies that have indistinguishable handling power.
- The hubs have restricted vitality and after scatter there is no battery charging capacities.
- Each hub has an underlying worth which is Emax and BS has no limitations on vitality, memory what's more, correspondence.
- Links are symmetric that is two hubs v1 and v2 can utilize a similar transmission capacity to interface [11].

8.5 PSO Grouping Issue

Two primary issue of bunching utilizing PSO technique is the union to neighborhood ideal and moderate combination speed, which is attempted to be illuminated by utilizing two thoughts of mayhem hypothesis and increasing speed procedure [12].

8.6   Proposed Method

Our proposed algorithm is composed of two clustering and data transmission phases.

8.6.1   Grouping Phase

In bunching stage, the particles are produced arbitrarily. At that point, the best focuses are chosen as the group heads and different hubs which are situated close to each bunch head turns into the individual from the bunch, and afterward, wellness capacity is determined for each group head. In the event that the wellness capacity is superior to anything worldwide best, it is substituted. This procedure is accomplished for age of 1,000. At that point, every hub readies a control message that contains personality and estimation of its lingering vitality and sends it legitimately to the BS. The BS which gets the data performs grouping activity [12, 13].

8.6.2   Proposed Validation Record

As recently referenced, the grouping is increasingly attractive in which intra-bunch thickness is higher, and in another word, the groups are progressively strong and between bunch thickness is lower [14]. In view of this guideline, the proposed strategy is to gauge the ideal number of bunches. The principal select the quantity of bunches. Additionally, to gauge pace of bunches division, the diverse separation between groups than absolute focal point of informational index for the quantity of groups is considered and after that determined the proportion between two, since the grouping is progressively attractive. The groups are increasingly smaller and more distant separated. So, for the quantity of groups where the list is most extreme, the bunching is increasingly alluring and the ideal number of groups is accomplished. Approval list is composed of two parts, F1 and F2:
Validity = max (F1 + F2)
Entomb: between bunch separation for which more remote is better.
Intra: intra-group separation for which closer is better.

8.6.3   Data Transmission Stage

After bunch arrangement and group heads race of each group, information can be transmitted by the typical hubs to comparing group heads. In this stage, every ordinary hub is associated with the closest bunch head. Group heads are doled out with the usage of a TDMA timetable to each bunch part. Every hub in the apportioned interim sends its information to group head as information message [15, 16].

8.7   Bunch Hub Refreshing Calculation Dependent on an Improved PSO

Lately, numerous advancement calculations have been generally utilized in the WSN. The molecule swarm enhancement (PSO) calculation is a populace-based stochastic improvement method created by Dr. Eberhart and Dr. Kennedy in 1995, roused by social practices of feathered creature rushing of fish tutoring. The framework is instated with a populace of irregular arrangements and scans going for optima by refreshing ages. PSO has no development administrators, for example, hybrid and change. In PSO, the potential arrangements, called particles, fly through the issue space by following the present ideal particles [17].

Attributable to its basic idea and high proficiency, PSO has turned into a generally received improvement system and has been effectively connected to some true issues, especially multimodal issues [18]. Subsequently, it is a successful calculation to take care of the bunching issues of vitality proficiency and negligible transmission separations for the grouping arrangement stage. In our past work, we use PSO calculation to take care of programming characterized organize issues effectively. In any case, PSO performs inadequately as far as nearby search with untimely combination, particularly for complex multi-crest search issues. So, as to manage this particular situation, we improved the customary PSO calculation by changing the inertial load to dodge particles being caught in neighborhood optima and utilized the improved PSO calculation to amplify the wellness elements of [5] and [8]. As a result, increasingly appropriate group heads and transfer hubs are chosen, which makes the convention more vitality effective. This area depicts how the improved PSO calculation is intended to ideally group the WSN in the bunching arrangement stage. The methodology comprises of the accompanying five primary advances:

1) Instate the enhancement issue and calculation parameters. Create a specific number of particles. The size of the molecule is characterized as M, every molecule I has a speed vector vi = [vi1; vi2; : ; vid], and a position vector xi = [xi1; xi2; : ; xid] is utilized to demonstrate its present state, where I is a positive number ordering the molecule in the swarm and d alludes to the elements of the issue.

2) Compute the wellness esteems. The particles search in a d-dimensional hyperspace, ascertaining the wellness estimations of every molecule dependent on (5) and (8). During the hunt procedure, every molecule monitors the individual best (pbest) arrangement Pi D [pi1; pi2; : ; pid] without anyone else and the worldwide best (gbest) arrangement Pg D [pg1; pg2; : ; pgd] accomplished by any molecule in the swarm. At that point, the neighborhood best position and the worldwide position will be found.

3) Update speed and position vectors. Each progression impacts the speed of every molecule toward its pbest and gbest positions.

4) Change the inertial weight. To dodge the calculation falling into a neighborhood ideal, we utilize an improved molecule swarm enhancement calculation, which alters the inertial load as appeared in (13) in order to maintain a strategic distance from particles being caught in nearby optima.

5) Go to stage 3 until the end rule is met. The present best arrangement is chosen after the end basis is met. This is the answer for the enhancement issue defined [18].

8.8 Other SI Models

While ACO and PSO are two of the most widely recognized instances of improvement methods enlivened by swarm insight, there are a few other enhancement procedures dependent on SI standards that have been proposed in the writing, including Artificial Bee Colony, Bacterial Foraging Cat Swarm Optimization, Artificial Immune System, and Glowworm Swarm Optimization, among numerous others. All these SI models naturally share the foremost motivational beginning of the knowledge of various swarms in nature, for example, swarms of *E. coli* microscopic organisms as in Bacterial Foraging, swarms of cells and particles as in Artificial Immune System, and the astonishing swarms of bumble bees as in the Artificial Bee Colony System [19].

Considerably more astoundingly, the sensory system of much fledgling spotter honey bees has been inside adjusted to evaluate the gainfulness of nourishment sources that are dependent on various elements:

(i) The sugar substance of their nectar;

(ii) Their good ways from the province; and

(iii) The simplicity with which nectar (or dust) can be gathered. After enrollment specialist, honey bees survey these variables; they settle on two things: right off the bat, if the nourishment source worth rummaging for (independent from anyone else), and besides in the event that it worth enlisting progressively bumble bees [19].

The scrounging conduct of a bumble bee settlement can be condensed as pursues: When a forager honey bee finds a nourishment source, it first comes back to the hive and gives up its nectar to working drones to store it in the hive. By then, the forager honey bee has three alternatives/choices to take.

(I) It can turn into an enrollment specialist honey bee and plays out a waggle move to select more honey bees (the move devotees) to go along with it in scavenging for the nourishment source, on the off chance that it is advantageous.

(ii) It can stay as a forager honey bee by simply returning to the nourishment source and keep scavenging there, independent from anyone else, on the off chance that it is not generally worth promoting for.

(iii) It can turn into an uncertain supporter by deserting the nourishment source when it is totally depleted—for this situation, the uncertain adherent honey bee begins to look for any waggle moves being performed by other selection representative honey bees and conceivably become a move devotee honey bee.

8.9   An Automatic Clustering Algorithm Based on PSO

Huge research has gone in the previous couple of years to develop the groups in complex datasets through transformative processing strategies. In any case, some work has been taken up to decide the ideal number of groups simultaneously. A large portion of the current grouping systems, in light of developmental calculations, acknowledge the quantity of classes K as a contribution as opposed to deciding the equivalent on the run. By the by, in numerous commonsense circumstances, the suitable number of gatherings in another dataset might be obscure or difficult to decide even around. For instance, while bunching

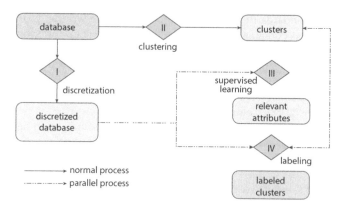

Figure 8.5 Process of automatic clustering [23].

a lot of reports emerging from the question to a web index, the quantity of classes K changes for each arrangement of archives that outcome from cooperation with the internet searcher [20].

8.10   Steering Rule Based on Informed Algorithm

Low-energy adaptive clustering hierarchy is a great steering calculation and it right off the bat acquainted bunching with accomplish vitality effective. In LEACH, CHs are irregularly chosen and the hub picked the nearest CH as its goal by single expectation correspondence. Filter is significantly more vitality proficient than some level steering conventions, for example, flooding, netting, SPIN, and DD since it stays away from the immediate correspondence among sensors. Nonetheless, the technique for arbitrary CHs choice realizes the uneven appropriation of CHs and it is not reasonable for huge scale WSNs [20].

Fluffy logic–based hexagonal geographical adaptive fidelity is a steering strategy which uses the fluffy rationale framework and topography data to accomplish the objective of vitality effective and vitality balance. The fundamental commitments of the work can be abridged as pursues. It partitions the entire sensor field into a few ordinary hexagons as per correspondence go and subjective hubs in nearby hexagons could intercommunicate. Along these lines, every hexagon could just keep up one dynamic hub and keep different hubs dozing to reduce information repetition and monitor vitality. Fluffy rationale framework is used to adjust the vitality utilization in every hexagon field. Investigation results show that the introduced strategy outflanks some conventional calculations [21].

In straight-line directing utilization, arbitrary walk is proposed. The fundamental thought of this convention is that the occasion and question ways are straight and they are probably going to enthusiasm for a plane. In this convention, an up-and-comer zone is guaranteed by within and outside groups which are dictated by the neighbor separation. The hub with the most remote neighbor separation and greatest leftover vitality in the up-and-comer zone is select as the following jump. Reproduction results exhibit that it beats some great irregular walk directing conventions [21].

Portable sink could further adjust the system's vitality utilization. An information gathering outline called Energy-Aware Path Construction (EAPC) is proposed, utilizing portable sink for vitality effective. The mapping is made out of three sections to ascertain a moving way for the portable sink. During the underlying stage, a negligible spreading over tree is built to associate all the sensor hubs. At that point, a lot of gathering focuses (CPs) are chosen agreeing for the advantage file during the CP determination stage and the common tree is deteriorated into numerous subtrees. At long last, an arched polygon is developed that is dependent on the CPs. The versatile sink moves along the arched polygon to get to each CP and assembles the information in each round. Reenactment result demonstrates that the displayed pattern possesses an improved exhibition in parts of lifetime [22].

A progressive directing calculation which is dependent on group chain is proposed in the calculation contains three stages to build the topology of the system. During the grouping and chain arrangement stage, every hub computes its bunch head choice worth (CHSV) as per the remaining vitality, neighbor separation, and the measure of information age. The hub with maximal CHSV will be chosen as the group head. At that point, the voracious calculation is acquainted with structure chains for intracluster correspondence. At last, a portable operator (MA) is utilized to gather information from CHs along a powerful way which is dictated by sign quality, lingering vitality level and way misfortune. Reproduction results depict that they proposed calculation beats some comparable work [22].

A unique course modification strategy is proposed in the calculation that isolates the hubs into a few gatherings as per the area data and picked the hub with most lingering vitality as the CH among each gathering. An insatiable calculation is utilized for CHs to produce a chain to transmit information to the portable sink and the CH which is closest to the versatile sink is the chain head [23].

8.11   Routing Protocols Based on Meta-Heuristic Algorithm

Subterranean ACO which is propelled by ants searching has been embraced by a few written works for directing way choice. The creators proposed a calculation joined the fluffy sensible framework with ACO. The fluffy consistent framework is utilized for the CHs choice as indicated by the info highlights, for example, separation to BS, leftover vitality, and hub degree. The ACO is utilized for ideal steering way disclosure for every hub by utilizing the likelihood work. The creators utilize the sorted two fluffy sensible frameworks joined with ACO to further improve the system's exhibition, and the Sugeno fluffy supplement administrator is utilized to refresh the pheromone focus. The creator characterizes the CHs steering issue in WSN as the voyaging sales representative issue (TSP) and ACO is used to look for an ideal direction with most limited separation [23].

Particle swarm advancement is another meta-heuristic calculation broadly connected among numerous enhancement issues. Kuila *et al.* proposed a vitality effective directing pattern. The work commitment is to set up the mapping connection among particles and sensors. The system is built by two distinct kinds of sensors, conventional hubs, and entryways, and every molecule speaks to the entire answer for the steering way. The component of the molecule is the quantity of entryways and each measurement speaks to the list of the applicant transfer hub. The wellness work for the most part contains two sections, Maxdis and Maxhop, and a definitive objective is to limit the wellness work. The creators proposed vitality effective and vitality adjusted calculation that is dependent on Kuila *et al.* What's more, they give more consideration to the vitality balance. In a novel bunching strategy is made by utilizing district parcel line spoken to by a tuple L = (x, y, θx, θy). PSO calculation is utilized to change the locale parcel line so as to accomplish better organize execution. In a calculation called VD-PSO is exhibited by Wei Wang *et al.* In VD-PSO, the component of every molecule is twofold the quantity of meeting focuses and it stores the arrangement of CHs. Because of the vulnerability of the quantity of the meeting focuses, the component of particles is unique; along these lines, the writers proposed an uncommon method to refresh the speed and area of the particles. In the creator proposed an inclusion gap fixing plan utilizing PSO to look through inclusion openings and fix it with a portable operator [24].

8.12 Routing Protocols for Avoiding Energy Holes

Vitality gaps in WSNs are, for the most part, brought about by the lopsided vitality utilization of hubs, and they may incredibly abbreviate the lifetime of the system on the off chance that they are not very much tended to. Numerous works intend to take care of the issue of vitality openings. In the creators propose a technique to protect hubs close to vitality gaps by maintaining a strategic distance from the topology transformation overhead. In the creators receive an exceptional strategy to separate the entire system into numerous concentric round tracks and areas which diminishing the vitality utilization by means of sifting repetitive information. In, the creators present arbitrary walk (RW) into system vitality adjusting. Then, the normal correspondence separation among hubs and the normal correspondence separation among RWs and sink are enhanced to diminish the vitality utilization. In sink versatility innovation is received to address the vitality openings issue [24, 25].

8.13 System Model

8.13.1 Network Model

Different cells' area is applied as the system structure of our introduced composition, and a maximum of sensors is conveyed utilizing an irregular way. We, at first, set the sink at the focal point of the sensor field. In each round, every hub needs to transmit its sensor information to the sink by single- or multi-jump transmission. A sensor can pick a CH inside its correspondence go else; it will transmit the information to a hand-off hub for sending [26]. CHs are normally hubs with high vitality and circulate equitably by the PSO calculation referenced in Section 8.4, and they assume the liability for information combining and transmit the intertwined information to the sink. To encourage the trials, we make the accompanying suppositions:

- The sink has the geology data of all the sensors, and in each round, every sensor will report its remaining vitality to soak in transmitted information.
- We accept that the system is in a great transmission condition and we do not think about the crash during the transmission. The radio channel is symmetric.
- The timekeepers of sensors are synchronized, utilizing a GPS module or a period synchronization strategy, for example, Flooding Time Synchronization Protocol (FTSP) or Glossy [27].

8.13.2   Power Model

We embrace a similar energy model to compute the vitality utilization. When the sign is created by the transmitter, the enhancer will fortify it, utilizing distinctive power as per the transmission separation. In this manner, we receive two unique models for transmission [28].

References

1. Balakrishnan, B. and Balachandran, S., FLECH: fuzzy logic based energy efficient clustering hierarchy for nonuniform wireless sensor networks. *Wireless Communications and Mobile Computing*, 1–13, 2017.
2. D. Karaboga, An idea based on honey bee swarm for numerical optimization, Technical Report TR06, Erciyes University, Engineering Faculty, Computer Engineering Department, 2005.
3. Darougaran, L., Shahinzadeh, H., Ghotb, H. and Ramezanpour, L. Simulated annealing algorithm for data aggregation trees in wireless sensor networks and comparison with genetic algorithm. *International journal of electronics and electrical engineering*, 62, 59–62, 2012.
4. Dhasian, H. R. and Balasubramanian, P. Survey of data aggregation techniques using soft computing in wireless sensor networks. *IET Information Security*, 7(4), 336–342, 2013.
5. E. Yang, T. Ahmet, T. Arslan and N. Barton, An Improved Particle Swarm Optimization Algorithm for Power-Efficient Wireless Sensor Networks, IEEE 0-7695-2919-4/07, 2007.
6. H.Ö. Tan and İ. Körpeoğlu, Power efficient data gathering and aggregation in wireless sensor networks, *ACM SIGMOD Record*, vol. 32, no. 4, pp. 66–71, Dec. 2003.
7. HevinRajesh, D. and Paramasivan, B. Fuzzy based secure data aggregation technique in wireless sensor networks. *Journal of Computer Science*, 8(6), 899–907, 2012.
8. Islam, O., Hussain, S. and Zhang, H. Genetic algorithm for data aggregation trees in wireless sensor networks. In *3rd international conference on Intelligent Environment, IEEE*, 312–316, 2007.
9. J. Kennedy, R. Eberhart, Particle Swarm Optimization, *IEEE International Conference on Neural Networks*, 1995.

10. J. Shanbehzadeh, S. Mehrjoo, A. Sarrafzadeh, An intelligent energy efficient clustering in wireless sensor networks, Lecture Notes in Engineering and Computer Science: *Proc. of The International MultiConference of Engineers and Computer Scientists* 2011, IMECS 2011, 16–18 March, 2011, Hong Kong, pp. 614–618.

11. K. Ferentinos, T. Tsiligiridis, and K. Arvanitis, Energy optimization of wirless sensor networks for environmental measurements, In Proc. of the International Conference on Computational Intelligence for Measurment Systems and Applicatons, 2005.

12. Kim, J. Y., Sharma, T., Kumar, B., Tomar, G. S., Berry, K. and Lee, W. H. Intercluster ant colony optimization algorithm for wireless sensor network in dense environment. *International Journal of distributed sensor networks*, 10(4), 1–10, 2014.

13. Kulkarni, R. V. and Venayagamoorthy, G. K. Particle swarm optimization in wireless-sensor networks: A brief survey. IEEE Transactions on Systems, Man, and Cybernetics, Part C (Applications and Reviews), 41(2), 262–267, 2011.

14. Kumar, H. and Singh, P. K. Analyzing Data Aggregation in Wireless Sensor Networks, 4th International Conference on Computing for Sustainable Global Development INDIACom, IEEE :4024–4029, 2017.

15. Kumar, H. and Singh, P. K. Node Energy Based Approach to Improve Network Lifetime and Throughput in Wireless Sensor Networks. *Journal of Telecommunication, Electronic and Computer Engineering (JTEC)*, 9(3–6), 79–88, 2017.

16. Lu, Y., Comsa, I. S., Kuonen, P. and Hirsbrunner, B. Probabilistic Data Aggregation Protocol Based on ACO-GA Hybrid Approach in Wireless Sensor Networks. In IFIP Wireless and Mobile Networking Conference (WMNC), 235–238, October 2015.

17. Lu, Y., Comsa, I. S., Kuonen, P. and Hirsbrunner, B Probabilistic Data Aggregation Protocol Based on ACO-GA Hybrid Approach in Wireless Sensor Networks. In *IFIP Wireless and Mobile Networking Conference* (WMNC), 235–238, October 2015.

18. Misra, R. and Mandal, C. Ant-aggregation: ant colony algorithm for optimal data aggregation in wireless sensor networks. In *IFIP International Conference on Wireless and Optical Communications Networks*, 1–5, April 2006.

19. Mohsenifard, E. and Ghaffari, A. Data aggregation tree structure in wireless sensor networks using cuckoo optimization algorithm. *Journal of Information System and Telecommunication* (JIST), 4 (3), 182–190, 2016.

20. Nayak, P. and Vathasavai, B. Energy Efficient Clustering Algorithm for Multi-Hop Wireless Sensor Network Using Type-2 Fuzzy Logic. *IEEE Sensors Journal*, 17(14), 4492–4499, 2017.

21. Neamatollahi, P., Naghibzadeh, M. and Abrishami, S. Fuzzy-Based Clustering-Task Scheduling for Lifetime Enhancement in Wireless Sensor Networks. *IEEE Sensors Journal*, 17(20), 6837–6844, 2017.

22. Ni, Q., Pan, Q., Du, H., Cao, C. and Zhai, Y. A novel cluster head selection algorithm based on fuzzy clustering and particle swarm optimization. *IEEE/ACM transactions on computational biology and bioinformatics*, 14(1), 76–84, 2017.

23. Norouzi, A., Babamir, F. S. and Orman, Z. A tree based data aggregation scheme for wireless sensor networks using GA. *Wireless Sensor Network*, 4(08), 191–196, 2012.

24. RejinaParvin, J. and Vasanthanayaki, C. Particle swarm optimization-based clustering by preventing residual nodes in wireless sensor networks. *IEEE Sensors Journal*, 15(8), 4264–4274, 2015.

25. S. Jin, M. Zhou and A. Wu, Sensor network optimization using a genetic algorithm, In *Proc. of the 7th World Multiconference on Systemics, Cybernetics and Informatics*, 2003.

26. S. Lindsey and C.S. Raghavendra, Pegasis: Power-efficient gathering in sensor information systems, in *Proc. IEEE Conf.* Aerosp, Big Sky, MT, Mar, vol. 3, pp. 1125–1130, 2002.

27. Singh, S. P. and Sharma, S. C. A Particle Swarm Optimization Approach for Energy Efficient Clustering in Wireless Sensor Networks. *International Journal of Intelligent Systems and Applications*, 9(6), 66–74, 2017.
28. Sudarmani, R. and Kumar, K. S. Particle swarm optimization-based routing protocol for clustered heterogeneous sensor networks with mobile sink. *American Journal of Applied Sciences*, 10(3), 259–269, 2013.

9

Swam Intelligence–Based Resources Optimization and Analyses and Managing Data in IoT With Data Mining Technologies

Pooja Dixit[1]*, Palvadi Srinivas Kumar[2] and N. Gayathri[3]

[1]Sophia Girls College Ajmer, Ajmer, Rajasthan, India
[2]Department of Computer Science Engineering, University of Madras, Chennai, Tamilnadu, India
[3]School of Computing Science and Engineering, Galgotias University, Greater Noida, Uttar Pradesh, India

Abstract

This chapter presents three interesting and growing domains: Swarm Intelligence, Internet of Things (IoT), and Data Mining. IoT is a device which generates massive amount of valuable and accurate data, but it is difficult to handle or extract the required information. For this purpose, Data Mining plays a vital role that allows extracting data or knowledge from the connected things, whereas SI is a new subfield of AI which is based on collective groups of intelligent agents. It is based on social behavior which can be observed by the nature and basic behavior of the birds like ant colonies and flocks of birds. The main focus of this chapter presents some biological motivation and some basic concepts of SI using two models: ACO and PSO. These are probabilistic technique which help to solving computational problems and find out the optimistic solution.

Keywords: Swarm Intelligence, Ant Colony Optimization, PSO model, IOT, data mining, clustering, KDD

9.1 Introduction

9.1.1 Swarm Intelligence

A swarm is an enormous set of identical, primary fundamental specialists connecting to each other locally and with the similar conditions that does not contain any focal control which are intriguing enable to globally behavior to arise. Swarm technique computation is inspired by nature, native-based computation which is furnished to communicate least attempts and is also capable for giving optimistic solution for any critical problems. SI technique can be categorized as an integral part of the AI which is applied to exhibit the

---

Corresponding author: poojadixit565@gmail.com

Abhishek Kumar, Pramod Singh Rathore, Vicente Garrcia Diaz and Rashmi Agrawal (eds.) Swarm Intelligence Optimization: Algorithms and Applications, (143–164) © 2021 Scrivener Publishing LLC. ISBN 978-1-119-77874-5

composite deportment or properties of communal swarm disposition. Ant colonies, honey bees, and bird flocks are the main example of the swarm techniques. Regardless of the type of agent like insects, swarm individuals, and people, they all are lonely moderately unrefined with regulated capabilities. They all cooperate simultaneously with specific standards to complete the principal pledge for the survival.

The social community interaction can be direct and indirect among swarm individuals. Direct interaction can be phenomenal or sound contact, such as swing orchestics of honey bees and indirect interaction arises when one specifically changes the atmosphere and another individual one reacts to the new environment. It is just like a pheromone trails of ants that they are store for search the food source in their way.

This type of indirect interaction is also designated as stigmergy that signify the transmission through the natural world or environmental nature. The focal purpose of this part is to discuss the most popular SI model that is basically inspired by ants' stigmergic behavior and birds flocking behavior.

Due to this incredible behavioral of the social insects, biological and normal researchers have been recitation of the basic behavioral of communal moth. In the late 80s, the scientists of computer science introduced the insights, which are based on the research of the naturalistic swarm method in the region of AI. In 1989, G. Beni and J. Wang were first to demonstrate the SI. It is a set of algorithm that is based on global optimization framework that control robotic swarm.

After 1991, M. Dorigo and partners were proposed the "ACO" technique that proposed the basic novel nature which was based on metaheuristic solutions of difficult combinational problems. In 1995, J. Kennedy et al. presented "practical swarm optimization" and initially mentioned for imitation of the bird flocking social behavior. In the end of 90s, these two most plausible SI algorithms start to attempt a unblended scientific intrigue and to penetrate the area of genuine utilization.

It should be noted here, after many years later, in 2005, D. Karabago presented an Artificial Bee Colony Algorithm like a recent family of SI. After the computational demonstration of swarms, which was introduced, there has been a consistent accretion in the amount of research papers disclose the profitable utilization of SI computation in a some enhancement undertakings and research problems. The standards of Swarm Intelligence effectively applied in an classification of different areas including function optimization problems, search best routes, scheduling, structural optimization, and image and data analysis. Swarm computational modeling has been used in broad-range of different field that include machine learning, bioinformatics and medical informatics, dynamic system, and also use in operation search. This technology has also used in business and finance [1].

Swarm Intelligence Models

In the literature review, swarm intelligence model basically is a technique that adopts the nature of swarm behavior like insects, bacteria, and fish [2]. It is a computational model that initiates the distributed optimization problem in a swarm model like CPSs. This process follows the state of-the-art process which describes nature as inspired in Figure 9.1. Generally, a nature-inspired engineer designs this identical systems and adopts similar algorithms that are used to solve complex real-world problems in different domain.

In SI model analysis, closer view is taken with all the actions, and creation of this model is based on the analysis of observations. The simulation then gives an assessment of behavior on how to achieve intended results with given behavior. Generally, this assessment usually

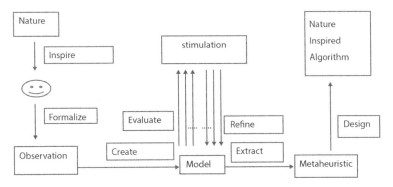

Figure 9.1 Process of designing a swarm intelligence model and the corresponding algorithm.

gives through a fitness value. At last, an algorithm is applied with the summary of the given intended values and designs a bio-inspired swarm intelligence model.

Generally, all SI model is based on individual, simple agents. They can communicate and cooperate directly or indirectly without any central control, but they only depend on their collective behavior that helps to solve the complex problems. So, in brief, there are some following characteristics of the SI model.

- Emergent conduct emerges from basic collaborations among people in a swarm.
- Individuals act as indicated by straightforward and neighborhood conduct.
- Organized conduct develops naturally.
- There is no focal control.

Five fundamental standards set the reason for swarm knowledge models (Chee Peng and Dehuri, 2009):

1. Proximity: capacity to perform basic calculation of reality and react to ecological boosts.
2. Quality: respond to quality (wellness) factors.
3. Diverse response: disseminate undertakings.
4. Stability: keep up the group behavior when there is a condition to emerge an incident of ecological changes.
5. Adaptability: change the group behavior when there is a condition to emerge an incident of ecological changes [3].

9.1.1.1 Swarm Biological Collective Behavior

The best examples of swarm intelligence behavior that we can see are in bird flocks, fish mosquitoes, and midges. Numerous animal creatures like fish instruct and birds flocks clearly show basic anatomical instruct; they deal with the organisms so they amalgamate and they can transform their appearance and direction, and they seem to walk as an individual entity. The fundamental principles of collective behavior are shown in Figure 9.2.

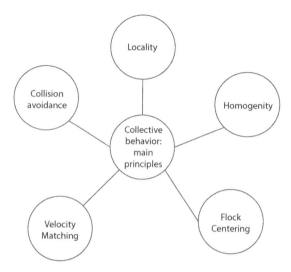

Figure 9.2 The main principle of collective behavior.

- Homogeneity: All birds in the flock do the common behavior. They move in the flocks barring any leader.
- Locality: The speed of each bird depends and influences by its nearby flocks mate. View considers vast signification scenes for society of flock.
- Collision avoidance: These types of collision are avoided with nearest flock mates.
- Velocity Matching: Flocks speed and velocity are measured or match by with nearest flocks mates.
- Flock Centralization: In this type, they try to stay closer to the nearer flock mates.

In flocks model at all times, an individual tries to maintain the minimal distance between themselves and others. The highest priority of this rule is that it frequently observes the animals' common behavior in nature. If any individual does not follow the behavior or not performing maneuver, then they tend with other individuals to follow the behavior and can avoid to be isolated. They adjust themselves according to the neighbors. Couzin *et al.* distinguished four collective dynamical behaviors as described in Figure 9.2.

- Swarm: They are combined by solidarity, yet inferior degree of parallel alignment into their fellow.
- Torus: People interminably pivot around a vacant center (processing). But, the rotation of direction is random.
- Difference between dynamic parallel clusters and individual element is that: in the dynamic parallel collection, the individual in a group is polarized and walks as a sequential collection, but individual in a group can move anywhere without any boundary in the collective set of clusters which density and collective form can fluctuate.

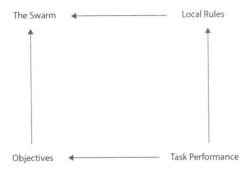

Figure 9.3 Models of collective behavior of Swarm Intelligence.

- Highly parallel group: They are more static as compared to dynamic parallel clusters in which high variety in density and form is minimal.

A swarm is represented as the set of operators which have some objective and work such operations from which they achieve their objective (see Figure 9.3). This aggregative or collection of information seems to increased up based on what are often enormous gatherings of generally straightforward specialists. These operators utilize straightforward principles or rules to work their exercises and by mean of the correspondence of the whole gathering. The swarm achieves its goals [4].

9.1.1.2   Swarm With Artificial Intelligence Model

9.1.1.2.1   Ant Colony Optimization

Swarm Intelligence model is an advanced model for solving the computational problems that's why this model is also referred to as computational model which solves any problem by natural swarm system. According to this literature, several swarm intelligence model have been proposed until date, and that models are widely used in real-world applications. Some examples of SI models are Ant Colony Optimization (ACO), Particle Swarm Optimization, (PSO) Artificial Bee Colony, Bacterial Foraging, Cat Swarm Optimization, Artificial Immune System, and Glowworm Swarm Optimization [5].

The first idea of ACO originates from the observing the behavior of searching food for ants. Ants separately have restricted intellectual capacities, but they are capable to find out the most brief way for searching food collectively and return their home. During their turn, they set down pheromone that makes way for following path by other ants. This means that other ants follow this pheromone and strengthen it, since they additionally set down pheromone. Thus, shorter ways to nourishment have more pheromone and are bound to be pursued. Accordingly, this positive feedback in conclusion allows to ants for follow a single path. ACO technique is a probabilistic technique or algorithm that solve the computational problems in an efficient way and that are based on to find out the best path by using graph that help ants for searching food. Figure 9.4 describes the simple flow scheme of a swarm.

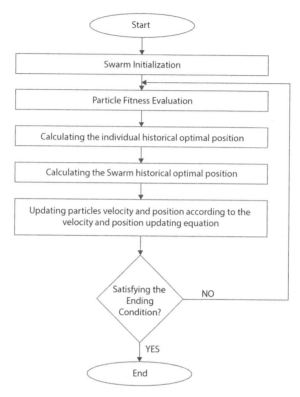

Figure 9.4 The simple flow scheme of a swarm.

- ACO technique is enlivened by the contemplation of the basic conduct of ants. Generally, in ant colony, simple behavior of individual ants is not capable to find the solution of complex problem. For example, construct optimal nest structure, find the food source by using choosing shortest path, construct a chain of ants, or arrangement of drops of ants have been observed. As mentioned figure above, when ants walking for search food source from their nest and follow a path x, they collect some chemical substance that's called pheromone (it is a chemical substance which is produced and released by an animal especially by insect, through which other insect follow this chemical and follows certain path) on the ground. The pheromone deposited that chemical and structures a path Y (State 1 in Figure 9.5). That chemical actually helps for individual ants to discover the nourishment sources that have been already discover by different ants. Pheromones' trails disappear if other ants do not follow the path and not join fortify their power. When ants locate the most brief way route for food, then they come back their nest as quicker than other ants (State 2 in Figure 9.5). Therefore, this chemical helps to other new ants that come out to find the food, and they are guided by this pheromone path and take a short route. So, it has been notice here that all

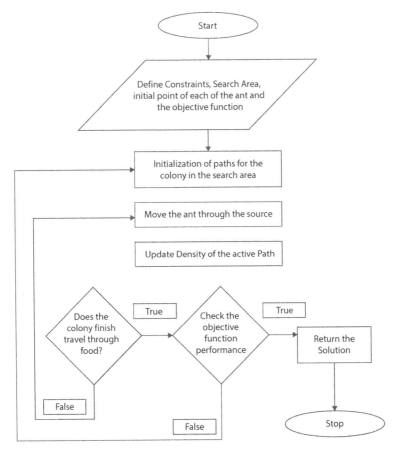

Figure 9.5 Food finding procedure followed by ants.

searching ants choose shortest path route for nourishment source (State 3 in Figure 9.5) [6].

- Explaining ACO Through an Example

Simple way of understanding working mechanism of ACO is by taking an example. We consider the example of traveling salesman problem. Traveling Salesman Problem is the problem in which set of areas (e.g., cities) and the distance are given between them. This issue is based on finding out the shortest path in minimal length that is based on the closer tour in which visitors visit city one time and just once.

For embed TSP on ACO, visitor find the shortest path by using graph defined by set of cities which are associated with vertices groups of graph. In Traveling Salesman Problem, it is conceivable to move one city to another city using shortest path. The graph construction is completely associated with number of vertices of cities. Visitors find the minimal distance of the cities by setting the length of the edges between vertices (nodes).

The length of edges is set between the vertices, which is proportional to the deviation between the urban areas using these vertices, and afterward, we associate pheromone esteems and heuristic value by using the graph edges. Pheromone value can be modified at run-time that shows the accumulated behavior of ACO, whereas heuristic values are issue subordinate qualities which are group in the reverse of the length of edges in case of TSP. The ants construct the chemical solutions as follows. Each ant selects the vertex of random city to start the construction of graph. At that point, it proceeds together with the graph edges in every steps of structure. Each ant is capable to maintain the memory of each steps of path, and after that, in subsequent steps, it does not choose the path steps that has already chosen or visited. Generally, an ant makes a chemical construction once, when it visits every vertices of the graph [7].

At every development stage, an insect probabilistically select the edge to seek after surrounded by them which led the unvisited vertices yet. The probabilistic rule is single sided by pheromone recognition and heuristic data: the excessive the pheromone and the heuristic worth identified with an edge, the higher the probability a subterranean insect will pick that particular edge.

At the point, when all of the ants have completed their visit, the edges of the pheromone are revived/refreshed. The pheromone esteems are at first decreased by a particular rate. Each edge by then gets an additional pheromone comparative with the idea of the responses for which it belongs.

This procedure is repeatedly used until an ended condition is not fulfilled [8].

9.1.1.2.2 PSO Model

In 1995, Russell Eberhart, who was an electrical architect, and James Kennedy, who was a social clinician, presented PSO. PSO is a second victorious Practical Swarm Optimization (PSO). Generally, non-persistent enhancement issues are handle by PSO. For instance, PSO has been successfully applied in dynamic frameworks, examine human tremor, register 3D-to-3D biomedical picture, advance loads, and structure of neural systems, figuring out how to play games and creation of music. As a matter of fact, PSO draws up motivation from the sociological conduct that related with birds flocking.

It is a naturalistic contemplation that birds can fly in large group and in long distance. They are also capable to maintain the limited distance between themselves and their neighbors. This zone shows a few insights concerning flying creatures in nature and graphs their capacities, just as their sociological running conduct.

9.1.1.3   Birds in Nature

The most noteworthy sense for flock association is considered the vision. Generally, bird's eyes are upon the two sides of their heads, through which they are able to see the objects and also capable to protests on each side simultaneously. The larger size of eyes of bird creatures for other creatures and animals is an inspiration that make the bird creature as one of the most incredibly created senses of vision in the group of all creatures. For example, the pigeon can view 300° barring diversion in their head, same as the vision of American Woodcocks is extraordinarily, which can able to view of whole 360°. Generally, all feathered creatures are pulled in by nutrition; they have astonishing limits in hurrying synchronously for nutrition looking and strapping partition for movement. Flying animals are moreover capable for social affiliation; they engage them to have the option to do: (i) they can flying without any chance of crash even while all of a sudden change the direction, (ii) they can respond quickly any type of outer dangers like quickly grouping and scattering rapidly, and (iii) avoiding predators.

Birds Flocking Behavior

Swarm growth and group learning and communicating with agents, for example, feathered creatures, fish, penguins, etc., have long cabal a wide range of researchers from different orders accompanied creature conduct, physics, communal psychology, sociable science, and computer science for a long time. Winged animal rushing can be described like the social cumulous movement conduct of an enormous number of cooperating flying creatures with a typical gathering objective. The neighborhood collaborations among feathered creatures (particles) for the most part rise the common movement heading of the swarm, as appeared in Figure 9.6 [9].

That type of interactions is based on the nearest neighbor law. In this type of algorithm, birds adhere to some fix flocking rules to coordinate their pace that include position and velocity without any pivotal coordination. In 1886, Craig Reynolds was introduced the rule of bird flocking behavior. Three flocking rules were proposed by Reynolds. He implemented the rules in his research investigation which is based on birds' actions or behavior. (i) Flock concentrates in which group individuals endeavor to remain nearby to close by flock mates by flying toward a path that put them closer to the centroid of the close by flock fellow, (ii) collision rectification (in which group individuals maintain a strategic distance from crashes with close by flock fellow dependent upon proportionate position), and (iii) speed coordinating (group individuals endeavor to coordinate speed with close by flock mates) [10].

Explaining PSO Algorithm

Basically, PSO is considered as a complex algorithm for solving the problem, but actually, it is a very simple algorithm technique, which includes a number of iterations, a group of clusters variables that contain their qualities values, adjusting their behavior according to the closer member of the group. Suppose that bird flocks make a circle over an area, where

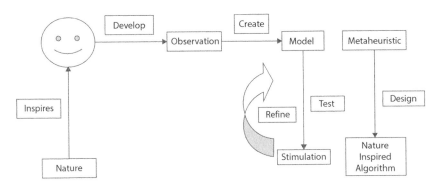

Figure 9.6 Ants stigmergic conduct in finding the smallest route among food and nest.

they can find a hidden food with help of smell. When someone in group is closest to the food, then they chirp loudly and other group member follows them. This fixing example proceeds until one of the group member impinge stumbles over the nourishment. So, this is a simple algorithm that is convenient to implement the basic structure of PSO is described in Figure 9.7. The algorithm keeps track of three worldwide factors:

- Reach destination value or status.
- Global optimum value that pointing which data particles is presently available and near to the pursuit.
- Barrier value indicates that when the algorithm should put on hold if the target is not discover.
- Each particle comprises with:
- Representation of data for giving an optimized solution.
- A velocity esteem demonstrating how much the data can be changed (http://mnemstudio.org/particle-swarm-introduction.htm).

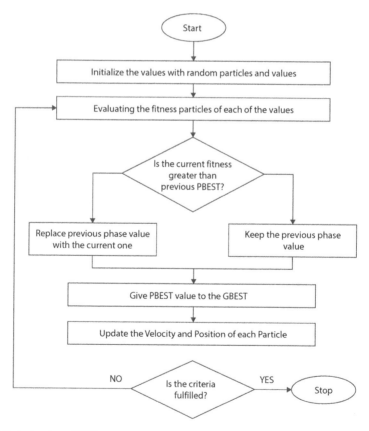

Figure 9.7 Basic structure of PSO.

An individual best (pBest) esteem showing that the nearest the molecule's data has ever gone to the target.

9.1.1.4   Swarm with IoT

Today, Internet of Things (IoT) points the higher points as an example of worldwide according to everything which is present around our surroundings, i.e., traffic light system and water pump distribution. With the capacity of sensing ability, technology and capacity of communicating IoT converts these above things into smart things. Internet plays important role in converting such things into smart things. This type of research includes two type of entities name as physical or digital entities. These entities are like peoples, objects, machines, and these are interconnected through internet. In this way, allowance to create new different things or classes of applications and to understand such applications and handle these services is too difficult because IoT-based framework does not provide flexible nature to solve complex problems. Beside this, Swarm Intelligence provides better understanding among applications and services by providing robust and flexibility in nature neither complicated and dynamic nature. This flexible and robust nature is capable to create effective design of patterns for algorithm for solving complex problems like in IoT-based framework. This change in solving complex problems in applications and services in IoT-based framework to Swarm Intelligence is more effective to create robust and flexible applications [11].

9.2   IoT With Data Mining

The idea of IoT concept rises from the importance to operate, robotize, and find out new appliance, devices, and sensors on the planet. So, in order to build intellectual verdicts for both human beings and for the items in IoT, DM techniques are accompanied by IoT innovations for essential decision-making and framework streamlining the basic roadmap of Data Mining with IoT is shown in Figure 9.8. DM includes discover novels, fascinating, and potentially advantageous practical patterns through data and embedded that information which help to find the hidden information with three types of different view: knowledge view, technique view, and application view. Knowledge view comprises with characterization, cluster grouping, association analysis, timing arrangement investigation, and outlier analysis. Application view combines the average DM application, incorporate online

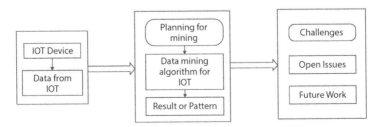

Figure 9.8 Roadmap of Data Mining with IoT.

business, production, human administrations like social insurance, and open help. The knowledge view and application view group together and comprises technique view. These days, Big Data is a hot discussed subject for data mining and IoT [12].

9.2.1 Data from IoT

Clearly, IoT may make information comprising of a lot of helpful data. But, in recent time, technical issues and defiance are significant disquisition topic alongside with various strategies for taking care of this information. It is acceptable to take care of the issue of enormous IoT data that is used to design sensors that are capable of collecting useful and important information. The recent research trend is trying to decrease complexity of input data. For data handling, distributed computing, cloud computing, and selection of features are famous methods.

Besides, how to deal with huge information acquired from IoT gadgets and finding concealed data from the information is significant job. As mentioned, sensors are used for analyzing of data and gadgets are used to building up certain valuable framework for developing a smart city or smart home. Numerous potential implementation are conceivable to be created from the huge information examination process. For satisfying the undertaking of finding concealed data from huge information, knowledge discovery data (KDD) effectively used into various areas. KDD has ability of discovering "anything" or "fascinating example" by using IoT, which uses an assistance of mentioned advances: collect the information, preprocessing, information mining, and assessment or basic leadership [13].

9.2.1.1 Data Mining for IoT

The following area depicts connection in between big data and data mining using IoT and point-by-point investigation and outline of various data mining methods for the IoT.

Basics of Using Data Mining for IoT
It is easier to utilize the data mining techniques for IoT for creating and analyzing data. Today, numerous ways are used to solve finding big data on IoT problem, without utilizing powerful and productive explication tool. Today, big data is enormously utilized. Generally, KDD frameworks and most traditional calculations are difficult to embed legitimately on the large amount of IoT data [14]. Figure 9.9 describe the basics use of Big Data Mining system for IoT.

For building up an elite information module of KDD mining for IoT, the suitable mining technique is to be tackled by KDD procedure: These are objective, features of data, and mining calculation.

Objective: It is critical to determine the relevant data from the massive amount of data and it is also challenging to extract the hidden important data patterns and information from database.

Data: Features of data, for example, delivery, portrayal, size, etc., play a fundamental job in information mining. Different information should be handled in an unexpected way. For instance, Ri and Rj might be comparative or not; however, they should be break down contrastingly if the syntax and semantics of the information is different.

Mining Algorithm: Data mining includes the certain algorithms for finding the most relevant data from the huge amount of data. By these algorithms, most frequently used data and

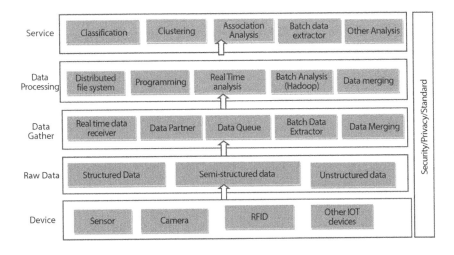

Figure 9.9 Big Data Mining system for IoT.

hidden patterns can be easily extracted. Some Data Mining techniques are: Classification, Clustering, and Association Rule Mining.

Classification: It is utilized to classify or identify the unlabeled patterns or information. Labeled data essentially take into the bit of unlabeled information with few data, class, or label identified with it. For instance, the image of any animal is stated as the piece of unlabeled information except if any data about it, its name, or label like its voice is not clearly referenced. Labeled data are accomplished by building decisions about acquirable segment of unlabeled data [15]. The basic Classification process is shown in Figure 9.10.

Clustering: It is utilized to create the clusters or group of similar type of data patterns or information. Figure 9.11 explains the clustering process. The unlabeled patterns are

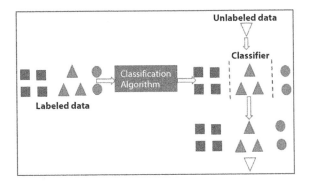

Figure 9.10 Classification process.

the examples of characteristic or human-made facts. Notwithstanding these realities, the unlabeled patterns incorporate with photographs, videos, sound recordings, x-rays, tweets, news stories, etc. There is no particular learning regarding the intermediary of the unlabeled patterns; however, it is just restrain information about data.

Association: It is utilized to find the frequently used information or data patterns. The main section of association rule mining is sequential patterns that actually applied to discover an occasion from the pattern of input that happen in specific order.

There are total 12 numbers of possible combinations that we can apply to extract big data by using IoT that is described in the following Table 9.1.

The main objective of finding hidden patterns can be different which particularly depend on the goal. The main endeavor of numerous analysts is to furnish better administrations that modulate with many mining techniques. For doing all this require overall study and design according to the system needed because this all are not possible with single mining technique or algorithm and not possible to extract valuable data for decision-making. So, we have to combine the mining technologies [16].

Figure 9.12 utilizes the Data Mining techniques such as Classification and Clustering for finding the hidden data patterns. Figure 9.13 shows probabilistic annexation of data mining technologies which could request to extract hidden patterns. The primary combination describes the utilization of clustering algorithm and then use classification algorithm. The second combination describes the use of classification algorithm and then that apply clustering algorithm on the data. The first classification is performed on input data or pattern for classify. The second combination, arrangement, is for apply technique, clusters, and classifiers. On the arrangement of the classifier, clustering calculation applied to include new

Table 9.1 Combination of algorithm.

Algorithm	Possible Combination	
Clustering	Clustering → Classification	Clustering → Classification → Frequent Pattern
	Clustering → Frequent Pattern	Clustering → Frequent Pattern → Classification
Classification	Classification → Clustering	Classification → Frequent Pattern → Clustering
	Classification → Frequent Pattern	Classification → Clustering → Frequent Pattern
Frequent Pattern	Frequent Pattern → Clustering	Frequent Pattern → Clustering → Classification
	Frequent Pattern → Classification	Frequent Pattern → Classification → Clustering

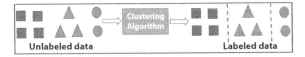

Figure 9.11 Clustering process.

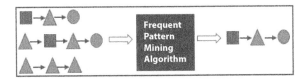

Figure 9.12 Frequent pattern mining process.

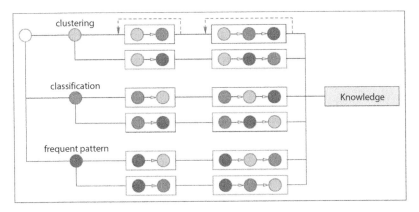

Figure 9.13 Different combination of mining technologies for the IoT.

modern classifier and make another pattern. It is the combination of various mining technologies that empowers the conceivable outcomes of taking care of patterns or knowledge which are come into the IoT steadily.

For instance, perceiving the human countenances or conduct not already in the learning knowledge database (the arrangement of classifiers). The different mixes that can be used are:

Clustering (making similar type groups) → classification (classify data according to predefined rule) → frequent pattern (extract this as output).

9.2.2   Data Mining With KDD

Data mining is a methodology used by association to change raw data into helpful or meaningful information. Software that is use to find useful patterns in tremendous clusters of data

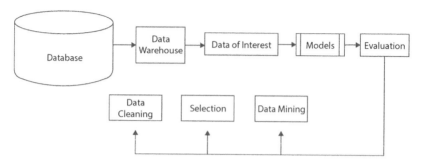

Figure 9.14 Steps of the knowledge discovery process.

and association can become familiar with their clients to learn powerful and effective show-casing procedures, agreement increment, and decrease costs. Data mining depends upon effective and powerful combination of data, warehousing, and PC handling (ALEXANDRA TWIN, 2019). Previously, the idea of discovering significant patterns in data by using some techniques such as data mining, extraction of knowledge, data discovery, data harvesting, information archaic exploration, and data pattern processing.

Generally, Data Mining terminology has been used by analysts, experts, and management information system (MIS) communities. The first KDD term was introduced at the first KDD workshop in 1989 (Piatetsky-Shapiro 1990) which underline that "knowledge" play an important role and final result of an information driven disclosure. It has been promoted in machine learning and AI. Information mining is the utilization of using distinct algorithm for extricating designs patterns from data. In Figure 9.14, KDD includes main steps like data preparation, selection of data, data cleansing, consolidating proper earlier information, and appropriate translation of the result of mining; these all are used for extracting useful patterns or information from the data. Dazzle application of data mining methods can be hazardous action that promoting the discover the irrelevant or meaningful patterns.

KDD covers the AI with machine learning and recognize the pattern by using certain data mining principal and algorithm: means for data modeling and extracting patterns. KDD mainly emphasizes on the discovering comprehensible model that can be translated as helpful or fascinating information and put a solid accentuation on operating with huge group of real-world data. Subsequently, properties of scaling algorithm to enormous data sets are of fundamental interest.

In the KDD procedure, Data Mining is a stage that comprising of using data analysis and disclosure algorithm that, under satisfactory computational productivity restrictions, making a specific identification of patterns over the data.

Steps of Knowledge Discovery
Evaluate the application area and gather the important prior information and find out the objective of the KDD procedure from the customer point of view.

1. Creating a collection of target data set: This is the basic or first stage for Knowledge Discovery. In this step, important information is collected from tradition or prior data or focus on the information data samples, on which searching procedure is to be execute.

2. Cleaning of data and preprocessing: After gathering information from prior data, cleaning and preprocessing step is done on gathered information in which noise is removed from the data or we can say that unnecessary data is removed.

3. Data decrease and projection: discovering cooperative highlights features that representing tile information relying on the tile objective of tile task. Utilizing the dimensionality reduce or transformation strategies to reduce tile successful number of factors viable or to discover invariant portrayals for the information.

4. Coordinating the objectives of tile Knowledge Discovery in Database process (step 1) to particular strategy of data mining: e.g., summarization, classification, regression, clustering, etc.

5. Select the algorithm for data mining(s): After coordinating the objective Knowledge Discover various algorithms are used to finding the data patterns. This incorporates choosing that which patterns and parameters might be appropriate and coordinating a specific data mining technique with the general standard of the KDD process.

6. Data mining: This step provides the basic techniques for gathering, finding important information such as classification rules or trees, regression, clustering, and so on.

7. Translating mined examples, this process can also include perception of the extricated examples/models, or characterization of the information given the extracted models.

8. Consolidating searching knowledge: It is necessary that make the learning information is more stronger into further framework for another activity, or simply archiving it and explaining it to invested individuals. This besides include inspect for and resolving possible scramble with recently recognized (or extracted) knowledge [17].

Swarm Intelligence and Knowledge Discovery
Data mining and PSO technique are able to appear that they do not share numerous properties for all intents and purpose. Be that as it may, they can be utilized together to shape a strategy which frequently prompts the outcome, in any event, when different strategies would be excessively costly or hard to execute.

9.2.3   PSO With Data Mining

PSO is the enhancement strategy which is used in pattern recognition and image processing. PSOs resolve the optimization issues by behavior of bird flocks. PSO is simple to execute and used to solve the complex optimization problems. Omran recommends in his paper that PSOs are utilized to create effective, powerful, and adaptable calculations to resolve a specific group of complicated issues that arise in the field of pattern recognition and image processing. In Data Mining, the clustering technique is important for pattern recognition and machine learning. It is the fundamental procedure in Artificial Intelligence. Clustering algorithm is used in many applications like image segmentation, vector and color quantization, spectral unmixing, data mining, image compression, and so on. Along these lines, finding a productive clustering algorithm is significant for scientists in a wide range of disciplines.

A visual augmented simulation–based data mining method broadening the idea of 3D displaying to relational structures. It is inclinable to the comprehension of enormous heterogeneous, unfinished and uncertain information, just as different types of organized and unstructured learning. Expanding the data generation rates, information types (social, realistic, logical, geometrical, and so on), and pattern relationships (geometrical, logical, etc.) requires the improvement of methodology encouraging progressively quick and instinctive comprehension of intrinsic data structure. In addition, the expanding multifaceted nature of examination of information makes it progressively hard for a customer (not truly a mathematician or information mining master), to fetch valuable results from the processed results produced by the using numerous strategies. This makes visual portrayal clearly engaging.

Growing data production rates, data types (social, realistic, symbolic, etc.), and pattern relationships (geometrical, logical, etc.) require the evolution of methods that encouraging progressively fast and natural comprehension of data structure.

Sousa *et al.* have introduced the utilization of PSO that is a technique for classification and clustering techniques in data mining. For other three variations of PSO, new developmental algorithm is introduced named as Genetic Algorithm (GA) which solves the problems by certain steps like: Selection, Crossover, and Mutation. Classification tasks are viewed as basic tools for decision support system which is going from the business industry, trade, military, and scientific and logical fields. The data sources utilized here for exploratory testing are usually utilized and considered as an accepted standard for rule revelation calculations dependability positioning. The outcomes acquired in these areas appear to demonstrate that PSO calculations are focused with other transformative methods and can be effectively applied to all the more requesting issue domain.

Recommender frameworks are new web-based programming tools, intended to assist clients with finding their way by using the present complex web-based online shops and diversion sites. This chapter depicts another recommender framework, which utilizes a PSO algorithm to understand individual inclinations of clients and give custom fitted proposals. Analyses are done to observe the exhibition of the framework, and results are contrasted with those acquired from the GA recommender framework and norms, and non-adaptive system is hooked in to the Pearson calculation. Recommender structure gives one strategy for bypassing this problem. Because the name suggest, their job is to suggest or recommend object or things to the customer reliant on their inclinations. These structures are much of your time employed by E-commerce sites as promoting devices to expand income by showing things that the customer is presumably getting to buy. An online webpage utilizing a recommender system can exploit knowledge of customer's' inclinations to collect a cognizance of their individual needs and thus increase customer dependability. This chapter focuses on the utilization of PSO algorithm to calibrate a profile-planning figuring inside a recommender structure, fitting it to the tendencies of individual customers. This engages the recommender structure to make continuously correct desires for customer's inclinations and, subsequently, better proposition to customers.

nPSO is used in the area of cascading classifiers. Cascading classifiers used to solve the pattern recognition problems. The main objective of using this methodology is to the improvement of arrangement exactness and the decrease of the unpredictability and multifaceted nature. Class-related reject thresholds issues are the main problem for cascading system. According to the literature review, the class-related reject threshold give an error-reject trade-off superior to a single worldwide threshold. The utilization of the PSO was proposed by Oliveira, Britto, and Sabourin for discovering thresholds so as to recover the error-reject trade-off produce by class-related reject thresholds. It has been demonstrated to be extremely effectual in taking care of genuine worldwide optimization issues. So as to demonstrate the advantages of that algorithm, the authors have used it to enhance the thresholds of a cascading classifier framework committed to perceive handwritten digits. In a cascading classifier, the information sources dismissed through the main initial stage are taken care of by the following ones utilizing costlier highlights or classifiers.

Challenges

It is major challenge of the present classification of PSO-based research whose primary objective depends on model types: rule-based models, nearest neighbor classifiers, and black box SVMs, and all these have various types of issues like binary to multiclass issues and hierarchical classification. This is presumably determined by the bigger capability of improvement issues in the persistent space. Regardless, for both classification and clustering, an orderly examination of the explanations behind the (elevated) execution is to a great extent missing. Since the utilization of PSO demand numerous decisions, the commitment of everyone should be studied.

9.3 ACO and Data Mining

ACO is combined with the Data Mining that means that this supports the classification and clustering for decision-making tasks. It means that any task is solved by the decision-making through Data Mining techniques. Classification and clustering modeling used like a graph finding issues permits the utilization of ACO for search ideal answers for these Data Mining tasks.

The main objective of the ant miner is to extract classification rules from data. The algorithm is based on the behavior of the ant colonies and some Data Mining techniques for extracting rules, principles, and policies. This chapter proposed an ACO calculation for the classification task of data mining. In this undertaking, the goal is to distribute all case (records, instance, and object) into single class. With regard to the classification task of data mining, found information or knowledge is frequently referred as IF-THEN rules that are as follows:

IF <Condition> THEN <class>.

The standard predecessor IF part contains a set of conditions part, which is commonly represented by a AND logical conjunction operator. In this term, the standard predecessor is a logical combination of terms that is represented in the form:

IF term1 AND term2 AND so on.

The clustering algorithm is based on Ant Colony that was proposed by mirroring various kind of normally happening emergent phenomena. This chapter portrays a basic social calculation, to be trailed by every specialist that creates an arranging procedure. Arranging is accomplished without requiring either outer heterogeneities (for example, temperature or stickiness), various leveled basic leadership, correspondence between the people or any worldwide portrayal of the earth. We likewise stress that the ants/robots have, without a doubt, extremely neighborhood data about the earth and a momentary memory, and moreover move arbitrarily, no situated development being vital.

9.4 Challenges for ACO-Based Data Mining

Data management positions as, probably, the greatest obstacle for Accountable Care Organizations. Reliable data works as an establishment for responsible consideration. But, analyzing unreliable data, breaking it down, and imparting it to different suppliers inside an ACO, these are things that most of medicinal services suppliers do not have the expertise or capacity to do effectively. Thus, ACOs face a few difficulties. Data management tasks are very challenging because, generally, medical providers are not literate about to discover the irrelevant data. One explanation of information by the board is testing it on the grounds that therapeutic suppliers are not prepared in mining understanding information. While data mining is certainly not a new science technology, insurance agencies have been digging claims information for a considerable length of time, abstracting information from electronic wellbeing health records, claims, and registries; something that most suppliers do not have a clue on how to do it nor do they have the time to figure out how to do it.

Another issue is that the information framework is regularly not set up to effectively share and to get information over a responsible consideration of organization network of suppliers. Generally, an ACO covers a thousands of patients and incorporates several physicians and experts. But, numerous electronic frameworks cannot communicate with each other so the information is not effectively available and sharable. This leads to breakdowns in care coordination that reduce the efficiency. ACO members ought to have the option to use information to help them flawlessly treat patients, increment productivity, and diminish care costs. In any case, getting your hands on the correct information at the opportune time is the key to all of this. ACO pioneers additionally need access to information so as to monitor patient care and measure execution of the suppliers in the network.

So, the central major issue is, if the requirement for data exists but the capacity to effectively gather and utilize the information does not, what is the solution? For most providers, the appropriate response is to redistribute information the management. Either that, or become a specialist at mining patient data and analyzing performance of data.

References

1. Admane, L., Benatchba, K., Koudil, M., Siad, L., Maziz, S., AntPart: an algorithm for the unsupervised classification problem using ants. *Appl. Math. Comput.*, 180, 1, 16–28, 2006. http://dx.doi.org/10.1016/j.amc.2005.11.130.

2. Alexandra Twin, Updated Aug 18, 2019 Investopedia https://www.investopedia.com/terms/d/datamining.asp
3. Craig W. Reynolds Symbolics Graphics Division "A Distributed Behavioral Model" Published in Computer Graphics, 21(4), July 1987, pp. 25-34. (ACM SIGGRAPH '87 Conference Proceedings, Anaheim, California, July 1987).
4. Grosan, C., Abraham, A., Chis, M., *Swarm Intelligence in Data Mining" Studies in Computational Intelligence* (SCI), 34, January 2007. https://www.researchgate.net/publication/225589418
5. Martens, D., Baesens, B., Fawcett, T., "Editorial Survey: Swarm Intelligence fo Data Mining." Article in Machine Learning. January 2011. DBLPhttps://www.researchgate.net/publication/220343951
6. Chen, F., Deng, P., Wan, J., Data Mining for the Internet of Things: Literature Review and Challenges, August 30, 2015.
7. Ahmed, H.R. and Glasgow, J.I., Swarm Intelligence: Concepts, Models and Applications, February 2012.
8. http://mnemstudio.org/particle-swarm-introduction.htm
9. Michelakos, I., Mallios, N., Papageorgiou, E.I., Vassilakopoulos, M., Ant Colony Optimization and Data Mining. June 2011.
10. Stankovic, J.A., Research Directions for the Internet of Things. *IEEE*, 2014.
11. Freeman, K., The ACO Data Management Challenge, 10.8.2015.
12. Dorigo, M., Ant colony optimization" Marco Dorigo. *Scholarpedia*, 2, 3, 1461, 2007.
13. Schranz, M., (Lake) CPswarm initial swarm modeling library Ref. Ares(2017)5343783 - 01/11/2017.
14. Oliveira, L.S., Britto, A.S., Jr., Sabourin, R., Improving Cascading Classifiers with Particle Swarm Optimization. *International Conference on Document Analysis and Recognition (ICDAR 2005)*, Seoul, South Korea, pp. 570–574, 2005.
15. Prajapati, P., Vasa, J., Patel, J., A Research Direction on Data Mining with IOT, March, 2017.
16. Bin, S., Yuan, L., Xiaoyi, W., "Research on Data Mining Models for the Internet of Things" IEEE. April 2010. https://www.researchgate.net/publication/261457602
17. Fayyad, U., Piatetsky-Shapiro, G., Smyth, P., Knowledge Discovery and Data Mining: Towards a Unifying Framework. *KDD-96 Proceedings*, 1996.

10

Data Management and Mining Technologies to Manage and Analyze Data in IoT

Shweta Sharma[1], Satya Murthy Sasubilli[2*] and Kunal Bhargava[3†]

[1]MDSU Ajmer, Ajmer India
[2]Huntington, Columbus, Ohio
[3]AIFLY Technology Ajmer, Ajmer India

Abstract

Internet of Things (IoT) is a significant piece of the new age data innovation. Information of the executives for IoT assumes a pivotal job in its powerful activities and has become a key research subject of IoT. We present a layered reference model for IoT information of the board. IoT has become a functioning zone of research, since IoT guarantees, among others, to improve nature of live and security in Smart Cities, to make asset flexible and squander the executives progressively effective, and to advance traffic including grouping, bunching, affiliation investigation, and time arrangement examination, and the most recent application cases are likewise reviewed. IoT Strategic Research and Innovation Directions is not a functional but yet rather an accepted requirement.

Keywords: Internet of Things, data management, data mining

10.1 Introduction

The Internet of Things (IoT) is a powerful and worldwide framework, wherein "Things" subsystems and individual physical and virtual components are recognizable, independent, and self-configurable. "Things" are relied upon to impart among ourselves and interface with the earth by interchange information made by detecting, although at the same time responding to occasions and activating activities to management the physical world. The perception that the IoT ought to endeavor to accomplish is to give a standard stage to making pleasing organizations and applications that saddle the total force of benefits accessible over the individual "Things" and any subsystems proposed to maintain the recently referenced "Things". The point of convergence of these advantages is the plenitude of data that can be made open by the mix of information that is conveyed persistently similarly as data set aside in ceaseless stores. This information can make the acknowledgment of inventive and eccentric applications and worth included administrations conceivable and will give a priceless source to incline examination

---

*Corresponding author: Satya.Murthy@huntington.com
†Corresponding author: kunalbhargava@live.com

Abhishek Kumar, Pramod Singh Rathore, Vicente Garrcia Diaz and Rashmi Agrawal (eds.) Swarm Intelligence Optimization: Algorithms and Applications, (165–188) © 2021 Scrivener Publishing LLC. ISBN 978-1-119-77874-5

and key chances. An exhaustive administration structure of structure of data that is made and set aside by the things inside IoT is thusly expected to achieve this target.

Information of the executives is a broad thought implying the structures, rules, and approach for decent organization of the data lifecycle necessities of a particular organization. With respect to IoT, data of the board ought to go about as a layer between the things producing the information and the applications getting to the information for assessment purposes and administrations. Our gadgets can be organized within subsystems or subspaces with self-ruling administration and inward various levels of the executives. The usefulness of information given through the particular subsystems is to cause accessiblity to the IoT arrangement, contingent upon the degree of security wanted besides the subsystem proprietors [1].

IoT knowledge has unmistakable qualities that compose of popular social established database of the executives in an out-of-date preparation. An enormous volume of heterogeneous, gushing, and geologically dispersed consistent data will be made by a large number differing contraptions intermittently sending recognitions about certain watched wonders or detailing the occasion of certain or peculiar events of interest. Occasional perceptions are generally requesting as far as correspondence overhead and capacity because of their spilling and nonstop nature. Although, occasion's current time strain by start-to-finish reaction times depends upon the criticalness of the reaction appropriate for the occasion. Moreover, there is metadata that portrays "Things" notwithstanding the information that is produced by "Things" object conspicuous evidence, zone, methodology, and organizations that are given as an instance of such data. IoT information will statically stay in fixed or versatile layout databases and wander the framework from effective and adaptable articles to storing centers. This will progress until it lands at united knowledge stores. Correspondence, stockpiling, and procedure inclination along these lines are characterizing components in the structure of information of the executives' answers for IoT [2].

Information of the executives' structure for IoT is displayed that fuses a layered, information driven, and united worldview to join the free IoT subsystems in a versatile and consistent information arrangement. Right now, "Things" layer is made out everything being equal and subsystems that can create information. Crude information, or basic totals, is then shipped through an interchanged layer to information vaults. These information stores are either guaranteed by affiliations or opened, and they can be arranged at explicit helpers or on the cloud. Affiliations or individual customers approach these stores through inquiry and alliance layers that process questions and examination assignments, choose which archives hold the necessary data, and arrange support to secure the information. What's more, constant or setting mindful questions are taken care of through the league layer by means of an expert's layer that flawlessly handles the disclosure and commitment of information experts. The entire structure in this manner permits a two-way distributing and questioning of information [3]. This permits the framework to react to the prompt information and preparing solicitations of the end clients and gives documented capacities to later long haul examination and investigation of significant worth included patterns.

10.2 Data Management

Conventional information of the executive frameworks handles the limit, recuperation, and update of basic data things, records, and reports. With respect to IoT, data of the board frameworks must condense data on the net while offering storing, logging, and evaluating works for detached assessment. This broadens the possibility of data the administrators from separated limit, requests dealing with, and trades the board exercises into online-detached correspondence/accumulating twofold errands. We, at first, portray the data lifecycle inside the setting of IoT and, a while later, plot the imperativeness use profile for all of the stages in order to admit a prevalent intelligence of IoT information of the board (Figure 10.1) [4].

10.3   Data Lifecycle of IoT

The lifecycle of information inside an IoT framework showed continuously from information creation to collection, move, alternative filtering and preprocessing, and for all time, to limit and documenting. Questioning and investigation are the end focuses that start (demand) and expend information creation, yet information creation can be set to be "pushed" to the IoT devouring administrations. Creation, assortment, total, separating, and some basic addressing and starter handling functionalities are seen as, on the web, correspondence concentrated exercises. Escalated preprocessing, long stretch amassing, and true and all around taking care of assessment are viewed as separated accumulating concentrated exercises [5].

Capacity tasks target making information accessible on the long haul for steady access/refreshes, although authentic is worried about read-just information. After all, some IoT frameworks can produce, process, and store information in arrangement for continuous and restricted administrations, by no convincing reason to engender this information further up to center concentrations in the framework; "edges" that join both handling and capacity components can exist as self-sufficient entities in the cycle (Figure 10.2).

Questioning: Data-escalated frameworks depend on questioning as the center procedure to get to and recover information. With regard to IoT, an inquiry can be given either to demand constant information to be gathered for worldly checking purposes or to recover a specific perspective on the information put away inside the framework. The principal case is common when (for the most part limited) an on-going solicitation for information is required. The subsequent case speaks to more globalized perspectives on information and top-to-bottom examination of patterns and examples.

Creation: Data creation includes detecting and moving information through the "Things" inside the IoT structure and detailing this information to invested individuals intermittently (as in an upfront investment/prompt model), pushing it up the system to collection focuses

Figure 10.1 Data management IoT.

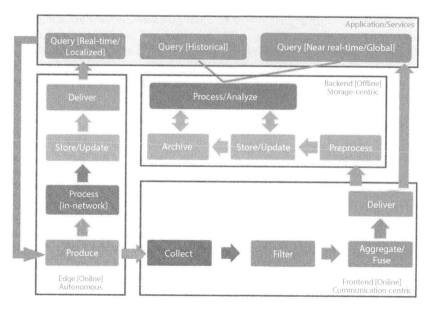

Figure 10.2 IoT data life cycle.

and in this way to database servers, or mailing it as a reaction activated through inquiries that demand the information from sensors and keen articles. Information is normally time-stepped and conceivably geo-stepped and can be as basic key esteem sets, or it might incorporate rich sound/picture with fluctuating intensities of multifaceted nature in the middle.

Assortment: The sensors and brilliant articles inside the IoT can store the information for a specific time interim or detail it to administering segments. Information might be gathered at fixation focuses or doors inside the system where it is additionally sifted and handled and potentially combined into minimal structures for productive transmission. Remote correspondence advances, for example, Wi-Fi, Zigbee, and cell, are utilized through items to deliver information to assortment focuses.

Conglomeration: Transmitting all the rough data out of the structure consistently is regularly restrictively pricey given the expensive expanding data spilling, the extending data spilling rates, and the compelled movement speed. Collection and combination procedures convey synopsis and blending activities progressively to pack the volume of information to be put away and transmitted.

Conveyance: As intelligence is separated, assembled, and conceivably handled, this one at the fixation focuses or at the self-governing virtual units inside the IoT, the after effects of these measures can be sent further up the structure, either as definite reactions or for capacity and top-to-bottom investigation. Wired or remote broadband correspondences might be utilized there to move information to perpetual information stores [6].

Preprocessing: IoT information determination originates from various sources with fluctuating organizations and frameworks. Information ought to be preprocessed to deal by missing data, remove redundancies, and fuse data from different sources toward a bound together blueprint before being focused on capacity. This preprocessing is a common technique in data mining termed as data cleaning. Blueprint reconciliation does not suggest savage power fitting of the considerable number of information into a fixed social (tables) outline, but instead, an increasingly dynamic meaning of a predictable method to get to the information without modifying approach for each sources information format. Possibilities at various levels in the chart can be added at this stage to IoT information things so as to deal with vulnerability that can be accessible in information or to manage the absence of trust that can endure in information authority [7].

Capacity Archiving: This stage handles the effective stockpiling and association of information just as the persistent restoring of information by new data as it gets accessible. Chronicling alludes to the disconnected long haul stockpiling of information that is not promptly required for the framework's progressing tasks. The center of incorporated stockpiling is the organization of capacity frameworks that adjust to the different information forms and the recurrence of information catch. Social database of the board frameworks is a famous decision that includes the association of information toward a table diagram by predefined inter-relationships and meta-data for proficient recovery at next stages. Nosql key esteem stores are picking up prevalence as capacity advancements for their help of large information stockpiling by no dependence on social composition or solid flexibility prerequisites normal of social database structures. Capacity can likewise be decentralized for independent IoT organizations, where information is stored at the articles that produce it and is not sent up the framework. Be that as it may, because of the constrained abilities of such items, stockpiling limit stays restricted in contrast with the incorporated stockpiling model [7, 8].

Preparing/Analysis: This stage includes the continuous recovery and examination tasks performed and put away and documented information so as to pick up experiences into verifiable information and foresee future patterns or to perceive varieties from the standard in the knowledge that may trigger further assessment or action (E. Rumelhart, 1986). Undertaking unequivocal preprocessing can be relied upon to channel and clean information before significant errands happen. Right when an IoT subsystem is self-overseeing and does not require enduring limit of its data, yet it rather keeps getting ready and limit in the framework, and by then, in orchestrating this, taking care of information may be acted, considering progressing or constrained inquiries.

Capacities for IoT information the executives

- Versatile availability and capacity to deal with information assortment: IoT frameworks have an assortment of principles and IoT information clings to a wide scope of conventions (MQTT, OPC, AMQP, etc.). Additionally, most IoT information exists in semi-organized or unstructured arrangements. Thusly, your information of the board framework must have the option to associate with those frameworks and hold fast to the different conventions so you can ingest information from those frameworks. It is similarly significant that the arrangement bolster both organized and unstructured information.
- Edge preparing and enhancements: A great information of the board arrangement will have the option to sift through incorrect records originating from the IoT frameworks, for example, negative temperature readings—before ingesting it into the information lake. It ought to likewise have the option to

improve the information with metadata, (for example, timestamp or static content) to help better examination.

- Big information preparing and AI: Because IoT information comes in exceptionally huge volumes, performing continuous investigation requires the capacity to run advancements and ingestion in sub-second idleness with the goal that the information is fit to be devoured progressively. Likewise, numerous clients need to operationalize ML models, for example, inconsistency discovery progressively with the goal that they can make preventive strides before it is past the point of no return.

- Address information float: Data originating from IoT frameworks can change after some time because of occasions, for example, firmware redesigns. This is called information float or diagram float. It is significant that your information of the board arrangement can consequently address information float without intruding on the information the executives' procedure [9].

- Real-time checking and alarming: IoT information ingestion and preparing never stops. Accordingly, your information of the executives' arrangement ought to give continuous observing stream representations to show the status of the procedure whenever regarding execution and throughput. The information of the executives' arrangement ought to likewise give alarms in the event that any issues emerge during the procedure [9, 10].

Challenges for IoT Data Management (Figure 10.3)
IoT foundation faces the accompanying difficulties during execution:

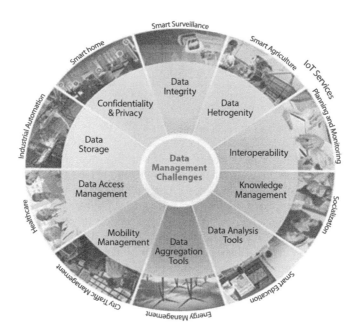

Figure 10.3 Data management challenges.

Versatility
Information gathered utilizing IoT sensors are depended upon to create in volume expo-nentially. It is IoT devices that would make more than 500 zettabytes of data for consistently before the completion of 2019. Subsequently, associations can go up against a critical issue of decreasing additional room in IoT data the board. Furthermore, business pioneers need to explore how they can share and improve the gathered data. Therefore, business pioneers can ask themselves the going with requests:

- Can the current foundation handle huge volumes of information?
- Which stage can be utilized to deal with the acquired information?
- Who can get to the gathered information?
- What will be the normal pace of information development throughout the following 5 years?

These inquiries can help business pioneers comprehend foundation that needs to help IoT information of the executives. Additionally, rising information volumes can offer ascent to another issue called information gravity. As the volume of IoT information develops, different applications and capacities will begin discovering an incentive in the information. Be that as it may, the rising number of utilizations will build information volume significantly more.

Security
The age of enormous information volumes can pull in cybercriminals, who wish to increase illicit access to critical information. A few major players, for example, Google, Facebook, Marriott, and British Airways, have been casualties of modern digital assaults. Delicate information of a huge number of clients was undermined in these digital assaults. Programmers can likewise tar-get operational information, which could incapacitate basic procedures in an association [11].

Different system vulnerabilities and recently made malware strains can misuse escape clauses in an association's security convention to wrongfully get to information. Programmers can likewise dispatch mechanized digital assaults to hack into an association's system. Moreover, absence of educated staff may tap on phishing messages and download vindictive documents, uncovering touchy business information [12].

10.4   Procedures to Implement IoT Data Management

Recognize use cases
Before embracing IoT arrangements, business pioneers must distinguish potential IoT use cases for different business strategies. For example, a retailer may utilize IoT information to comprehend client conduct, while an assembling firm may utilize it for prescient upkeep. With this methodology, business pioneers can settle on educated choices while picking IoT arrangements and comprehend their information stockpiling and the executives' necessities.

Contract talented experts
To execute IoT arrangements and IoT information of the board effectively, business pioneers should contract talented experts. These experts can help in creating and executing compelling IoT reception procedures. Moreover, business pioneers can allot venture chiefs for their IoT ventures.

Distribute adequate spending plan
Business pioneers need to painstakingly comprehend a few necessities, for example, foundation and assets for fruitful IoT information of the board. By examining these necessities, organizations can allot adequate spending plan for their venture. If there should arise an occurrence of lack of spending plan, business pioneers can gather private ventures.

Comprehend information prerequisites
Before starting the information assortment process, associations need to comprehend which sort of information they will require and how a lot of information stockpiling they possess. Business pioneers need to dissect how various informational collections can correspond to each other to use accessible information effectively and limit stockpiling necessities. Also, engineers and business pioneers need to work together to make sense of how gathered information can be improved and coordinated with big business frameworks.

Execute security conventions
Organizations need to execute a multifaceted methodology for information security. First of all, associations can scramble their information to guarantee information trustworthiness. Associations ought to likewise limit access to touchy information by giving information just to get concerned gatherings. Also, associations must teach their representatives about information security [13].

Teach and train representatives
Organizations must teach their representatives about IoT arrangements, their advantages, and IoT information of the executives. For this reason, associations can likewise boost teaching different workers about IoT (Figure 10.4) [14].

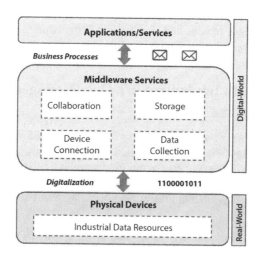

Figure 10.4 Industrial data management.

10.5 Industrial Data Lifecycle

Mechanical information is a significant asset that can be progressively basic for overall assembling business forms and the wellspring of immense riches whenever took care of appropriately. Dealing with this information requires high handling and capacity abilities because of its gigantic, complicated, and unstructured nature. The lifecycle of current data with the help of admire three phases, physical, middleware, and applications, can be described. The whole mechanical condition has been partitions into two sub-portions that go for the real and propelled world. In obvious circumstances, the unrefined present day knowledge with different information categorization, gatherings, and different estimations is created with different physical pieces of sharp creation lines. The physical contraption fragment incorporates each and every real datum sources, for instance, sensors, net-created information, databases, and pariah operations. This portion is, in any case, called data disclosure. In the wake of completing the digitalization and mixture frames, this data transforms into a bit of the propelled world in matched structure, where middleware and application portions attempt different organizations to maintain it [15]. The middleware section keeps an eye on interoperability across various assembling plant devices, contraption disclosure, flexibility, the officials of tremendous data, setting care, and the security appearances of the IoT condition [16].

In the middleware stage, the information assortment component legitimately associates by the physical gadgets and trade double information utilizing directions/reaction technique. The information is legitimately or by implication obtained by logical and business requests from every single substantial source. Subsequent to applying separating, arranging, total, and order methods, the prepared information is sent to the capacity module for all time putting away into accessible archives for later use. As of late, these vaults use distributed computing frameworks to store modern information and give quality characteristics, for example, unwavering quality, accessibility, security, versatility, and vigor. All industrial facility gadgets have been conveyed with the IoT framework over the gadget association module. This module reacts to standard and occasion information current appropriately, for instance, each pre-preparing functionalities are tested first for normal information flow (disconnected information) and afterward put away in lasting archives, though explicit occasions (online information) are legitimately broadcast to the operation server for a speedy reaction. The joint effort component offers types of assistance to the shopper of information for explicit approach to the physical gadgets independently. With this accomplishment, a client may discover the metadata around gadgets (i.e., type and area). The function segment cooperates including the middleware with getting demand messages and mailing reactions to the particular solicitations. This stage additionally gives the stage to software engineers and experts to make the accessible information valuable and create new chances and administrations. The information is analyzed with the objective to upgrade forms, remove helpful bits of knowledge, and settle on better and early choices [17].

10.6   Industrial Data Management Framework of IoT

10.6.1   Physical Layer

The physical layer consists of each information maker substances of the assembling framework and modulus. These substances may be stream robots, meters, servo meters, transport lines, machine dreams, brilliant compartments, installed chips, and different gadgets on the shop floor. A constant information is obtained from manufacturing plant address and floor to the upper layer with different connectors, utilizing cutting edge modern correspondence convention termed as Open Platform Communication Unified Architecture (OPC-UA). The particular connectors have been sent for various sensors, for example, climate, acoustic, vibration, pressure, rotational quickness, torque, force, and vitality discharge to screen the genuine status of machines in advanced structure. Each physical gadget on the shop floor is incorporated by one another and all gadgets have special distinguishing proof so each information shopper can get to them separately. We favored area that established distinguishing proof as it is progressively effective for adaptable information procurement inside a circulated domain. Neighborhood collection has been tested at this layer to limit the capacity and communication cost of the rough mechanical information. The neighborhood accumulation components gained information from information sources and abridged this with disposing of the less significant or homogeneous information streams. This additionally assists with transmitting information productively with least postponement and ensures the on-going information obtaining framework (Figure 10.5) [18].

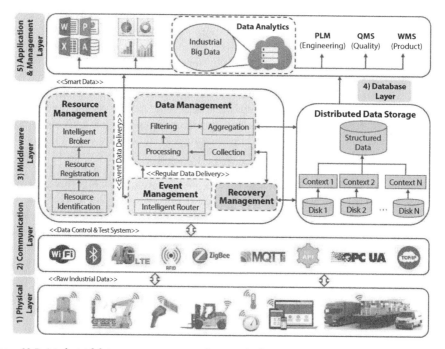

Figure 10.5 A industrial data management system framework of an IoT.

10.6.2   Correspondence Layer

The correspondence layer gives human machines interface, associates each layers of the proposed structure, and attempts transportation that connects between information makers and shoppers. This layer likewise handles correspondence between disseminated plant gadgets inside a tremendous mechanical territory to think information assortment, preparing, perception, and capacity. Ordinarily, the intensity of mechanical gadgets is stored little, which decline their computations and handling abilities. Besides, the greater part of these gadgets is controlled by batteries, so that vitality of the board is additionally a basic problem for them. To defeat these problems, a WSN is actualized for checking of mechanical gadgets through remote sensor systems. The WSN attempts adaptability and adaptability, and it has capacity to work with numerous gadgets cooperatively to accomplish the shared objectives. The modern information ought to be productively gathered from the physical layer and conducted it for high throughput and low inactivity rate to upper layers for additional procedures and examination. For this reason, the correspondence layer gives a few arrangements as a focal center point. Different correspondence advancements, for example, Wi-Fi, RFID, 4G LTE, Zigbee, Bluetooth, z-wave, and so on, are present, that are utilized to move substantial information traffic by dormancy assurance and large data transfer capacity support. These advancements have capacity to development and store information by a little level for an impressive time length. This layer guarantees the information preservation and workers protection by shielding the system from unapproved approach and ensures safe transmission of information on each period of the information lifecycle [19].

10.6.3   Middleware Layer

A tremendous system of interconnected processing plant gadgets, a significant number of occasions created with shop floor machines, and complicated IoT innovations address new difficulties for improvement of IoT applications. Right now, middleware layer offers different administrations for function improvement by incorporating heterogeneous registering and specialized gadgets. This layer bolsters interoperability inside the assorted functions and administrations running on these gadgets. A number of frameworks are working to be created with the help of IoT middileware arrangements; however, constrained frameworks are accessible for assembling conditions. As of late, middleware arrangements are increasing more significance because of the key job in rearranging the development of new administrations and applications [20].

10.7   Data Mining

Information mining process alludes to the procedure of semi-automatically breaking down huge databases for design mining which are creative, authentic, valuable, and justifiable, which is otherwise called Knowledge Discovery in Databases (KDD). Information mining or KDD process incorporates issue plan, information assortment, information cleaning for example preprocessing, change, picking mining task/technique, and result assessment/representation. Information disclosure is an iterative procedure. Information mining covers with different fields like measurements, AI, man-made brainpower, and databases; yet, for the most part, it centers around computerization of taking care of enormous heterogeneous information, calculation, and versatility of number of highlights and occurrences. Starting late, an extending number of rising applications oversee endless sensor data in IoT as a result of a wide collection of sensor contraptions on identifying layer. The broad scaling of heterogeneous sensor makes an issue of information taking care of which is one of key issues for the IoT system application. Sensors in IoT functions sense the tangled situation and deliver a colossal data that must be isolated and cleaned so it will, in general, be deciphered, and customer will be outfitted with bits of information on the data accumulated in sort of models. Across various framework establishments, IoT licenses identifying the things and remotely finding a good pace engages open entryways for an unrivaled compromise among real and electronic world. It results into an improved adequacy, precision, and better monetary results. Each question can be perceived particularly by the usage of its introduced enrolling system. However, these items can interoperate inside the present foundation of the Internet. Appraisals suggest that IoT will be an aggregation including about 50 billion items before the completion of 2020. The route toward finding and exploring accommodating examples in an IoT of data is the thing that we allude it as Data Mining. Information mining can, in like manner, be described as a reasonable technique that is utilized to examine and glance through broad proportion of colossal data in order to find increasingly important data in it. Till date, the example discovering strategies were not full-fledge used and the data assembled was just a static aggregation of databases. In any case, with the strategy for discovering designs in the data, more utilization of the data is being obtained which chooses better decisions for the headway of the business or social angle [21].

Figure 10.6 portrays unmistakably that IoT assembles information from different origins, which may accommodate information for the IoT itself. KDD, when associated with

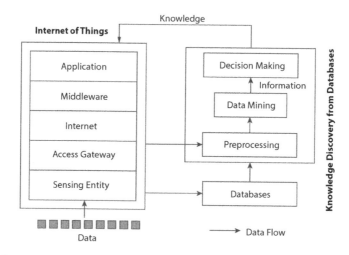

Figure 10.6 Data mining integrated IoT architecture.

IoT, will change over the information accumulated by IoT toward significant data that would then have the option to be changed over into learning. The information diving step is accountable as removing structures from the yield of the information getting ready advance and, after that, empowering them within the essential initiative advance, which manages changing its commitment to significance data. It is basic to observe that each mean of the Knowledge Discovery of Database (KDD) technique can have a strong effect on the past phase of mining, for example, not all the characteristics of the information are important for mining; right now, assurance is typically used to pick the key characteristics from any record in the database for mining. The outcome is that data mining estimations can encounter genuine troubles to find important information (e.g., putting frameworks with applicable get-togethers) if the picked properties cannot totally address the characteristics of the data [22]. It is, in like manner, indispensable to observe that the information mix, generous scale information, knowledge transmission, and decentralized preparing problems can strongly influence the structure execution and advantage the idea of IoT than data mining or KDD estimations alone can admit on the standard functions [23].

The principle challenge is to choose a reasonable calculation for a certain IoT framework, as there a few procedure and calculations accessible in information mining. The primary reason for any information mining system is to set up an efficient prescient or enlightening portrayal of huge information that not just best fits or depicts it, even so ready to sum up to recently produced information [24]. Information mining for the most part classified into two procedures. One is Descriptive information mining and the other is Predictive information mining. In illustrative information, mining information is depicted in a brief and totaled manner and gives noteworthy general properties of the information. In prescient information, mining information is broke down in a succession to manufacture a solitary or a loT of information models and tries to anticipate the conduct of recently produced informational indexes by utilizing methods like relapse, order, and pattern examination. Information mining can be seen as a basic strategy over the span of information disclosure. This procedure is an iterative grouping of the accompanying advances:

- Data cleaning—In this grouping, clamor and conflicting information is evacuated.
- Data combination—This progression joins different information sources.
- Data choice—In this procedure, information is recovered which is important to the examination procedure.
- Data change—In this progression outline or collection, activities are performed so information is changed or solidified into proper for information removing.
- Data mining—In this procedure, wanted information designs are separated by utilizing canny techniques.
- Pattern assessment—In this procedure, disclosure of fascinating examples that speaks to the information relying upon some alluring measures.
- Knowledge introduction—In this procedure, mined information is exhibited to the client by utilizing perception and information portrayal systems.

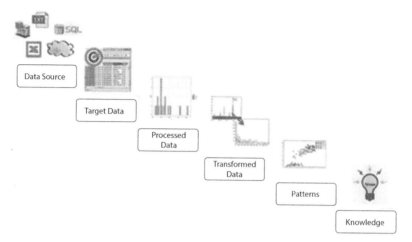

Figure 10.7 Data mining process.

Utilizations of IoT With Data Mining (Figure 10.7)

A. Smart City Applications

There are a few IoT frameworks in savvy city that identify with the suitable information mining functionalities used to make existing framework more brilliant and better.

Traffic Control—IoT gadgets or things, for example, advanced mobile phones, vehicle sensors, and GPS, are utilized everywhere throughout the city that can be filled in as information focuses, for example, time of voyaging, frequency of overwhelming vehicles, clumsy zones, and development regions. Familiarity with the causes behind traffic impediment in the chose region is known with the assistance of these information focuses. To take care of the traffic blockage issue, we can utilize order calculation. The chose regions can be grouped dependent on the higher, lower, or medium odds of car influx occurrences in a predetermined area. For the expectation of the time in a day where the hindrance will occur at the most noteworthy rate and conceivable course that has no traffic blockage used to land at the goal is accomplished by Classification strategy. To stay away from clog, characterization will scatter the traffic [25].

Rural Electronic Meters—Traditional meters are supplanting with keen electronic meters with a quick pace, since brilliant meters can offer point by point depiction about on-going vitality utilization data in an advanced manner by means of email or PDAs. Regardless, Time Series examination is applied on time arrangement information that is consequently gathered at various time interims everywhere throughout the day and can be utilized to anticipate vitality utilization and sends messages promptly if any oddity is distinguished in vitality utilization. Manufactured information which is utilized for guaging might be produced accessible genuine information. Pipeline Leak Detection—For civil partnerships, support of water pipe spillages is troublesome, all the more absolutely with old funnels. Utilizing anomaly location calculation alongside utilization of sensors, sound of water development can be investigated to spot spills.

B. Smart Home Applications

For Governments, IoT offers Smart city applications (like reconnaissance, force and lighting, leaving meter, versatile traffic the executives, catastrophe the board, occasions control, asset of the executives, and crisis reaction framework), Smart transportation applications (like associated vehicles, armada the executives, roadways, rail transport, port, and aeronautics), Smart lattice applications (like electrical cable productivity and request reaction), Smart water applications (like waste water of the board and household waterworks), Smart foundation applications, and Environment-based applications (for example, air quality, ecological checking, and landfill and waste administration). IoT gadgets produce information; by mining this information, we can create important examples which can additionally be utilized to foresee future episodes for mechanized client association. This is accomplished with order and time arrangement examination models to characterize the intuitive gadgets that are associated together dependent on their use. Information created by these gadgets can be put away with their relative timeframes, by applying direct relapse on this information can conjecture future occasions [26].

C. Enterprise Applications
On the undertaking side, IoT offers administrations like Energy-based applications (for example, working administration, as apparatuses and wells prescient support, spill mishap of the board), Smart medicinal services applications (for example, crisis rescue vehicle administration, medical clinic the executives, crisis room, facility based, medical procedure, lab analysis, home consideration, inquire about, senior consideration, charging gear proficiency, mechanical IoT, and resource the board), Smart retails (like self-checkouts, store offers, advanced marks, misfortune counteraction, design enhancement, stock control, and client relationship of the board), Smart horticulture applications (for example, following steers, remote sensor on water, and natural nourishment affirmation), Smart financial applications (for example, ATM machine upkeep, online vehicle, home advances and e-proclamation, and so on.), Smart structure and Smart development, Smart training, Smart protection, Smart coordinations, and Smart assembling applications [27].

D. Health Care Applications
With the progressions of IoT frameworks, benefits in medicinal services industry are obviously improved. Social insurance framework in a joint effort with IoT frameworks offers a various types of assistance for patients like successive checking of the level circulatory strain, diabetes, pulse, weight subtleties, and heartbeat related data. Every one of this information will be put away the on cloud kept up by concerned medical clinic. A savvy framework ought to be created to incorporate this different information and give precisely exact insights regarding quiet [28]. With the assistance of content mining, we can analyze patient's medicinal history based on specialist's solution and finish up about the state of patient. Bunching can be utilized for treatment of the patient.

10.7.1 Functionalities of Data Mining

Functionalities of data mining are fuse portrayal, connection assessment, clustering, time game plan examination, and exemption examination.

- Grouping is the path toward data, a ton of models or limits that delineate and perceive information classes or thoughts, to envision the class of articles whose class name is dark.
- Grouping separates data objects without directing an acknowledged class model.

- Affiliation assessment is the exposure of alliance rules demonstrating quality worth conditions that as frequently as conceivable happen together in a given game plan of data.
- Time course of action assessment incorporates methodologies and techniques for separating time plan data to evacuate significant bits of knowledge and various qualities of the data.
- Exception assessment delineates and models consistency or examples as objects whose lead development later [29].

10.7.2 Classification

Portrayal is huge for the officials of dynamic. Given an article, it is predefined to one of target classes or class that is termed game plan. The objective of solicitation is to totally imagine the objective class for any case in the information. For instance, a depiction model could be utilized to isolate the improvement of candidates as low, medium, or huge credit risks.

The target class for any case in the data of request is to absolutely envision through the target.

The particular various techniques to arrange the information, along with decision tree acknowledgment, diagram established or rule-positioned ace structures, dynamic course of action, and neural frameworks [30].

Bayesian framework and support vector machines (SVMs):

- A decision tree is a stream layout like tree architecture, where any inside center is implied with square shapes and leaf centers that are implied for ovals. Each subjective center point has, in any event, two child centers. Every single inside focus point contains parts, which test the estimation of an announcement of the properties. Bends from an inward center point to its children are set apart by undeniable aftereffects of the test. Each leaf community has a class name similar with it. ID3 or Iterative Dichotomiser 3 is a fundamental decision tree training computation. C4.5 calculation is an improved change of ID3; it uses gain extent as separating criteria. The qualification, some place in the scope of C4.5 and ID3 figuring, is such ID3 usage combined parts, while C4.5 counts usage multiway parts. Supervised learning in quest (SLIQ) is fit for dealing with huge instructive records effectively and lesser time multifaceted nature, Scalable Parallelizable Induction of Decision Tree computation (SPRINT) is furthermore brisk and significantly versatile, and SPRINT is no limit basic on greater educational assortments. More development investigates endure flawless. Portrayal and (CART) regression trees are an estimation of non-parametric decision tree. It makes either portrayal or backslide trees, considering if the return variable is total or tenacious. Chi squared modified joint effort identifier (CHAID) and the improvement researcher revolve around isolating an educational assortment into select and complete bits that change by recognition to the return variable [31].
- The K-Nearest Neighbor (KNN) calculation is presented with the nearest neighbor calculation which is intended to discover the closest purpose of the watched matter. The principle thought of the calculation of KNN is to discover the K-closest focuses. There are a variety of enhancements for the customary calculation of KNN, for example, the (WKPDS) wavelet-based K-nearest neighbor

partial distance Search calculation, (ENNS) Equal-Average Nearest Neighbor Search calculation, (EENNS) Equal-Average Equal-Norm Nearest Neighbor code word Search calculation, the (EEENNS) Equal-Average Equal-Variance Equal-Norm Nearest Neighbor Search calculation, and different upgrades [32].

- Bayesian frameworks obtain composed non-cyclic diagrams whose center points address sporadic elements in the Bayesian sense. Edges address unforeseen situations, center points which are not related address elements that are prohibitively liberated from one another. In perspective on Bayesian frameworks, these classifiers have various characteristics, like exhibit interpretability and settlement to complex knowledge and portrayal issue frameworks [33]. The investigation fuses sincere Bayes, K-dependence Bayesian classifiers, one-dependence Bayesian classifiers, semi-naïve Bayes, specific naïve Bayes, Bayesian structure extended gullible Bayes, boundless Bayesian classifiers, and Bayesian multinets.

- SVM figuring is overseen as learning model for related learning counts that dismember information and see structures, which relies upon quantifiable learning theory. SVMs produce an equal classifier, the supposed perfect disconnecting hyperplanes, over an extremely nonlinear mapping of the data vectors into the high-spatial component space. SVM is commonly used in content gathering, displaying, structure affirmation, and remedial finding. A lot of further research is done, granular assistance vector machines (Gsvm), feathery assistance vector machines (Fsvm), twin assistance vector machines (TWSVMs), regard in risk reinforce vector machines (VaR-SVM), and situating help vector machines (RSVM) (Figure 10.8) [34].

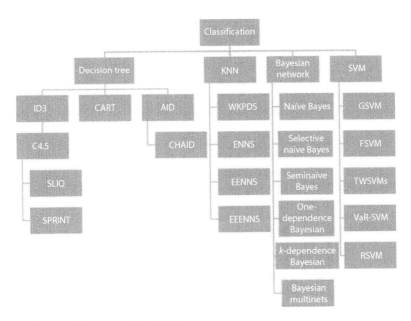

Figure 10.8 The research structure of classification.

10.8 Clustering

Batching estimations disengage data into critical social occasions with the objective that structures in a comparative get-together are practically identical in few sense and models in various get-together endure exceptional in a comparable sense. Searching for bunches incorporates solo learning. In instruction recuperation, for objects, the web crawler bundles billions of website pages toward various social occasions, for instance, news, reviews, accounts, and sounds. One direct instance of grouping issue is to parcel centers into different social events [35].

- Progressive clustering strategy solidifies information items into subgroups; the particular subgroups join within greater and noteworthy level get-togethers, and so forth, and structure a hierarchy of leadership tree. Different level gathering procedures have two game plans: (top-down) problematic and (base up) agglomerative and approaches. The agglomerative gathering starts by one-point packs and recursively merges at any rate two of the bundles. The problematic bundling strikingly is a top-down philosophy. It starts by a singular gathering consists of entire data centers and recursively items that bunch within reasonable subclusters. Fix clustering usage representatives and singular value decomposition (SVD) are ordinarily investigated.
- Dividing figurings discover packs either with iteratively moving concentrations between subgroup or with perceiving districts seriously populated by information. The relevant analysis fuses k-medoids, snob, mclust, and k-infers–related analysis. Thickness established separation methodologies that attempt to discover low-dimensional information, which is thick related, termed as structural data. The related research consolidates density-based spatial clustering of applications with noise (DBSCAN). System-based allocating use different level agglomeration as one time of getting ready and perform space division and a while later absolute legitimate bits; asks about fuse BANG.
- In solicitation to manage straight out data, authorities modify information gathering to preclustering of things or out trademark characteristics; normal research fuses ROCK.
- Adaptable bundling research faces flexibility issues for enlisting time and consciousness requirements, along with BIRCH and DIGNET.
- High spatial information packing strategies are proposed to manage information by a few characteristics, along with MAFIA and DFT [36].

10.9 Affiliation Analysis

Connection rule mining is based on the available container assessment or trade data examination, and its objective disclosure of rules demonstrates trademark worth affiliations that happen once in a while and, besides, helps in the time of logically wide and abstract data which, in this manner, also powerfully helps. The assessment structure of connection examination is showed in Figure 10.9.

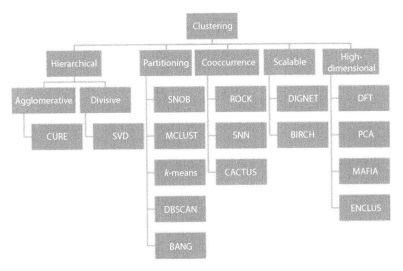

Figure 10.9 Structure of clustering.

- For the fundamental rundown of alliance assessment computations, the information will be arranged basically. The previous based estimations have been used to discover intratransaction affiliations and, a while later, discover relationship. There are heaps of expansion computations. As demonstrated by the information record gathering, it bundles into two sorts: horizontal database format algorithms and vertical database format algorithms, the normal computations consolidate LAPIN-SPAM and MSPS. Model advancement computation is logically stunning yet may be speedier to figure given immense numbers of information. The common figuring is Fp-Growth estimation.
- In any area, the data would be a movement of events, and right now, issue is discover event plans that happen as a rule together. It isolates into two areas: event-based counts and event-organized computations; PROWL is the normal estimation.
- In solicitation to abuse scattered equivalent PC systems, a couple of counts are made, for example, Par-CSP [37].

10.10   Time Series Analysis

A period course of action is a combination of common knowledge dissents; the components of time game plan data consolidate tremendous information size, large capacity, and reviving continually. Typically, time course of action task relies upon 3 bits of fragments, including depiction, equivalence parts, and requesting (Figure 10.10) [38].

- One of the critical clarifications behind time game plan depiction is to diminish the estimation, and it segregates toward three orders: model-based

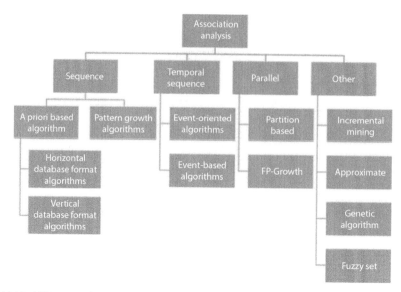

Figure 10.10 Affiliation analysis research structure.

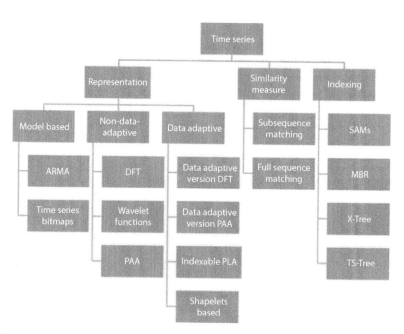

Figure 10.11 Structure of time series analysis.

depiction, non-data adaptable depiction, and information flexible depiction. The model-based depictions use to find specifications of essential model for a depiction. Noteworthy exploration works join and the time course of action bitmaps investigate. In non-data flexible depictions, the specifications of the change proceed as before for each time course of action paying little regard to its tendency, related research including DFT, wavelet limits related points. In data flexible depictions, the specifications of a change will development as showed by the data available and associated works along with depictions variation of DFT and indexable PLA.

- The likeness extent of time course of action examination is ordinarily finished in an expected manner; the investigation direction joins subsequent organizing and full progression planning.
  - The requesting of time game plan examination is immovably including by depiction and closeness measure part, the investigation point fuses Spatial Access Methods (SAM) and Ts-tree [39].

References

1. Baldi, Autoencoders, unsupervised learning, and deep architectures. *ICML unsupervised and transfer learning*, vol. 27, p. 1, 2012.
2. Becker, Indoor positioning solely based on user's sight, in: *International Conference on Information Science and Applications*, Springer, pp. 76–83, 2017.
3. Bengio, *et al.*, Learning deep architectures for AI. *Found. Trends R Mach. Learn.*, 2, 1, 1–127, 2009.
4. Borkowski, Schulte, S., Hochreiner, C., Predicting cloud resource utilization, in: *Proceedings of the 9th International Conference on Utility and Cloud Computing*, ACM, pp. 37–42, 2016.
5. Bottou, Large-scale machine learning with stochastic gradient descent, in: *Proceedings of COMPSTAT'2010*, Springer, pp. 177–186, 2010.
6. Chauvin, and Rumelhart, D.E., *Backpropagation: theory, architectures, and applications*, Psychology Press, 168, 1995.
7. Chung, Gulcehre, C., Cho, K., Bengio, Y., Empirical evaluation of gated recurrent neural networks on sequence modeling, arXiv preprint arXiv:1412.3555v1 [cs.NE], Recurrent neural networks are able to. perform. 169, 170, 176, 183, 2014.
8. Dai, Fidler, S., Urtasun, R., Lin, D., Towards Diverse and Natural Image Descriptions *via a Conditional GAN*, in: *Proceedings of the IEEE Conference on Computer Vision and Pattern Recognition*, pp. 2970–2979, 2017.
9. Deng, A tutorial survey of architectures, algorithms, and applications for deep learning. *APSIPA Trans. Signal Inf. Process.*, 3, 1–29, 2014.
10. Doersch, Tutorial on variational autoencoders, arXiv preprint arXiv:1606.05908v2 [stat.ML], 2016.
11. Kahou, E., Bouthillier, X., Lamblin, P., Gulcehre, C., Michalski, V., Konda, K., Jean, S., Froumenty, P., Dauphin, Y., BoulangerLewandowski, N. *et al.*, Emonets: Multimodal deep learning approaches for emotion recognition in video. *J. Multimodal User Interfaces*, 3, 99–111, 2016.
12. Rumelhart, E., Hinton, G.E., Williams, R.J., Learning representations by back-propagating errors. *Nature*, 323, 6088, 533, 1986.
13. Fragkiadaki, Levine, S., Felsen, P., Malik, J., Recurrent network models for human dynamics, in: *Proceedings of the IEEE International Conference on Computer Vision*, pp. 4346–4354, 2015.

14. Gantz, and Reinsel, D., *The digital universe in 2020: Big data, bigger digital shadows, and biggest growth in the far east*, vol. 2007, no. 2012, pp. 1–16, IDC iView: IDC Analyze the future, 2012.

15. Goodfellow, Pouget-Abadie, J., Mirza, M., Xu, B., Warde-Farley, D., Ozair, S., Courville, A., Bengio, Y., Generative adversarial nets, in: *Advances in Neural Information Processing Systems*, pp. 2672–2680, 2014.

16. Gu, Chen, Y., Liu, J., Jiang, X., Semi-supervised deep extreme learning machine for wi-fi based localization. *Neurocomputing*, 166, 282–293, 2015.

17. Hada-Muranushi, Muranushi, T., Asai, A., Okanohara, D., Raymond, R., Watanabe, G., Nemoto, S., Shibata, K., A deep-learning approach for operation of an automated realtime flare forecast. *Space Weather*, 173, 174, 180, 2016.

18. He, Mendis, G.J., Wei, J., Real-time detection of false data injection attacks in smart grid: A deep learning-based intelligent mechanism. *IEEE Trans. Smart Grid*, 2017.

19. He, Zhang, X., Ren, S., Sun, J., Deep residual learning for image recognition, in: *Proceedings of the IEEE conference on computer vision and pattern recognition*, pp. 770–778, 2016.

20. Hermans, and Schrauwen, B., Training and analysing deep recurrent neural networks, in: *Advances in neural information processing systems*, pp. 190–198, 2013.

21. Hochreiter, and Schmidhuber, J., Long short-term memory. *Neural Comput.*, 9, 8, 1735–1780, 1997. [32] Mikolov, T., Joulin, A., Chopra, S., Mathieu, M., Ranzato, M., Learning longer memory in recurrent neural networks, arXiv preprint arXiv:1412.7753v2 [cs.NE], 2014.

22. Liu, J., Gu, Y., Kamijo, S., Joint customer pose and orientation estimation using deep neural network from surveillance camera, in: *Multimedia (ISM), 2016 IEEE International Symposium on*, IEEE, pp. 216–221, 2016.

23. Kang, and Kang, J.-W., Intrusion detection system using deep neural network for in-vehicle network security. *PLoS One*, 11, 6, e0155781, 2016.

24. Krizhevsky, Sutskever, I., Hinton, G.E., Imagenet classification with deep convolutional neural networks, in: *Advances in neural information processing systems*, pp. 1097–1105, 2012.

25. Lane, Bhattacharya, S., Georgiev, P., Forlivesi, C., Kawsar, F., An early resource characterization of deep learning on wearables, smartphones and internet-of-things devices, in: *Proceedings of the 2015 International Workshop on Internet of Things towards Applications*, ACM, pp. 7–12, 2015.

26. Li, Zhang, Y., Marsic, I., Sarcevic, A., Burd, R.S., Deep learning for rfid-based activity recognition, in: *Proceedings of the 14th ACM Conference on Embedded Network Sensor Systems*, ACM, pp. 164–175, 2016.

27. Liu, Racah, E., Correa, J., Khosrowshahi, A., Lavers, D., Kunkel, K., Wehner, M., Collins, W., Application of deep convolutional neural networks for detecting extreme weather in climate datasets. *Int'l Conf. on Advances in Big Data Analytics*, 2016.

28. Liu, Zhang, L., Liu, Q., Yin, Y., Cheng, L., Zimmermann, R., Fusion of magnetic and visual sensors for indoor localization: Infrastructure-free and more effective. *IEEE T. Multimedia*, 19, 4, 874–888, 2017.

29. Liu, Cao, Y., Luo, Y., Chen, G., Vokkarane, V., Ma, Y., Chen, S., Hou, P., A new deep learning-based food recognition system for dietary assessment on an edge computing service infrastructure. *IEEE Trans. Serv. Comput.*, 2017.

30. Lu, Zhang, J., Zhao, X., Wang, J., Dang, J., Multimodal sensory fusion for soccer robot self-localization based on long short-term memory recurrent neural network. *J. Ambient Intell. Hum. Comput.*, 7, 1–9, 2017.

31. Metz, and Collins, K., How an A.I. 'Cat-and-Mouse Game' Generates Believable Fake Photos. 180, 2018. (Accessed on 2018-02-09). [Online]. Available: https://www.nytimes.com/interactive/2018/01/02/technology/ai-generated-photos.html.

32. Mittal, Yagnik, K.B., Garg, M., Krishnan, N.C., Spotgarbage: smartphone app to detect garbage using deep learning, in: *Proceedings of the 2016 ACM International Joint Conference on Pervasive and Ubiquitous Computing*, ACM, pp. 940–945, 2016.

33. Neverova, N., Wolf, C., Lacey, G., Fridman, L., Chandra, D., Barbello, B., Taylor, G., Learning human identity from motion patterns. *IEEE Access*, 4, 1810–1820, 2016.

34. Ordónez, and Roggen, D., Deep convolutional and lstm recurrent ¯ neural networks for multimodal wearable activity recognition. *Sensors*, 16, 1, 115, 2016.

35. Werbos, P.J., Backpropagation through time: what it does and how to do it. *Proc. IEEE*, 78, 10, 1550–1560, 1990.

36. Kingma, P., Mohamed, S., Rezende, D.J., Welling, M., Semisupervised learning with deep generative models, in: *Advances in Neural Information Processing Systems*, pp. 3581–3589, 2014.

37. Pascanu, Gulcehre, C., Cho, K., Bengio, Y., How to construct deep recurrent neural networks, arXiv preprint arXiv:1312.6026v5 [cs.NE], 2013.

38. Pigou, Van Den Oord, A., Dieleman, S., Van Herreweghe, M., Dambre, J., Beyond temporal pooling: Recurrence and temporal convolutions for gesture recognition in video. *Int. J. Comput. Vision*, 6, 1–10, 2015.

39. Price, Glass, J., Chandrakasan, A., A scalable speech recognizer with deep-neural-network acoustic models and voice-activated power gating, in: *Proceedings of the IEEE ISSCC2017*, 2017.

40. Rasmus, Berglund, M., Honkala, M., Valpola, H., Raiko, T., Semi-supervised learning with ladder networks, in: *Advances in Neural Information Processing Systems*, pp. 3546–3554, 2015.

41. Shokri, and Shmatikov, V., Privacy-preserving deep learning, in: *Proceedings of the 22nd ACM SIGSAC conference on computer and communications security*, ACM, pp. 1310–1321, 2015.

42. Sladojevic, Arsenovic, M., Anderla, A., Culibrk, D., Stefanovic, D., Deep neural networks based recognition of plant diseases by leaf image classification. *Comput. Intell. Neurosci.*, 2016, 187, 2016.

43. Soto, Jentsch, M., Preuveneers, D., Ilie-Zudor, E., Ceml: Mixing and moving complex event processing and machine learning to the edge of the network for iot applications, in: *Proceedings of the 6th International Conference on the Internet of Things*, ACM, pp. 103–110, 2016.

44. Tao, Wen, Y., Hong, R., Multi-column bi-directional long shortterm memory for mobile devices-based human activity recognition. *IEEE Internet Things J.*, 2016.

45. Tokui, Oono, K., Hido, S., Clayton, J., Chainer: a next-generation open source framework for deep learning, in: *Proceedings of workshop on machine learning systems (LearningSys) in the twenty-ninth annual conference on neural information processing systems (NIPS)*, 2015.

46. Toshev, and Szegedy, C., Deeppose: Human pose estimation *via* deep neural networks, in: *Proceedings of the IEEE Conference on Computer Vision and Pattern Recognition*, 2014, pp.

47. Valpola, From neural pca to deep unsupervised learning, in: *Advances in Independent Component Analysis and Learning Machines*, pp. 143–171, 2015.

48. Wang, Gao, L., Mao, S., Pandey, S., Deepfi: Deep learning for indoor fingerprinting using channel state information, in: *2015 IEEE Wireless Communications and Networking Conference (WCNC)*, IEEE, pp. 1666–1671, 2015.

49. Yuan, Lu, Y., Wang, Z., Xue, Y., Droid-sec: deep learning in android malware detection. *ACM SIGCOMM Comput. Commun. Rev.*, 44, 4, 371–372, ACM, 2014.

50. Zhang, Liu, K., Zhang, W., Zhang, Y., Gu, J., Deep neural networks for wireless localization in indoor and outdoor environments. *Neurocomputing*, 194, 279–287, 2016.

Swarm Intelligence for Data Management and Mining Technologies to Manage and Analyze Data in IoT

Kapil Chauhan[1*] and Vishal Dutt[2†]

[1]Aryabhatta College of Engineering and Research Center, Ajmer, India
[2]Aryabhatta College, Ajmer, India

Abstract

The huge information created using the Internet of Things (IoT) are assuming of business strategy worth, and data mining calculations can be imposed to IoT to concentrate concealed data from information. In this paper, we supply an orderly technique to audit facts mining in getting to know view, device view, and alertness see, including characterization, bunching, affiliation examination, time association research, and exception investigation. We evaluated these calculations and mentioned problems and open studies problems. Finally, an endorsed significant record mining framework is proposed.

Artificial Intelligence (AI) calculations improve the capacity for huge information investigation and IoT stages to offer some incentive to every one of these market fragments. The creator sees three distinct sorts of IoT data:

1. Unstructured data.
2. Information about information (meta data).
3. Transformed information. Man-made brainpower (AI) will be helpful on the side of dealing with every one of these information types regarding distinguishing, ordering, and basic leadership.

Information mining and other computerized reasoning techniques would assume a basic job in making more astute IoTs, but with numerous difficulties.

Keywords: Data management, data mining (information), optimizing, big data, Swarm Intelligence, big data analytics

*Corresponding author: kapilajmer86@gmail.com
†Corresponding author: vishaldutt53@gmail.com

Abhishek Kumar, Pramod Singh Rathore, Vicente Garrcia Diaz and Rashmi Agrawal (eds.) Swarm Intelligence Optimization: Algorithms and Applications, (189–206) © 2021 Scrivener Publishing LLC. ISBN 978-1-119-77874-5

11.1   Introduction

Creating propels starting late and genuine moves up to Internet shows and enrolling systems have made correspondence between different contraptions less complex than whenever in ongoing memory. Internet of Things (IoT) is a blend of installed advancements including wired and remote correspondences, sensor and actuator gadgets, and the physical items associated with the Internet. One of the long-standing goals of registering is to disentangle and improve human exercises and encounters (e.g., see the dreams related with "The Computer for the 21st Century" or "Figuring for Human Experience"). IoT expects information to either speak to better administrations to clients or upgrade the IoT structure execution to achieve this insightfully. Thusly, frameworks ought to have the option to get to crude information from various assets over the system and break down this data so as to separate learning [1].

Data science is combine of different coherent fields that uses data mining, Artificial Intelligence (AI), and various techniques to find structures and new bits of information from data. These techniques consolidate a broad extent of estimations material in different zones. The route toward applying data assessment methodologies to explicit domains incorporates portraying data types, for instance, volume, collection, and speed; data models, for instance, neural frameworks, gathering and batching procedures, and applying beneficial computations that match with the data traits. By following our reviews, coming up next is determined: First, since information is created from various sources with explicit information types, it is essential to embrace or create calculations that can deal with the information qualities. Second, the extraordinary number of assets that creates information progressively is not without the issue of scale and speed [2]. At long last, finding the best information model that fits the information is one of the most significant issues, for example, acknowledgment and for better investigation of IoT information. These issues have opened countless open doors in extending new advancements.

The intriguing practices saw, in nature structure, a fascinating wellspring of motivation for taking care of true issues. Swarm Intelligence–based calculation is so significant in bio-roused calculation which spotlights on the aggregate conduct of decentralized, self-composed frameworks. It is roused by the conduct of certain creatures or bugs, for example, ants, termites, winged animals, and fishes. It is described by its eminent practices that came about because of the nearby associations among people and produce smart practices at the gathering level. A few SI-based calculations were proposed and applied effectively in a tremendous scope of issues. More up to date, few ones have been proposed and still under examination to demonstrate their efficiency. In contrast to the current surveys on SI, this audit paper accumulates exemplary and new SI-based calculations each with its extent of utilizations and reports them in a brief and succinct manner. This can push the perusers to effortlessly limit their examination by furnishing them with direct access to the related writing. Additionally, this audit may be utilized as an underlying perusing point to investigate numerous SI-based calculations and related IoT-based applications [3].

IoT targets elevating a worldview as indicated by which everything around us (for example, traffic lights or water dissemination siphons) are changed into a keen thing with the capacity of detecting, handling, conveying, as well as impelling and are constantly associated. It is an examination field in which both computerized and physical substances (for example, people, objects, and machines) are interconnected through Internet, along these lines empowering an entirely different class of utilizations an administrations. To acknowledge

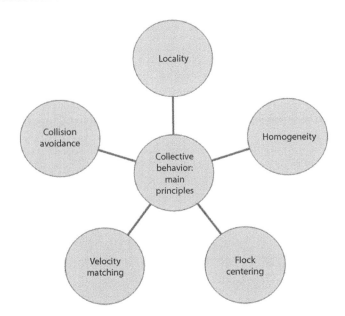

Figure 11.1 Data management and principles of analyze data.

such applications and administrations, numerous significant difficulties must be defeated in light of the fact that IoT-based frameworks are perplexing and dynamic in nature. Power and flexibility make SI an effective structure worldview for calculations that manage progressively complex issues, for example, IoT-based frameworks. In this manner, SI establishes a wellspring of motivation for IoT-based frameworks that can be demonstrated as a swarm of more straightforward gadgets or can incorporate SI-based calculations to accomplish some worldwide objectives. Along these lines, beginning from straightforward guidelines for individual practices and cooperations among people, a worldwide ideal can be accomplished at framework level. This self-association capacity is expected to adjust frameworks to fluctuating natural conditions, to scale efficiently, and to give versatile activity to the maintainability of the framework [4]. For IoT-based savvy urban communities, the exchange of information is utilized to settle on compelling choices for enormous information analytics. Data is put away and prepared on cloud servers after accumulation and collection of information from keen gadgets on IoT systems. Further, to process the enormous volume of information, there is a requirement for programmed exceptionally versatile cloud innovation, which can further improve the exhibition of the frameworks.

Writing detailed that current cloud-based information handling frameworks are not ready to fulfill the exhibition necessities of IoT applications when a low reaction time and inactivity is required. Besides, different explanations behind an enormous reaction time and dormancy are land dispersion of information and correspondence disappointments during exchange of information. Distributed computing frameworks become bottlenecked because of ceaselessly getting crude information from IoT gadgets. Consequently, a bio-propelled calculation–based enormous information examination is an elective worldview that gives a stage between figuring frameworks and IoT gadgets to process client information in a proficient way.

11.2   Information Mining Functionalities

Functionalities of data mining fuse portrayal, gathering, alliance assessment, time game plan examination, special case examination, etc.

(a) Grouping is the way toward searching a great deal of systems or limits that depict and perceive data classes or thoughts, to envision the class of articles which is class name is dark.

(b) The process of clustering separates data module without advising an acknowledged batch module.

(c) Association assessment is the exposure of alliance standards indicating property estimation conditions that as frequently as conceivable happen together in a given course of action of data.

(d) Time plan examination includes systems and procedure for determining course of action information in a way to expel huge estimations and various significance of the information/data [5].

11.2.1   Classification

Plan is basic for the director basic power. Given an article, doling it out to one of predefined target classes or classes is called game plan. The goal of strategy is to precisely foresee the objective class for each case in the information. For instance, an approach model could be utilized to see advance up-and-comers as low, medium, or high credit dangers. There are different methods to portray the information, including choice tree enlistment, format-based or rule-based pro-structures, diverse leveled assembling, neural systems, Bayesian system, and support vector machines (see Figure 11.2).

- The K-Nearest neighbor computation is involved by the Nearest Neighbor figuring which is planned to find the nearest one point of the watched article. The proposal for the KNN count is to find the K nearest centers SVM figuring is overseen learning models with related learning estimations that explore data and see structures, which relies upon genuine learning speculation. SVM produces a parallel classifier and assumed perfect disengaging hyper planes, through an incredibly non-straight mapping of the data vectors into the high-dimensional part space. SVM is commonly used in content course of action, advancing, plan affirmation, and helpful investigation [6].

11.2.2   Clustering

Packing counts separate data into noteworthy social events with the objective that models in a comparable get-together are near in common way and models in different get-together are divergent in a comparable sense. Searching for bunches incorporates independent learning. In data recuperation, consider as an example, the web list packs billions of webpage pages into different social events, for instance, news, overviews, accounts, sounds, and so forth. One direct instance of bundling issue is to hole centers into different social occasions.

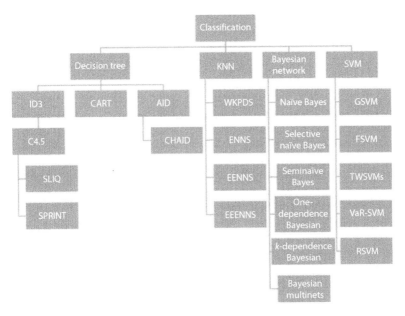

Figure 11.2 The research structure of classification.

- In solicitation to manage hard and fast data, pros change data gathering to pre-packing of things or full scale trademark characteristics, ordinary research consolidates ROCK, etc.
- Scalable gathering investigation faces adaptability issues for handling time and memory essentials.
- High dimensionality data gathering methodologies are planned to manage data with numerous qualities, join DFT [7].

11.3   Data Mining Using Ant Colony Optimization

Ants assemble things to frame stores (grouping of dead cadavers or burial grounds) saw in the types of *Pheidole Pallidula* and *Lasius Niger*. The fundamental component basic to this kind of collection wonder is a fascination between dead things intervened by the subterranean insect laborers: little bunches of things develop by pulling in laborers to store more things. It is this positive and auto-reactant criticism that prompts the arrangement of bigger and bigger bunches. The general thought for information grouping is that confined things ought to be gotten and dropped at some other area where more things of that type are available. Dai, B. *et al.* [8] proposed ACLUSTER calculation to pursue genuine insect like practices, however much as could reasonably be expected. In that sense, bio-propelled spatial change probabilities are joined into the framework, evading arbitrarily moving specialists, which urge the conveyed calculation to investigate areas clearly without premium. The system enables controlling ants to discover groups of items in a versatile manner. So as to show the conduct of ants related with various errands (dropping and grabbing objects), the utilization of mixes of various reaction edges was proposed. The learning calculation tends to the issue of information securing as far as principles from model cases by creating and keeping up the learning base using basic system, pheromone trail data grid, and utilization of accessible heuristic data. The presentation of a subterranean insect province classifier is contrasted and the notable choice tree–based C4.5 calculation as far as the prescient precision on experiments and the straightforwardness of guidelines found. [9] proposed a novel subterranean insect–based grouping strategy by joining versatile, heterogeneous ants, a period ward shipping movement, and a technique that changes the spatial installing created by the calculation into an unequivocal apportioning. Observational outcomes exhibit the capacity of insect-based bunching and arranging to naturally distinguish the quantity of groups inalienable to an information gathering and to deliver excellent arrangements. Be that as it may, the presentation of the calculation for topographic mapping was not so much excellent [10].

Web use mining endeavors to find helpful learning from the auxiliary information acquired from the communications of the clients with the Web. Web use mining has turned out to be exceptionally basic for compelling Web webpage for the board, making versatile Web locales, business and bolster administrations, personalization, arrange traffic stream investigation, etc. Abraham and Ramos proposed a subterranean insect bunching calculation to find Web utilization designs (information groups) and a direct hereditary programming way to deal with dissect the guest patterns. Exact outcomes unmistakably demonstrate that subterranean insect province bunching performs well when contrasted with a self-sorting out guide (for grouping Web use designs).

11.3.1 Enormous Information Investigation

The informational index of the huge information cannot be dealt with by run of the mill social or article arranged database, typical PCs, or conventional work area application programming. It needs tremendous parallel handling intensity of PC bunches. For the most part, the enormous information handling depends on a nonlinear framework whose conduct, in some cases, gives off an impression of being capricious or irrational. For a direct framework, it fulfills the superposition rule—the additively and homogeneity properties as underneath:

$$F(P1 + P2 + \dots) = F(P1) + F(P2) + \dots$$

$$F(aP) = aF(P) \text{ for scalar } a$$

In contrast to a straight framework, the yield of a nonlinear framework is not legitimately relative to the info. It needs to utilize the information from numerous sources with various measurements, so it would seem that turbulent and irregular; however, it is not constantly arbitrary and some shrouded learning can be found.

Five significant parts of enormous information, which start with character "V," are underscored in huge information examination. These angles incorporate volume, assortment, speed, veracity, and worth. These five angles speak to the various challenges in breaking down the enormous information [11].

The subtleties of five angles are as follows:

(i) Volume: a lot of information;
(ii) Variety: the scope of information types and sources;
(iii) Velocity: the speed of information changes;
(iv) Veracity: the vulnerability because of information irregularity, deficiency, as well as model approximations; and
(v) Value: the estimation of the bits of knowledge and advantages.

The huge information looks into expect to get the experiences or advantages from the enormous measure of progressively evolving information. The enormous sum and quickly changing information expands the hardness of issue. Notwithstanding for a straightforward sort or search activity, the issue with the huge information is considerably more troublesome than an issue with moderately little information.

The huge information investigation is likewise to consequently separate learning from tons of data. It can be understood because of the mining or preparing of the large data in storehouses for utilization of information or examples [12]. Information mining is a piece of the greater procedure of the learning revelation in databases (KDD). KDD is the way toward changing over crude information into helpful data [13]. Figure 11.1 demonstrates the general procedure of KDD. Information mining is the basic investigation venture of KDD. The strategies in information mining field could be used in enormous information examination, for instance, information grouping, information bunching, expectation, and illustrative statistic, just to give some examples [14].

11.3.2 Data Grouping

Information grouping, or named as information order, is an issue that discovers right class (or classifications) for articles (for example, information) by giving a lot of classes (subject, points) and an accumulation of informational collection. Information arrangement can be considered as a mapping f: D → C, which is from the item space D onto the arrangement of classes C. The goal of a classifier is to get an exact arrangement results or expectations with high certainty. The huge information may contain numerous sorts of unstructured or semi-organized information; now and again, this information should be changed into organized information. Every datum record with numerous properties or highlights is changed as a vector with numerous measurements. The element of the element space is equivalent to the quantity of various characteristics that show up in the informational collection. Diverse weight can be appointed to each component. The strategies for doling out loads to the highlights may shift. The least difficult is the double technique wherein the element weight is it is possible that one—if the comparing highlight is available in the information—or zero generally [15].

The information bunching investigation is a method that partitions information into a few gatherings (groups). The objective of grouping is to order items being comparative (or identified with) each other into a similar bunch, and put articles being inaccessible from one another in various groups [16].

Bunching is the way toward gathering comparable articles. From the viewpoint of AI, the bunching investigation is now and again named as solo learning. In the conceptualize improvement calculation, each arrangement is spread in the hunt space. The circulation of arrangements can be used to uncover the scenes of an issue. From the grouping investigation, the indexed lists can be acquired.

Estimation 1 Search Approach with effective way

1. discuss search space with the ultimate objective that region describes an answer (part)
2. Set issue parameters
3. while no all-out course of action do
4. search space parameters are initialize
5. while no association of swarm do
6. swarm individuals are select
7. every picked individual in swarm do
8. request space enough researching new regions while manhandling extraordinary game plans found as of not long ago, upgrading objective work
9. end for
10. The search space parameters are updated
11. end while
12. include game plan (part) and update issue variables
13. end while

Count 2 Approach of Data Organizing

1. Discuss two-dimensional component space F
2. Issue parameters are set
3. search space parameters are initialize
4. while no get together of swarm do
5. Select some swarm individuals
6. for each picked individual in swarm do
7. Update neighboring data item(s)' location(s), propelling objective work f
8. end for
9. The variables of search space is update
10. end while

11.4 Computing With Ant-Based

11.4.1 Biological Background

Ants convey not straightforwardly with one another, yet rather by implication through their condition. This roundabout correspondence, known as stigmergy, permits a province of ants with constrained memory and capacities to come to smart answers for complex issues. All the more explicitly, ants impart by dropping a substance called pheromone on their way, along these lines giving an input instrument to draw in different ants. Ways with higher pheromone levels are bound to be picked and consequently fortified. Then, again, the pheromone trail power of ways that are not picked is diminished by dissipation. These standards are outlined for finding the most brief way between a nourishment source (right) and the home (left). Two ants start from their home (left) and search for the most brief way to a nourishment source (right). At first, no pheromone is available on either trails, so there is a 50-50 possibility of picking both of the two potential ways. Assume one subterranean insect picks the lower trail and the other one the upper trail. The subterranean insect that has picked the lower (shorter) trail will have returned quicker to the home, bringing about twice as much pheromone on the lower trail as on the upper one. Subsequently, the likelihood that the following insect will pick the lower, shorter trail will be twice as high, bringing about more pheromone; in this way, more ants will pick this trail, until inevitably (nearly) all ants will pursue the shorter way.

The general advances are outlined in the nonexclusive ACO meta-heuristic as appeared in Algorithm.

Algorithm: ACO Meta-heuristic

    a. Initialize variable, initialize pheromone trails
    b. while termination condition not met do
    c. create an optimal results
    d. apply local search optional
    e. update pheromones
    f. end while

11.5 Related Work

There are not many works introducing regular AI and information mining rules that have been utilized in IoT situations. This is use to various grouping, bunching, and continuous example digging determining for the IoT foundation and administrations. In any case, that work did not consider DL that draws near, which is the focal point of our study. Additionally, their emphasis is for the most part on disconnected information mining, while we likewise think about learning and digging for both ongoing (i.e., quick) and enormous information examination. In this way, the user determining AI techniques in the important parts of wireless sensor network, for example, directing, limitation, and grouping, just as nonpractical necessities, for example, security and nature of administration. They assessed a few calculations in administered, unaided, and support learning draws near. The main aim centers around the framework of WSN (which is one potential foundation for executing IoT applications), while our work is not reliant on the wellsprings of information and spreads a wide scope of IoT applications and administrations. Additionally, the focal point of was on conventional AI strategies, while this article centers around cutting edge and deep learning procedures. At long last, Fadlullah *et al.* tended to deep learning approaches in system traffic control frameworks. While this work fundamentally centers around the foundation of system, it varies from our work that spotlights on the utilization of deep learning in IoT applications. In the past, particularly those dealing with the IoT, Qiu *et al.* investigated a few customary AI systems alongside a few propelled strategies which are use deep learning for handling basic enormous information. In explicit, they featured the association of various AI systems with sign preparing advances to process and examine auspicious huge information applications [17].

11.6 Contributions

We know that this paper anticipated IoT researchers and creators who need to fabricate assessment, AI structures, and learning plans over their IoT establishment, using the rising DL AI that moves close. The responsibilities of that mechanism can be dense as seeks after:

- In solicitation to get deep learning strategy in the IoT natural frameworks, we perceive the important factor of IoT information.
- We analyze some related work in the composing that have kept an eye on AI for IoT, and we review the state-of-the-craftsmanship deep learning procedures and their real nature in the IoT space both for gigantic data and spilling data assessment.
- A wide extent of IoT applications that have utilized deep learning in their interesting condition. We also give a relationship and a standard for using different sorts of DNN in the diverse IoT regions and applications.
- We analyze the continuous strategies and advances for sending deep learning on all degrees of IoT dynamic framework from resource constrained contraptions to the cloudiness and the cloud.
- The main focus is troubles and upcoming research course for the viable and profitable meeting of deep learning and IoT device [18].

11.7 SI in Enormous Information Examination

The huge data determination is another exploration scope of data preparing; be that as it may, the focus of enormous information investigation has been contemplated in other research fields for quite a long time under an alternate title. The qualities of the huge information examination are condensed into a few words with introductory "V," which are volume, assortment, speed, veracity, and worth. These complexities are an accumulation of various research issues that are existed for a considerable length of time. Relating to the SI, the volume and the assortment mean huge scale and high-dimensional information; the speed indicates that data and information are quickly changing, similar to an enhancement issue in powerful condition; the veracity implies that information are conflicting or potentially deficient, similar to a streamlining issue with commotion or guess; and the worth is the goal of the huge information examination, similar to the wellness or target work in an advancement issue. The huge information examination is an expansion of information mining methods on a lot of information. Extracting of data has been a famous scholarly point in software engineering and measurements for a considerable length of time [19].

11.7.1   Handling Enormous Measure of Information

The enormous data examination requires a brisk mining for a tremendous scope instructive assortment, i.e., the massive proportion of data should be set up in a limited chance to reveal supportive information. As the figuring power improves, the more volume of data can be readied. The more data are recouped and taken care of, the better cognizance of issues can be gotten. The scientific issue can be demonstrated as an advancement issue. The SI calculations—or all the more extensively, the transformative calculations—are a pursuit procedure dependent on the past encounters. To uncover learning from an enormous volume of information inside the huge information setting, the hunt scopes of the tackled issue must be augmented and even reached out to the outrageous.

A snappy sweep is basic to require care of the difficulty with huge informational indexes. The SI calculations are likewise systems hooked in to the inspecting of the pursuit space. Through the meta-heuristics rules, information tests are browsed the monstrous information space. From these delegate information tests, the difficulty structure might be gotten. In light of the SI, we could locate a sufficient arrangement with a high search speed to tackle the difficulty with a huge volume of data [20].

11.7.2   Handling Multidimensional Information

When all is claimed in done, the development focus searching the simplest accessible arrangement (s) for a given issue inside suitable time, and therefore, the issue may have a couple of or various ideal arrangements, of which many are neighborhood ideal arrangements. Regularly, the difficulty will end up to be increasingly troublesome with the event of the number of things and goals. Extraordinarily, issues with a huge number of things, e.g., in more than thousand factors, are named as huge scale issues.

Numerous enhancement techniques handle the improper effects of the scourge of dimensionality, which results that their presentation weakens rapidly as the component of the hunt space expands.

The course of action space of an issue normally increases exponentially with the issue estimation, and in this way, continuously beneficial request systems are required to explore each promising region inside a given time spending plan. The formative figuring or SI relies upon the correspondence of a social affair of courses of action. The promising areas or the location of issues are very difficult to reveal by little game plan tests (differentiated and the amount of each and every conceivable course of action) [21].

The attributes of an issue may likewise change with the scale. The issue will turn out to be increasingly troublesome and complex when the measurement increments. Rosenbrock's capacity, for example, is unimodal for two-dimensional issues, however progresses toward becoming multimodal for higher dimensional issues. Due to such an exacerbating of the highlights of an improvement issue coming about because of an expansion in scale, a formerly fruitful hunt system may never again be fit for finding an ideal arrangement. Luckily, an inexact outcome with a rapid might be superior to a precise 653 Big information investigation with SI downloaded by Shaanxi Normal University at 22:09 18 May 2017 (PT) result with a late speed. The SI calculations can locate an adequate arrangement quickly, which is the quality of the SI in taking care of the enormous information investigation issues [22].

11.8 Requirements and Characteristics of IoT Data

IoT information can be spilled always or gathered as a wellspring of immense information/data. Spouting data implies the data made or got inside little between times of time and ought to be immediately analyzed to evacuate brief encounters or possibly choose speedy decisions. Tremendous data insinuates monstrous datasets that the normally used gear and programming stages are not prepared to store, manage, procedure, and separate. Finally, two procedures should be managed differently since their necessities for intelligent response are not the equal. Learning from huge data assessment can be passed on following a couple of long stretches of data age; anyway, understanding from spouting data examination should be set up in an extent of couple of a few milliseconds to couple of minutes. Data blend and sharing expect a fundamental activity in making all inclusive conditions subject to IoT information. This activity is dynamically fundamental for time-delicate IoT task where a helpful mix of data is relied upon to bring all bits of data together for assessment and along these lines giving strong and definite huge bits of information [23].

11.8.1 IoT Quick and Gushing Information

In this scenario, spilling data assessment that can be, in a general sense, passed on first class enlisting structures was proposed. The spouting information assessment on such frameworks relies upon data parallelism and unfaltering planning. By parallel entity/information, a gigantic dataset is allotted into a couple of more diminutive datasets, on which parallel assessment are played out at the same time. Enduring getting ready implies carrying a little bunch of data to be dealt with quickly in a pipeline of computation assignments. In spite of the way that these frameworks reduce time inactivity to reestablish a response from the spilling data methodical structure, they are not the best response for time-stringent IoT applications. By bringing spouting data examination closer to the wellspring of data (i.e., IoT devices or edge devices), the prerequisite for data parallelism and continuous taking care of small amount data as the size of the data in the source empowers it to be arranged rapidly. Regardless, expediting fast examination IoT contraptions exhibits its own special challenges, for instance, scope of figuring, storing, and control resources at the wellspring of data [24].

11.8.2 IoT Big Information

IoT is notable to be one of the real wellsprings of huge information, as it depends on interfacing a colossal number of keen gadgets to the Internet to report their much of the time caught status of their surroundings. Perceiving and removing important examples from tremendous crude info information is the center utility of enormous information examination as it brings about more significant levels of bits of knowledge for basic leadership and pattern expectation. Consequently, removing these experiences and information from the huge information is of outrageous significance to numerous organizations, since it empowers them to increase upper hands. In sociologies, Hilbert thinks about the effect of huge information examination to that of the development of the telescope and magnifying lens for space science and science, individually. A few works have depicted the general highlights of huge information from various viewpoints as far as volume, speed, and assortment.

Be that as it may, we receive the general meaning of huge information to portray the IoT huge information through coming up with the next "6V's" highlights [25].

- Volume: It is a deciding element to consider a dataset as large information or customary huge/exceptionally enormous information. The amount of produced information utilizing IoT gadgets is substantially more than previously and plainly fits this component.
- Velocity: The pace of IoT huge information generation and preparing is sufficiently high to help the accessibility of huge information progressively. This legitimizes the requirements for cutting edge devices and advances for investigation to effectively work given this high pace of information generation.
- Variety: The huge information comes in various structures and types. It might comprise of organized, semi-organized, and unstructured information. A wide assortment of information types might be created by IoT, for example, content, sound, video, tangible information, etc.
- Variability: This property alludes to the various paces of information stream. Contingent upon the idea of IoT applications, various information producing segments may have conflicting information streams. Besides, it is feasible for an information source to have various paces of information burden dependent on explicit occasions. For instance, a stopping administration application that uses IoT sensors may have a pinnacle information load in times of heavy traffic.
- Value: Value is the change of huge information to helpful data and bits of knowledge that carry upper hand to associations. An information esteem exceptionally relies upon both the basic procedures/administrations and how information is dealt with. For instance, a specific application (e.g., therapeutic essential sign checking) may need to catch all sensor information, while a climate gauge administration may require simply irregular examples of information from its sensors. As another model, a Visa supplier may need to keep information for a particular timeframe and dispose of them from that point.

Performing examination over ceaseless information streams is regularly alluded to as stream preparing or, in some cases, complex occasion handling in the writing [26].

11.9   Conclusion

The compilation of difficult data is a big aspect. It has pulled in a regularly expanding number of contemplations starting now. A huge segment of the huge data asks about focus on the monstrous proportion of data, in any case, communicate with sensitive information and the different goals are furthermore huge in dealing with immense data issues. The colossal data examination issue has various difficulties, which have been investigated autonomously for a long time with different names, for instance, the sensitive information, aspect of heterogeneous data, dynamic issues, just to give a few models. In view of the properties of immense data issues, it is difficult to use some "independent and vanquish" frameworks to deal with these issues. The SI count is such a figuring and information procedure, which have gotten incredible execution on the request and improvement issues, especially for the issues that the standard system cannot light up or are very difficult to handle. This paper centers on the connection between colossal data assessment, and SI frameworks are discussed. The uses of multitude Intelligence in the colossal data assessment and the tremendous data examination ways in Swarm Intelligence are destitute down. The gigantic data assessment issues are detached into four segments: dealing with a great deal of data, managing high-dimensional data, dealing with dynamical data, and multi-target improvement. Most certifiable gigantic data issues can be shown as a colossal scale, dynamical, and multi-target issues. With the conceivable cross-treatment of the two fields of enormous information investigation and the SI, we examined a case of a true product steering issue in the port. The calculation has been utilized to demonstrate the attainability of the Swarm Intelligence strategies. This paper is the initial phase in our exploration to use the SI calculation to a major information examination issue. Because of the multifaceted nature of the genuine item directing frameworks in the port, the task is a progressing one. We just got a huge static informational index to show the genuine framework and to confirm the pursuit capacity of the Swarm Intelligence calculation. The underlying outcomes have demonstrated that the unfilled stacking rate is fundamentally diminished contrasted and the current calculation. In any case, it is hard to supplant the present sub-framework with our calculation. The primary hindrance is that the test informational collection is a static one; however, the information is progressively powerful and stochastic in true framework (for example, the vehicles may have a few mishaps). The subsequent impediment is that the present port framework is huge and complex. The port framework has numerous assignments and distinctive mechanical procedures. To maintain a strategic distance from tumult in the port framework, it might require many testing work to use another strategy on the genuine framework. In this examination, we introduced a correlation of various PSO strategies on benchmark issues. Our future research will think about the presentation of our strategy and fit it in a powerful genuine framework. Another intriguing occurrence is the financial burden dispatch issue in the arrangement and plan of current power framework. With enormous measure of information and the non-curved/non-smooth nature of target capacities and additionally imperatives, SI calculations can take care of such issues viably. These models could be comprehended as cutting edge IT or information preparing advancements; be that as it may, their fundamental system could be the SI calculations. With the uses of the SI, increasingly fast and powerful strategies can be intended to take care of enormous information issues [27].

References

1. Baldi, Autoencoders, unsupervised learning, and deep architectures. *ICML unsupervised and transfer learning*, vol. 27, no. 37–50, p. 1, 2012.
2. Kunhoth, J., Karkar, A., Al-Maadeed, S. *et al.* Indoor positioning and wayfinding systems: A survey. *Hum. Cent. Comput. Inf. Sci.*, 10, 18, 2020. https://doi.org/10.1186/s13673-020-00222-0
3. Bengio, *et al.*, Learning deep architectures for AI. *Found. Trends R Mach. Learn.*, 2, 1, 1–127, 2009.

4. Borkowski, Schulte, S., Hochreiner, C., Predicting cloud resource utilization, in: *Proceedings of the 9th International Conference on Utility and Cloud Computing*, ACM, pp. 37–42, 2016.

5. Bottou, Large-scale machine learning with stochastic gradient descent, in: *Proceedings of COMPSTAT'2010*, Springer, pp. 177–186, 2010.

6. Parker, D. B., Learning-logic (Invention Report S81-64, File I). Stanford, CA: Office of Technology Licensing, Stanford University, 1982.

7. Bastien, F., Lamblin, P., Pascanu, R., Bergstra, J., Goodfellow, I.J., Bergeron, A., Bouchard, N., Bengio, Y., Theano: new features and speed improvements. Deep Learning and Unsupervised Feature Learning NIPS 2012 Workshop, 2012.

8. Dai, B., Fidler, S., Urtasun, R., Lin, D., Towards Diverse and Natural Image Descriptions *via* a Conditional GAN, in: *Proceedings of the IEEE Conference on Computer Vision and Pattern Recognition*, pp. 2970–2979, 2017.

9. Deng, A tutorial survey of architectures, algorithms, and applications for deep learning. *APSIPA Trans. Signal Inf. Process.*, 3, 1–29, 2014.

10. Kingma, D.P. and Welling, M., Auto-encoding variational Bayes. ICLR, 201

11. Kahou, E., Bouthillier, X., Lamblin, P., Gulcehre, C., Michalski, V., Konda, K., Jean, S., Froumenty, P., Dauphin, Y., Boulanger Lewandowski, N. *et al.*, Emonets: Multimodal deep learning approaches for emotion recognition in video. *J. Multimodal User Interfaces*, 10, 2, 99–111, 2016.

12. Rumelhart, E., Hinton, G.E., Williams, R.J., Learning representations by back-propagating errors. *Nature*, 323, 6088, 533, 1986.

13. Fragkiadaki, Levine, S., Felsen, P., Malik, J., Recurrent network models for human dynamics, in: *Proceedings of the IEEE International Conference on Computer Vision*, pp. 4346–4354, 2015.

14. Gantz and D. Reinsel, The digital universe in 2020: Big data, bigger digital shadows, and biggest growth in the far east, IDC iView: IDC Analyze the future, no. 2012, pp. 1–16, 2007.

15. Goodfellow, Pouget-Abadie, J., Mirza, M., Xu, B., Warde-Farley, D., Ozair, S., Courville, A., Bengio, Y., Generative adversarial nets, in: *Advances in Neural Information Processing Systems*, pp. 2672–2680, 2014.

16. Gu, Chen, Y., Liu, J., Jiang, X., Semi-supervised deep extreme learning machine for wi-fi based localization. *Neurocomputing*, 166, 282–293, 2015.

17. Yu, D., Huang, X., Wang, H., Cui, Y., Short-Term Solar Flare Prediction Using a Sequential Supervised Learning Method. *Solar Physicals*, 91 -105, 2009.

18. He, Zhang, X., Ren, S., Sun, J., Deep residual learning for image recognition, in: *Proceedings of the IEEE conference on computer vision and pattern recognition*, pp. 770–778, 2016.

19. Hermans, and Schrauwen, B., Training and analysing deep recurrent neural networks, in: *Advances in neural information processing systems*, pp. 190–198, 2013.

20. Hochreiter, and Schmidhuber, J., Long short-term memory. *Neural Comput.*, 9, 8, 1735–1780, 1997. [32] Mikolov, T., Joulin, A., Chopra, S., Mathieu, M., Ranzato, M., Learning longer memory in recurrent neural networks," arXiv preprint arXiv:1412.7753v2 [cs.NE], 2014.

21. Liu, J., Gu, Y., Kamijo, S., Joint customer pose and orientation estimation using deep neural network from surveillance camera, in: *Multimedia (ISM), 2016 IEEE International Symposium on*, IEEE, pp. 216–221, 2016.

22. Kang, and Kang, J.-W., Intrusion detection system using deep neural network for in-vehicle network security. *PLoS One*, 11, 6, e0155781, 2016.

23. Krizhevsky, Sutskever, I., Hinton, G.E., Imagenet classification with deep convolutional neural networks, in: *Advances in neural information processing systems*, pp. 1097–1105, 2012.

24. Lane, Bhattacharya, S., Georgiev, P., Forlivesi, C., Kawsar, F., An early resource characterization of deep learning on wearables, smartphones and internet-of-things devices, in: *Proceedings of*

the 2015 *International Workshop on Internet of Things towards Applications*, ACM, pp. 7–12, 2015.

25. Li, Zhang, Y., Marsic, I., Sarcevic, A., Burd, R.S., Deep learning for rfid-based activity recognition, in: *Proceedings of the 14th ACM Conference on Embedded Network Sensor Systems*, ACM, pp. 164–175, 2016.

26. Liu, Racah, E., Correa, J., Khosrowshahi, A., Lavers, D., Kunkel, K., Wehner, M., Collins, W., Application of deep convolutional neural networks for detecting extreme weather in climate datasets. *Int'l Conf. on Advances in Big Data Analytics*, 2016.

27. Liu, Zhang, L., Liu, Q., Yin, Y., Cheng, L., Zimmermann, R., Fusion of magnetic and visual sensors for indoor localization: Infrastructure-free and more effective. *IEEE T. Multimedia*, 19, 4, 874–888, 2017.

28. Desai, A. and Lee, D.J., Visual odometry drift reduction using SYBA descriptor and feature transformation. *IEEE Trans. Intell. Transp. Syst.*, 17, 1839–1851, 2016.

29. Conti, F., Pullini, A., Benini, L., rain-inspired classroom occupancy monitoring on a low-power mobile platform in: *Proceedings of the IEEE Conference on Computer Vision and Pattern Recognition Workshops*, 2014, pp. 610–615.

30. Alexe, B., Deselaers, T., Ferrari, V., What is an object?, in: *Proceedings of the IEEE Conference on Computer Vision and Pattern Recognition*, 2010.

31. Neverova, N., Wolf, C., Lacey, G., Fridman, L., Chandra, D., Barbello, B., Taylor, G., Learning human identity from motion patterns. *IEEE Access*, 4, 1810–1820, 2016.

32. Ordóñez, and Roggen, D., Deep convolutional and lstm recurrent ‾ neural networks for multimodal wearable activity recognition. *Sensors*, 16, 1, 115, 2016.

33. Werbos, P.J., Backpropagation through time: what it does and how to do it. *Proc. IEEE*, 78, 10, 1550–1560, 1990.

34. Kingma, P., Mohamed, S., Rezende, D.J., Welling, M., Semisupervised learning with deep generative models, in: *Advances in Neural Information Processing Systems*, pp. 3581–3589, 2014.

35. El Hihi, S. and Bengio, Y., Hierarchical recurrent neural networks for long-term dependencies. In NIPS 8. MIT Press, 1996.

36. Price, Glass, J., Chandrakasan, A., A scalable speech recognizer with deep-neural-network acoustic models and voice-activated power gating, in: *Proceedings of the IEEE ISSCC2017*, 2017.

37. Rasmus, Berglund, M., Honkala, M., Valpola, H., Raiko, T., Semi-supervised learning with ladder networks, in: *Advances in Neural Information Processing Systems*, pp. 3546–3554, 2015.

38. Shokri, and Shmatikov, V., Privacy-preserving deep learning, in: *Proceedings of the 22nd ACM SIGSAC conference on computer and communications security*, ACM, pp. 1310–1321, 2015.

39. Soto, Jentsch, M., Preuveneers, D., Ilie-Zudor, E., Ceml: Mixing and moving complex event processing and machine learning to the edge of the network for iot applications, in: *Proceedings of the 6th International Conference on the Internet of Things*, ACM, pp. 103–110, 2016.

40. Tao, D., Wen, Y., Hong, R., Multicolumn bidirectional long shortterm memory for mobile devices-based human activity recognition. *IEEE Internet of Things Journal*, 3, 6, 2016.

41. Tokui, Oono, K., Hido, S., Clayton, J., Chainer: a next-generation open source framework for deep learning, in: *Proceedings of workshop on machine learning systems (LearningSys) in the twenty-ninth annual conference on neural information processing systems (NIPS)*, 2015.

42. Toshev, and Szegedy, C., Deeppose: Human pose estimation *via* deep neural networks, in: *Proceedings of the IEEE Conference on Computer Vision and Pattern Recognition*, 2014, pp.

43. Valpola, From neural pca to deep unsupervised learning. *Advances in Independent Component Analysis and Learning Machines*, pp. 143–171, 2015.

44. Wang, Gao, L., Mao, S., Pandey, S., Deepfi: Deep learning for indoor fingerprinting using channel state information, in: *2015 IEEE Wireless Communications and Networking Conference (WCNC)*, IEEE, pp. 1666–1671, 2015.

45. Zhou, y. and Jiang, X., Dissecting android malware: characterization and evolution. In IEEE S&P'12, pages 95–109, 2012.

12

Swarm Intelligence–Based Energy-Efficient Clustering Algorithms for WSN: Overview of Algorithms, Analysis, and Applications

Devika G.[1]*, Ramesh D.[2] and Asha Gowda Karegowda[3]

[1]*Department of CSE, SAHE Tumakuru, Tumakuru, Karnataka, India*
[2]*Department of MCA Associate Prof., Department of MCA Sri Siddhartha Institute of Technology Tumakuru, Tumakuru, Karnataka, India*
[3]*Department of MCA, Siddaganga Institute of Technology, Tumakuru, Karnataka, India*

Abstract

The industrial and scientific communities have witnessed an amplified interest for wireless sensor networks (WSNs) from few years concerning much on potential application under various domains. However, WSN has got corner of attention concerning mainly with factor of energy, in addition to assuring non-redundant data without compromising with QoS and transmission time. This shortcoming can be rectified with adaptation of energy-efficient strategies to facilitate extension of WSN lifetime with avoidance of unnecessary delays as much as possible. Among the various approaches for optimizing energy consumption, clustering techniques stand ahead among all sensor networks. Clustering technique influences strongly with greater work on energy conservation with its architectural design. One part of artificial intelligence is Swarm Intelligence (SI) which is inspired and designed looking on to different physical and chemical properties of multi-agents to solve optimization problems. The solution for WSN optimization problems based on SI clustering models are proving powerful, effective, and simple in order to improve lifetime of WSN. This chapter answers more frequent SI questions what, why, how, and where SI can be applied so as to optimize n/w energy utilization. The chapter covers over almost 60+ SI algorithms applications in brief. Furthermore, various issues of WSN clustering and WSN services are briefed for the sake of completeness. The major contribution is the survey of various SI techniques applied for WSN, in particular, for cluster formation and CH selection. The study reveals that among the various SI algorithms, PSO has been extensively applied for WSN cluster formation followed by use of ABC, CS, BFO, and ACO. We have categorized SI algorithms based on social behavior of insect, bacteria, bird, fish, animal, and others, among which, our survey (covering papers from 2000 to 2019) unfolds that almost 50% work is contributed by insects based SI. There is still lot of scope to explore new SI-based WSN in particular for cluster formation.

Keywords: Wireless sensor networks, lifetime, artificial intelligence, swarm intelligence, optimization, clustering techniques

---

Corresponding author: sgdevika@gmail.com

Abhishek Kumar, Pramod Singh Rathore, Vicente Garrcia Diaz and Rashmi Agrawal (eds.) Swarm Intelligence Optimization: Algorithms and Applications, (207–262) © 2021 Scrivener Publishing LLC. ISBN 978-1-119-77874-5

12.1 Introduction

One of the areas of artificial intelligence is Swarm Intelligence (SI) is a budding technology initiated and developed as of social behavior similar to biological systems like ants, bees, birds, fish, monkeys, etc. [1]. In 1989, Gerardo Beni and Jing Wang explained SI applicability in robotic system similar to cellular system (4, wiki). Different SI algorithm has different rules representation to communicate, based on artificial network of agents/particles [2]. In this sense, SI plays a pivotal role in achieving coordination among all agents/particles. Swarm consists of or designs huge collection of same category species/agents which may interact among them locally or globally but most of SI algorithms look for local concern in view of global environment conducts [3]. In recent years, swarm algorithms are being developed as independent nature-inspired division. The productivity of population-based algorithms is alertness, easy accessibility, smart, low cost, and adaptable to different natured problems from simple to complex [4]. Collectively going on with all SI features tries to resolve any problem through models of social agents/swarm to name few instances similar to gathering of honey by bee, collective actions of ants, walk of wolf, communication among birds, and others [5]. In all on going activities, swarm will exchange messages via direct or through another agent [6].

Normally, WSN can sense, communicate, and perform some fundamental tasks as soon as data are collected at nodes [7]. WSNs are pool of small-sized low-cost computational nodes used to estimate or access local or remote environmental characteristics or any assigned parametric factors that need to be conveyed for appropriate processing for required location/devices [8, 9]. Technological advancement has provided increased ability to sensors, made available at low cost, and estimate different parameters remotely as of sensing live with minimized work and errors. In spite of many improvements, WSNs are required to be operated in an energy-efficient manner as being deployment in human unattended environments [10–12]. WSN domain motivates researchers to make up their minds through dire need in data collection and processing then forth according to problem under concern [13–15]. Routing problem of WSN expect solution not only for one layer but for multiple and multi-layer rather than only for single or optimized route between nodes. WSN routing problem is better solved with application of SI. The different or variable needs of network paradigms can be easily manageable with application of SI algorithms. SI algorithms can generate similar result for passive or active network with any topologies and results are not affected with traffic delay or variations. Algorithms tries to optimize route if it is not optimized at least balance in network will happen.

The main principles of SI include the following: i) Awareness: SI members will have complete knowledge regarding its surrounding; ii) Autonomy: each member are autonomous in their work; iii) Solidarity: the members will work in coordinated manner; iv) expandability: more provision to include new members; and v) Resiliency: they have ability to operate under any conditions. These key principles of SI assist WSN in many key operations: clustering, scheduling, optimization, and fault tolerance. This chapter mainly concentrates on the SI for WSN in cluster formation which includes cluster head selection and routing so as to escalate the network lifespan.

12.1.1   Scope of Work

During 2018–2030, SI is predicted to generate $447.5 million by global SI at a CAGR rate of 40.9%. The global wireless sensor network (WSN) market size was 50 million US$ and is expected to reach 70 million US$ by the end of 2025, with CAGR of 14% throughput forecast period during 2019–2025 by US watch market survey report (MarketFuture) in 2018 and highest growth rate is expected in regions of Asia-Pacific. McKinsey's report on global economic impact of sensor network [16] estimates a continuous growth of $2.7 to $6.2 trillion in 2025. Indeed, SI will have effects on jobs and labor force since many of these will be taken care by WSN applications which will operate independent of human intervention. The increase in usage of sensors and WSN also create increased demand for SI-based algorithms, products, platforms, and tasks. In McKinsey's report under section Knowledge work automation economic impact of intelligence is described. Devices with sensors can be applied to perform tasks that rely on analysis, judgment, and creative problem solving for real-time. This chapter will focus on usage of cluster-based techniques in WSN and studies on SI-based improvement in resource utilization with the incorporation of clustering techniques in WSN under different applications. The survey will focus on SI-based WSN clustering, and henceforth, other aspects of SI such as fault tolerance and security issues are concealed.

12.1.2   Related Works

Top among many issues of WSN is routing, which is mainly responsible for deciding the network longevity. Umpteen numbers of researchers have worked in this direction. In [17], WSN routing protocols state of the art and process from path identification to data forwarding is analyzed for research works in 1999–2000. The methods identified for compassion were all based on classical routing techniques. The review process similar to [17] but with quite lot more routing protocols were surveyed in [18, 19]. The surveyed routing protocols are once again fall to classical category. The routing protocols up to 2004 were compared and presented structurally good in [20]. Creamy routing protocols among those presented in [20] are reviewed in detail in [21] in the very same year. [22] is a recent work that carried on in similar direction concerning only to classical routing protocols, and critical and application-based review is presented. Continuing with survey work in [23], both classical and bio-inspired protocols were reviewed. Classical routing algorithms were given prominence compared to bio-inspired algorithms. Comparisons of algorithms were restricted to design. In same trend, most recent survey work is [24], which includes swarm routing techniques for WSN. Performance merits for WSN routing if switching over to swarm techniques from classical routing techniques are presented. Simulation environment and application-related issued of WSN were included. Energy-efficient protocols classical and bio-inspired protocols of only promising routing protocols were reviewed in [25]. Pure survey work for only SI routing protocols was initially included in [26]. Comparison of protocols was only based on simulation environment and design. Work from [27] discusses few commonly applied SI algorithms but comparison is not covered. Survey work of [28] tries to connect SI and WSN. Most of WSN operational areas were covered under review and future directions stated to concentrate more on improving performance of WSN routing and data processing tasks of WSN. Review of [29] was restricted only for ant-based approaches in

Table 12.1 Summarization of survey works on routing protocols in WSN.

Author	Key survey concept	Year	Ref. no.
Akyildiz *et al.*	Conventional Routing	2002	[17]
Karaki and Kamal	Conventional Routing	2004	[18]
Akkaya and Younis	Conventional Routing	2005	[19]
Yang and Mohammed	Conventional Routing	2005	[20]
Singh *et al.*	Conventional Routing	2010	[21]
Celik *et al.*	Swarm Intelligence Routing	2010	[22]
Villalba *et al.*	Conventional Routing	2010	[23]
Baranidharam *et al.*	Conventional Routing	2010	[24]
Saleem *et al.*	Swarm Intelligence Routing	2011	[25]
Hazem and Janice	Swarm Intelligence Routing	2012	[26]
M Vergin & R Ganeshan	Swarm Intelligence Routing	2015	[27]
T Gui *et al.*	Swarm Intelligence Routing	2016	[28]
Tina *et al.*	Swarm Intelligence Routing	2016	[29]
SR Shinge *et al.*	Swarm Intelligence Routing	2019	[30]
D W Sambo *et al.*	Swarm Intelligence Routing	2019	[31]

increase efficiency of WSN. More elaborate work in review process includes in [30, 31] for meta-based optimization algorithms of WSN. Even though most of survey works state all classical and SI routing protocols for WSN were included, they only refine works present during those time or might not review covering all aspects. Most of the review works are completely narrow downed to one topic are survey in wide range missing critical review features. Hence, there is need to review SI algorithms only for routing in WSN. Table 12.1 highlights the contribution of few of research scholars with the key survey concept.

12.1.3   Challenges in WSNs

The unique challenges in WSN feature from inherent design of sensor network and its corresponding applied fields. Sensor-specific applications are having increased impact on different issues from design to practical deployment significantly. Most of sensors usage is related to applications of real-time and hence have different design issues and requirements. The complexity will also increase in WSN, and hence, challenges will also be more; thus, there is a requirement to answer these challenges of WSN. Currently, most works are considered part of application requirements to increase performance in different in different networks of sensor.

The key stimulating aspects of sensor networks are overviewed below.

- Energy source limitations: Prominent challenge in WSN is to minimize energy consumption of sensor nodes. Majority of applications related to WSN are either real-time or remote access in nature and requires size to be very less. Due to these application requirements, the battery size is also very less in sensor as well in most cases often replacement or recharge option cannot be provided for nodes of WSN [31]. For instance, if sensors like Smart dust mote or MicaZ or Mica2 are powered with very less capacity of 33 mAh and 1400 to 3400 mAh battery [32], respectively. Power issues of WSN have led to different research biases from software to hardware related to WSN.

- Redundancy management: Applications of WSN opt for similar natured sensors being deployed within networks and also sensor nodes are required to carry on work under limited energy. Sensors placed nearby collect or in on time messages forwarded from upper placed nodes used to send redundant data. WSN data redundancy hence requires processing within to once again minimize usage of energy, as in most cases, sensors are placed in uninterruptable regions of interest. Another possible redundancy handling is by avoiding link failure or through handling disruptions in communication links.

- Ensuring data aggregation: Data is common component of WSN as sensing is main aim. Loss or overlap in data situations has to be handled in WSN. All problems of data related issues more energy to overcome sensor from that situation. Best solution to avoid all possible data issues or problems is to process data locally which may not be possible always. Data need to be at minimum as much as possible while forwarding as it requires less energy to forward. The data size is proportional to energy consumption as can be seen in processors executing instructions. Aggregation techniques can be applied at different levels by grouping sensors possible to reduce through basic operations.

- Routing: Sensors will not have IDs as can be the case of nodes of physical network. Nodes are accessed in data centric class no need to use unique IDs. Data sensed by nodes will be communicated to BS at regular intervals or on call from the BS. If either of the case is chosen, path identification is basic step. All sensors are involved in similar task for a given application; hence, data can be reduced and processed locally through basic operation or via query model. Sensor operations are data centric; hence, traditional or MANETs routing techniques are not best choice. Routing protocol and data aggregation support for processing and collaboration of data in locally considering all neighborhood nodes.

- Non-distributed algorithms: Protocols are of distributed in nature. They cannot sustain any delay, overhead, collection of information for all collection, or dissemination affects overall performance. As nodes are more populated and limited in resources non-distributed algorithms with central controlled algorithms are of best choice. Data and other resources require attention while designing algorithms.

- Scalability: WSN and its applications will vary in dimension from on to another. In all such cases, processing will remain constant in spite of size variation. The sensing and data processing activities also vary from applications and duration of task being carried on. All protocols of WSN hence required to be flexible enough to perform similarly according to network size or any other variations.

- Management of faults: Failures are common issue of any application, for it, WSN is not exception. Sensors data can be misinterpret leading to failure to fault of system. Failure in link or data or device will finally lead to failure of system. Catastrophic nature of failure cause overall system affected from deployment to data exchange operation of complete system. Hence, to guarantee normal operation of sensor network, fault avoidance is better option.

- Self-configuration: Because of inherent feature and application requirement of WSN, all nodes to be self-regulating and self-operational independent of any human or device being intervened to function it. Hence, operations nearly to be automated.

- Communication overhead: WSN sensors capable of handling very less computations under limited storage environment. The messages being exchanged need also be at minimum in order to balance network energy. All protocols of different operations hence need to put on eye to this features before developed. Nodes are capable to sense only limited region so hardware limitations also to be considered in design. The computations support from hardware side is also minimal.

- Selection of communicational methodology: WSN requires either direct communication with BS or indirect based on applicational requirement and size of the application under consideration. However, if it use, direct or indirect communication performance should not alter.

- Efficient and balance use of energy: Energy is key factor in sensor as all operations require energy, but which is not unlimited. Sensor required to sense, process, manage, store, and forward data to different nodes and zoned of WSN. The deployment of sensors should be in such a way as to support all nodes to use energy in efficient and balanced way. Operations of sensors balance usage of energy between them in order to prolong network life time of WSN. Routing is one more suitable option to make energy usage in better way. If energy is balance between operations in individual sensor and balance of energy using connectivity merely solve the problem. Hence, energy usage in efficient manner and balanced manner will make WSN to carry out its task for longer time.

- QoS: All application-specific devices or techniques should look for parameters of service such as quality of data being processed in optimized manner and others. Delay has to be at minimum in all carried-out operations as much as possible from one sensor to another. Identification of best path to BS will improve all QoS parameters to certain extent. Other QoS constraints such as extendibility, reliability, and security should be considered as challenge factors in the design of WSN protocols.

- Hot-spot problem: WSN will be operational all the time which leads to failure and faults. Among most problems of routing, hot spot problem is major as it affects overall performance of network in terms of life time. In this problem, sensor which is more active, i.e., near to BS or nodes performing more tasks, will likely to lose energy faster compared to others. As they lose energy, easy functioning of network will disappear hence routing protocols should handle such situation of WSN. The routing algorithm should be capable of handle as well this problem.

12.1.4   Major Highlights of the Chapter

In order to adopt SI approaches in the WSN domain for different applications, one has to initially identify major features, issues, and problems of WSN. The chapter includes the following key aspects:

Initially, fundamental concepts of WSN and literature review of prominent works have been addressed of SI techniques for WSN covering application and challenges of it.

Survey of a WSN routing algorithms applied with bio-inspired design and their context is done.

Suitable guidelines are provided for SI with clustering for various WSN domains and applications through comparison.

- An evaluation of current techniques, tools, and skills for employing clustering at various stages of WSN design problems with resource constrained environments.
- Further amalgamation benefits and issues that are generatable with SI and WSN highlights are provided.

The next sections of this chapter are organized as follows. In Section 12.2, the SI characteristics and requirements will be described. In Section 12.3, brief structural design of common and successful SI techniques will be provided. It will also provide advancements toward actual real-time and reckless SI algorithm designs and issues related to state-of-art algorithms which can combine with WSN. The frameworks and tools which support for SI clustering capabilities in WSN are provided in Section 12.3. A detailed review of SI clustering techniques to the WSNs different functionalities is also included in Section 12.3. In Section 12.4, future research directions and open challenges for SI and WSN domains will be presented followed by conclusion in Section 12.5.

12.2   SI-Based Clustering Techniques

A branch of artificial intelligence is SI which deals on collective cooperative features and activities of meta-agent swarms with single or multiple populated swarms from different plant to animal species or multiple swarm individual group behavior. Large set of homogenous or heterogeneous, simple or complex agent interacting locally or globally interior or exterior, part or in environment, control through distributed or central mechanism is known as swarm. Collins Dictionary states SI as follows "an artificial-intelligence approach to problem solving using algorithms based on the self-organized collective behavior of social insects". All research activists related to SI can be categorized into different individual units based on their computational or structural or parametric aspects of involved swarm [33]. Likewise, generally, clustering can be grouped by means of features such as grid or partition or density or hierarchical techniques applied to network [34]. Among these, hierarchical techniques are applied most and also most suitable to WSN as it is more versatile, possible to build random number of clusters [32]. Algorithms based on swam techniques are recently the best choice for complex applications in producing less energy used, firm and robust optimal resolutions [35]. Direct or indirect communication for interaction among swarms can be used [36], for instance, direct communication of honey bees or indirect communication as in ant colony through pheromone trails [37].

The biologists and scientists from last decade are studying social behaviors of insects as of astounding techniques of these systems of swarm in nature. In 1989, manifestation of SI was for introduced firstly by Beni G and Wang J for global optimization in controlling robotic [38]. Then, in 1991, M Dorigo bring forth concept of ant colony optimization (ACO) as solution for hard combinatorial optimization. In 1995, J Kennedy put forth theory of particle swarm optimization (PSO) similar to bird flock social behavior. Then, after gap of 10 years, D Karabago introduced artificial bee colony (ABC) algorithm for SI group [39]. From then, there is a steady increase in SI research papers based social behavior of organisms; the principle behavior such as flocking, stigmergy, social behavior, firefly, navigation behavior, foraging, or any other can be applied to implement/form collective groups with intelligence. In terms of application view, SI can be viewed through five fundamental principles: proximity, quality, diverse, stability, and adaptability principles. Principles of SI are currently been applied for various problems under all domains from house hold to industry to explore route in communication network, analysis of mages, formation of group based activities, scheduling, data analysis, machine and deep learning problems, medical and bioinformatics, operation research, and others [40].

12.2.1 Growth of SI Algorithms and Characteristics

The comparison of SI-based research work is briefed in this section. Figure 12.1 shows the percentage of papers published in Scopus between 2000 and 2019 sourced Web of Science. The survey shows that the maximum utilized algorithmic technique is PSO. So, there is scope of implementation for others techniques in different domain applications. The PSO, ABC, BFO, and CSO algorithms are most frequent used and have applied under different domains for problems ranging from optimization to design.

The increase in complexity is addressed in progress of time for different SI algorithms as shown in Figure 12.2. Conceptual SI algorithms distribution designed by various researchers between 2000 and 2019 is shown in Figure 12.2. Most of the SI techniques have derived inspiration from insect's behavior as nearly 50% of our survey papers covers. Fish, bird, animal, bacterial, and others occupy next position in order and still require exploration in this direction. Conceptual SI algorithm distribution designed by various researchers between 2000 and 2019 is shown in Figure 12.3. Most of the SI techniques have derived inspiration from insect's behavior as nearly 50% of our survey papers covers. Fish, bird, animal, bacterial, and others occupy next position in order and still require exploration in this direction.

Roots of SI take us to pure science and engineering domains. The problem solutions can be given to various fields which are emerging or advanced can be applied with SI

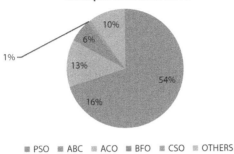

Figure 12.1 Relative comparison of SI-based algorithms during 2000–2019.

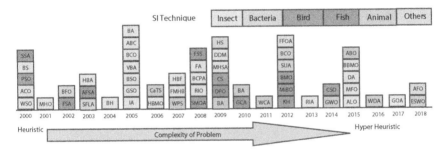

Figure 12.2 Swarm intelligence algorithms (see Table 12.3 for abbreviations).

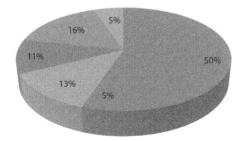

Figure 12.3 Conceptual distribution of SI techniques from 2000 to 2018.

techniques. Lot of matures SI algorithms can be applied in wireless network, production and construction management, science of information and security, e-commerce, informatics in focus on decisions at design and operational stage, functional, business, education, corporate decision, agriculture, town layout, civil construction, military, health care, governance, and other application domain [41]. The SI algorithm can be readily espoused to various engineering and manufacturing level application and solution development but, much of exploration has ended in developmental environment rather than true applications, this is because probably lack of available pseudo-code which can ease the implementation. Many applications domains like industries can embrace many practical applicable SI algorithms such as ACO, PSO, ABC, firefly optimization, nightmare bat, bacterial foraging, frog leaping, flower pollination, and other social swarm optimization algorithms. The medium complex level applications such as government, enterprise, and social application can be explored by means of new SI algorithms through theoretical understanding in suitability and applicability with these applications. The new upcoming algorithms which are less explored such as amoeba-based algorithm [42], bean optimization algorithm [43] and swarm techniques which are based on doves and eagles are reviewed and implemented [165, 166]. Fruit fly, wasp, and glowworm distinct insect grounded algorithms discussed in [44–46] and monkey, shark, wolf, and lions feature grounded algorithms implemented and briefed in [47–51] are being explored in as of looking into their natural activates from environment of dwelling to emulate behavior to different applicational requirements in various operational requirements. Key characteristics and roles of corresponding SI algorithms are presented in Figure 12.4 [52].

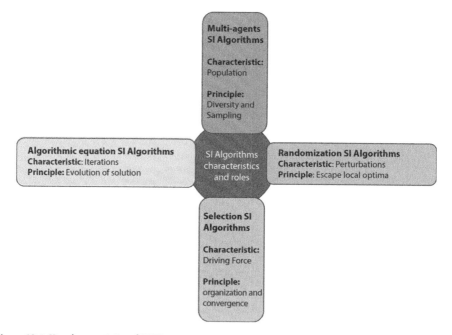

Figure 12.4 Key characteristics of WSN.

Table 12.2 Comparison of typical SI algorithms frequently applied for clustering.

Algorithm	Inspiration	Applicable system	Purpose of utilization	Searching mechanism	Control parameters	Communication model
PSO	Behavior such as flock of animals	Distributed Optimization	Local optima minimization	The flying points and weight of inertia are co-related	Particle number, element, range, and inertia weight	Broadcasting like
ACO	Foraging Behavior	Continuous Optimization	Robust indicator, Memory model to record previous regions completely transfer the neighborhood structures to the next iteration	Not robust indicator, Memory model to record previous search regions did not completely transfer the neighborhood structures to the next iteration	Ants count, evaporation of pheromone, reinforcement	Broadcasting like
FFO	Attraction on the basis of flash light	Continuous Optimization	Fire flying drive in direction of attractiveness	Best firefly identification through random method	Number of fireflies, and optimization parameter, attractiveness, absorption coefficient	Broadcasting like

(Continued)

Table 12.2 Comparison of typical SI algorithms frequently applied for clustering. (*Continued*)

Algorithm	Inspiration	Applicable system	Purpose of utilization	Searching mechanism	Control parameters	Communication model
Cuckoo	Brood parasitism behavior	Continuous Optimization	It lose iteration in identification optimum of local and perform poor convergence to the local optimum	It does not lose iteration in identification of global optimum, better convergence toward global optimum	Count of pigeon, two operators, factor of map and compass	Broadcasting like
BAT	Behavior of bat echolocation	Continuous Optimization	Low loudness with increased pulse value	Loudness is more	Bat count, rate of loudness	Broadcasting
ABC	Bee foraging	Continuous Optimization	Food source search based neighborhood identification	Scout bee identification using random method	employed and onlooker bee count, cycle number	Broadcasting like
DA	NP-D Dimensional Real-valued vector.	Continuous Optimization	Low Convergence speed but a good performance	High convergence speed but a poor performance	Number of dragonfly, radii of range, maximum duty cycles	Direct
GSO	Behavior of lighting worms	Continuous Optimization	Give a swarm position update	Find neighbor phase discussed by sensor image	Number of worms, randomization parameter, absorption coefficient	Broadcasting like

12.2.2   Typical SI-Based Clustering Algorithms

Table 12.2 compares on most frequently used SI techniques for clustering. Inspiring factor for SI techniques is included. Model applicability is compared in terms of either continuous or distributed supported in optimizing application either forms of data being processed either continuous or distributed. Both the kinds of application are suitable of WSN environment. The key SI features exploitation and exploration are discussed for each techniques as utilization and searching. The purpose of utilization technique utilized in corresponding algorithms is briefly described and search optimizations are included. Finally, clustering key parameter considered in construction and regulation of clusters with suitable communication medium.

12.2.3   Comparison of SI Algorithms and Applications

This sub-section provides a comparison of SI algorithms from different classes from flora to fauna. The techniques differ from one to another in terms of inspiration drawn, SI technique being applied, appropriate solution update mechanism and their applications. The possible SI techniques adopted in design are multi-agent, selection, randomization, and algorithmic techniques as shown in Figure 12.4. The inspiration drawn in development of SI algorithms is significant to be noted in development of any applications. The appropriate applicability of different SI techniques is shortlisted, which will provide future directions for still unexplored techniques for implementation and evaluation. Table 12.3 provides information of major used and proven SI techniques in various applications ranging from home to industry and from small scale to large scale problems.

12.3   WSN SI Clustering Applications

This section will provide detailed conceptual study on SI algorithms application environment performed by different researchers applying clusters especially to WSN. Clustering is a critical mission of WSN for energy efficiency and network constancy. It is a very familiar data processing technique being used in WSN's from long time. The clustering techniques are proved to be suitable in WSN. The clustering technique is widespread methods which utilize to minimize the energy consumption in WSNs. They give better state of the art for beginners and also they have been critically reviewed as well compared with other protocols. Clustering procedures are organizing the sensor nodes into specific sets known as clusters. Among all nodes, one single node will get chosen as CH which becomes major node for that particular cluster. The CH has many function in addition to sensing the environment such as; data gathering form all cluster member and convey it to BS, convey other CHs data to next hop, make fusion cluster data, and sometimes control the cluster based on clustering method [53]. The key advantage of clustering is in minimizing the energy consumption and thereby prolong average time of sensors for all iterations of WSN. An illustration of simple cluster in WSN is shown in Figure 12.5. Considering the structure of cluster and how to improve it is a first challenge that faced the developers, because it represents as a base for design the cluster-based routing protocol.

Table 12.3 SI techniques applied to WSN and other domains.

Algorithm	Full name	SI technique	Best solution update mechanism	Inspired function	Applications	Ref.
WSO	Wasp swarm optimization	Multi-agent	Equation	Collective behavior of wasp	WSN, image processing, maintenance, security, segmentation, classification, scheduling, gaming	Theraulaz, 1997
ACO	Ant colony optimization	Multi-agent	Rule	Foraging behavior of ants	Security, detection, peer-to-peer networks, VWAN, WAS, programming optimization, performance analysis, remote sensing, resource management, construction planning, optimization of RFID	Dorigo, 1992
PSO	Particle swarm optimization	Multi-agent	Mixed	Group behavior of birds	To reduce NP problems, distributed networks, power problem, monitoring, WSN, WMN, median problem	Ahamadi, 2015
BS	Bee system	Selection	Rule	Searching of food	Robot design, scheduling, feature selection, fake detection, planning, network issues, WSN, modeling of optimization problems	Sato, 1997
SSA	Shark search algorithm	Randomized	Mixed	Crawling behavior of shark	Machine learning, e-commerce, WSN, automation, forecasting, acoustic science, robot movement, fuzzy, optimization	Hersovici, 1998

(Continued)

Table 12.3 SI techniques applied to WSN and other domains. (*Continued*)

Algorithm	Full name	SI technique	Best solution update mechanism	Inspired function	Applications	Ref.
MHO	Marriage in honey bees optimization	Selection	Eq.	Marriage in real Honey-bee	Satellite communication, scheduling problems, data management, feature selection, planning, WSN, allocation planning	Abbass, 2012
FSA	Fish swarm algorithm	Multi-agent	Rule	Group behavior of fish	Power management, security, prediction, underwater WSN, fuzzy related issues, frequency and time management	LI, 2003
BFO	Bacterial foraging optimization	Randomized	Rule	Searching nutrients by bacteria	Routing and security issues of WSN, cellular technology, grid technology, image processing, threshold level fixing, image error detection and optimization edge detection, face detection	Passino, 2002
SFLA	Shuffled frog leaping algorithm	Selection	Mixed	Leaping and shuffling behavior of frogs	WSN, packing and unpacking industry, amplifier technology, parameter testing, VWAN, image processing, recognition technology	Mutazono, 2012; Eustiff, 2003
AFSA	Artificial fish swarm algorithm	Multi-agent	Mixed	Natural social behavior of fish Schooling	Image processing, production and construction planning, WSN, fuzzy logic, ANN, robot optimization, composite function	Filho, 2008

(*Continued*)

Table 12.3 SI techniques applied to WSN and other domains. (*Continued*)

Algorithm	Full name	SI technique	Best solution update mechanism	Inspired function	Applications	Ref.
HBA	Honey bee foraging	Algorithmic	Rule	Movement of bee in search	WSN, multi- level threshold resistance problems	Nakrani, 2003
BH	Beehive	Randomized	Mixed	Group gossip in hive	Bioinformatics, WSN, faced pose elimination	Wedde, 2004
TA	Termite algorithm	Multi-agent	Rule	Group behavior in termite hill	Allocation algorithms, WSN , image processing, remote sensing, MIMO under water problems, link selection in WSN	Roth, 2005
GSO	Glow worm swarm optimization	Multi-agent	Mixed	Light gossiping behavior	Identification, sensitivity analysis, classification of image, data related problems, routing	Krishnananda, 2005
BSO	Bee swarm optimization	Multi-agent	Rule	Group intelligence in honey collection	Identification, sensitivity analysis, classification of image, data related problems, water management, WSN	Drais, 2005

(*Continued*)

Table 12.3 SI techniques applied to WSN and other domains. (*Continued*)

Algorithm	Full name	SI technique	Best solution update mechanism	Inspired function	Applications	Ref.
VBA	Virtual bee algorithm	Randomized	Rule	Social group support	Optimization problem based, WSN search based	Yang, 2005
BCO	Bee colony optimization	Algorithmic	Rule	Formation of honey comb	Parameter estimation, location search, optimization problems	Mirjalili, 2016
ABC	Artificial bee colony	Algorithmic	Mixed	Foraging behavior of honey bee	Classification and prediction problems, noise removal from images, feature selection and identification	Karaboga, 2005
BA	Bee algorithm	Selection	Rule	Food related operations in hive	Identity proofing, WSN, faced pose elimination	Pham, 2005
HBMO	Honey bee mating optimization	Selection	Mixed	Selection of honey bee in mating process	Traffic light management, optimization of path in network, data structure, NP-hard problems	Haddad, 2006

(*Continued*)

Table 12.3 SI techniques applied to WSN and other domains. (*Continued*)

Algorithm	Full name	SI technique	Best solution update mechanism	Inspired function	Applications	Ref.
CaTS	Cat swarm optimization	Multi-agent	Eq.	Natural behavior of cats	WSN, image processing, maintenance, security, segmentation, classification, scheduling, gaming	Chu, 2006
WPS	Wolf pack search	Multi-agent	Mixed	Formation of wolf pack	Security, detection, peer-to-peer networks, VWAN, WAS, programming optimization, performance analysis, remote sensing, resource management, construction planning, optimization of RFID	Liu, 2011
FMHB	Fast marriage in honey bee optimization	Multi-agent	Mixed	The mating and fertilization tasks in bees	WSN energy maintenance, sensor placement, security and monitoring problems, satellite selection, classification problems, e-commerce, cancer classification	Mutazono, 2012
HBF	Honey bee foraging	Multi-agent	Eq.	Foraging of honey bees	Routing and security issues of WSN, cellular technology, grid technology, image processing, threshold level fixing, image error detection and optimization edge detection, face detection	Baig, 2007

(*Continued*)

Table 12.3 SI techniques applied to WSN and other domains. (*Continued*)

Algorithm	Full name	SI technique	Best solution update mechanism	Inspired function	Applications	Ref.
SMOA	Slime mould optimization	Randomized	Eq.	Molding property of slimes	Localization, classification, image processing, threshold fixing, forecasting	Monismith, 2008
RIO	Roach infestation algorithm	Selection	Mixed	Communication behavior of cockroaches insects	Optimization problem, stability based, constrains based, WSN, image processing, VLSI	Havens, 2008
MA	Monkey Algorithm	Randomized	Mixed	Behavior of a monkey climbing trees. Solving specific	Numerical optimization, VWAN, planning, calibration, WSN, location identification	Zhao, 2008
BCPA	Bee collecting pollen algorithm	Randomized	Rule	Form of Pollen collection bee	Light and power management, fault detection, image processing, record preferencing, site allotment MIR scan image classification.	Lu, 2008

(*Continued*)

Table 12.3 SI techniques applied to WSN and other domains. (*Continued*)

Algorithm	Full name	SI technique	Best solution update mechanism	Inspired function	Applications	Ref.
FA	Firefly algorithm	Multi-agent	Eq.	Flashing behavior of fireflies	WSN, medical problems, crack detection, feature estimation	Yang, 2008
FSS	Fish school algorithm	Multi-agent	Eq.	Movement of fish schools and bird flocks	Building planning, node identification, search optimization, quality maintenance	LI, 2003
BA	Bat algorithm	Multi-agent	Mixed	Echolocation characteristics of micro-bats	Data mining, energy management, image compression, ANN, fuzzy, classification, scheduling	Yang, 2010
DPO	Dolphin partner optimization	Multi-agent	Mixed	Biological characteristics of dolphin	Supply chain, inventory, manufacturing, power management, ANN, mathematical equation formulation	Shiqin, 2012
CS	Cuckoo search	Randomized	Eq.	Breeding behavior of cuckoo bird	Feature estimation and reduction, civil construction related issues, estimation, prediction of image, value for image enhancement	Yang, 2009

(*Continued*)

Table 12.3 SI techniques applied to WSN and other domains. (*Continued*)

Algorithm	Full name	SI technique	Best solution update mechanism	Inspired function	Applications	Ref.
MHSA	Mosquito host seeking algorithm	Selection	Rule	Host-seeking behavior of mosquitoes	Network, target detection, clustering, VWAN	Feng, 2009
BCO	Bee colony optimization	Multi-agent	Rule	Groups formation in bee	Cellular technology, forensics, manufacturing problems, color management, project scheduling, manipulation prediction	Teodorovi, 2005
HS	Hunting search	Randomized	Rule	Catching of animals	Optimization, energy management, water and soil maintenance, segmentation, threshold fixing, fuzzy and node calibration problems	Oftadeh, 2009
GEA	Group escaping algorithm	Randomized	Rule	Escaping techniques of prisoners from prison	WSN, image error minimization, Cellular technology, forensics, manufacturing problems, color management, project scheduling, manipulation prediction	Saremi, 2017

(Continued)

Table 12.3 SI techniques applied to WSN and other domains. (*Continued*)

Algorithm	Full name	SI technique	Best solution update mechanism	Inspired function	Applications	Ref.
BA	Beaver algorithm	Multi-agent	Eq.	Probabilistic actions of swarm	Mathematical Optimization functions, energy management, water and soil maintenance, segmentation, threshold fixing, fuzzy and node calibration problems	Ayesh, 2009
WCA	Wolf colony algorithm	Multi-agent	Eq.	Hunting technique and the social hierarchy of grey wolves	Traffic management, remote sensing, spatial image conversion, WSN, network security, multi-objective functions	Mirjalili, 2014
KH	Krill herd algorithm	Multi-agent	Mixed	Heading behavior of krill	To reduce NP problems, distributed networks, power problem, monitoring, WSN, WMN, median problem	Gandomi, 2012
LA	Lion Algorithm	Multi-agent	Rule	Lion's territorial defense and territorial takeover	Robot design, scheduling, feature selection, fake detection, planning, network issues, WSN, modeling of optimization problems	Rajakumar, 2012

(*Continued*)

Table 12.3 SI techniques applied to WSN and other domains. (*Continued*)

Algorithm	Full name	SI technique	Best solution update mechanism	Inspired function	Applications	Ref.
MiBO	Migrating bird optimization	Algorithmic	Rule	Group migration in birds	Machine learning, e-commerce, WSN, automation, forecasting, acoustic science, robot movement, fuzzy, optimization	Duman, 2012
BMO	Bird mating optimization	Selection	Rule	Mating of birds	Satellite communication, scheduling problems, data management, feature selection, planning, WSN, allocation planning	Askarzadeh, 2012
BCO	Bacterial colony optimization	Randomized	Mixed	Searching of nutrients in group	Power management, security, prediction, underwater WSN, fuzzy related issues, frequency and time management	Teodorovi, 2012
FFOA	Fruit fly optimization	Selection	Rule	Sensing and perception behavior of fruit fly	Routing and security issues of WSN, cellular technology, grid technology, image processing, threshold level fixing, image error detection and optimization edge detection, face detection	Pan, 2012

(*Continued*)

Table 12.3 SI techniques applied to WSN and other domains. (*Continued*)

Algorithm	Full name	SI technique	Best solution update mechanism	Inspired function	Applications	Ref.
BLA	Bee life algorithm	Selection	Rule	Food foraging, reproduction and neighbor searching behaviors of bee	WSN, packing and unpacking industry, amplifier technology, parameter testing, VWAN, image processing, recognition technology	Bitam, 2013
GWO	Glow worm optimization	Multi-agent	Rule	Foraging behavior of glowworm Swarm	Image processing, production and construction planning, WSN, fuzzy logic, ANN, robot optimization, composite function	Mirjalili, 2014
CSO	Chicken swarm optimization	Multi-agent	Mixed	Maintenance of hierarchical behavior	To reduce NP problems, distributed networks, power problem, monitoring, WSN, WMN, median problem	Meng, 2014
ALO	Ant lion optimization	Selection	Mixed	The hunting action of ant lions	Robot design, scheduling, feature selection, fake detection, planning, network issues, WSN, modeling of optimization problems	Mirjalili, 2015a
MFO	Moth flame optimization	Randomized	Mixed	Angle movements of moths	Machine learning, e-commerce, WSN, automation, forecasting, acoustic science, robot movement, fuzzy, optimization	Mirjalili, 2015b

(*Continued*)

Table 12.3 SI techniques applied to WSN and other domains. (*Continued*)

Algorithm	Full name	SI technique	Best solution update mechanism	Inspired function	Applications	Ref.
DA	Dragon fly algorithm	Selection	Rule	Dynamic and static swarming in flies	Satellite communication, scheduling problems, data management, feature selection, planning, WSN, allocation planning	Mirjalili, 2015
BBMO	Bumble bee mating optimization	Selection	Rule	Bumble bee are clever bee, their marriage behavior	Power management, security, prediction, underwater WSN, fuzzy related issues, frequency and time management	Marinakis, 2010
ABO	African buffalo optimization	Randomized	Mixed	Fittest identification among	Routing and security issues of WSN, cellular technology, grid technology, image processing, threshold level fixing, image error detection and optimization edge detection, face detection	Odili, 2015
WOA	Whale optimization algorithm	Randomized	Rule	Actions involved in catching preys	WSN, packing and unpacking industry, amplifier technology, parameter testing, VWAN, image processing, recognition technology	Mirjalili, 2016

(*Continued*)

Table 12.3 SI techniques applied to WSN and other domains. (*Continued*)

Algorithm	Full name	SI technique	Best solution update mechanism	Inspired function	Applications	Ref.
LOA	Lion optimization algorithm	Selection	Mixed	Lion cooperation characteristics	Image processing, production and construction planning, WSN, fuzzy logic, ANN, robot optimization, composite function	Yazdani, 2016
GOA	Grasshopper optimization algorithm	Multi-agent	Mixed	The social interactions in hoppers	Optimization WSN, classification, problems, TSP, image segmentation, ANN, video compression	Krishnanand, 2005
ESWA	Elephant swarm water search Algorithm	Multi-agent	Mixed	Elephant herd search for water	Image processing, image recognition, power management, optimization, field remote maintenance, optimization	Mandal, 2018
AFO	Artificial flora optimization	Algorithmic	Rule	Migration and reproduction in flora	WMN, distribution of water in pipeline, fault detection, data related problems, classification and prediction problem planning, WSNs	L Cheng, 2018

As in Figure 12.5, CH will be major node of cluster will control and coordinate all activities of other nodes clusters. Messages will be exchanged within cluster in accordance with CH instructions. Currently, cluster process over traditional methods is progressing prove to be better in term of energy-efficiency and extended lifetime. Clustering of sensor nodes is very important to explain many problems QoS problems such as extendibility, delay management, scalability, and other issues of sensor networks. In few situations, clusters will include gateway or intermediate nodes to forward data to BS from CH. This alternate mechanism will extend life time of CH and average energy of nodes in cluster will also be balanced. In addition, energy maintenance will be formed through another layer or by CH itself to collect data and further use using simple mathematical functions to reduce data being conveyed between nodes thereby minimizing need for energy for processing larger sized data [54]. Nesting of cluster will be constructed to optimize network in network that is wider in size.

12.3.1   WSN Services

The services provides by WSN is presented in Figure 12.6. The outer most layer is the presentation of data from different applications to provide better software in order to translate or to present information is various forms. The next service layer guarantees QoS in terms of availability, efficiency, security, and other parameters related to communication of data with network and across networks. The data forwarded expect synchronization of data requires compression and aggregation, security, and fault tolerance. The basic functionalities and services of WSN are included in lower layer for coverage, identification, generation of carrier frequency, required detection of level path, modulation, deployment, localization, and data encryption.

12.3.2   Clustering Objectives for WSN Applications

The clusters can be equal or unequal based on the application requirements. In WSN, unequal clusters are preferred over equal since it overcomes the problem of hop spot. The most common objectives of clustering to be considered in designing WSN are as follows:

- Scalability: [55] clustering increases number of nodes to scale size of network and to minimize/maximize of routing problem.
- Tolerance to fault: [56] transmission of data in an error free manner (Heinzelman *et al.*, 2002), CH rotation will result proper load balancing with minimized data faults.
- Data Aggregation/fusion: [57] it amplifies needed data and suppress noise either in single or multi-hop.
- Load balancing: [58] the clustering guarantees uniform distribution of resources.
- Stabilized network topology: the tracking of nodes and data, to consider any random changes in topology of network.
- Increased lifetime: [59] it increase the capability of routing thereby increasing lifetime of network.

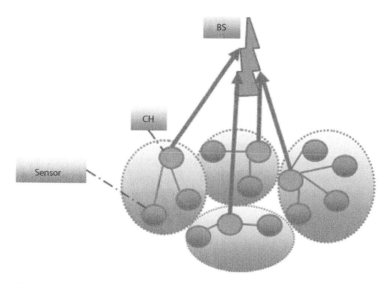

Figure 12.5 Typical nodes cluster formation.

- Multiple routing paths: more than one path can be generated between nodes or between node and BS.
- Speed: adaptability to changing network paradigms.
- Route recovery: if any identified route fails, new routes will be recomputed to minimize network fault.
- Distributed: inherently, SI is distributed in nature help to achieve easy control mechanism in network.

The clustering issues and network of WSN are shown in Figure 12.7.

12.3.3 SI Algorithms for WSN: Overview

This section will provide details on usage of SI algorithms for network of sensors designed with hierarchical topology. The hierarchical clusters will minimize route from CH to BS which results in reduced energy consumption. Initial countenance of SI was given by Beni and Wang with an illustration of cellular system of robotics. A multi-agent self-organized and decentralized behavior of computational intelligence in restricted environment on collective behavior of elements in natures is presented in initial version which became base for next level works of SI. The core SI design includes simple agents interact locally. SI will also include global behaviors of search and optimization problem. Swarms will interact locally or globally, any interaction methodologies can be used to structure out design. Meanwhile, controlling can be done either through branch or fixed methods in SI. Organisms' interaction in nature will be modeled or simulated in SI as algorithms or computation models. Among SI algorithms, most prominent are idealizing ant, bee, particle, wolf, cuckoo, fish school, and others. The major works and utilization of SI algorithm are for optimization under different domains in various research and practical areas are optimization algorithm

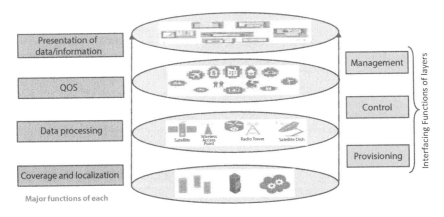

Figure 12.6 Key services of WSN.

from ant colony to novel swarm algorithms. Currently, more works are ongoing in WSN using SI to optimize route between CH and BS as well between CH and its members. Further works can be extended with SI and WSN to improve performance in the direction pertaining to QOS parameters (scalability, reliability, and delay), data transmission optimization, formations and cluster, and others. As energy is consumed more in data transmission or processing, SI algorithms can be adopted to minimize data locally as much as possible in order to increase residual energy of sensors and network [60]. Another nature inspired collection can be utilized in packet transmission as it is trust area of WSN [61].

12.3.4 The Commonly Applied SI-Based WSN Clusterings

12.3.4.1 ACO-Based WSN Clustering

ACO principle is used to reduce redundant data within clusters [62]. The processing includes two phases: CH selection in first phase followed by data traversal in redundant fashion for next phase. Nodes are allowed to sense data within specified radii sensing areas. Nodes left with energy level utmost are the one which is identified as CH. Remaining nodes are enabled to enter sleeping mode. This ant-based protocol provides an optimal path selection and energy maintenance within network in construction of intra-clusters. In [63], major operations of their work include: selection of CH, formation of varied size clusters, and path identification in multi-path format in all identified clusters. Majority of algorithms works in phased manner to minimize complexity similarly tasks are been carried on in three phases initial cluster identification, finding neighbors in order to select shortest path and last is to sense and disseminate information to end point of concern. CSMA MAC protocol is used to collect data or to communicate with neighbor and every node will build its own non-persistent detail. During steady phase, the selection of CH, clustering and data delivery are processed. The CH are elected fuzzy based and shorter path with in cluster for communication through ACO. Residual energy, number of neighbors, and quality of node link are taken as measurable parameters during identification of CH which ensures

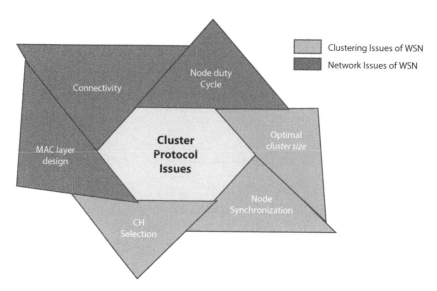

Figure 12.7 Key issues of WSN.

reliability. Fitness function looks for CH to BS link cost and distance and energy levels in all nodes. The protocol is compared with ACO-based algorithms for WSN yields 41%, 63%, and 15% increase in energy, network life time, and throughput in comparison to it. A hybrid approach of fuzzy and ACO for WSN to improve routing presented in [64]. Clusters formed are distributed in nature as of fuzzy in nature. The formation of clusters is according to rules of fuzzy and selection of CH based on ACO. The goal is to optimize WSN performance by relating all nodes. In formation of clusters, route cost is considered, wherein the high cost is assigned if routes are near to more neighbors. Integration of chain and cluster routing techniques applied in [65] in aim of minimizing average energy consumption of cluster and network. The cluster-based routing protocol with both chain and cluster is developed using ACO. The design is developed with an aim to eliminate redundant data so as to increase energy efficiency. The distance between nodes and energy level are considered in formation of clusters. Cluster formation for dense environment based on ACO introduced in [67]. Nodes require exchange of message across cluster to facilitate ACO principles are adopted. The algorithm proposed is based on pheromone deposition pattern of ant colony identification in routing data packets from CH to BS with an aim to minimize the efforts wasted in transferring the redundant data sent by the sensors. The nodes are placed with less space in between so as to simulated dense environment and every takes mimics LEACH from identification to information exchange between CH and BS. Similar to method of [66] tasks are carried on in phased manner but here it includes two. First phase is to segregate nodes into different clusters and next to exchange data in and out of clusters. Protocol has taken measures to minimize redundant data transmission. Routing of data based on ACO is performed within the cluster. Activities of network are carried on until all the nodes are dead. Hierarchical Data Dissemination in WSN [68] is developed concentrating on data transmission using ACO. The protocol has been developed using ACO SI principles in formation of clusters. The network area is divided into zones. The node with consumes less time for communication will get selected as CH for particular zone; the next part of operations is similar to leach. Even though algorithm reduces energy in formation of clusters with identification of zone, it is not better choice for dynamic and larger networks. Protocol designed in a goal to improve QOS and minimize energy consumption by cluster formation. The clusters are formed by three stages, hop tree–based algorithm, cluster formation, and route discovery. Optimization of energy using ACO in WSN [69] of sensor nodes is given importance. The formations of clusters are based on ACO techniques. Energy-efficient algorithm named Power Aware Scheduling and Clustering Algorithm based on ACO (PASC-ACO) is proposed. Network is partitioned into different zones of unequal sizes. Nodes will enter to sleep for certain time before becoming CH in any round later they will enter to active state and are ready to become CH for that round. Nodes with least delay from every zone will be selected as CH for that zone. All other nodes in each zone will send request message after node get select as CH along with its information once node make announcement as CH for that particular round. Rather than single hop communication, multi-hop message transmission is used during exchange of information from CH to BS to increase reliability. Ant-based routing effect in energy for WSN in [70] is concern to reduce load and energy with in network. Protocol uses routing table to maintain details of neighbor and nodes nearby. Routing table will also assist in faster identification of path for communication. Later paths will be identified from source node to BS utilizing information stored in routing at the beginning of phase one. Memory M_k of every node will store necessarily two records. Each node is as ant maintains last two visited nodes record. The path followed in their memories will always create receive and sent packet. The next node will restart timer to save required information if no record is found in immediate next node. The ants are traced backward until route details are present in different ants. Once the ants are found with record that contains identification, these are found in all eliminated node to search in memory of all ants. Once record is found in ant, the information will be updated in all traversed ants. The energy level minimized will be erased from forward ants with vector Ek and average energy until all nodes are minimized from current to node to BS. Each node receives information from forward ants and ant reaches node used to calculate trail of pheromone from corresponding ant in backward. The strength of nodes will determine source node. Node closer to BS will consist of more pheromone trials than other backward ants. Hence, nodes near to BS will have more pheromone level than other nodes far from BS which helps in identification of paths. The mobile and multiple BS is a problem in this protocol. In parameter adaptation for ant colony system in WSN [71], a cluster algorithm is designed in validating performance of WSN based on ACS. The algorithm evaluated with features such as throughput, energy consumption, and latency. The ACO algorithms have major drawback in energy absorption is more in initial route identification has in most of methods reviewed.

12.3.4.2   PSO-Based WSN Clustering

The PSO-enabled WSN clustering works that are topic of this sub-section are reviewed. [72] presented a routing algorithm of bacteria foraging and PSO techniques hybrid WSN. Bacteria foraging is applied for cluster formation of CH selection captivating residual energy of nodes among various clusters is featured parameter. During processing stage of

WSN, CH obtains local best and global best. The position in search area with PSO to identify suitable synchronous update is considered to establish optimized solution. The synchronous updates included in this protocol faces problem in loosely connected nodes that have feedback that will not be sent to non-immediate offsprings based on PSO. [73] proposed protocol with an objective to use WSN energy efficiently based on PSO principle for clustering with mobile sink. Remaining energy of nodes and placement of nodes are prime parameters to be notified for CH selection. The mobile sink is assumed to move near CH of interest and collect data. The simulations are conducted in comparison with LEACH in metric to transmission delay and network lifetime. WSN is partitioned into two areas according to fitness function applied to nodes as of PSO. The communication with sink is applied randomly by estimations method to minimize energy usage in operations and henceforth is the major concern of proposed protocol. The improved PSO is followed to partition the tasks of network into different clusters to carry out different operations with an aim to increase number of alive nodes in WSN. Results of simulation obtained are compared with LEACH and PSO-based WSN. The data duplication problem still exists in the protocol. [74] has used PSO for cluster formation built with objective function using parameters of residual energy and distance. Gravitational search algorithm with PSO is applied for communication between CH and sink. Selection of CH is based on distance to BS. Simulation results are compared with LEACH and PSO. The protocol does not form uniform clusters. SI principle–influenced energy-efficient PSO algorithm for WSN routing is implemented in [75] that has adopted PSO for cluster formation. The set of nodes are randomly picked for selection of CH, and then, their intra-cluster distance, energy level of all nodes every iteration, and distance to BS from all nodes are considered to decide the selection of CH. The process of selection is time leading, and also as randomly selected in larger sized network, it is not suitable as may lead to unbalanced clusters. PSO strategy applied in formation of clusters and identification of gateway nodes, to optimize energy consumption which, in turn, helps in global optimal CH selection to aggregate data. The data is routed from CH to sink by identifying link according to harmony-based search algorithm. Energy Balanced Unequal Clustering for WSN protocol creates unequal clusters, commonly used for periodical data gathering applications in a centralized way [76]. The PSO algorithm is applied in selection of CH candidate followed by cluster formation. The routing technique considered in design is inter-cluster communication considering all features on greedy algorithm. In efficient identification of CH, energy left in every nodes and its distance to BS and distance from relay nodes featured in fitness function. This procedure will avoid frequent need for selection of new CH and reduce the energy requirement in the network. Energy-efficient PSO used WSN clustering and routing algorithms as discussed in [77] protocol are implemented applying PSO and works in three phases. Bootstrapping phase assigns IDs to all nodes and gateways. The load balanced in routing are applied for forming balanced clusters. The protocol is compared with original PSO and GAR considering WSN outing performance metrics which includes from life time of sensor, count of dead nodes, and number of messages being forwarded from nodes or BS. An increased LEACH efficient algorithm for WSN through PSO principles was presented in [78]. The PSO-based sensor networks are constructed in forming clusters with an aim to extent lifespan. The nodes assigned to different clusters considering geographical radii. [79] form cluster in WSN using adaptive PSO for selection of the CH in aim to balance overall energy of sensors in a network. CH selection, if based on fitness function, in turn, uses PSO function to form cluster and to identify CH. All CHs will intimate selection to all other nodes through broadcast. The rest of nodes on receiving messages from CH look for more suitable CH for it through metrics of distance and cost required for each communication to it. The next processes are normally carried out similar to LEACH. An enhanced WSN of PSO is used in identification of unequal clusters. Traditional PSO and hot spot problems are reduced. Network set up and message exchange phase for different iterations of WSN will be carried out as of LEACH protocol. Each node will keep track of its information to be sent to BS. BS is responsible in identification of better CH. Formation of cluster and CH selection is as usually part of first phase of each round. The intra-cluster communication takes place in accordance with TDMA schedule, and hence, every member of cluster should communicate in their respective slots itself. The design consumes less energy in later rounds compared to initial rounds. Centralized protocol constructed with a goal to minimize energy consumption inside WSN through PSO principles is discussed in [80]. The PSO will be used to divide network of sensors into different clusters and core part of the algorithm will be similar to LEACH. During every operation of protocol considers energy availability in nodes and distance to two communicating nodes. The Euclidean distance used to compute distance between nodes. The selection of node as CH using PSO will guaranteed in selection of node with sufficient energy to handle as CH gets select. Results of comparison between LEACH and LEACH-C are also presented as of performance metrics of WSN routing. Similar to this protocol, centralized hierarchical clustering for WSN using PSO is presented in [81]. CH is selected in such a way as to extend the life time of network through by avoiding number of iterations. The algorithm is also capable of extending as it support for two-hop communication, i.e., during communication of CH to BS, two intermediate nodes will be considered. Nodes selected as CH will be in active state unceasingly. Protocol is compared with traditional algorithm to show advantage of Si algorithm. In [82], WSN has developed GAPSO protocol utilized PSO, genetic algorithm, and BFO in formation of cluster and selection of CH. The techniques are applied individually in identification of nearby nodes in order to form clusters. Then, PSO and GA are used in selection of CH for identified clusters. The total time required in formation of cluster is more. Energy-Efficient Clustering in Multi-hop WSNs applies differential evolutionary MOPSO [83]. The MOPSO protocol aims at developing energy-efficient WSN applying multi-objective PSO in combination with differential evolution technique for selection of CH is done. PSO-based WSN routing with an aim to solve hot spot problem is discussed in [84]. In beginning of every round, tentative CH is elected which is considered to consist of more energy. Later, CH will be elected using fitness function features with parameters such as energy and distance to BS from node. To minimize burden on CH alternate node in cluster selected as intra-node. Intra-node will assist in CH in collection data from all nodes. The nodes are selected between transmission paths from CH to BS which minimize hot-spot problem. The nodes at all levels will be chosen according to PSO. PSO-based energy-aware cluster-based WSN is presented in [85]. Routing is performed via elected CH. the CH is elected using cost function of PSO. Multi-path communication is used to communicate to BS unlike direct communication thereby reducing communication cost. The nodes are centrally controlled by BS. BS monitors all nodes energy level at regular interval to guarantee uninterruptable operations with in network. CH will collect information from its member nodes. Once CH receives all data from its counter parts, it will combine all data into one frame and forward to BS. In [86], routing protocol is developed in aim to reduce energy consumption of nodes in WSN. PSO algorithm is utilized in construction of cluster to identification of CH. In the process of identification, energy level of other nodes and distances are considered. To avoid energy loss of far nodes with in clusters intra-nodes, they are identified via communication with CH. Similar to LEACH nodes are randomly picked for CH election process. Evolving a hybrid k-means clustering algorithm for WSN using PSO and GAs has included in design [87]. The clusters are formed applying PSO and GA techniques. PSO is used to form arbitrary number of clusters, and selection of best CH is carried out by GA. The PSO algorithms comparatively consume less energy compared to ACO, but most of works concentrate on only single hop. The distance and iterations remaining energy are not considered in most of works in formation of clusters.

12.3.4.3   ABC-Based WSN Clustering

An energy-efficient, centralized, multipath, and scalable routing protocol for WSN has developed protocol supports multipath intra-communication and formation of dynamic clusters on event based on principles searching conducts of natural bee mimics as artificial bees [88]. Algorithm is designed with an aim to minimize overheads improving QoS capability. Nodes with minimum residual energy are kept aside in formation of clusters. The design of topology is considered for both single and dynamic events scenario. The reliability on transmission of messages is less. A bio-inspired clustering scheme in WSNs, Bee WSN [89], and Honey bee algorithm is applied in CH node identification from set of nodes of WSN. The algorithm works in two phases. Fitness function is computed and applied in initial phase and cluster head selection done in second phase. The computation of objective function considers node energy, degree, speed, and direction into consideration. The selection time is more and network life is more if network size is less. Energy-efficient clustering protocol based on improved metaheuristic in WSN [90] adopted ABC-based improved algorithm is enhanced solution search equation with an aim to increase usage abilities. A global convergence development model applied to from clusters. The algorithm has tried to maintain memory requirements. Honey Bee Mating principle–based clustering algorithm is presented in [91]. The formation of initial round cluster is through k-means algorithm. Other computations and operations are similar to LEACH. The optimization algorithm has convergence problem. WSN protocol designed using enhanced exploration capabilities of ABC in [92]. The metaheuristic capabilities are improved by introducing new distribution technique. Distribution technique is capable of sampling. Sampling combination of store and compute operations. This method is suitable for limited hardware requirements of WSN in view of authors. ABC-based formation of cluster and packet forward concept for WSN applied in [93] using ABC algorithm. ABC is to optimize the use of energy applying ABC for cluster formation. Artificial bee colony optimization performance improvement based on clustering protocol for WSN [94] has designed algorithm applying ABC for original LEACH algorithm. The environment considered is very similar to bee's group as employed, scouts, and onlooker. At beginning, one half consists of employed bee and remaining half consist of onlooker bee. The employed bee looks for distance among all neighbors along with onlooker bee. The bee with more nectar, i.e., is residual energy considered in formation of CH. After all data collection, onlooker will select CH node. The cost function of new one is contest with the old one and best solution is stored until the utmost number of cycle is attained. CH selected taking multiple features into consideration and evaluation using alive and dead nodes, distance from BS to other initiating node. Comparison of each parameter from conventional LEACH is also presented. The simulation has been done in MATLAB. The proposed protocol utilizes ABC and ACO approaches [95]. ABC is applied in CH selection and ACO to for data transmission. The protocols are designed to enhance stability period of network. Sub-CH is elected in each cluster in addition to CH for transmission of data to BS. LEACH and WSNCABC are used to compare in terms of throughput. The main merit of ABC is its variation in design techniques and its suitability in WSN. The most of the algorithms developed optimizes toward local optimization rather than global optimization in ABC.

12.3.4.4   CS Cuckoo–Based WSN Clustering

Cuckoo-based WSN clustering and routing protocol [96] has introduced an improved selection of CHs with an objective function adopting cuckoo search optimization principles. The communication between CH and sink node is routed, applying harmony search in against to traditional TDMA. Performance is improved in energy factors but at a cost of time. Improvement aimed at extending lifetime of network, learning dead nodes and alive nodes. A cuckoo-based approach followed in formation of clusters [97]. Nodes of heterogeneous type considered to minimize energy utilization and to pictorize real-time network. Network is assumed to be deployed with normal energized nodes of 80% and remaining 20% are considered to be more than the normal range of energy level. The protocol does not from uniform clusters as always CH will be selected from nodes with higher energy level itself. Cuckoo bird species with an aim to increase the lifetime of the network using a clustering protocol based on the breed parasitism are presented [98]. The CHs and non-CH nodes are selected in the network. The selection is as similar to LEACH. CHs are will be selected using cuckoo principles. All nodes in the network will get to know about CH selection, and thereby, other nodes will join to cluster knowing its distance to CH from it and cost of energy required for communication to it. After computations, non-CH will send to its optimized CH a join request message. The CH node will gather all join messages and allot time schedule to communicate with it. The selection of CH is based on all requests that are generated to accept or reject according to threshold and random probability. The changes from different iterations and reception of request to accept or reject are based on whether the rejection probability crosses the threshold or not. The selection of CH presented is of rejection or acceptance of cuckoo eggs as cuckoo bird with certain probability. CH will accept node as its member only if requesting non-CH node has more threshold level than CH. Once all non-CH nodes are assigned to CH, cluster formation round will be completed and followed by it WSN will enter into steady phase communication. The transmission of sensed information happens between the nodes and the BS. Authors have proposed energy-efficient routing algorithm ACEED LEACH in [99]. Presented algorithm is implemented using ant colony and cuckoo search optimization to increase LEACH process. Algorithm is being developed in two-phase manner, first phase for grouping and next for sensing. ACO pheromone composition principles are utilized in selection of CH. Cluster formation is based on cuckoo bird egg strategy. The hybrid algorithm performs better for WSN in utilization of average energy of cluster and network. Dropping of nearby nodes is more or assignment of nodes to any group is better if nodes are spaced less in cuckoo optimization. Hence, if nodes are loosely spaced, then it has effects on the performance.

12.3.4.5 *Other SI Technique-Based WSN Clustering*

12.3.4.5.1 Grey Wolf Optimization (GWO) Wolf–Based WSN Clustering

Energy Optimization in WSNs uses Grey Wolf Optimizer [100]. The energy optimization in a WSN is attempted using hybrid SI algorithms: grey wolf optimization and GA for communication. The formation of clusters is done using GWO exploration methods and CH selection using GA. A wolf-based centralized, energy-aware cluster–based algorithm called WOA-Clustering (WOA-C) is developed by [101]. Node with high energy is selected as CH to form clusters which are uniformly distributed throughout the entire sensor plot. The proposed algorithm has three main components: network model, energy model, and cluster head selection model which are explained in the following sections.

12.3.4.5.2 BFO (Bacteria)–Based WSN Clustering

Data aggregation in addition to BFO-based CH selection resulted in an improved WSN energy [102]. The delay in formation is more. BFO has also been applied by [103] for CH selection. The selection of CH is based on principles of BFO to show better performance. The comparison performed in terms of number of clusters and average end-to-end delay in MATLAB is performed. The protocol suffers from higher average packet drop ratio. [104] have extended their previous work by CH selection in WSN using hybrid BFO and bee swarm optimization in a pipeline mechanism. The performance is measured in terms of number of cluster formation, packet drop ratio, and lifetime of network.

12.3.4.5.3 Bat-Based WSN Clustering

Improved low-energy adaptive hierarchy protocol based on local centroid bat algorithm (ILEHP) for designing bat algorithm. In this paper, [105] authors have applied a bat algorithm technique to solve some disadvantage in LEACH like random selection of CH, taking no account of the remaining energy and position of nodes, along with an aim to improve the poor local search capability of the algorithm. The improved protocol divides the CH selection process into optimization of temporary CH and formal CH selection. In this protocol, they will generate temporary CHs by following traditional LEACH protocol at the first round. Later on, they optimize these CHs based on LCBA and select formal CHs based on residual energy.

12.3.4.5.4 Firefly Optimization–Based WSN Clustering

Cluster head selection [106] introduces new cluster-based communication network that will be organized between sensors and sink node. The among sensor nodes best node will be selected as CH applying firefly cyclic grey wolf optimization to stimulate optimal CH selection framework with an objective to stabilization of energy, minimization of distance between nodes and minimizing delay. The FF and GWO algorithms are hybridized to improve performance. Hybrid SI-based clustering algorithm for energy management in WSN [107] designed algorithm based on two SI technique shuffled frog and firefly. Firefly algorithm is applied to from equal sized cluster and shuffled frog technique for adding individuals to clusters. The algorithm is design to work on event generation from sink. SFFA computes required number of nodes to become CH considering distance and residual energy. CSMA/CA and MAC layer protocols rules are applied in formation of clusters, and TDMA is used for communication once clusters are formed. The neighboring information collected will be sent to CH once event message is sent to network. Likewise, the details of selected CH will also be sent to CH. The simulations are performed to compare algorithm with LEACH, SFA, and FFA. The setup phase is lengthier and consumes more energy. In formation of clusters, distance of all nodes is considered as clusters are of equal size. The aggregation is not employed as CH. A Firefly-Inspired Micro and Macro Clustering Approach for WSNs [108] forms clusters based on Firefly principles. The protocol includes micro and macro clustering phases. In self-micro clustering phase, nodes self-organize themselves into clusters and during macro clustering are refined to integrate small neighboring cluster distance wise. The CH will be decided in macro phase based on distance. The results show improvement in residual energy level as are self-organized. The self-organization is not optimal solution to from clusters in network consisting of spread of nodes in wide range. Fire-LEACH: A Novel Clustering Protocol for WSNs based on Firefly Algorithm [FL] [109] approach used for improving the LEACH protocol for reducing in steady state energy consumption. The BS broadcasts the percentage of CHs requirements for the entire network. Based on this randomly, CHs are selected as in LEACH. All the CHs learn about the ordinary nodes and other CHs in the plot. Then, they broadcast the packet of interest by introducing the intensity value that is calculated based on intensity value of all nodes in network for that round. The firefly algorithm is applied to compute this value using distance of CH and non-CH nodes, which serves to be an objective function for all sensor nodes. All the CHs store the maximum of the intensity values calculated with all the other non-CH nodes in the network belonging to a particular round. The non-CH nodes now compare their intensity values with all the other CHs intensity values and attach to a CH that is having more intensity value than their values, by sending a join request packet. This process leads to a cluster formation. After the formation of the clusters, the network enters to the steady state phase; further steps are same as in LEACH. Hybrid Approach for Energy Optimization in WSNs (HAEOW) routing protocol based on firefly and ABC [110] hybrid clustering approach is proposed to minimize the energy of the network so as to increase the life time of WSN. The cluster-based firefly and artificial bee colony (ABC) algorithm are implemented. Two problems are concentrated like selection of CH and cluster formation. Initially, the selection of CH and CH formation of cluster remains same as LEACH for first round. The existing CHs are checked for residual energy if CH is eligible to continue as CH for next round, if it as with firefly technique, it will continue as CH for next round; else, the selection of next CH is done with highest residual energy in the cluster. This process is repeated for all clusters in the network. Then, selection of CH done based on optimization of ABC using residual energy of the current CH; then top required n nodes with highest residual energy are set as CHs. The steady phase remains same as LEACH. A Nature Inspired Optimal Path Finding Algorithm to Mitigate Congestion in WSNs [111] with aim is to avoid congestion in network by applying techniques of firefly to select optimal route communication with BS. The clusters are formed once and they will be static. The balancing of nodes is main issue in this protocol. The cluster-based data transfer enables the WSN to Firefly Algorithm for Cluster Head Selection in WSN. [112] introduces a modified firefly heuristic, and synchronous firefly algorithm is proposed to improve the network performance.

12.3.4.5.5   Frog-Based WSN Clustering

Shuffled Frog Leaping Algorithm–based Unequal Clustering Strategy for WSN [113] formed clusters with principles of shuffled frog leaping algorithm. The CH is exchanged based on time and nodes weight. The relay nodes are identified to communicate between CH and sink. The sink is considered to be mobile to avoid hot spot problem. The performance of algorithm is compared with LEACH and EBUCP. SI Fuzzy Clustering (SIF) is a centralized clustering protocol [114], which utilizes Mamdani fuzzy system to select CHs at each round. SIF uses three input variables including energy level, distance to the sink, and distance to the cluster centroid. At first, all nodes are clustered via fuzzy c-means algorithm, and then, in each cluster, one node is selected as CH via the Mamdani fuzzy inference system. [115] designed a Shuffled frog-leaping algorithm (SFLA)–based Clustering Algorithm (SBCA) for mobile ad hoc networks. They showed how SFLA could be useful in raising the performance of clustering algorithm. It has the ability to find the optimal or near-optimal cluster heads to manage the resources of the network more efficiently. They modified SFLA by replacing the complex evolution with the single point crossover operation. Fuzzy SFLA (FSFLA) [116] employs the SFLA algorithm together with fuzzy inference system in a central CPU positioned at the sink to select CHs for single-hop schemes. It considers the remaining energy, the distance from the sink, the number of neighboring nodes, and node histories in CH-selection procedure. Genetic Algorithm–based Energy-Efficient Adaptive Clustering Hierarchical Protocol (GAEEP) identifies number and position of CH applying genetic algorithm [117]. The protocol is designed in rounds considered with two phases: setup and steady phase. In first phase, BS will execute GA and determine optimal number of CHs and its position. The second phase identifies the communication path from CH to BS. The nodes which are near to BS will communicate data directly to BS instead of CH. CDMA code is used in inter communication to reduce collision. The designed protocol is compared with LEACH, SEP, ERP, LEACH-GA, and DEU for both homo and heterogeneous networks. Sink Mobility–based Energy Balancing Unequal Clustering Protocol [118] has introduced a balance the energy consumption using Shuffled Frog Leaping Algorithm (SFLA) to elect CHs to form unequal clusters. The residual energy is considered in selection to minimize the reclustering overhead. The exchange time and node weight are continuously monitored by CH. The two phases are considered in design cluster establishment and data transmission. The greedy algorithm applied to identify relay node for communication with multi-hop inter cluster routing. The sink node with mobility is assumed in design. The comparison with LEACH and EBUCP protocols is simulated. Novel Chemical reaction optimization–based unequal clustering and routing algorithm for WSNs (nCROU-CRA) [119] is a distributed methodology in design reduces the problem of hot spot. The chemical reaction optimization is used for section of CHs and cluster members to join CH based on cost function. The unequal clusters are formed to communicate with BS. The molecular structure encoding and potential energy function are applied in selection of CH and formation on clusters. The algorithm is compared with CRO-UCRA with parameters residual energy, lifetime, number of alive nodes, and convergence rate and achieves higher performance in all terms. An Unequal Multi-hop Balanced Immune Clustering protocol for WSN (UMBIC) utilizes inter- and intra-cluster communications that are considered in design of WSN for nodes and BS. The unequal clustering and multi-objective immune algorithm mechanism applied in construction. The algorithm is developed considering residual energy and distance factors. The connectivity and low communication cost are key factors identified in design. The computational complexity is reduced. The threshold energy level is keep tracked to go for next iteration or not.

12.3.4.5.6   Glowworm Optimization–Based WSN Clustering

Hybrid-based CH selection for maximizing network lifetime and energy efficiency in WSN [120] selects CH based on principles of Glowworm swarm and fruitfly algorithm. The fitness function for selection of CH considers neighbors with maximum residual energy based on glowworm swarm optimization. It includes four stages: initialization, Luciferin-update, movement, and neighborhood range update. The route identification selection formed applying fruitfly optimization algorithm. The algorithm is compared in terms of performance other existing methods like PSO, Genetic Algorithm (GA), Artificial Bee Colony (ABC), GSO, Ant Lion Optimization (ALO), and Cuckoo Search (CS) of alive node analysis, energy analysis, and cost function, and the betterments of proposed work are also proven.

12.3.4.5.7   Fish-Based WSN Clustering

A novel energy–aware node clustering algorithm for WSNs using a modified artificial fish swarm algorithm [123] form cluster applying local and global searches, applying artificial fish algorithm. The base algorithm is combined with new convergence speed technique by applying search based technique of fish swarm. Whale optimization–based WSN clustering Whale Optimization–Based Energy-Efficient Cluster Head Selection Algorithm for WSNs [124] developed algorithm based on whale optimization–based algorithm. The selection of CH is made considering residual energy into consideration. The model is developed by applying three phases, network, energy, and CH selection.

12.3.4.5.8   Flower Optimization

Flower Pollination Optimization Algorithm for WSN Lifetime Global Optimization (FPOAW) [125] is an energy-aware clustering mode designed in an objective to achieve the global optimization for WSN lifetime. A candidate CH is to be selected for every cluster from the flower pollination clustering. The CH is selected as the node inside the cluster with the most remaining energy. It searches for optimal distribution of nodes on clusters. The objective fitness function is employed to minimize the intra-cluster compactness with minimum distance between nodes in same cluster. In flower pollination optimization, the number of cluster is formed based on distance between CH and nodes in a cluster with a goal to find the number of cluster centers that minimize the intra-cluster distance. The steady phase of the protocol remains unchanged.

12.3.4.5.9   Nature-Based WSN Clustering

A new BBC-based LEACH Algorithm for Energy-Efficient Routing in WSN (ANBLE) is a based on big bang crunch. The protocol consider traditional LEACH algorithm's cluster formation using big bang crunch–based metaheuristic algorithm with an objective to optimize battery utilization. The proposed protocol applies the fitness function on nodes and selects the CH where all the nodes are considered as particles are arranged into an order by way of a convergence operator center of mass and then cluster members are joined around the center mass of CH by adding or subtracting a normal random number whose value decreases as the iterations elapse.

Achieving energy efficiency in WSN using Gravitational Search algorithm (GSA) (AEEWG) [126] is applied for CH selection based on Newtonian law of gravity and the law of motion. Here, agents are considered as objects and their performance based on its masses. All objects are attached to one another by a gravitational force which causes the movement of objects globally. While forming clusters, GSA clustering method is used. CH for each cluster is selected based on the nodes distance from BS in the cluster, node being in central position in cluster, and remaining energy.

The comparison of SI-based metaheuristic WSN clustering is summarized in Table 12.4. Comparison parameters are grouped as pure cluster and general parameters. Parametric values are symbolized in order to avoid space as variable (V), fixed (F), single hop (S), multi-hop (M), Yes (Y), No (N), aggregation (A), relay (R), high (H), medium (M), good (G), and low (L).

12.4 Challenges and Future Direction

This section provides challenges and future directions for SI in WSN, in particular for cluster formation. Wide ranges of applications beginning from monitoring, processing, and to controlling of feature extracted from sensors are recently being applied for disaster management, military surveillance, and other inhabitant-based applications. Sustained duration of sensor life can be prolonged with energy garnering new features obtained from new energy sources. In addition to CH selection, there is scope for selection of SI-based vice CH selection, inter and intra-relay nodes. Furthermore, there is also scope for SI-based data aggregation so as to reduce the amount of data transfer without comprising on QOS and delay parameters. Data aggregation directly leads to increased network life span.

The main challenging part in applying most of the SI algorithm is lack of clarity in understanding of working of these algorithms and difficult for implementation. In addition, the biggest challenge is this SI-based WSN being applied to real-time applications. As of now, most of the work published is the outcome of simulation results. Yet, lot more to explore in this direction to improve clustering identifying in pragmatic WSN few among them are as follows:

- Concentration on real-time distributed WSN
- Optimization of data and energy at CH either by aggregation or decision or mining basis
- Making centralized control in taking major decisions
- Design which are time and space intensive
- Integration with new technological platforms like cloud, high broad adoptions, and other upcoming network embedded technologies, coverage, and connectivity issues

A review of articles establishes that a lot of research scope can still be exploited and explored in area of WSN addressing problems in addition to clustering like multi-hop, mobility based, and QOS parameters. It was observed that ACO, PSO, and ABC SI have been explored extensively for WSN clustering issue. Furthermore, it is observed that CSO, GWO, and FFO are currently being explored. There is still lot of scope of other newly designed SI algorithms in formation clusters for small embedded devices applications like WSN or IoT.

The demand for real-time application events anticipates an efficient and effective QoS-based cluster for fast data delivery from the network infrastructure wise. The reliability and delay are the issues which demand more attention. In addition to identifying the optimal route to BS, there is a need for scalable and less time consumable cluster formation design in real time. In this direction, the survey reveals that the hybrid SI algorithms like PSO-ABC, BFO-MPSO, and others have shown positive response to issues like delay, packet loss, and QOS in an energy-efficient manner.

In future, design of SI algorithms can be developed addressing the following issues:

- Adoption of mobility in the network
- Designing clustering methods for reactive networks
- Scalability
- Designing new heuristic-based clustering approaches
- Application of QoS requirements of a WSN
- Energy-harvesting in sensor networks
- Implementation of SI-based WSN for real-time applications

12.5   Conclusions

This chapter provides comprehensive insight to innumerable SI applications for various fields, in particular for clustering issue in WSN for which the main objective of extending the WSN lifespan. WSN clustering of SI techniques is proved to be promising by their inherent design composition sand computational optimization principles from construction to controlling firm clusters followed by optimal routing. During all these processes, WSN with SI algorithms is minimizing consumption of energy as established by many researchers in their theories and practical demonstrations from sensing to message exchange process with BS. The assessment of different SI clustering techniques on WSN using comparable feature like number of cluster, topological differences, characteristics of nodes, etc., were summarized. The paper also addresses the various challenges and future direction which would of great support for the researchers wanting to work in the much to be explored arena of SI-based WSN. The study reveals that among the various SI algorithms, PSO has been extensively applied for WSN cluster formation followed by use of ABC, CS, BFO, and ACO. We have categorized SI algorithms based on social behavior of insect, bacteria, bird, fish, animal, and others among which, our survey (covering papers from 2000 to 2019) unfolds that almost 50% work is contributed by insect-based SI. There is still lot of scope to explore new SI-based WSN in particular for cluster formation.

Table 12.4 Appraisal of swarm intelligence based metaheuristic WSN clustering.

Reference	SI technique applied	Clustering approach						CH selection approach					Algorithm general feature								
		No. of clusters	Type of topology	Communication b/w CH and BS	Node type	Homogeneous nodes	Data sent to CH	Original energy	Remaining energy	Inter node distance	Energy of cluster	Other factors	Nodes distribution	Overhead message	Energy distribution	Efficiency	Expandability	Delay in transmission	Complexity	Usage of data aggregation	Experimental\simulation tool
Bhaskaran, 2017	FFO	V	S	S	F	Y	A	N	Y	N	Y	Light intensity	Random	H	M	G	M	M	M	Y	MATLAB
Ashwin	WHALE O	V	S	S	F	Y	R	N	Y	N	N	Sum of energy of adjacent nodes	Random	L	L	G	L	M	M	Y	MATLAB
Chavan, 2018	ACO	V	M	M	F	Y	R	N	N	N	N	Location information	Random	L	M	G	M	M	H	N	MATLAB
Prassad, 2016	PSO + DE	F	S	S	F	Y	A	N	Y	Y	N	–	Random	M	M	H	L	L	M	N	Sim
Azizi1, 2015	AFSO (Fish)	F	S	S	F	Y	A	N	N	Y	N	Intra cluster distance	Random	M	M	H	L	L	M	N	Sim
Jabinian, 2018	GWO + GA	V	S	S	F	Y	A	N	Y	Y	N	–	Random	M	M	H	M	H	M	Y	Sim
Boucetta, 2015	ACO	V	S	S	F	Y	A	N	Y	Y	N		Random	L	M	G	M	L	L	Y	MATLAB
Sheta, 2015	ACO	V	S	S	F	Y	A	Y	Y	N	N		Random	L	L	M	M	M	M	Y	MATLAB
Ramluckun, 2018	ACO	F	S	S	F	Y	A	N	Y	Y	N		Random	L	L	M	M	L	M	Y	MATLAB
Gambhir, 2018	ABC	V	S	S	F	Y	R	N	Y	N	Y	Route path distance	Random	L	M	G	L	L	H	N	MATLAB
Kaur, 2018	GA+PSO	V	S	S	F	Y	R	N	Y	N	N		Random	M	M	H	M	M	H	N	MATLAB

(Continued)

Table 12.4 Appraisal of swarm intelligence based metaheuristic WSN clustering. (*Continued*)

Reference	SI technique applied	Clustering approach						CH selection approach					Algorithm general feature								
		No. of clusters	Type of topology	Communication b/w CH and BS	Node type	Homogeneous nodes	Data sent to CH	Original energy	Remaining energy	Inter node distance	Energy of cluster	Other factors	Nodes distribution	Overhead message	Energy distribution	Efficiency	Expandability	Delay in transmission	Complexity	Usage of data aggregation	Experimental\simulation tool
Mann, 2017	ABC	V	S	S	F	Y	R	N	N	Y	N		Random	L	M	M	L	M	L	N	MATLAB
Navanath, 2018	GWO + Fruit fly	V	S	S	F	Y	A	N	N	Y	N		Random	L	M	G	H	M	L	Y	MATLAB
Ahmada, 2018	Bee	V	S	S	F	N	R	Y	Y	Y	N		Random	L	M	G	M	M	M	N	EstiNet 8.1.
Kuila, 2015	PSO	V	S	S	F	N	R	N	Y	Y	N		Random	M	M	G	M	M	M	Y	Sim
Fan, 2016	Frog	V	S	S	F	N	R	N	Y	Y	Y		Random	M	L	G	M	M	H	N	Sim
Veena, 2017	PSO	V	S	S	F		R	N	Y	Y	N		Random	M	M	G	L	M	L	N	Sim
Kumar, 2016	ABG+ACO	V	S	S	F	N	R	N	Y	N	N		Random	L	M	M	L	M	M	Y	Sim (MATLAB)
Adnan, 2016	Cuckoo	V	S	S	M/F	N	R	N	Y	N	N		Random	L	Low	M	M	L	H	Y	Sim
Rao, 2017	PSO	V	S	S	M/F	Y	A	Y	Y	N	Y		Random	L	M	G	L	L	H	N	Sim
Parvin, 2015	PSO	V	S	S	F	Y	A	N	Y	Y	N		Random	L	M	G	H	M	L	Y	Sim
Gupta, 2018	Cuckoo based	V	S	S	F	Y	A	N	Y	Y	N		Random	L	L	G	M	M	L	N	Sim (MAt)

(*Continued*)

Table 12.4 Appraisal of swarm intelligence based metaheuristic WSN clustering. (Continued)

Reference	SI technique applied	Clustering approach						CH selection approach					Algorithm general feature								
		No. of clusters	Type of topology	Communication b/w CH and BS	Node type	Homogeneous nodes	Data sent to CH	Original energy	Remaining energy	Inter node distance	Energy of cluster	Other factors	Nodes distribution	Overhead message	Energy distribution	Efficiency	Expandability	Delay in transmission	Complexity	Usage of data aggregation	Experimental\simulation tool
Jabeura, 2016	Firefly	F	S	S	F	Y	R	Y	N	N	Y	–	Random	L	M	M	L	M	M	N	Sim (JAVA)
Salehian, 2016	IPSO	V	S	S	F	Y	R	N	N	Y	N	Classification	Uniform	G	M	M	M	M	M	Y	Sim (JAVA)
Wang, 2016	PSO	V	S	S	F	Y	R	N	Y	N	N	Position of node	Random	G	M	M	M	L	H	Y	Sim
Kim, 2014	ACO	V	S	S	F	Y	R	N	Y	N	N	Sensing Radii	Random	G	M	G	M	M	M	Y	sim
Elhabyan, 2015	PSO	V	S	S	F	N	R	N	Y	Y	N		Random	G	M	G	M	L	M	Y	sim
Cai, 2015	Bee	F	S	S	F	Y	R	N	Y	Y	Y		Random	G	M	G	M	M	M	N	sim
Pitchaimanickam, 2014	PSO + BFO	V	M	S	F	Y	A	N	N	Y	N		Random	G	M	H	M	M	M	Y	sim
Tina, 2016	MSO(Monkey)	F	S	S	F	Y	R	N	Y	N	N	Location of node	Uniform	G	L	H	L	M	M	Y	Sim
Barzin, 2019	Frog+ firefly	V	S	S	F	N	A	N	Y	Y	N		Uniform	G	L	G	M	M	M	Y	Sim (MATLAB)
Siew, 2013	PSO	V	S	S	F	Y	A	N	Y	N	Y		Uniform	G	L	M	L	L	M	N	Ommet
Suiew, 2013	PSO	V	S	S	F	Y	R	N	N	Y	N		Uniform	L	M	M	L	L	L	Y	NS2
Amin, 2014	PSO	V	S	S	F	Y	A	N	Y	N	N		Random	G	M	M	L	L	M	N	Sim
CAO, 2014	PSO	V	S	M	F	Y	A	N	Y	Y	Y		Uniform	G	L	L	M	M	H	N	Sim

(Continued)

Table 12.4 Appraisal of swarm intelligence based metaheuristic WSN clustering. (Continued)

Reference	SI technique applied	Clustering approach						CH selection approach					Algorithm general feature								
		No. of clusters	Type of topology	Communication b/w CH and BS	Node type	Homogeneous nodes	Data sent to CH	Original energy	Remaining energy	Inter node distance	Energy of cluster	Other factors	Nodes distribution	Overhead message	Energy distribution	Efficiency	Expandability	Delay in transmission	Complexity	Usage of data aggregation	Experimental\simulation tool
Jung-yoon, 2014	PSO	F	S	S	F	Y	A	N	Y	Y	N		Random	G	M	M	M	H	M	N	sim
Nasir, 2019	ACO	V	S	S	F	Y	A	N	Y	N	N		Random	M	M	M	L	L	M	Y	Sim
Gajjar, 2015	ACO	V	S	S	F	Y	A	Y	Y	Y	N		Uniform	L	M	G	L	M	H	Y	Sim
Arya, 2015	AC	V	S	S	F	Y	R	N	Y	Y	N		Random	L	M	G	M	L	M	N	Prowler
Rathi, 2013	PSO	F	M	S	F	Y	A	N	N	N	Y	–	Uniform	L	M	G	L	L	L	Y	MATLAB
Godbole, 2012	PSO	V	S	S	F	Y	R	Y	Y	N	N		Uniform	L	Low	G	L	M	M	N	MATLAB
Myoung, 2008	ACO	V	S	S	F	Y	R	N	N	Y	N	Distance to BS	Random	L	M	G	L	M	H	Y	Omnet
Ramluckun, 2018	ACO	V	S	S	F	Y	R	N	Y	Y	N		Uniform	L	M	M	L	M	H	Y	Omnet
Cao, 2014	LCB (bat)	V	S	S	F	Y	R	N	N	Y	Y	–	Random	L	L	M	H	M	L	N	MATLAB
Archna, 2014	BBC	F	S	S	F	Y	A	N	N	N	N	Arrangement of nodes	Random	M	M	G	L	M	L	N	MATLAB
HAEOW	FF + ABC	V	S	S	F	Y	A	N	N	Y	N	–	Random	L	M	G	L	L	M	Y	NS2
Kumar, 2014	CWO	V	S	S	F	Y	R	N	Y	Y	N		Grid	L	L	G	H	M	M	Y	Sim
Sharaw, 2014	FPO	V	S	S	F	Y	R	N	Y	N	N		Uniform	L	M	M	L	L	H	Y	MATLAB

(Continued)

Table 12.4 Appraisal of swarm intelligence based metaheuristic WSN clustering. *(Continued)*

Reference	SI technique applied	Clustering approach						CH selection approach					Algorithm general feature								
		No. of clusters	Type of topology	Communication b/w CH and BS	Node type	Homogeneous nodes	Data sent to CH	Original energy	Remaining energy	Inter node distance	Energy of cluster	Other factors	Nodes distribution	Overhead message	Energy distribution	Efficiency	Expandability	Delay in transmission	Complexity	Usage of data aggregation	Experimental\simulation tool
S. Kumar, 2014	FF	F	S	S	F	Y	R	N	Y	N	N	Intensity value	Grid	M	M	M	L	M	M	N	Sim
Aksher, 2019	GSA (GRAVITATION)	V	M	S	F	Y	A	N	Y	Y	N	Center position within cluster	Random	M	M	M	L	M	H	Y	NS2
Vinutha, 2017	PSO	V	S	S	F	Y	A	N	Y	Y	N		Random	L	M	M	L	M	H	Y	MATLAB
Garg, 2014	PSO	V	S	M	F	Y	A	N	Y	Y	N		Uniform	L	M	G	H	M	L	N	Omnet
Lingxia, 2013	QTE	V	S	S	F	Y	A	N	Y	Y	N		Grid	L	M	M	L	L	L	N	MATLAB
Bipendeep, 2014	BGO	V	S	S	F	Y	R	Y	N	Y	N		Random	L	L	M	L	M	M	Y	Sim
Ayan, 2009	AOC	V	S	S	F	Y	R	N	N	Y	Y		Random	L	L	M	H	L	M	Y	Sim
Rich, 2014	ABC	V	S	S	F	Y	R	N	Y	Y	Y		Random	L	L	M	H	M	M	Y	NS2
Parual, 2014	ABC	V	M	S	F	Y	A	N	Y	N	Y		Random	L	M	M	H	M	H	Y	MATLAB
Huang, 2008	ABC	V	M	S	M/F	Y	A	N	Y	Y	N		Uniform	L	L	L	H	M	M	N	MATLAB

References

1. Mohammed, A., Burhanuddin, M.A., Alkhazraji, A., Basiron, H., IoT Devices and Sensors Management Framework for Mobile E-health Applications. *J. Adv. Res. Dyn. Control Syst.*, 10, 02–Special Issue, 2157–2161, 2018.

2. Colorni, Dorigo, M., Maniezzo, V., Trubian, M., Ant System for Job-shop Scheduling. *Belg. J. Oper. Res. Stat. Comput. Sci.*, 34, 1, 39–53, 1994.

3. Hassan, H., Shah, W.M., Iskandar, M.F., Talib, M.S., Abdul-Jabbar Mohammed, A., K nearest neighbor joins and mapreduce process enforcement for the cluster of data sets in bigdata. *J. Adv. Res. Dyn. Control Syst.*, 10, 4, 690–696, 2018.

4. Engelbrecht, P. (Ed.), *Computational Intelligence: An Introduction*, The University of California, Wiley, pp13-288, 2010.

(a) Islam, A. K. M. M., Zeb, A., Wada, K., "Communication protocols on dynamic cluster based wireless sensor networks", 2013, *International Conference on Informatics, Electronics and Vision*, Dhaka, pp. 1–6, 2013.

5. Abbass, H., MBO: Marriage in honey bees optimization-a Haplometrosis polygynous swarming approach, in: *Proceedings of the 2001 IEEE Congress on Evolutionary Computation (IEEE Cat. No.01TH8546)*, Seoul, Korea, vol. 1, pp. 207–214, 27–30 May 2001.

6. Abo-zahhad, M., Ahmed, S.M., Sabor, N., A new energy-efficient adaptive clustering protocol based on genetic algorithm for improving the lifetime and the stable period of wireless sensor networks. *Int. J. Energy Inf. Commun.*, 5, 47–72, 2014. http://dx.doi.org/10.14257/ijeic.2014.5.3.05.

7. Adnan, Md. A., Razzaque, *et al.*, A novel cuckoo search based clustering algorithm for wireless sensor networks, in: *Proceedings of ICOCOE-2015, Advanced Computer and Communication Engineering Technology*, Springer International Publishing, pp. 621–634, 2016.

8. Ahmadi, R. and Masdari, M., Providing an efficient algorithm for wireless sensor network routing with hybrid particle swarm optimization and LEACH. *Acad. R. Sci. D Outre-Mer Bull. Seances*, 4, 3, 80–88, 2015.

9. Akkaya, K. and Younis, M., A Survey on Routing Protocols for Wireless Sensor Networks. *Ad Hoc Networks* (Elsevier), 3, 3, 325–349, 2005.

10. Akkaya, K. and Younis, M., An energy-aware QoS routing protocol for wireless sensor networks, in: *Proceedings of the IEEE workshop on mobile and wireless networks (MWN '03)*, Providence (RI), 2003, 2003.

11. Akyildiz, I.F., Su, W., Sankarasubramaniam, Y., Cayirci, E., Wireless sensor networks: A Survey. *Comput. Networks*, 38, 4, 393–422, 2002.

12. Barzin, A., Sadegheih, A., Zare, H.K., Honarvar, M., Hybrid swarm intelligence-based clustering algorithm for energy management in wireless sensor networks. *J. Ind. Syst. Eng.*, 12, 3, 78–106, 2019.

13. Amit, S. and Senthil, M.T., Cluster head selection for energy efficient and delay-less routing in wireless sensor network. *Wirel. Netw.*, Springer, 25, 1, 232–244, 2017.

14. Anandamoy, S., Swarm Intelligence Based Optimization of MANET Cluster Formation. A Thesis submitted to the Faculty of Electrical Engineering, The University of Arizona, 2006, Available from: http://www.aims.arizona.edu/PUBLICATIONS/PDF/Thesis_Sen.pdf.

15. Anandaraman, C., Madurai Sankar, A.V., Natarajan, R.A., New Evolutionary Algorithm Based on Bacterial Evolution and Its Application for Scheduling A Flexible Manufacturing System. *J. Tek. Ind.*, 14, 1–12, 2012.

16. Kar, A.K., Bio inspired computing –A review of algorithms and scope of applications. *Expert Syst. Appl.*, 59, 20–32, 2016.

17. Karegowda, A., Devika, G., Premsudha, B.G., A Pragmatic Study of Evolutionary Techniques Based Energy Efficient Hierarchical routing protocols - LEACH And PEGASIS. *Int. J. Appl. Eng. Res.*, 10, 5, 38274–38285, 2015.

18. Askarzadeh, A. and Rezazadeh, A., A new heuristic optimization algorithm for modeling of proton exchange membrane fuel cell: bird mating optimizer. *Int. J. Energy Res.*, 37, 1196–1204, 2012.

19. Ayesh, A., Beaver algorithm for network security and optimization: Preliminary report, in: *Proceedings of the 2009 IEEE International Conference on Systems, Man and Cybernetics*, San Antonio, TX, USA, 11–14 October 2009, pp. 3657–3662.

20. Christian, B. and Daniel, M., *Swarm intelligence. introduction and applications, Natural Computing Series*, pp. 1–6, Springer, Kingdom, August 2010.

21. Shio kumar singh, MP singh, D K singh, Routing protocols in WSN: A survey, *International journal of computer science and engineering survey*, vol. 1, no. 2, 2010.

22. Panigrahi, B.K., Shi, Y., Lim, M.-H. (Eds.), *Handbook of Swarm Intelligence. Series: Adaptation, Learning, and Optimization*, vol. 7, Springer, Springer-Verlag Berlin Heidelberg, 2011.

23. Pitchaimanickam, B. and Radhakrishnan, S., A hybrid bacteria foraging using Particle Swarm Optimization algorithm for clustering in wireless sensor networks. *Science Engineering and Management Research (ICSEMR), 2014 International Conference on*, IEEE, 2014.

24. Rajakumar, B., The Lion's Algorithm: A New Nature-Inspired Search Algorithm. *Procedia Technol.*, 6, 126–135, 2012.

25. Wang, B., Jin, X., Cheng, B., Lion pride optimizer: An optimization algorithm inspired by lion pride behavior. *Sci. China Inform. Sci.*, 55, 10, 2369–2389, 2012.

26. Baig, A.R. and Rashid, M., Honey bee foraging algorithm for multimodal & dynamic optimization problems, in: *Proceedings of the 9th Annual Conference on Genetic and Evolutionary Computation (GECCO '07)*, London, UK, 7–11 July 2007, ACM Press, New York, NY, USA, p. 169, 2007.

27. Bastos Filho, C.J.A., de Lima Neto, F.B., Lins, A.J.C.C., Nascimento, A.I.S., Lima, M.P., A novel search algorithm based on fish school behavior, in: *Proceedings of the 2008 IEEE International Conference on Systems,Man and Cybernetics*, Singapore, 12–15 October 2008, pp. 2646–2651. Appl. Sci. 8, 1521 30 of 31

28. Bitam, S. and Mellouk, A., Bee life-based multi constraints multicast routing optimization for vehicular *ad hoc* networks. *J. Netw. Comput. Appl.*, 36, 981–991, 2013.

29. Gui, T., Ma, C., Wang, F., Wilkin D. E., Survey on swarm intelligence based routing protocols for WSN, *International conference on industrial technology*, IEEE, Vol 16, pp. 1944-1949, 2016.

30. Blum, and Merkle, D. (Eds.), *Swarm Intelligence – Introduction and Applications. Natural Computing*, Springer, Berlin, 2008.

31. Boucetta, Idoudi, H., Saidane, L.A., Ant Colony Optimizationbased hierarchical data dissemination in WSN, in: *2015 InternationalWireless Communications and Mobile Computing Conference (IWCMC)*, IEEE, pp. 782–787, 2015.

32. Lim, C.P., Jain, L.C., Dehuri, S., *Innovations in Swarm Intelligence: Studies in Computational Intelligence*, vol. 248, 1–7, Springer, 2009.

33. Celik, F., Zengin, A., Tuncel, S., A Survey on swarm intelligence based routing protocols in wireless sensor networks. *Int. J. Phys. Sci.*, 5, 14, 2118–2126, 2010.

34. Chu, S.C., Tsai, P.W., Pan, J.S., Cat Swarm Optimization, in: *Pacific Rim International Conference on Artificial Intelligence*, Springer, Berlin/Heidelberg, Germany, pp. 854–858, 2006.

35. Devipriya, Rajesh Shyamala Devi, B., Thenkumari, K., Efficiency Improvement in Wireless Sensor Networks using ABC Algorithm for Cluster-based Packet Forwarding. *Indian J. Sci. Technol.*, 9, 30, 152–156, 2016.

36. Karaboga, and Basturk, B., A Powerful And Efficient Algorithm ForJ Numerical Function Optimization: Artificial Bee Colony (ABC) Algorithm. *J. Global Optim.*, Springer Netherlands, 39, 3, 459–471, 2007.

37. Karaboga, An Idea Based On Honey Bee Swarm for Numerical Optimization, Technical Report-R06, Erciyes University, Engineering Faculty, Computer Engineering Department, 2005.

38. Prasad, R., Naganjaneyulu, P.V., Satya Prasad, K., *Energy Efficient Clustering in Multi-hop Wireless Sensor Networks Using Differential Evolutionary MOPSO*, vol. 59, pp 134–145, January-December, 2016.

39. Corne, W., Reynolds, A., Bonabeau, E., Swarm Intelligence, in: *Handbook of Natural Computing*, G. Rozenberg, T. Bäck, J.N. Kok (Eds.), pp. 1599–1622, Springer, 2012.

40. Devika, G., Premasudha, B.G., Gowda, A., A comparative study of energy efficient hierarchical wireless sensor network protocols. *Int. J. Appl. Res. Inf. Technol. Comput.*, 6, 3, 189–196, 2015.

41. Dorigo, M., Learning and Natural Algorithms. Ph.D. Thesis, Politecnico di Milano, Milano, Italy, 1992.

42. Drias, H., Sadeg, S., Yahi, S., Cooperative Bees Swarm for Solving the Maximum Weighted Satisfiability Problem, in: *International Work-Conference on Artificial Neural Networks (IWANN)*, pp. 318–325, Springer, Berlin/Heidelberg, Germany, 2005.

43. Duman, E., Uysal, M., Alkaya, A.F., Migrating Birds Optimization: A new metaheuristic approach and its performance on quadratic assignment problem. *Inf. Sci.*, 217, 65–77, 2012.

44. Brynjolfsson, Zungeru, A.M., Ang, L.-M., Seng, K.P., Classical and swarm intelligence routing protocols for wireless sensor networks: A survey and comparison. *J. Netw. Comput. Appl.*, 35, 5, 1508–1536, 2012. https://www.marketresearchfuture.com/reports/wireless-sensor-networks-market-1805.

45. Eusuff, M.M. and Lansey, K.E., Optimization of Water Distribution Network Design Using the Shuffled Frog Leaping Algorithm. *J. Water Resour. Plan. Manag.*, 129, 210–225, 2003.

46. Fan, X. and Du, F., Shuffled frog leaping algorithm based unequal clustering strategy for wireless sensor networks. *Appl. Math. Inform. Sci.*, 1426, 1415–1426, 2015.

47. Feng, X., Lau, F.C.M., Gao, D.A., New Bio-inspired Approach to the Traveling Salesman Problem, in: *International Conference on Complex Sciences*, Springer, Berlin/Heidelberg, Germany, pp. 1310–1321, 2009.

48. Beni, and Wang, J., Swarm intelligence in cellular robotic systems, in: *NATO Advanced Workshop on Robots and Biological Systems*, Il Ciocco, Tuscany, Italy, 1989.

49. Sunitha, G.P., Vijay Kumar, B.P., Dilip Kumar, S.M., A Nature Inspired Optimal Path Finding Algorithm to Mitigate Congestion in WSNs. *Int. J. Sci. Res. Netw. Secur. Commun.*, 6, 3, 50–57, 2018.

50. Gajjar, S., Sarkar, M., Dasgupta, K., FAMACRO: Fuzzy and ant colony optimization based MAC/routing crosslayer protocol for wireless sensor networks. *Procedia Comput. Sci.*, 46, 1014–1021, 2015.

51. Gambhira, Payala, A., Arya, R., Performance analysis of artificial bee colony optimization based clustering protocol in various scenarios of WSN Ankit. *Procedia Comput. Sci.*, 132, 183–188, 2018.

52. Gandomi, A.H. and Alavi, A.H., Krill herd: A new bio-inspired optimization algorithm. *Commun. Nonlinear Sci. Numer. Simul.*, 17, 4831–4845, 2012.

53. González, J.R., Pelta, D.A., Cruz, C., Terrazas, G., Krasnogor, N. (Eds.), pp. 305–318, Springer, Berlin/Heidelberg, Germany, 2010.

54. Gupta, G. and Jha, S., Integrated clustering and routing protocol for wireless sensor networks using Cuckoo and Harmony Search based metaheuristic techniques. *Eng. Appl. Artif. Intell.*, 68, 101–109, 2018.

55. Haddad, O.B., Afshar, A., Mariño, M.A., Honey-Bees Mating Optimization (HBMO) Algorithm: A New Heuristic Approach for Water Resources Optimization. *Water Resour. Manag.*, 20, 661–680, 2006.

56. Havens, T.C., Spain, C.J., Salmon, N.G., Keller, J.M., Roach Infestation Optimization, in: *Proceedings of the 2008 IEEE Swarm Intelligence Symposium*, St. Louis, MO, USA, 21–23 September 2008, pp. 1–7.

57. Heinzelman, W.R., Chandrakasan, A., Balakrishnan, H., Energy efficient communication protocol for wireless microsensor network, in: *Proceedings of the 33rd annual Hawaii international conference on systems science*, vol. 2, pp. 3005–3014, 2000.

58. Hersovici, M., Jacovi, M., Maarek, Y.S., Pelleg, D., Shtalhaim, M., Ur, S., The shark-search algorithm. An application: Tailored Web site mapping. *Comput. Netw. ISDN Syst.*, 30, 317–326, 1998.

59. Kennedy, and Eberhart, R.C., Particle Swarm Optimization, in: *Proceedings of IEEE International Conference on Neural Networks*, Perth, Australia, pp. 1942–1948, 1995.

60. Naeimi, Soroush *et al.*, A survey on the taxonomy of cluster-based routing protocols for homogeneous wireless sensor networks. *Sensors*, vol. 12, no. 6, pp. 7350–7409, 2017.

61. Manyika, Chui, M., Bughin, J., Dobbs, R., Bisson, P., Marrs, A., *Disruptive technologies: Advances that will transform life, business, and the global economy*, vol. 180, McKinsey Global Institute, San Francisco, CA, 2013.

62. Wang, Cao, Y., Li, B., Kim, H.-j., Lee, S., Particle swarm optimization based clustering algorithm with mobile sink for WSNs. *Future Gener. Comput. Syst.*, 76, 452–457, 2016. http://dx.doi.org/10.1016/j.future.2016.08.004.

63. Kim, J.-Y., Sharma, T., Kumar, B., Tomar, G.S., Berry, K., Lee, W.-H., Inter cluster ant colony optimization algorithm for wireless sensor network in dense environment. *Int. J. Distrib. Sens. Netw.*, 2014.

64. Jabeura, N., A Firefly-Inspired Micro and Macro Clustering Approach for Wireless Sensor Networks. *The seventh International Conference on Emerging Ubiquitous Systems and Pervasive Networks (EUSPN)*, 2016.

65. Jain, A.K., Data clustering: 50 years beyond K-means. *Pattern Recognit. Lett.*, 31, 651–666, 2010.

66. Jiang, C.J., Shi, W.R., Xiang, M., Tang, X.L., Energy-balanced unequal clustering protocol for wireless sensor networks. *J. China Univ. Posts Telecommun.*, 17, 94–99, 2010. http://dx.doi.org/10.1016/S1005-8885(09)60494-5.

67. Dattatraya, K.N. and Raghava Rao, K., Hybrid based cluster head selection for maximizing network lifetime and energy efficiency in WSN. *J. King Saud Univ. - Comp. Info. Sci.*, 1, 1–10, 2018.

68. Karaboga, D., An Idea Based on Honey Bee Swarm for Numerical Optimization; Technical Report, Erciyes University, Engineering Faculty, Computer Engineering Department, Kayseri, Turkey, 2005.

69. Karaki, J.N. and Kamal, A.E., Routing Techniques in Wireless Sensor Networks: A Survey. *Wireless Commun., IEEE*, 11, 6, 6–28, 2004.

70. Kavitha, G. and Wahidabanu, R., Foraging optimization for Cluster Head Selection. *J. Theor. Appl. Inf. Technol.*, 61, 3, 571, 2014 March.

71. Krishnanand, K. and Ghose, D., Detection of multiple source locations using a glowworm metaphor with applications to collective robotics, in: *Proceedings of the IEEE Swarm Intelligence Symposium*, Pasadena, CA, USA, 8–10 June 2005, pp. 84–91.

72. Li, X.L., A New Intelligen Optimization-Artificial Fish Swarm Algorithm. Ph.D. Thesis, Zhejiang University, Hangzhou, China, 2003.

73. Li, X.L., Shao, Z.J., Qian, J.X., An Optimizing Method based on Autonomous Animate: Fish Swarm Algorithm. *Syst. Eng. Theory Pract.*, 22, 32–38, 2002.

74. Liu, X.Y., Ant colony optimization algorithm based on dynamical pheromones for clustering analysis. *Int. J. Hybrid Inf. Technol.*, 7, 2, 29–38, 2014.

75. Liu, C., Yan, X., Liu, C., Wu, H., The Wolf Colony Algorithm and Its Application. *Chinese J. Electron.*, 20, 664–667, 2011.

76. Cheng, L., Wu, X., Wang, Y., Artificial Flora (AF) Optimization Algorithm. *Appl. Sci.*, 8, 329, 2018.

77. Lu, X. and Zhou, Y.A., Novel Global Convergence Algorithm: Bee Collecting Pollen Algorithm, in: *Advanced Intelligent Computing Theories and Applications. With Aspects of Artificial Intelligence*, pp. 518–525, Springer, Berlin/Heidelberg, Germany, 2008.

78. Belal, Gaber, J., El-Sayed, H., Almojel, A., Swarm Intelligence, in: *Handbook of Bioinspired Algorithms and Applications. Series: CRC Computer & Information Science*, vol. 7, Chapman & Hall, (Ed.), 2006.

79. Dorigo, Bonabeau, E., Theraulaz, G., Ant algorithms and stigmergy. *Future Gener. Comput. Syst.*, 16, 8, 851–871, 2000.

80. Dorigo, and Birattari, M., Swarm intelligence. *Scholarpedia*, 2, 9, 1462, 2007.

81. Dorigo, M., Optimization, learning and natural algorithms (in Italian), Ph.D. Thesis, Dipartimento diElettronica, Politecnico di Milano, Italy, 1992.

82. Dorigo, M., Maniezzo, V., Colorni, A., Positive feedback as a search strategy, Tech. Report 91-016, Dipartimento di Elettronica, Politecnico di Milano, Italy, 1991.

83. Yazdani, M. and Jolai, F., Lion Optimization Algorithm (LOA): A natureinspired metaheuristic algorithm. *J. Comput. Des. Eng.*, 3, 1, 24–36, 2016.

84. Baskaran, M. and Sadagopan, C., Synchronous Firefly Algorithm for Cluster Head Selection in WSN(). *Hindawi Publishing Corporation Sci. World J.*, Article ID 780879, 7, 2015.

85. Majhi, S.K. and Biswal, S.A., Hybrid Clustering Algorithm Based on K-means and Ant Lion Optimization, in: *Emerging Technologies in Data Mining and Information Security*, pp. 639–650, Springer, Singapore, 2019.

86. Mandal, and Sadhana, S., *Elephant swarm water search algorithm for global optimization*, Springer, 2018.

87. Kaur, M. and Sohi, B.S., Comparative Analysis of Bio Inspired Optimization Techniques in Wireless Sensor Networks with GAPSO Approach. *Indian J. Sci. Technol.*, 11, 4, 83–96, 2018.

88. Mann, P.S. and Singh, S., Energy efficient clustering protocol based on improved metaheuristic in wireless sensor networks. *J. Netw. Comput. Appl.*, 83, 40–52, 2017.

89. Marinakis, Y., Marinaki, M., Matsatsinis, N., A Bumble Bees Mating Optimization Algorithm for Global Unconstrained Optimization Problems, in: *Nature Inspired Cooperative Strategies for Optimization (NICSO 2010)*.

90. Ahmada, M., Ikramb, A.A., Wahid, I., Inamc, M., Ayubd, N., Ali, S., A bio-inspired clustering scheme in wireless sensor networks: BeeWSN, The 9th International Conference on Ambient System, Networks and Technologies (ANT 2018). *Procedia Comput. Sci.*, 130, 206–213, 2018.

91. Meng, X., Liu, Y., Gao, X., Zhang, H.A., New Bio-inspired Algorithm: Chicken Swarm Optimization, in: *Advances in Swarm Intelligence*, pp. 86–94, Springer, Cham, Switzerland, 2014.

92. Min, H. and Wang, Z., Group escape behavior of multiple mobile robot system by mimicking fish schools, in: *Proceedings of the IEEE International Conference on Robotics and Biometrics (ROBIO)*, Tianjin, China, 14–18 December 2010, pp. 320–326.

93. Mirjalili, S., Dragonfly algorithm: A new meta-heuristic optimization technique for solving single-objective, discrete, andmulti-objective problems. *Neural Comput. Appl.*, 27, 1053–1073, 2015.

94. Mirjalili, S., Moth-flame optimization algorithm: A novel nature-inspired heuristic paradigm. *Knowl.-Based Syst.*, 89, 228–249, 2015.

95. Mirjalili, S., The Ant Lion Optimizer. *Adv. Eng. Softw.*, 83, 80–98, 2015.

96. Mirjalili, S. and Lewis, A., The Whale Optimization Algorithm. *Adv. Eng. Softw.*, 95, 51–67, 2016, Appl. Sci. 2018, 8, 1521 31 of 31.

97. Gurpreet Kaur Bhatti, Jatinder Pal Singh Raina, Cuckoo based Energy Effective Routing in Wireless Sensor Network, *International Journal of Computer Science and Communication Engineering*, Vol.3, No.1, PP.92-95, 2014.

98. Mirjalili, S., Mirjalili, S.M., Lewis, A., GreyWolf Optimizer. *Adv. Eng. Softw.*, 69, 46–61, 2014.

99. Monismith, D.R. and Mayfield, B.E., Slime Mold as a model for numerical optimization, in: *Proceedings of the 2008 IEEE Swarm Intelligence Symposium*, St. Louis, MO, USA, 21–23 September 2008, pp. 1–8.

100. Moon, S.H., Park, S., Han, S.J., Energy efficient data collection in sink-centric wireless sensor networks: A clustering approach. *Comput. Commun.*, 101, 12–25, 2017.

101. Mukhdeep, S.M. and Singh, S.B., Firefly Algorithm Based Clustering Technique for Wireless Sensor Networks. *WiSPNET Conference*, IEEE Press, 2016.

102. Mutazono, A., Sugano, M., Murata, M., Energy efficient self-organizing control for wireless sensor networks inspired by calling behavior of frogs. *Comput. Commun.*, 35, 661–669, 2012.

103. Shigei, Miyajima, H., Morishita, H., Energy Consumption Reduction of Clustering Communication Based on Number of Neighbors for Wireless Sensor Networks. *IAENG Int. J. Comput. Sci.*, 37, 3, 136–144, 2010.

104. Nagpal, A., Jatain, A., Gaur, D., Review based on data clustering algorithms, in: *Proceedings of the Conference on Information & Communication Technologies*, Thuckalay, Tamil Nadu, India, 11–12 April 2013, pp. 298–303.

105. Nakrani, S. and Tovey, C., On Honey Bees and Dynamic Allocation in an Internet Server Colony, in: *Proceedings of the 2nd International Workshop on The Mathematics and Algorithms of Social Insects*, Atlanta, GA, USA, 15–17 December 2003, pp. 1–8.

106. Nasir, H.J.A., Ku-Mahamud, K.R., Kamioka, E., Parameter adaptation for ant colony system in wireless sensor network. *J. Inf. Commun. Technol.*, 18, 2, 167–182, 2019.

107. Ramluckun, N. and Bassoo, V., Energy-efficient chain-cluster based intelligent routing technique for WSN. *Appl. Comput. Inform.*, 1, 1–10, 2018.

108. Niu, B. and Wang, H., Bacterial Colony Optimization. *Discret. Dyn. Nat. Soc.*, 2012, 698057, 2012.

109. Zedadra, *et al.*, Swarm intelligence-based algorithms within IoT-based systems: A review. *J. Parallel Distrib. Comput.*, 1, 1–12, 2018. https://doi.org/10.1016/j.jpdc.2018.08.007.

110. Boyinbode, O., Le, H., Mbogho, A., Takizawa, M., Poliah, R., A Survey on Clustering Algorithms for Wireless Sensor Networks. *Proceedings of 2010 13th International Conference on Network-Based Information Systems*, p. 358364, 2010.

111. Odili, J.B., Kahar, M.N.M., Anwar, S., African Buffalo Optimization: A Swarm-Intelligence Technique. *Procedia Comput. Sci.*, 76, 443–448, 2015.

112. Oftadeh, R. and Mahjoob, M.J., A new meta-heuristic optimization algorithm: Hunting Search, in: *Proceedings of the 2009 IEEE Fifth International Conference on Soft Computing, Computing with Words and Perceptions in System Analysis, Decision and Control*, Famagusta, Cyprus, 2–4, pp. 1–5, September 2009.

113. Reddy, and Babu, R., An Evolutionary Secure Energy Efficient Routing Protocol in Internet of Things. *Int. J. Intell. Eng. Syst.*, 10, 3, 337–346, 2017.

114. Pan, W.T., A new Fruit Fly Optimization Algorithm: Taking the financial distress model as an example. *Knowl.-Based Syst.*, 26, 69–74, 2012.

115. Passino, K., Biomimicry of bacterial foraging for distributed optimization and control. *IEEE Control Syst. Mag.*, 22, 52–67, 2002.

116. Pham, D., Ghanbarzadeh, A., Koc, E., Otri, S., Rahim, S., Zaidi, M., The Bees Algorithm. Technical Note; Technical Report, Manufacturing Engineering Centre, Cardiff University, Cardiff, UK, 2005.

117. Pratyay, K. and Prasanta, K.J., Energy efficient clustering and routing algorithms for wireless sensor networks: Particle swarm optimization approach. *Eng. Appl. Artif. Intell.*, 33, 127–140, 2014.

118. Eberhart, C. and Kennedy, J., A new optimizer using particle swarm theory, in: *Proceedings of the Sixth International Symposium on Micro Machine and Human Science*, Nagoya, Japan, pp. 39–43, 1995.

119. Elhabyan, S. and CE Yagoub, M., Two-tier particle swarm optimization protocol for clustering and routing in wireless sensor network. *J. Netw. Comput. Appl.*, 52, 116–128, 2015.

120. Zhao, R. and Tang, W., Monkey algorithm for global numerical optimization. *J. Uncertain Syst.*, 2, 3, 165–176, 2008.

121. Rajagopal, A., Somasundaram, S., Sowmya, B., Suguna, T., Soft computing based Cluster Head Selection in Wireless Sensor Network using Bacterial Foragin Optimization Algorithm. *Int. J. Electr. Comput. Energetic, Electron. Commun. Eng.*, WASET, 9, 3, 357–362, 2015.

122. Rajagopal, A., Somasundaram, S., Sowmya, B., Suguna, T., Cluster Head Selection in Wireless Sensor Network using Hybrid BFO-BSO Algorithm. *Int. J. Appl. Eng. Res.*, RI publications, 10, 17, 38245–36250, 2015.

123. Kumar, R. and Kumar, D., Hybrid Swarm Intelligence Energy Efficient Clustered Routing Algorithm for Wireless Sensor Networks. *Hindawi Publishing Corporation J. Sensors*, 2016, Article ID 5836913, 19 pages, 2016. http://dx.doi.org/10.1155/2016/5836913.

124. Aryaa, R. and Sharma, S.C., Analysis and optimization of energy of sensor node using ACO in WSN, International Conference on Advanced Computing Technologies and Applications (ICACTA-2015). *Procedia Comput. Sci.*, 45, 681–686, 2015.

125. Rao, P.C., Jana, P.K., Banka, H., A particle swarm optimization based energy efficient cluster head selection algorithm for wireless sensor networks. *Wirel. Netw.*, 23, 7, 2005–2020, 2017.

126. RejinaParvin, J. and Vasanthanayaki, C., Particle swarm optimization-based clustering by preventing residual nodes in wireless sensor networks. *IEEE Sens. J.*, 15, 8, 4264–4274, 2015.

127. Azizi, R., Sedghi, H., Shoja, H., Sepas-Moghaddam, A., A novel energy aware node clustering algorithm for wireless sensor networks using a modified artificial fish swarm algorithm. *Int. J. Comput. Netw. Commun. (IJCNC)*, 7, 3, pp. 105–116, May 2015.

128. Roth, M.H., Termite: A Swarm Intelligent Routing Algorithm for Mobile Wireless Ad-Hoc Networks. Ph.D. Thesis, Cornell University, Ithaca, NY, USA, 2005.

129. Oliveira, C., Andrade Duarte, G., Beltrao Cunha, H., Unified Coordination-Communication Strategy to Swarm Controlled Mobile Wireless Sensor Network. *IEEE Lat. Am. Trans.*, 12, 5, 951–956, 2014.

130. Guru, S., Halgamuge, S., Fernando, S., Particle swarm optimizers for cluster formation in wireless sensor networks, in: *Proc. Int. Conf. on Intelligent Sensors, Sensor Networks and Information Processing*, pp. 319–324, 2005.

131. Hasson, S.T. and Hasan, Z.Y., Roads clustering approach's in VANET models, in: *2017 Annual Conference on New Trends in Information and Communications Technology Applications, NTICT 2017*, March, pp. 316–321, 2017.

132. Sabor, S. and Abo-Sahhad, M., An Unequal Multi-hop Balanced Immune Clustering protocol for wireless sensor networks. *Appl. Soft Comput. J.*, 43, 372–389, 2016. http://dx.doi.org/10.1016/jasc.2016.02.016.

133. Sabor, N., Sasaki, S., Abo-Zahhad, M., Ahmed, S.M., A comprehensive survey on hierarchical-based routing protocols for mobile wireless sensor networks: Review, taxonomy, and future directions. *Wireless Commun. Mobile Comput.*, 1, 23, 2017.

134. Sahitya, G., Balaji, N., Naidu, C., Wireless sensor network for smart agriculture, in: *Applied and Theoretical Computing and Communication Technology (iCATccT), 2016 2nd International Conference on*, IEEE, pp. 488–493, 2016.

135. Saleem, M., Di Caro, G., Farooq, M., Swarm intelligence based routing protocol for wireless sensor networks: Survey and future directions. *Inf. Sci.*, 181, 4597–4624, 2011.

136. Salehian, S.K. and Subraminiam, S., Unequal clustering by improved particle swarm optimization in Wireless Sensor Network. *Procedia Comput. Sci.*, 62, 403–409, 2015, http://dx.doi.org/10.1016/j.procs.2015.08.433.

137. Saremi, S., Mirjalili, S., Lewis, A., Grasshopper Optimisation Algorithm: Theory and application. *Adv. Eng. Softw.*, 105, 30–47, 2017.

138. Sato, T. and Hagiwara, M., Bee System: finding solution by a concentrated search, in: *Proceedings of the 1997 IEEE International Conference on Systems, Man, and Cybernetics*, Orlando, FL, USA, 12–15 October 1997, vol. 4, pp. 3954–3959.

139. Shankar, D., Chavan, Kulkarni, A.V., Event based clustering localized energy efficient ACO for performance enhancement of WSN. *Eng. Technol. Appl. Sci. Res.*, 8, 4, 3177–3183, 2018.

140. Sheta, A. and Solaiman, B., Evolving a Hybrid KMeans Clustering Algorithm for Wireless Sensor Network Using PSO and GAs. *Int. J. Comput. Sci. Issues (IJCSI)*, 12, 1, 23–32, 2015.

141. Shiqin, Y., Jianjun, J., Guangxing, Y.A., Dolphin Partner Optimization, in: *Proceedings of the 2009 IEEE WRI Global Congress on Intelligent Systems*, Xiamen, China, 19–21 May 2009, pp. 124–128.

142. Shokouhifar, M. and Jalali, A., A new evolutionary based application specific routing protocol for clustered wireless sensor networks. *AEU – Electron. Commun.*, 69, 432–441, 2015.

143. Singh, M.P. and Singh, B.S., Improved metaheuristic based energy-efficient clustering protocol for wireless sensor networks. *Eng. Appl. Artif. Intell.*, 53, 142–152, 2017.

144. Singh, S.K., Singh, M.P., Singh, D.K., Routing Protocols in Wireless Sensor Networks – A Survey. *Int. J. Comput. Sci. Eng. Surv. (IJCSES)*, 1, 2, 63–83, 2010.

145. Salehian, S. and Subhraminiam, S.K., Unequal clustering by improved particle swarm optimization in WSN. *Internarional conferencde on soft computing ans software engineering*, SCSE, 2015.

146. Srinivasa Rao, P.C. and Banka, H., Novel chemical reaction optimization based unequal clustering and routing algorithm for Wireless Sensor Networks (nCROUCRA). *Wirel. Netw.*, 23, 3, 386–394, 2016, http://dx.doi.org/10.1007/s11276-015-1148-0.

147. Teimoury, E., Gholamian, M.R., Masoum, B., Ghanavati, M., An optimized clustering algorithm based on Kmeans using Honey Bee Mating algorithm. *Sensors*, 16, 65, 1–19, 2016.

148. Teodorović, D. and Dell'Orco, M., Bee colony optimization—A cooperative learning approach to complex transportation problems. *Adv. OR AI Methods Transp.*, 51, 60, 2005.

149. Theraulaz, G., Goss, S., Gervet, J., Deneubourg, J.L., Task differentiation in Polistes wasp colonies: A model for self-organizing groups of robots, in: *Proceedings of the First international Conference on Simulation of Adaptive Behavior on from Animals to Animats*, Paris, France, 24–28 September 1991, pp. 346–355.

150. Anand, V. and Pandey, S., Particle Swarm Optimization and harmony search based clustering and routing in Wireless Sensor Networks. *Int. J. Comput. Int. Sys.*, 10, 1252–1262, 2017.

151. Katiyar, V., Chand, N., Soni, S., A Survey on Clustering Algorithms for Heterogeneous Wireless Sensor Networks. *Int. J. Adv. Netw. Appl.*, 02, 04, 745–754, 2011.

152. Wedde, H.F., Farooq, M., Zhang, Y., BeeHive: An Efficient Fault-Tolerant Routing Algorithm Inspired by Honey Bee Behavior, in: *Ant Colony Optimization and Swarm Intelligence*,

M. Dorigo, M. Birattari, C. Blum, L.M. Gambardella, F. Mondada, T. Stützle (Eds.), pp. 83–94, Springer, Berlin/Heidelberg, Germany, 2004.

153. Cai, X. *et al.*, Bee-Sensor-C: An Energy-Efficient and Scalable Multipath Routing Protocol for Wireless Sensor Networks. *Int. J. Distrib. Sens. Netw.*, 1, 1–14, 2015.

154. Xunli, F.A. and Feiefi, D.U., Shuffled frog leaping algorithm based unequal clustering strategy for wireless sensor networks. *Int. J. Appl. Math. Inf. Sci.*, 9, 3, 1415–1426, 2015.

155. Xunli, F.A.N., and Feiefi DUShuffled Frog Leaping Algorithm based Unequal Clustering Strategy for Wireless Sensor Networks. *Appl. Math. Inform. Sci.*, 9, 3, 1415–1426, 1415, 2015.

156. Yang, C., Chen, J., Tu, X., Algorithm of Fast Marriage in Honey Bees Optimization and Convergence Analysis, in: *Proceedings of the 2007 IEEE International Conference on Automation and Logistics*, Jinan, China, pp. 1794–1799, 18–21 August 2007.

157. Yang, C., Tu, X., Chen, J., Algorithm of Marriage in Honey Bees Optimization Based on the Wolf Pack Search, in: *Proceedings of the 2007 IEEE International Conference on Intelligent Pervasive Computing (IPC 2007)*, Jeju City, Korea, pp. 462–467, 11–13 October 2007.

158. Yang, X.S., *A New Metaheuristic Bat-Inspired Algorithm. In Nature Inspired Cooperative Strategies for Optimization (NICSO 2010)*, vol. 284, pp. 65–74, Springer, Berlin/Heidelberg, Germany, 2010.

159. Yang, X.S., Engineering Optimizations *via* Nature-Inspired Virtual Bee Algorithms, in: *International Work-Conference on the Interplay Between Natural and Artificial Computation*, Springer, Berlin/Heidelberg, Germany, pp. 317–323, 2005.

160. Yang, X.S., Firefly Algorithm, in: *Nature-Inspired Metaheuristic Algorithms*, p. 128, Luniver Press, Beckington, UK, 2008.

161. Yang, X.S. and Suash, D., Cuckoo Search *via* Lévy flights, in: *Proceedings of the 2009 IEEE World Congress on Nature & Biologically Inspired Computing (NaBIC)*, Coimbatore, India, pp. 210–214, 9–11 December 2009.

162. Zahedi, Z., Akbari, R., Shokouhifar, M., Safaei, F., Jalali, A., Swarm intelligence based fuzzy routing protocol for clustered wireless sensor networks. *Expert Syst. Appl.*, 55, 313–328, 2016.

163. Zaman, N. and Abdullah, A.B., Energy efficient routing in wireless sensor network: Research issues and challenges, in: *IEEE International Conference on Intelligence and Information Technology*, United, 2010.

164. Jabinian, Z., Ayatollahitafti, V., Safdarkhani, H., Energy Optimization in Wireless Sensor Networks Using Grey Wolf Optimizer. *J. Soft Comput. Decis. Support Syst.*, 5, 3, 1–6, June 2018.

165. Su, M.-C., Su, S.Y., Zhao, Y.X., A Swarm inspired projection algorithm. *Pattern Recognit.*, 42, 11, 2764–2786, 2009.

166. Yang, X.S., Deb, S., Eagle strategy using levy walk and firefly algorithms for stochastv optimization, In: Gonzalez J.R, Pelta D A, Cruz C, Terrazas G, Krasnogor N, Nature inspired cooperative stratergies for optimization, studies in computational intelligence, Vol. 284, Springer, Berlin, Heiderlberg, 2010. https://doi.org/10.1007/978-3-642-12538-6_9

13

Swarm Intelligence for Clustering in Wireless Sensor Networks

Preeti Sethi

J.C. Bose University of Science & Technology, YMCA, Faridabad, Haryana, India

Abstract

Swarm Intelligence (SI) is the concept which explores the collaborative behavior of various decentralized units (e.g., mobile agents) to solve complex problems. It includes models that show the ability to acquire knowledge to adapt to different circumstances. Use of SI approach in wireless sensor network (WSN) is a promising approach because of the fact that it is a connected network of individual nodes which cooperatively bind themselves in a network. Clustering in WSN refers to grouping the sensors in near proximity in a logical unit called cluster. Each cluster is headed by a special sensor which is responsible for data collection from the individual sensors. The increasing use of sensors in applications like environment monitoring and health care applications has attracted the research community to ensemble SI in these units. The chapter presents a detailed description of how SI can be exploited for clustering in WSNs, thereby ensuring an energy-efficient data dissemination in a resource constrained network.

Keywords: Swarm Intelligence, clustering, mobile agents, data dissemination, fault tolerance, hierarchical network, sensors, intelligent sensing units (ISUs)

13.1   Introduction

The term "swarm" refers to a group of flying objects/insects which cooperatively work to achieve a common goal. The concept of *Swarm Intelligence* (SI) means "*collective intelligence*" inhibited by the group of units involved in a given network. SI owe its roots to the life of social insects (like wasps, ants, bees, and termites) which are known for their organization, having an efficient communication and warning system, maintaining an army and dividing labor. It has been found that the colonies (groups) of these social insects are very flexible and adaptive. These little living things are also looked upon for their feature where a "senior" worker performs the tasks of "junior" worker(s) in case of the need of the same arises. This flexibility allows the colony to be robust and maintain its life in spite of considerable disturbances. Interaction between individual insects in a colony of social insects like bee dancing during food procuring, ants' pheromone secretion, and performance of specific

Email: preetisethi22@gmail.com

Abhishek Kumar, Pramod Singh Rathore, Vicente Garrcia Diaz and Rashmi Agrawal (eds.) Swarm Intelligence Optimization: Algorithms and Applications, (263–274) © 2021 Scrivener Publishing LLC. ISBN 978-1-119-77874-5

acts which signal the other insects to start performing the same actions has also motivated the researchers to imbibe these concepts for both inter-cluster and intra-cluster communication. These communication systems between individual insects contribute to the formation of the "collective intelligence" of social insect colonies. Ant Colony Optimization (ACO) and Particle Swarm Optimization (PSO) are the two most popular optimization frameworks based on original notion of SI [1]. The above listed features of insects have attracted the researchers to a great level and several artificial agents have been created by setting analogy with social insects.

13.2   Clustering in Wireless Sensor Networks

A wireless sensor network (WSN) is defined as a particular class of *ad hoc* network consisting of several miniature sensing units called *sensors*. These miniature units, which are generally arbitrarily deployed in a given environment, sense the physical and environmental conditions such as sound, temperature, pressure, etc., and pass their sensed data through the network to other location(s) known as sink or destination. Figure 13.1 presents the basic architecture of WSN. The key advantage of using these small devices to monitor the surroundings is that it does not need infrastructure for gathering knowledge. The sensor nodes in the WSN continuously observe the environment and then depending on their application transfer the data by single-hop or multi-hop data transmission to the sink node [2].

WSN finds its application in various domains like traffic control system, military surveillance, environmental monitoring, forest fire detection, health care systems, etc., to name a few. Each of these applications exploits the sensing and communication capability of sensor units for collecting the information from the targeted area.

On the basis of network architecture, WSN is categorized into flat and/or hierarchical network. Figure 13.2 depicts 2 types of Wireless Sensor Network. Whereas in flat network, each sensor node transfers the data directly from source to the destination (via single hop

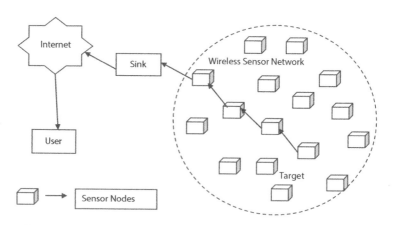

Figure 13.1 Architecture of WSN.

or multiple hops), hierarchical network organizes the nodes into smaller sub-groups called clusters. Individual sensor nodes submit their data to their respective cluster head, which further submit the same to the destination/sink for further analysis [3].

Clustering is defined as the task of grouping sensors on the basis of some parameter (distance, logical organization, etc.). The special sensor nodes elected as cluster head then transmit the information of its respective cluster to its immediate parent, thereby reducing the network traffic. Clustering reduces the number of nodes taking part in communication, ensures scalability for large number of nodes, and reduces the communication overhead for both single hop and multiple hops [15].

Organising sensor nodes into clusters has been excessively pursued by the research community in order to achieve one or the other of the following objectives.

- Load Balancing: One of the major objectives of clustering is to evenly distribute the randomly deployed sensors so as to achieve load balancing. Uniform distribution of these sensing units can also influence the delay factor of the data being communicated. When cluster heads of such equal sized clusters perform data aggregation, the combined data report becomes ready almost at the same time for further processing at the base station or at the next tier in the network [5, 16].
- Fault Tolerance: As the selected cluster heads are nothing but sensor nodes, they are prone to malfunction or fail. In order to prevent the loss of information due to the failure of sensor node in a given cluster, achieving fault tolerance is a desirable property especially in harsh and non-reachable environments. To achieve fault tolerance, dynamic clustering or (re)clustering is proposed in literature. Though dynamic clustering helps to achieve fault

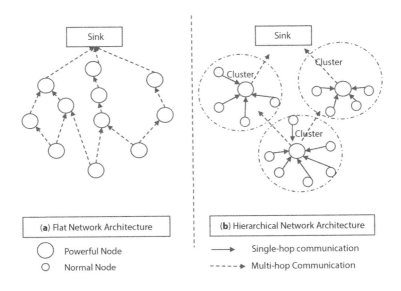

Figure 13.2 Types of Wireless Sensor Network.

tolerance, it causes additional burden on nodes and disruption to the on-going operation. Therefore, back-up cluster heads or rotation of CHs is done to achieve fault tolerance [17, 18].

- Increased Connectivity and Reduced Delay: To ensure maximum benefits as a result of clustering, inter-cluster communication is a major requirement in many applications. The goal of connectivity is not only restricted to guaranteeing the availability of a path from every cluster head to the base station but also be more restrictive by imposing a bound on Minimal Cluster Count on the path length. It is desired to minimize the count of elected cluster heads especially when they are resource rich nodes and there is inherent complexity in deploying such nodes. Reducing their count is also required when their size is large and their visibility is unwanted in applications like border protection, military surveillance, infrastructure security, etc., to name a few [19].

- Maximal Network Longevity: It is advantageous if the energy dissipated in intra-cluster communication is minimized. If the cluster heads are resource rich enough, energy minimization can be achieved if the CH is placed as closed to the sensors. However, when CHs are regular sensors, their lifetime can be extended by limiting their load [21].

- Minimal Cluster Count: It is desired to minimize the count of elected cluster heads especially when they are resource rich nodes and there is inherent complexity in deploying such nodes. Reducing their count is also required when their size is large and their visibility is unwanted in applications like border protection, military reconnaissance, and infrastructure security [6, 22].

13.3   Use of Swarm Intelligence for Clustering in WSN

The novel concept of SI has attracted the research community to a great extent and paved a way for using it to achieve the objectives of clustering in WSN. The network makes use of small moving units called *mobile agents* for the purpose of traversing the data from source to destination [14, 20]. This section firstly provides an in-depth description of mobile agents. It thereafter discusses the use of mobile agents for performing the task of clustering, thereby using SI [4].

13.3.1   Mobile Agents: Properties and Behavior

Mobile agents are special type of software agents which are mobile in nature, i.e., which can migrate and execute on different machines in a dynamic networked environment. A typical mobile agent can migrate from one machine to another under its own control and can suspend execution any time. Mobile agents are capable of executing on different machines in a dynamic networked environment and sense and (re)act autonomously and proactively in this environment to realize a set of goals or tasks. They are thus autonomous, social, and adaptable mobile entities. A mobile agent approach trades server computation and cost for savings in network bandwidth and client computation. This approach is advantageous when the server's CPU is not a bottleneck. These types of agents also provide a natural development environment for implementing free market trading services. The flexible distributed computing architecture integrated with mobile agents pave a way for a radical and attractive rethinking of the design process [24].

13.3.2 Benefits of Using Mobile Agents

The use of mobile agents has simplified the implementation of many applications in a networking environment. The various advantages incurred by using them are as follows.

- Reduction of Communication

The use of mobile agents reduces communication with respect to bandwidth, latency, and connection time at the expense of minimal overhead for sending agent code and its execution state across the network. Communication latency is reduced by sending an agent with a sequence of service requests across the network rather than issuing each service request by a separate remote procedure call. Similarly, communication bandwidth is controlled by migrating the agent across the network in order to deliver instructions for the generation of data on a remote host. It also gets reduced by moving the agent across the network to the source of data in order to reduce the data before transmission. An example for the reduction of communication by mobile code is the NeWS window system where clients communicate with the display server by sending brief PostScript programs instead of drawing a grid by sending several thousand messages for individual points [7].

- Asynchronous Tasks

Another advantage of mobile agent technology is the ability to perform tasks asynchronously. Using this technology, the client part of the application is relocated from the mobile device to immobile servers provided in the network. To an end user, it gives the view that the entire task is moved to the network, where it gets completed asynchronously.

- Dynamic Protocols and Intelligent Data

Mobile agents support dynamic protocols, i.e., new protocols which can be executed automatically and on need basis. Initially, however, to receive an agent, the client and server must share some standard protocol. Once the agent is running, though, it can make use of any specialized protocol for communicating back to its home server. Additionally, an executing agent can repetitively communicate with the server without intervention from the user, thereby permitting the use of dynamic services. One of the most widely used example of above mentioned concept is a news service which can transmit news updates to agents on distributed clients by using a special multicast protocol.

- Software Deployment

Mobile agents help to automate the software installation and updation process. These mobile entities are capable of gathering information about the environment, inquire the same from the user about their installation preferences, configure the system, create directories, and uncompress and compile the software. However, this approach to software deployment has its own restrictions as it might not be possible to capture each and very special case and error condition of the installation process and the programming of suitable deployment agents might become very complex. An improved approach to software deployment would be to use the agent language itself (Agent Tcl, Obliq, etc.), as it is, in particular, designed to prevent such damage.

- Temporary Applications

In addition to deploying software packages, the agent can be the application itself. In many of the cases, an application agent might be self-contained and has no communication needs at all. In that case, it is much smaller than a stand-alone application since it could exploit the infrastructure provided by the mobile agent system. Examples of such temporary applications are route planners which are downloaded on a mobile computer for a particular trip and rejected after its use. Upon arrival at a new location, the user might temporarily download services that are particular to this new scenario. Java-based applets are also the examples of applications of mobile agents [8].

- Distributed and Heterogeneous Computing

Mobile agents can also serve as the basis for general-purpose distributed and heterogeneous computing. They provide the necessary infrastructure for communication between the tasks in a heterogeneous environment. The agent system furthermore supports the independent compilation and initiation of agents so that further agents can be assigned to a task at runtime. Prospective applications for agent-based distributed computing are parallel algorithms with a reasonable low communication overhead compared to its computation requirement and particle or object-based simulation.

13.3.3   Swarm Intelligence–Based Clustering Approach

Because of the robust approach of the mobile agents, they are being embedded in sensor units for the purpose of data and/or information communication. They then work using the principle of SI to support the same. Numerous SI-based clustering algorithms have been proposed in literature for both inter and intra clustering [25, 26].

The chapter presents a depth study of a mobile agent–based architecture which makes use of SI for clustering. The work presents a detailed study of the above shown architecture. It is a novel architecture specially designed for non-deterministic environment. As shown in the figure, the complete architecture is divided into four phases, namely, mobility controlled communication phase, clustering phase, filtering phase, and fusion Phase (MC3F2) Figure 13.3 presents the Architecture of MC3F2. The detailed study of all the four phases is beyond the scope of this chapter. Interested readers can refer to [23] for the same. This chapter elaborates on how clustering is done using SI [9].

The work describes a clustering algorithm which makes use of mobile agents. These mobile agents are imbibed in the sensor units, thereby making them as intelligent Sensor Units (ISUs). This agent-based approach is rightly termed as Agent-Based Clustering (ABC) and is well suited to event driven applications especially in a non-deterministic area.

ABC approach for clustering runs every time an event is detected by an ISU. When an ISU detects an event, it initiates its corresponding agent to form cluster. This mobile agent (termed as initiator agent) considering itself to be a tentative cluster head generates a call for proposal (*cfp*) for all the ISUs which are within its communication range of its ISU. The communication range of a particular sensor is calculated using Equation (13.1) [10].

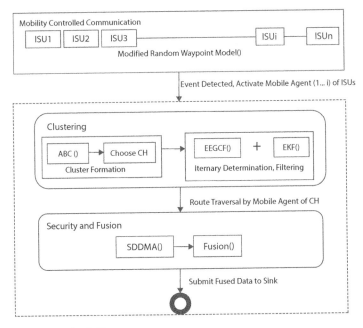

Figure 13.3 Architecture of MC3F2.

$$c = 2 \times r \tag{13.1}$$

where *c = communication range of ISU,*

r = sensing range of ISU.

Each ISU which receives the *cfp* responds with its residual energy and reliability value (RV) through its embedded mobile agent. The residual energy at any interval (say, t) is given by Equation (13.2)

$$E_{residual} = E_{maximum} - (E_{sensing} + E_{processing} + E_{transmission}) \tag{13.2}$$

The RV of an agent refers to its credibility to perform an assigned task. When two or more agents compete for a similar task, the one with the higher RV value is chosen to perform that specific task. The RV value of an agent has been calculated using RCNTEP. The initiator agent logs both these values from every responding sensor and compares its residual energy with each of the incoming residual energy values logged in as: $E_{residual[1....n]}$

Three possibilities arise:

a) The residual energy value of the initiator agent is larger than any of the respondent's residual energy. In such a case, the initiator agent considers its sensor to be a cluster head and broadcasts an "*election_won*" message to all the neighbors for which it generated a *cfp*.

b) The residual energy value of the initiator agent is less than any of the respondent's residual energy. In such a case, the initiator agent determines the sensor with the maximum energy and communicates it to carry out the task of clustering and generate a *cfp* for the same.

c) The residual energy value of the initiator agent is equal to any of the respondent's residual energy. This situation normally arises when clustering is being carried out for the first time in the network. In such a case, every sensor has maximum energy, i.e., $E_{residual} = E_{max}$. The initiator agent in this case thus uses the RV value of an agent to determine the cluster head. Figures 13.4 and 13.5 depict the working algorithm and flowchart of ABC [11].

Algorithm :Form_clusters()

    Input :

- n : no. of nodes in th e network
- Eresidual[1.....n] : Residual energies of all the nodes in the network
- *RVagent[1.........n] : Reliability value of the software agents of all the sensors in the network*

    Output : A Clustered Network

Begin

    . *Detect the event*

    For (i=1; i<=n; i++) // n is the no. of sensors which detected the event

        a. Sensor_Agent[i] = Tentative CH

        b. Sensor_Agent[i] broadcasts its sensing range(r) value to rest of the n - 1 sensors in the network and ask for their E_{res} value based on the equation : c = 2r

        c. Sensor_Agent[i] asks for Reliability value of the agent of each responding sensor

        d. Log in the incoming E_{res} value and Reliability Value of the sensors (say j sensors, where j<=n) and compare it with the E_{res} values of the parent/receiver sensor

    For (k=1; k<=j; k++)

    If any (E_{res}(k)) >E_{res} (parent sensor)

        cluster_head = k

    else if E_{res} (k) <Eres (parent sensor)

        cluster_head = parent sensor

    else if Eres (j) = Eres (parent sensor) = Emax

        cluster_head = sensor whose agent has max(RV)

End.

Figure 13.4 Working algorithm of ABC.

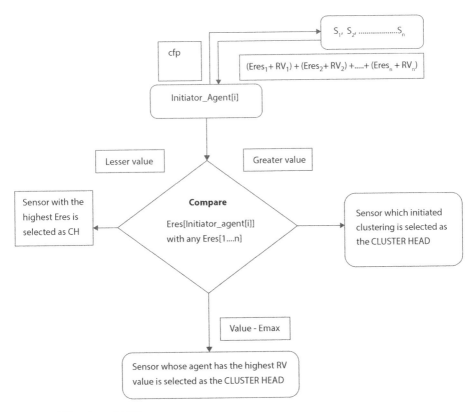

Figure 13.5 Flowchart of ABC.

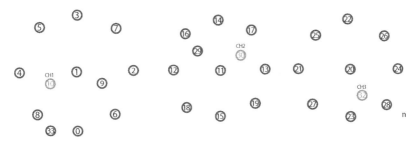

Figure 13.6 Randomly deployed clusters with elected cluster heads.

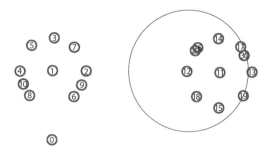

Figure 13.7 Clustered ISUs.

ABC protocol was simulated using MATLAB, and the snapshots of the simulation of ABC are shown in Figures 13.6 and 13.7, respectively [12].

13.4   Conclusion

The detailed study of the chapter reveals that the concept of SI clearly justifies that nature is still a continuous source of inspiration for human beings. The said concept is found to have incredible scope in the arena of WSNs. It has been found that the use of SI for the purpose of clustering leads to numerous benefits like increased speed of communication, execution on demand, reduced channel traffic, etc. Once the data has been collected from various clusters, it can henceforth be used for data analysis depending upon the application [13].

References

1. Abbasi, A.A. and Younis, M., A survey on clustering algorithms for wireless sensor networks. *Comput. Commun.*, 30, 14–15, 2826–2841, 2007.
2. Abbasi, S., Manteghi, S., Heidarzadegan, A., Nemati, Y., Parvin, H., A Robust Clustering *via* Swarm Intelligence, in: *International Conference on Computational Science and Its Applications*, Springer, Cham, pp. 55–70, 2015, June.
3. Abraham, A., Das, S., Roy, S., Swarm intelligence algorithms for data clustering, in: *Soft computing for knowledge discovery and data mining*, pp. 279–313, Springer, Boston, MA, 2008.
4. Zhao, X., Wang, C., Su, J., Wang, J., Research and application based on the swarm intelligence algorithm and artificial intelligence for wind farm decision system. *Renew. Energy*, 134, 681–697, 2019.
5. Aderohunmu, F.A., Deng, J.D., Purvis, M., Enhancing clustering in wireless sensor networks with energy heterogeneity. *Int. J. Bus. Data Commun. Netw. (IJBDCN)*, 7, 4, 18–31, 2011.
6. Ari, A.A.A., Labraoui, N., Yenké, B.O., Gueroui, A., Clustering algorithm for wireless sensor networks: The honeybee swarms nest-sites selection process based approach. *Int. J. Sens. Netw.*, 27, 1, 1–13, 2018.
7. Boveiri, H.R., Khayami, R., Elhoseny, M., Gunasekaran, M., An efficient Swarm-Intelligence approach for task scheduling in cloud-based internet of things applications. *J. Ambient Intell. Hum. Comput.*, 10, 9, 3469–3479, 2019.

8. Dorigo, M., Birattari, M., Li, X., López-Ibáñez, M., Ohkura, K., Pinciroli, C., Stützle, T. (Eds.), *Swarm Intelligence: 10th International Conference, ANTS 2016, Brussels, Belgium, September 7–9, 2016, Proceedings*, vol. 9882, Springer International Publishing, Switzerland, 2016.

9. Eberhart, R. and Kennedy, J., Particle swarm optimization, in: *Proceedings of the IEEE international conference on neural networks*, vol. 4, pp. 1942–1948, 1995, November.

10. El-Gamal, Y., El-Gazzar, K., Saeb, M., A Comparative Performance Evaluation Model of Mobile Agent Versus Remote Method Invocation for Information Retrieval. *Proc. World Acad. Sci.*, 7, 286–291, 2007.

11. Karaboga, D. and Akay, B., A survey: Algorithms simulating bee swarm intelligence. *Artif. Intell. Rev.*, 31, 1–4, 61–85, 2009.

12. Karaboga, D. and Ozturk, C., A novel clustering approach: Artificial Bee Colony (ABC) algorithm. *Appl. Soft Comput.*, 11, 1, 652–657, 2011.

13. Karim, L., Nasser, N., Sheltami, T., A fault tolerant dynamic clustering protocol of wireless sensor networks, in: *GLOBECOM 2009–2009 IEEE Global Telecommunications Conference*, IEEE, pp. 1–6, 2009, November.

14. Kassabalidis, I., El-Sharkawi, M.A., Marks, R.J., Arabshahi, P., Gray, A.A., Swarm intelligence for routing in communication networks, in: *GLOBECOM'01. IEEE Global Telecommunications Conference (Cat. No. 01CH37270)*, vol. 6, IEEE, pp. 3613–3617, 2001, November.

15. Kuila, P. and Jana, P.K., Energy efficient clustering and routing algorithms for wireless sensor networks: Particle swarm optimization approach. *Eng. Appl. Artif. Intell.*, 33, 127–140, 2014.

16. Kumar, D., Aseri, T.C., Patel, R.B., Multi-hop communication routing (MCR) protocol for heterogeneous wireless sensor networks. *Int. J. Inf. Technol. Commun. Convergence*, 1, 2, 130–145, 2011.

17. Kumarawadu, P., Dechene, D.J., Luccini, M., Sauer, A., Algorithms for node clustering in wireless sensor networks: A survey, in: *2008 4th International Conference on Information and Automation for Sustainability*, IEEE, pp. 295–300, 2008, December.

18. Li, D.A., Hao, H., Ji, G., Zhao, J., An adaptive clustering algorithm based on improved particle swarm optimisation in wireless sensor networks. *Int. J. High Perform. Comput. Networking*, 8, 4, 370–380, 2015.

19. Liu, C.M., Lee, C.H., Wang, L.C., Distributed clustering algorithms for data-gathering in wireless mobile sensor networks. *J. Parallel Distrib. Comput.*, 67, 11, 1187–1200, 2007.

20. Parpinelli, R.S. and Lopes, H.S., New inspirations in swarm intelligence: A survey. *Int. J. Bio-Inspir. Com.*, 3, 1, 1–16, 2011.

21. Rani, N.S., Rao, O.S., Prasad, M.K., Efficient implementation of data aggregation in wsns by mobile agent paradigm. *Int. J. Comput. Sci. Eng.*, 3, 9, 3254, 2011.

22. Senthilnath, J., Kulkarni, S., Raghuram, D.R., Sudhindra, M., Omkar, S.N., Das, V., Mani, V., A novel harmony search-based approach for clustering problems. *Int. J. Swarm Intell.*, 2, 1, 66–86, 2016.

23. Sethi, Juneja, Chauhan, *Deign of a Communication Strategy for Wireless Sensors in Non-Deterministic Environment using "Mobile Agent*, MEACSE Publications. http://www.meacse.org/ijcar 2014.

24. Sutagundar, A.V. and Manvi, S.S., Location aware event driven multipath routing in Wireless Sensor Networks: Agent based approach. *Egypt. Inform. J.*, 14, 1, 55–65, 2013.

25. Ünler, A., Improvement of energy demand forecasts using swarm intelligence: The case of Turkey with projections to 2025. *Energy Policy*, 36, 6, 1937–1944, 2008.

26. Xiao, R. and Chen, T., Relationships of swarm intelligence and artificial immune system. *Int. J. Bio-Inspir. Com.*, 5, 1, 35–51, 2013.

14

Swarm Intelligence for Clustering in Wi-Fi Networks

Astha Parihar[1*] and Ramkishore Kuchana[2]

[1]MDSU Ajmer, Ajmer, India
[2]HCL Technologies, Dallas, TX, India

Abstract

Wi-Fi networks or cellular networks are used in various fields such as healthcare and military. Due to its limited, miniature energy sources, power becomes the mist valuable resources for node in this type of networks. To enhance the usage of power sources, developer gives several ideas from assorted angles. Clustered nodes play a precious role in preserving energy. Clustering perspective targets resolving the collision rose in useful information broadcasting. In this segment, we defined some modern power adequate clustering approaches, to enhance the life of sensing networks. The suggested clustering techniques are: (a) fuzzy logic–based clustering lead selection, (b) efficient sleep job process for sensor nodes, (c) hierarchical clustering, and (d) estimating power service. Classical clustering perspective that is Small Power Adaptive Clustering Hierarchy (SPACH) and selected clustering methods are assumed for comparing the execution of suggested perspectives. The introduced current clustering outlook exhorts improved life related to the elected rules.

Keywords: Wireless sensor networks, clustering, energy, harvesting, fuzzy logic

14.1 Introduction

14.1.1 Wi-Fi Networks

In the on-going years, remote sensor systems (RSSs) have increase critical jobs in different applications and have pulled in the consideration of specialists because of their perplexing, different necessities that frequently concede intrinsic exchange offs. A remote sensor arrangement is comprised of sensor hubs associated through an impromptu and self-designing availability.

There is a fundamental area in remote system named as sink that is helpful and partially comprises the ecological parameters such as temperature, pressure also known as sensor hubs, and screen. That sink node of cellular network collects the information from the nerve center and dispatches the information to the client over the internet or any other private virtual system that is PVS.

Corresponding author: asthaparihar9@gmail.com

Abhishek Kumar, Pramod Singh Rathore, Vicente Garrcia Diaz and Rashmi Agrawal (eds.) Swarm Intelligence Optimization: Algorithms and Applications, (275–290) © 2021 Scrivener Publishing LLC. ISBN 978-1-119-77874-5

In general, cellular networks get feature and essential to specially appointed organization. Class of small range remote individuals region has a place in wireless network [1].

A sensor hub contains a radio handset; handset plays out the job of both the transmitter and collector. Vitality sources and sensors are related by the arrangement of microcontroller and electronic circuits. The expense and range of sensor hubs show a critical level of variety relying on the idea of the function. In numerous applications, sensor hubs request the individual association because of the arbitrariness present in uncontrolled, nondeterministic topologies [2, 3].

Various classifications of sensor hubs accommodate checking parameters, for example, temperature, dampness, sound, movement of articles, and so on. These classes are isolated upon the idea of utilizations. In future, sensor systems would pulverize an essential piece of human life and make existing PCs, porList specialized gadget, and other registering gadgets.

A sensor system might be made out of cognate or sensor hubs. They may screen either space or items or communications of these two [4]. In this day and age, sensor systems are utilized in fluctuated fields, for example, combat zone observation, clinical diagnostics, accuracy Longmin, climate checking, and local apparatuses force. Every sensor function requests its self-arrangement of prerequisites and attributes. Most sensor applications utilize reactors in the spot of common sensors to respond to the occasions in a proper way.

Plan of wireless sensor networks (WSNs) gives a few difficulties because of confinement of assets, for example, stockpiling, handling, and correspondence of messages. These assets become boundless in the greater part of the sensor systems. Hypothetical estimation could not be precise enough in numerous situations to anticipate and forestall disappointment of sensor systems. The plan multifaceted nature of WSNs increments with developing applications and their needs. Applications of sensors, its new commands, and new arrangements are required for traditional calculations of impromptu system, which is sufficiently for take into these sensors [5].

Remote sensing systems might be arranged into pre-determined and abandoned systems that depend over its utilization [6]. Previous classification of systems picks up the benefits of nature of administration (QoS), adaptation to internal failure, strength, and adaptability. In numerous sober minded situations, human oversight for sensor systems is constrained or precluded since the hubs are scattered in basic conditions, for example, more profound piece of wildernesses and submerged situations. These systems are called as unattended systems [7].

Likewise, a characteristic exchange off is seen in the midst of the guidelines used to decide the presentation of Wi-Fi networks. The applications barely coordinate with indistinguishable arrangement of guidelines. Comparing the prerequisites, they oppose summed up answers for their temperament of self-logical inconsistency and application-explicit regions [8]. Adaptability arrangement is tested when the self-governance of hubs increments. There is a joined requirement for quick assembly time and least vitality utilization of sensor hubs. At the point when the arrangements are slanted toward one or a lot of parameters, they normally bargain the remainder of the exhibition factors. This unpredictability prompts many intriguing questions and arrangements with regard to depicting the proficiency of a WSN. Cutting over the fleeting and spatial areas, the procedure turns out to be increasingly mind-boggling, multifaceted, and profoundly particular [9].

The life of a sensor organizations is devoted reliant upon vitality utilization, particularly place where there is no arrangement of human perspectives to the included sensor hubs.

Along these lines, numerous strategies have been suggested to limit vitality utilization in RSSs. Numerous difficulties related to this are displayed by remote sensing system [10].

The presentation of a remote sensor organization is multifaceted and inalienably imbalanced under one or constrained points of recognition. A comprehensive and reasonable methodology required an explicit and entire comprehension of sensor utilization [11].

14.1.2 Wi-Fi Networks Clustering

Clustering is one of the significant techniques for dragging out the system lifetime in RSS. It includes gathering of sensor hubs into groups and choosing bunch heads (CHs) for all the groups. CHs gather the information from separate bunch's hubs and forward the totaled information to base station.

Sensor hubs collect information and send it to a sink either legitimately or cooperatively over the different hubs. To reduce system traffic, adaptability and vigor sensor function bunched the hubs [12].

An example plan of bunching is appeared in Figure 14.1. Here, chunks are furnished by group of heads and these chunk heads send the totaled information to the related organization [13].

Versatility of execution over the growing sensor systems is the essential bit of leeway of bunching. Moreover, bunching perspective gives various auxiliary points of interest. It gives dependability and maintains a strategic distance from one-point disappointment because of its confined arrangements. To decrease power utilization appropriately for Wi-Fi networks a group of nodes will be recommended [14]. All sensor hubs are not necessary to be in active state and devour vitality in various sensor applications. Some nerve centers might be situated in the rest process when the light is fleeted and spatial, in which no vitality is destroyed [15]. A viable calendar can be contrived and conveyed to these sensor hubs

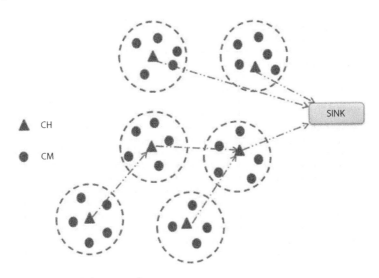

Figure 14.1 Clustering in wireless network.

through the sink or director. There are chosen sensor hubs named as "Bunch Head". Group head screens and directs the information stream across bunches for which impressive vitality is devoured. Therefore, to diminish the life of sensing system, re-clustering procedure and impression of group head is required [16].

One of the traditional bunching conventions named small vitality versatile grouping pecking order tends to the over-burdening of groups and it pivots the job of bunch heads between the sensor hubs that exist in a group. The huge disadvantage of small convention methodology is that no burden is given for the leftover vitality of the nerve center. The constraints of Small Power Adaptive Clustering Hierarchy (SPACH) persuaded specialists to return to and enhance the SPACH convention to receive QoS prerequisites of wireless network. When all is said and done, SPACH and its variations experience the ill effects of adaptability and burden adjusting regardless of their effortlessness [17].

A fluffy-based framework such as hubs and the hubs' center (for shape on request bundled) with specific information is used for utilization of bunching convention of rationale leveled grouping. This work motivated numerous analysts to re-quantify the job of group heads from the local bunch point of view in a various leveled sensor condition [18].

A bunching perspective to be specific, vitality mindful grouping plan with transmission power control for sensor organizations conveyed perspective for way determination to arrive at the sink [19]. This plan sets various degrees of transmission power for intra-group and between bunch correspondence to improve vitality investment funds.

A vitality collecting convention to be specific, vitality reaping and data transmission convention assess the vitality to be gathered dependent on the blackout likelihood.

The previously mentioned contemporary bunching perspectives for RSSs demonstrate the requirement for the new grouping arrangements from various points of view.

The coming of new advancements and rising patterns in operation improvement protest the exploration discoveries of execution in sensor networks, particularly to the vitality point of view [20]. A group of arrangements is expected to job with different kinds of neglected nerve systems where numerous limits are eccentric because of arbitrary sending of sensor hubs. Watching intently, center is necessary more around the correspondence upward of sensor hubs. Additionally, any proposal of bunching perspective ought to be tried for its versatility in a WSN domain.

14.2 Power Conscious Fuzzy Clustering Algorithm (PCFCA)

14.2.1 Adequate Cluster Head Selection in PCFCA

Vitality mindful fluffy grouping calculation (PCFCA) is a psychological method for non-adjective bunching procedure. In this procedure, the sensor hubs are used in an altered remote sensing application and grouped by the vitality point of view.

On the basis of trial conditions, the accompanying reasons are made.

Sending is completed in an irregular way by the sensors.

It is an altered condition.

All the sensor hubs are passive in nature.

The separation among two sensor hubs is estimated by the got signal quality

14.2.2   Creation of Clusters

The registered sensor hubs must be separate because of the consumption of sensor hubs. For this, our proposed perspective utilizes a component where a reference point signal is broadcast from the sink to the remainder of the sensor hubs. In light of the got signal quality, a sensor hub can ascertain its good ways from the sink. At that point, a gathering of conditional bunch heads is chosen from the sensor organizations in order to a particular portion of the whole system as folSmalls. An edge "T" is determined and sent to all the sensor hubs. Each sensor hub produces an irregular number and looks at the equivalent against the got limit esteem. Assume the created esteem is more than the edge, at that point, the sensor hub pronounces itself as a group head. Else, it turns into a standard sensor hub [21].

The proposed strategy brings about 2-bounce group arrangement, and a perpetual bunch head (CH) is chosen dependent on fluffy rationale which accentuates the accompanying three elements.

(1) Staying leftover vitality:
This framework is relied upon the larger for a qualified CH in an opposition stage same as vigorously connected with to local bunch and between group information crowds.

(2) Amount of nodes is two-jump inclusion:
This amount of 2 means the number of complete neighbors is situated in the 2-bounce good ways that is taken away to the conditional CH and is set as in (14.1). It is alluring for a speculative bunch head to have larger incentive guidelines to turn into a perpetual group head.

$$\text{2-jump hub degree} = |\text{S2-bounce nbs}(i)|/\#\text{Vertex} \qquad (14.1)$$

Here, s2-jump nbs(i) and gives the full counts of neighbors in order to the conditional bunch head in its multi-bounce inclusion. A run of the mill 2-bounce grouping condition in RSSs is spoken to in Figure 14.2.

(3) Cluster Head Centrality:
In order to looking a successful CH, the criterion should be small qualities to lessen vitality utilization due to the information collection and overloading forms. Centrality of a hub is determined utilizing in (14.2).

$$\text{Node Centrality} = \sqrt{(\Sigma js2\text{-hop-nba}(i)d2(I,j))/(|s2\text{-hop-nba}(i)|)} \qquad (14.2)$$

Here, the term "d(i,j)" speaks to the separation in the middle of two hubs "I" and "j", 0j is an individual from the set 2-jump nbs. The variable "A" speaks to zone of the system.

Utilizing conditional group heads (TCHs) that are recognized, and by utilizing fluffy rationale, essential bunch heads (PCHs) are chosen assuming the three previously mentioned parameters. The fluffy yield volatile "possibility" is registered for each speculative group head as appeared in List 14.1 to figure its likelihood to become to a lasting bunch head [22].

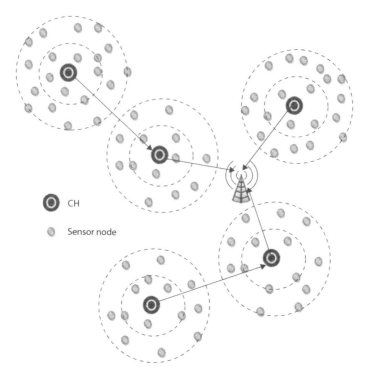

Figure 14.2 A multi-hop clustered Wi-Fi network.

Utilizing Mandeni strategy, the fluffy in the event that rules is prepared. Each provisional bunch head acquires its opportunity esteems and communicates the equivalent to all its 2-bounce neighbors. It occurs in ensuing phases of jump inclusion [23].

In this manner, a sensor hub can either turn into a bunch head or stays as a standard hub. A standard hub needs to recognize the reasonable bunch to join. Assume that it has gotten commercials from at least two bunch heads to join; at that point, it will pick the nearby group lead and accompanied gathering. This assumption is done by the vitality viewpoint. Two chunk leads that are situated on equivalent separation might be noticed at the specific events. In this type of cases, the sensor hubs will pick that bunch leads which are promoted, gotten before and join. Group of covering is kept away [24].

To produce the information from the sensor hubs, the following procedure is used. The bunch heads gather the information from the group hubs and total the information. Here, a group is shaped on 2-jump inclusion, and thus, the conglomeration should be possible for a bigger scope contrasted with the traditional 1-bounce bunching perspectives.

The group goes detailed collected information to the sink. In contrast to SPACH and numerous traditional calculations, the proposed calculation acquires the nearness of various jump hand-off in middle of the group lead and the sink [25]. This multi-jump transfer supports the determination of any one way dependent on little likelihood between different decisions and the chosen way is not really an ideal way as folSmalled in numerous methodologies [26]. The dreary works of a couple of mainstream ways which have been distinguished

List 14.1 Input and output variables in fuzzy sets.

Power	Multi-Hop ND	Node correspondence	Time	Power
Small	Small	Long	Very Shaky	Small
Small	Small	Moderate	Shaky	Small
Small	Small	Near	Slight Shaky	Small
Small	Moderate	Long	Shaky	Small
Small	Moderate	Moderate	Slight Shaky	Small
Small	Moderate	Near	Slight Shaky	Small
Small	Large	Long	Slight Shaky	Small
Small	Large	Moderate	Slight Shaky	Small
Small	Large	Near	Moderate	Small
Moderate	Small	Long	Slight Shaky	Moderate
Moderate	Small	Moderate	Slight Moderate	Moderate
Moderate	Small	Near	Moderate	Moderate
Moderate	Moderate	Long	Slight Moderate	Moderate
Moderate	Moderate	Moderate	Moderate	Moderate
Moderate	Moderate	Near	Large Moderate	Moderate
Moderate	Large	Long	Moderate	Moderate
Moderate	Large	Moderate	Large Moderate	Moderate
Moderate	Large	Near	Slight strong	Moderate
Large	Small	Long	Moderate	Large
Large	Small	Moderate	Large Moderate	Large
Large	Small	Near	Slight strong	Large
Large	Moderate	Long	Large Moderate	Large
Large	Moderate	Moderate	Slight strong	Large
Large	Moderate	Near	Strong	Large
Large	Large	Long	Slight strong	Large
Large	Large	Moderate	Strong	Large
Large	Large	Near	Very strong	Large

as proficient ways cause vitality consumption of hubs on these ways and force them to bite the dust early. Our concept of choosing minimum utilized or unutilized ways can successfully add to the conveyance of vitality utilization and delay the life of sensor hubs [26, 27].

14.2.3 Execution Assessment of PCFCA

Calculations of this presentation are accessed under three situations. First situation consisting that sink is situated in the middle of huge numbers that is 100, which are sent. Second situation contains that sink is situated at the inside when the quantity of sensor hubs was served as 200 tests to the system versatility. In situation third, the sink is situated outer the predefined Wi-Fi networks [28]. Limits and the system length are kept up as in situation 2. The exhibition of PCFCA calculation is looked at against the bench-marking conventions to be specific, small vitality versatile grouping chain of importance (SPACH), vitality mindful bunching convention utilizing fluffy rationale (PCPF), and vitality mindful bunching plan with broMSCAsting energy control for sensor systems (EACLE) [29].

Measurement utilization for registering the life of sensing systems that are early hub bites the dust (FND) and half of the hubs alive (HNA) measurements. The above-mentioned measurements are broadly embraced dependent at the perspective even if the vitality consumption of that measurement is absolute early hub in the system or half of the hubs demonstrate the demise of the system. Recreation results of proposed calculations show vitality recovery contrasted with SPACH, 46% of progress concerning EACLE and 30% of progress as for PCPF [30].

It is to be seen that SPACH shows the least fortunate exhibition among the chose bunching perspectives since it does not reappoint group heads from the vitality point of view and it keeps on being a probabilistic model. EACLE gives some reformation in vitality utilization as concentrated from the recreation outcomes. The addition in vitality proficiency is accomplished in EACLE as long as it utilizes various ways for between bunch traffic and delays the passing of sensor hubs. PCPF guarantees much more vitality enhancement as long as it receives a fluffy-based bunch head political decision. The outcomes saw across both FND and HNA metric affirms this case [31].

It lessens vitality proficiency by assuming important and adequate guidelines for a bunch head political race and accept a possible design in which 2-jump inclusion is given for each group head and multi-bounce hand-off is accomplished for between bunch correspondences [32]. The outcomes exhibit that PCFCA keeps WSN working for longer period other than different methodologies.

This work remains as an agent for psychological and successful group head political decision process. Such techniques uncover the sensor systems and its applications to the developing time of investigations and can be in the end marketed. Efficient Energy Harvesting Clustering assisted (EEHC) algorithm [33].

14.3 Vitality Collecting in Remote Sensor Systems

Life of remote sensor applications relies on the lifetime of the sensor hubs which are compelled by their vitality assets. These assets manage the overseen by the utilization of vitality reaping, using encompassing sources to drag out the battery life in remote sensor hubs. The productivity of this methodology relies on how much vitality is gathered. This can significantly impact the lifetime of sensor hubs and thusly that of the sensor organization [34]. In our proficient vitality gathering helped bunching (EEHC) for remote sensor organizations, the successful vitality reaping for RSSs is tested and concentrated through a productive vitality planning. The estimation of vitality utilization, vitality planning, and vitality gathering is introduced as folSmalls [35].

14.3.1   Power Utilization

A sensor hub devours vitality during detecting the information and sending this information to the bunch head. A bunch head expends the vitality in session to the gathering, information total, and sending the amassed information. The vitality utilization of a bunch part to detect and send 1-piece of data to the group head is assessed in (14.3).

$$E_{SN} = E_{Sensing} + E_{tx} \tag{14.3}$$

Accepting a detecting pace of "x," the all out information detected and broadcasted by "n" bunch individuals in a timespan "t" is assessed as shows in (14.4).

$$ECM = (n.x.t).E_{SN} \tag{14.4}$$

When the greatest counts of group individuals are situated at 1-bounce separation from the bunch head, it is expected that the information detected on time "t" and sends to the bunch head inside a similar stretch. Assume a group head gathers L-bit size of information on time "t" (i.e., L = x.t.n); at that point, the all out vitality protection for information gathering, total, and sending in that CH across timespan "t" is evaluated as shown in Eq. (14.5).

$$E_{CH} = (n.x.t)E_{rx} + (n.x.t) + E_{DA} + n.x.t\ /\alpha + E_{txr} \tag{14.5}$$

where α is aggregation ratio.
The total power acquired at time "t" for a cluster is shown in (14.6).

$$Ec = E_{CH} + E_{CM} \tag{14.6}$$

For a time hole "t," the whole cluster that is the entire cluster nodes along with the cluster head should produce the power similar to that of the approximated energy. Let us consider that there are "n" cluster representative and a cluster head, and then, the power that is expected to be produced by a sensor node in a cluster is shown in the Eq. (14.7).

$$Eh = Ecn + 1Eh \tag{14.7}$$

14.3.2   Production of Energy

Gathered vitality is determined for each time stretch "T" among time "t1" and "t1 + T." The three parts speak to the vitality of the hub at beginning time "t1," vitality collected on time span "T," and vitality spillage during this stretch. The element «τ» speaks to charging proficiency. Every sensor hub is given the capacity cushions to gather reaped vitality.

14.3.3   Power Cost

The energy devoured should be remunerated through the vitality gathered inside the limit of a group in some random time allotment that is the vitality spending plan should reap more vitality other than the vitality expended in each bunch intermittently [36]. A productive vitality financial plan ought to guarantee that the vitality utilization ought not to be expanded than the vitality collected over whenever cut.

14.3.4   Performance Representation of EEHC

The exhibition of our EEHC has been contrasted and an advanced grouping convention named vitality collecting and data transmission convention (EHITP) and the traditional bunching convention SPACH belongs to the three situations. In situation I, 100 sensor hubs are sent to the district of 200 × 200 m². In situations II and III, the number of inhabitants in sensor hubs and territory is multiplied progressively. The exploratory outcomes show that EEHC displays average correction of 91% and 67% when contrasted with SPACH and EHITP, individually.

Along these lines, the gathering can make proficient by proper planning in remote sensing systems and this planning continues affected through the idea of the sensor applications and basic powerful requirements.

14.4   Adequate Power Circular Clustering Algorithm (APRC)

14.4.1   Case-Based Clustering in Wi-Fi Networks

For the most part, RSSs are utilized for two purposes: ceaseless information observing and occasion checking. A model for the previous class is a climate observing sensor that estimates temperature, dampness, and so forth. An ordinary occasion–based sensor arranges territory checking, for example, observation of wild creatures and savvy home applications. But, a couple of utilizations in the subsequent class, a large portion of the hubs are keeps on rest manner so as to spare force and the powerful rest/wakeup planning calculations are required to decide the arrangement of sensor hubs that can be booked to lay down as for time.

The vitality proficient circular grouping (APRC) calculation is an occasion driven bunching calculation, i.e., on the event of an occasion, the groups are shaped to lessen vitality spread, in a circular style. The circular bunching perspective utilizes two phases of grouping process. The primary phase of grouping is trailed by further parcelling of bunches. At that point, CHs are chosen from vitality viewpoint.

14.4.2   Circular Clustering Outlook

The circular bunching perspective utilizes two phases of grouping procedure. Since the organization of sensor hubs, the separation among them is figured utilizing Euclidean separation. In view of the separation, "k" number of groups is framed which brings about the principal phase of bunches. Since the grouping procedure is displayed as circular procedure

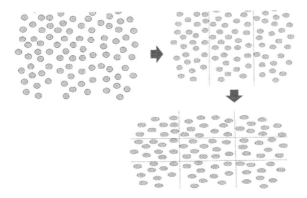

Figure 14.3 Circular clustering in Wi-Fi networks.

ahead, "k" count of bunches is separated in "j" count of groups dependent on the separation and span among the hubs which prompts the other phase of groups. An average procedure of this two-phase grouping is pictorially spoken to as appeared in Figure 14.3. After circular grouping procedure, CH is chosen dependent on vitality levels and utilizing cooperative booking calculation. In light of the calculations, the hub with least turnaround time and large vitality is chosen as the CH between the hubs in the bunch.

Information of particular 6-s round is detected by the hubs. Turnaround time is determined since the rounds are finished. The hub having the base turnaround time is chosen as the bunch head between the hubs in the group. Each hub sends the detected information to the bunch head. Bunch head contains information that is amassed and transmitted to the base station by the multi-jump steering. The totaled information in a group head prompts less transmission information, decline in overheads, and abatement in vitality utilization.

14.4.3   Performance Representation of APRC

The exhibition of our APRC has been assessed across the customary SPACH bunching perspective under three situations through recreation. In situation I, the quantity of sensor hub sent is 100 and so as to test the adaptability the situation II and situation III were thought of. In situation II, 250 sensor hubs and, in situation III, 500 sensor hubs have been thought of.

From the outcomes acquired for situation I, APRC perspective shows execution improvement when contrasted with the exemplary SPACH convention. For 100 hubs, there is 23.8% expansion in lifetime, 0.29% reduction in vitality utilization, 3.0% lessening setback, 1.49% expansion in transmission of time, 1.8% increment in good put, and 0.56% diminishing in overhead. In situation II, APRC displays the execution enhancement of 12.58% expansion in life, 0.402% decline in vitality utilization, 9.815% abatement in delay, 9.289% increment in devolution time, 0.524% increment in good put, and 0.554% reduction in overhead. In situation III, APRC displays execution enhancement of 11.03% expansion in lifetime, 0.619% abatement in vitality utilization, 5.735% lessening in delay, 9.289% increment in transmission time, 0.524% increment in good put, and 0.554% diminishing in overhead trash out.

Along these lines, the circular bunching strategy gives significant progress across different execution causes, continuing the harmony of the whole system.

14.5   Modifying Scattered Clustering Algorithm (MSCA)

14.5.1   Equivalence Estimation in Data Sensing

From a fleeting and structural point of view, methodology of grouping the sensor hubs is utilized in the similitude metric estimation. Similar and nearest sensing system generates comparable information. Essentially, this information created from a similar system can display likeness to significant stretch out of the exception of excellent situation of utilization. Likewise, information which is produced by similar sensor hubs at progressive time gaps of perception can uncover likeness. Repetition of that information age as well as its total, as adequately managed by this strategy, which are extensive adds vitality utilization in sensing system.

Segment of similitude measure in the midst of the information detected from sensor hubs makes the way for devise a viable rest timeList and spare vitality. This thought is promoted in the proposed versatile conveyed bunching calculation (MSCA).

14.5.2   Steps in Modifying Scattered Clustering Algorithm (MSCA)

It utilizes two significant stages: a bunch arrangement stage and a versatile rest obligation cycle stage. In the group arrangement stage, the information age rate and the likeness between information arrangement are broke down by the sink. In light of estimation, the hubs are assembled into different bunches. In each bunch, the group heads are chosen, dependent on the network and remaining vitality.

In functional situations, the groups may not be in equivalent size. In view of the comparability proportion of the time arrangement, the grouping is done in this methodology. By utilizing the comparability measure, the level of spatial relationship can be determined. For the most part, for two areas with large structural connection, their comparing time arrangement is related with large comparability estimation. Subsequently, in an exceptionally smooth sub-district, the watched measure includes just slight changes inside the sub-area. At the end of the day, the contrast between the perceptions at any two areas inside the sub-locale might be exceptionally slight and consequently unimportant.

Along these lines, without trading off the perception unwavering quality, the working sensor hubs inside this sub-locale could be meagre. Then, again, the working sensor hubs ought to be thick in a quick evolving sub-area. The spatial testing rate needs to coordinate the spatial variety of the watched physical episode by setting a suiList Nearness measure edge esteem. Thus, the likeness measure limit esteem incorporates a level autonomy. This worth may be turned to adjust the exchange off among unwavering quality and vitality utilization.

In the rest obligation period stage, the information age paces of bunch individuals are contrasted and a base limit level. The hubs with lower rates, smaller than the limit scale, are in total apportioned a rest obligation period that is already defined. The rest of plan is educated to each sensor hub. The booking is done with a reasonable and circulated way to control vitality utilization.

Each group head gathers the information from its individuals and checks for the nearness in the got information. In the event that it experiences a huge degree of progress, it gives description to the sink alongside the information. At that point, sink executes rescheduling of rest obligation round, if important. In this manner, a piece of the outstanding burden of the sink in periodical checking of the hubs is shared by the group heads.

The data values N_i and N_j are said to be equal, if

$$m_i = m_j, m_i = m_j \tag{14.8}$$

Here, m_i and m_j are the magnitudes of the values of N_i and N_j

$$D_{ij} < D_{Th} \tag{14.9}$$

where D_{ij} is the distance between N_i and N_j. D_{Th} is the distance threshold.

$$\delta_{ij} < \delta_{min}, \delta_R = ABS (R_j - R_i) \tag{14.10}$$

In (14.11) R_i and R_j are the transmitting rates of N_i and N_j, respectively. Calculated sending rates are mentioned in (14.11) and (14.12):

$$R_i = NP_i/TR_i = NP_i/T \tag{14.11}$$

$$R_j = NP_j/TR_j = NP_j/T \tag{14.12}$$

where NP_i is the number of packets in a time T.
δ_{ij} is the round of difference of sending rates of N_i and N_j.
δ_{min} is the minimum thresh-out for δ_{ij}.

The nodes can be showed as points in 3D. Node i has a set of coordinates (m_{ti}, D_i, and R_i) and Node j has coordinates (m_{tj}, D_j, and R_j). Therefore, the equal distance among the nodes N_i and N_j is given by (14.13).

$$SM_{ij} = \sum k = \ln(xik - xjk)2 \quad \sqrt{}, n = 3. SMij = \sum k = \ln xik - xjk2, n = 3.$$
$$\tag{14.13}$$

Here, xi1 = mti, xi2 = Di, xi3 = Ri and xj1 = mtj, xj2 = Dj, xj3 = Rj.
Here, n is the counts of similarity metrics.

14.5.3   Performance Evaluation of MSCA

The exhibition of the suggested MSCA calculation has been looked at contrast to a current grouping calculation termed as vitality effective dispersed bunching (EEDC) calculation. Counts of sensor hubs have been shifted from 20 to 100 of every reenactment zone of 500 by 500 m². The outcomes acquired display the presentation enhancement picked up through MSCA concerning EEDC as long as 25% vitality utilization, 18% delay, and 20% conveyance proportion from the average estimations of different runs.

In this manner, the compelling rest obligation cycle impressively decreases the vitality utilization in RSSs, guaranteeing that the overhead and deferral are not expanded under such situations.

14.6 Conclusion

WSNs are increasingly complex in their necessities and to give bunching answers for them requires satisfactory information on the idea of the applications, limit confinements of sensor hubs, the trade-off among the normal execution boundaries, and the impediments of rising advances. This part has sketched out four present day grouping draws near (EAFCA, EEHC, EERC, and ADCA) intended for remote sensor organizations, each from a recognizable viewpoint. The recreation results acquired for the proposed grouping approaches are empowering. This will arouse analysts to investigate further here. The excursion of exploration in this field has crossed noteworthy achievements, yet it has been left with many open-finished issues and unexplored streets because of the nearness of inalienable exchange-offs among the presentation variables and dynamic needs of sensor applications. The exhibition of a RSS can additionally be investigated through all-encompassing methodologies concocted or acquired from current mechanical progressions.

References

1. Balakrishnan, B. and Balachandran, S., FLECH: fuzzy logic based energy efficient clustering hierarchy for nonuniform wireless sensor networks. *Wireless Commun. Mobile Comput.*, 1–13, 2017.
2. Karaboga, D., An idea based on honey bee swarm for numerical optimization, Technical Report TR06, Erciyes University, Engineering Faculty, Computer Engineering Department, 2005.
3. Darougaran, L., Shahinzadeh, H., Ghotb, H., Ramezanpour, L., Simulated annealing algorithm for data aggregation trees in wireless sensor networks and comparison with genetic algorithm. *Int. J. Electron. Electr. Eng.*, 62, 59–62, 2012.
4. Dhasian, H.R. and Balasubramanian, P., Survey of data aggregation techniques using soft computing in wireless sensor networks. *IET Inf. Secur.*, 7, 4, 336–342, 2013.
5. Yang, E., Ahmet, T., Arslan, T., Barton, N., An Improved Particle Swarm Optimization Algorithm for Power-Efficient Wireless Sensor Networks, IEEE, 0-7695-2919-4/07, 2007.
6. Tan, H.Ö. and Körpeoğlu, İ., Power efficient data gathering and aggregation in wireless sensor networks. *ACM SIGMOD Rec.*, 32, 4, 66–71, Dec. 2003.
7. HevinRajesh, D. and Paramasivan, B., Fuzzy based secure data aggregation technique in wireless sensor networks. *J. Comput. Sci.*, 8, 6, 899–907, 2012.
8. Islam, O., Hussain, S., Zhang, H., Genetic algorithm for data aggregation trees in wireless sensor networks, in: *3rd international conference on Intelligent Environment*, IEEE, pp. 312–316, 2007.
9. Kennedy, J. and Eberhart, R., Particle Swarm Optimization. *IEEE International Conference on Neural Networks*, 1995.
10. Shanbehzadeh, J., Mehrjoo, S., Sarrafzadeh, A., An intelligent energy efficient clustering in wireless sensor networks. *Lecture Notes in Engineering and Computer Science: Proc. of The International MultiConference of Engineers and Computer Scientists 2011*, 16–18 March, 2011, IMECS, Hong Kong, 2011.

11. Ferentinos, K., Tsiligiridis, T., Arvanitis, K., Energy optimization of wirless sensor networks for environmental measurements, in: *Proc. of the International Conference on Computational Intelligence for Measurment Systems and Applicatons*, 2005.
12. Kim, J.Y., Sharma, T., Kumar, B., Tomar, G.S., Berry, K., Lee, W.H., Intercluster ant colony optimization algorithm for wireless sensor network in dense environment. *Int. J. Distrib. Sens. Netw.*, 10, 4, 1–10, 2014.
13. Kulkarni, R.V. and Venayagamoorthy, G.K., Particle swarm optimization in wireless-sensor networks: A brief survey. *IEEE Trans. Syst. Man Cybern. Part C (Appl. Rev.)*, 41, 2, 262–267, 2011.
14. Kumar, H. and Singh, P.K., Analyzing Data Aggregation in Wireless Sensor Networks. *4th International Conference on Computing for Sustainable Global Development INDIACom*, IEEE, pp. 4024–4029, 2017.
15. Kumar, H. and Singh, P.K., Node Energy Based Approach to Improve Network Lifetime and Throughput in Wireless Sensor Networks. *J. Telecomm. Electron. Comput. Eng. (JTEC)*, 9, 3-6, 79–88, 2017.
16. Lu, Y., Comsa, I.S., Kuonen, P., Hirsbrunner, B., Probabilistic Data Aggregation Protocol Based on ACO-GA Hybrid Approach in Wireless Sensor Networks, in: *IFIP Wireless and Mobile Networking Conference (WMNC)*, pp. 235–238, 2015, October.
17. Lu, Y., Comsa, I.S., Kuonen, P., Hirsbrunner, B., Probabilistic Data Aggregation Protocol Based on ACO-GA Hybrid Approach in Wireless Sensor Networks, in: *IFIP Wireless and Mobile Networking Conference (WMNC)*, pp. 235–238, 2015, October.
18. Misra, R. and Mandal, C., Ant-aggregation: ant colony algorithm for optimal data aggregation in wireless sensor networks, in: *IFIP International Conference on Wireless and Optical Communications Networks*, pp. 1–5, 2006, April.
19. Mohsenifard, E. and Ghaffari, A., Data aggregation tree structure in wireless sensor networks using cuckoo optimization algorithm. *J. Inf. Syst. Telecommun. (JIST)*, 4, 3, 182–190, 2016.
20. Mohsenifard, E. and Ghaffari, A., Data aggregation tree structure in wireless sensor networks using cuckoo optimization algorithm. *J. Inf. Syst. Telecommun. (JIST)*, 4, 3, 182–190, 2016.
21. Nayak, P. and Vathasavai, B., Energy Efficient Clustering Algorithm for Multi-Hop Wireless Sensor Network Using Type-2 Fuzzy Logic. *IEEE Sens. J.*, 17, 14, 4492–4499, 2017.
22. Nayak, P. and Vathasavai, B., Energy Efficient Clustering Algorithm for Multi-Hop Wireless Sensor Network Using Type-2 Fuzzy Logic. *IEEE Sens. J.*, 17, 14, 4492–4499, 2017.
23. Neamatollahi, P., Naghibzadeh, M., Abrishami, S., Fuzzy-Based Clustering-Task Scheduling for Lifetime Enhancement in Wireless Sensor Networks. *IEEE Sens. J.*, 17, 20, 6837–6844, 2017.
24. Ni, Q., Pan, Q., Du, H., Cao, C., Zhai, Y., A novel cluster head selection algorithm based on fuzzy clustering and particle swarm optimization. *IEEE/ACM Trans. Comput. Biol. Bioinf.*, 14, 1, 76–84, 2017.
25. Norouzi, A., Babamir, F.S., Orman, Z., A tree based data aggregation scheme for wireless sensor networks using GA. *Wireless Sens. Netw.*, 4, 08, 191–196, 2012.
26. RejinaParvin, J. and Vasanthanayaki, C., Particle swarm optimization-based clustering by preventing residual nodes in wireless sensor networks. *IEEE Sens. J.*, 15, 8, 4264–4274, 2015.
27. Jin, S., Zhou, M., Wu, A., Sensor network optimization using a genetic algorithm, in: *Proc. of the 7th World Multiconference on Systemics, Cybernetics and Informatics*, 2003.
28. Lindsey, S. and Raghavendra, C.S., Pegasis: Power-efficient gathering in sensor information systems, in: *Proc. IEEE Conf. Aerosp*, Big Sky, MT, Mar, vol. 3, pp. 1125–1130, 2002.
29. Singh, S.P. and Sharma, S.C., A Particle Swarm Optimization Approach for Energy Efficient Clustering in Wireless Sensor Networks. *Int. J. Intell. Syst. Appl.*, 9, 6, 66–74, 2017.
30. Sudarmani, R. and Kumar, K.S., Particle swarm optimization-based routing protocol for clustered heterogeneous sensor networks with mobile sink. *Am. J. Appl. Sci.*, 10, 3, 259–269, 2013.

31. Sun, Y., Dong, W., Chen, Y., An improved routing algorithm based on ant colony optimization in wireless sensor networks. *IEEE Commun. Lett.*, 21, 6, 1317–1320, 2017.

32. Heinzelman, W.B., Chandrakasan, A.P., Balakrishnan, H., An application specific protocol architecture for wireless microsensor networks. *IEEE Trans. Wireless Commun.*, 1, 4, 660–670, 2002.

33. Heinzelman, W., Chandrakasan, A., Balakrishnan, H., Energy efficient communication protocol for wireless micro sensor networks, in: *Proc. of the Hawaii International Conference on System Sciences*, 2000.

34. Wang, X., Li, X., Leung, V.C., Artificial intelligence-based techniques for emerging heterogeneous network: State of the arts, opportunities, and challenges. *IEEE Access*, 3, 1379–1391, 2015.

35. Xie, M. and Shi, H., Ant-colony optimization based in-network data aggregation in wireless sensor networks, in: *Pervasive Systems, 12th International Symposium on Algorithms and Networks (ISPAN)*, pp. 77–83, 2012, December.

36. Zhou, Y., Wang, N., Xiang, W., Clustering hierarchy protocol in wireless sensor networks using an improved PSO algorithm. *IEEE Access*, 5, 2241–2253, 2017.

15

Support Vector in Healthcare Using SVM/PSO in Various Domains: A Review

Vishal Dutt[1]*, Pramod Singh Rathore[2]† and Kapil Chauhan[2]‡

[1]Aryabhatta College, Ajmer, India
[2]Aryabhatta College of Engineering and Research Center, Ajmer, India

Abstract

The Particle Swarm Optimization (PSO) is motivated by social conduct of winged animal rushing and fish tutoring. It is a stochastic optimization algorithm. In this algorithm, each key is regarded as a particle and each particle has a fitness value calculated by a function called objective function. This idea came from the bird behaviors, as multiple birds have a common objective, i.e., piece of food. They do not have any idea about where the food is. But, they surprisingly know that the distance of the food from their current location. Here, each particle performs their best individually as birds do. As same as the swarm behavior, our data particle adjusts their speed for best performance. Attributable to the changes the current world obtaining, it is one in every of the best methodology for approximating the available future outcomes. Aboard leading edge investigates in care large of information area unit accessible; nevertheless, the principle bother is the manner by which to develop the extant information into a valuable practices. To change surface of this obstacle, the thought of information mining is that the most acceptable. Data processing has an unbelievable potential to empower care frameworks to utilize information all the additional proficiently and adequately. Consequently, it improves care and reduces prices. This paper audits totally different inquiries concerning on PSO in care space.

Keywords: PSO, SVM, PHMS, HHV-8, Regression, LDA, SAS, ANN

15.1 Introduction

Particle Swarm Optimization (PSO) may be a heuristic overall streamlining system place forth initially by [1, 2]. Swarm insight depends upon the overall direct of redistributed, self-sifted through structures. It is going to be traditional or faux. Standard samples of Swarm Intelligence are unit hymenopteron settlements, fish mentoring, winged animal running, bumble bee swarming, and so on. Aside from multi-automation systems, some computer programs for coping with improvement and knowledge assessment problems

Corresponding author: vishaldutt53@gmail.com
†*Corresponding author:* pramodrathore88@gmail.com
‡*Corresponding author:* kapilajmer86@gmail.com

Abhishek Kumar, Pramod Singh Rathore, Vicente Garrcia Diaz and Rashmi Agrawal (eds.) Swarm Intelligence Optimization: Algorithms and Applications, (291–308) © 2021 Scrivener Publishing LLC. ISBN 978-1-119-77874-5

are unit models for a few human trinkets of SI. The simplest swarm data systems are unit PSO and hymenopteron colony advancement. In PSO, every particle flies through the third-dimensional area and changes its circumstance in each movement with its own one among a form comprehension which of companions toward an ideal course of action by the complete swarm. Consequently, the PSO problem solving may be a person from Swarm Intelligence.

In PSO, community, understood as particles in square measure are "flown" through hyper-dimensional. Changes to the circumstance of particles within the chase house rely on the social-mental tendency of people to duplicate the accomplishment of others. The movements to a particle within the swarm square measure are thus influenced by the expertise, or data, of its neighbors. The chase direct of associate degree atom is suitably stricken by that of varied particles within the swarm (PSO is afterward a sort of useful pleasing estimation). The consequence of showing this social lead is that the request strategy is with the final word objective that particles random confederate come toward effectively productive areas within the request house.

15.2 The Fundamental PSO

People in a PS pursue a basic conduct: to imitate the achievement of neighboring people and their own victories. The aggregate conduct that rises up out of this straightforward conduct is that of finding ideal areas of a high-dimensional inquiry space. A PSO calculation keeps up a swarm of particles, where every particle speaks to a potential arrangement. In relationship with transformative calculation ideal models, a swarm is like a populace, while a particle is like a person [3].

In the essential PS enhancement calculation, PS comprises of n particles, and the situation of every particle reactants the potential arrangement in D-dimensional space. These particles can change its state in accordance with three basic principles.

- To keep its obtuseness.
- To change the fitness as indicated by its most confident person location.
- To change the fitness as indicated by the swarm's most confident person location.

The circumstance of each particle in the swarm is affected both by the most cheerful individual location in the midst of its improvement and the circumstance of the most certain individual particle in its enveloping (close association). Right when the whole PS is enveloping the particle, the most confident individual location of the incorporating is comparable to the one of the whole most sure individual particle; this computation is known as the whole PSO. In case the confined including is used in the computation, this figuring is known as the midway PSO. In basic terms, the particles are "flown" through a multidimensional pursuit space, where the location of every particle is balanced by its very own involvement and that of its neighbors. Let $\mathbf{p}_j(m)$ signify the situation of particle I in the pursuit space at time step t; except if generally expressed, t means discrete time steps. The situation of the particle is changed by including a speed, $\mathbf{s}_j(m)$, to the extant location, for example:

$$P_j(m + 1) = P_j(m) + s_j(m + 1)$$

$$\text{with } P_j(0) \sim Q\,(P_{min}, P_{max})$$

Basically, it is the speed vector that drives the enhancement procedure and reflects both the experiential learning of the particle and socially traded data from the particle's neighborhood. The experiential learning of a particle is by and large alluded to as the subjective segment, which is relative to the separation of the particle from its very own best location found since the first run through advance [4]. The socially traded data is alluded to as the social segment of the speed fitness.

15.2.1 Algorithm for PSO

```
For each p
      Initialize p
End for
Loop
      For each p
            Now estimate the value for fitness (Fv)
            If (Fv>pBest)
            cv = pBest`
End loop
  // Now select p along with the pBest value for every
  single particle as the gBest
For each p
      Now calculate the Speed on the behalf of equation
      (v [ ]=v[ ]+c1 * rand() * (pBest [] - extant [ ] +c2
      * rand() * (gBest[ ] - extant [ ]))
      Now update the particle location on the behalf of
      equation (extant [ ]=extant [ ] + v [ ]
End
```

15.3 The Support Vector

A Support Vector Machine (SVM) is AN analytic classifier formally pictured by a secluding hyperplane. Basically, it is a supervised rule for machine learning procedures. This calculation is basically used for classification problems [5]. In an exceedingly manner of speaking,

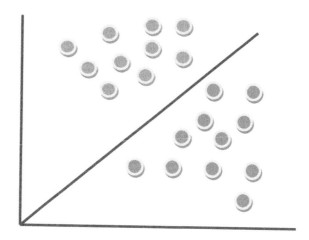

Figure 15.1 The support vector concept.

given named information of regulated finding out (Training Data), the estimation yields an ideal hyperplane that categories new points of reference. In two-dimensional areas, this hyperplane could be a line analytic plane in two areas wherever in every category lay in either facet (Figure 15.1) [5, 6].

Studies in Healthcare Using PSO

Advanced mobile phones and handheld computation devices have progress status scattered benefits anywhere. A private solider will perform very important everyday assignments whereas his eudemonia is recorded, controlled, and ready, perpetually utilizing on body sensors and actuators with the inescapable medicative services framework. In such a state of affairs, immaculate and n="qtiperar" title="is significant is important" id="tip_17"> is critical. For worldwide good of PHMS, it should be tried and confirmed for his or her protected, long-standing time use and solid activity underneath totally different more and more evolving things. This paper proposes a completely a unique procedure to interrupt down a PHMS with PSO underneath skillfulness initiated dynamic changes within the unique state of affairs and steady association of the medicative widget with the build. Consequences demonstrate that human movability that initiated setting changes will cause dangerous fit-nesss, for instance, tranquilize dose [7].

They designed up a framework within which PSO is lifeless as the PHMS sceptered therapeutic framework; massive volume information of knowledge is formed intermit-tently and also the information is screw-topped off with current information. Thanks to the voluminous information of knowledge, the existence multifarious nature emerges once taking care of that information utilizing these registering devices [8]. Therefore, on investi-gated and acquired progressively precise outcomes, the purchasers ought to utilize another computation framework. To beat the disadvantages of this framework, we tend to advocate another framework which will dissect the body sensing element information naturally. The body sensing element information are like pulse, sugar level, heartbeat, and so forth. Are place away into the information within the current and also the new PHMS framework will organize typical and strange cases by utilizing the PSO calculation? PSO may be a kind of development calculation and it is applicable to huge measures of knowledge and has usually wonderful time execution, and consequently, it fits the rationale for WBAN information examination in an exceedingly PHMS domain. For instance, to quantify pulse, we tend to use couple care circulatory strain sensing element that is formed by GENEXEL MEDICAL and T-bit is used for remote correspondence [9]. The PSO has been reinvigorated by the mutual exercises of creatures, for instance, fish tutoring, creepy crawly swarming, and winged animal running. It includes numerous particles that are instated haphazardly within the hunt area of a goal work. These particles are alluded to as swarm. Each molecule of the swarm describes a possible arrangement of the advance issue. The particles fly through the pursuit area and their locations are rested hooked in to the simplest places of individual particles in each cycle. The health estimations of particles are gotten to make your mind up, that location within the inquiry area is the best. In the kth stress, the swarm is rested, utilizing the related fitness:

$$V_i^{k+1} = \rho^k V_i^k + c_1 r_1 \left(P_i^k - X_i^k \right) + c_2 r_2 \left(P_g^k - X_i^k \right) \tag{15.1}$$

$$X_i^{k+1} = X_i^k + V_i^{k+1} \tag{15.2}$$

where Xi and Vi relate to this location and speed vectors of the ith molecule, separately; Pi is the best past state of affairs of the ith molecule and Pg is the best worldwide state of affairs among each one of the particles within the swarm; r1 and r2 square measure 2 uniform irregular groupings made from interval [0,1]; c1 and c2 square measure the psychological and social scaling parameters, on an individual basis; and rk is the dormancy substance accustomed that limit the past speed of molecule safeguarded. The latency substance r^k can be characterized or varied directly from a most extreme price rmax to a base price r^{min}. Speed vector Vi is strained to a boundary Vl associated with a boundary Vu. Before enjoying out the real arrangement, a procedure for conglomeration is needed to diminish the live of device data. This is often finished by problem solving the traditional of each hour data and isolated into the movement time frame (day time) and intermission (evening time). Likewise, thus, on breaking down the device data for every day, the traditional of device data for each day is set [10].

The top of execution consequences is in request to substantiate the adequacy of the planned strategy on top; we have a tendency to took some trials, utilizing a re-enactment state of affairs [11].

Measurements: The exhibition of the planned PHMS with PSO calculation is assessed with the incidental to measurements: truth, quality, and affectability. These equal measures are characterized, utilizing True Negative (TN), True Positive (TP), False Positive (FP), and False Negative (FN).

Exactness: It alludes to the all out range of records that square measure accurately organized by the classifier.

$$\text{Accuracy} = (TP + TN) / (TP + FP + TN + FN) \tag{15.3}$$

OR

Accuracy = (TP + TN) / N; where, TP + FP + TN + FN = N = Total Population.

Sensitivity: It is the ratio of people who are identified as having disease.

$$\text{Sensitivity} = TP / (TP + FN) \tag{15.4}$$

Specificity: It is the ratio of healthy people who have no diseases.

$$\text{Specificity} = TN / (TN + FP) \tag{15.5}$$

Time Complexity: It quantifies the amount of time taken by the algorithm.

It was the primary UN agency that gave the concept of SVM. Among all the accessible calculations, it provides extraordinarily precise outcomes. It is learning prominence since it could also be effectively extended to problems known with multiclass but it had been, for the foremost, half created for problems known with double order [34]. Thus, on be valuable for various powerful and productive assignments, it is appropriate creating single even as various hyperplanes in high-dimensional house [12]. The principle purpose of constructing hyperplane by SVM thus isolates the data focuses. There are two other ways of corporal punishment SVM. The principal methodology utilizes scientific programming and second system includes bit capacities. With the help of getting ready datasets, non-direct capacities may be effectively mapped to high-dimensional house. Such circumstance should be conceivable once we use bit capacities. Gaussian, polynomial, sigmoid, and so on are a number of instances of portion capacities. For the grouping of data focuses, hyperplane is employed [13]. The essential assignment of hyperplane is to spice up the detachment between data focuses. Bolster vectors are used, thus, on developing the hyperplane. There are totally different points of interest of SVM. A number of them are pursued: initial one is that, it is viable in high-dimensional areas. Another is that, it is compelling in things wherever range of measurements is additional outstanding than the amount of tests. Third one is that, it is memory good on the grounds that it utilizes a set of getting ready focuses within the alternative capability (called bolster vectors), and next is that, it is versatile in light substance of the very fact that numerous half capacities may be determined for the selection capability. A little of the burdens of SVM are pursued: initial one is that, on the off probability that the quantity of highlights may be a ton additional outstanding than number of tests, at that time, SVM is sure to provide horrifying showings, and therefore, the another is that, it does not squarely provide chance gauges. These are determined, utilizing a sweeping 5 overlap cross-approval [14].

We've utilized varied varieties of techniques. During the exploration/trial examinations of LibSVMs, C4.5, BaggingC4.5, AdaBoostingC4.5, and Random Forest on seven tiny scale cluster malignancy informational collections were directed utilizing 10-overlay cross approval approach on the informational collections non-inheritable from Kent Ridge Bio- Medical Dataset depot. Take a look at consequences, it has been discovered that Random Forest order strategy performs superior to the assorted used characterization ways. Bosom malignant growth is one among the deadly and unsafe ailments in girls. Potter *et al.* had performed, probing the bosom illness informational assortment utilizing Maori hen equipment, and later examined the exhibition of assorted classifier utilizing 10-overlay cross approval technique [15].

Building on a cross-breed SVM-based analysis model, thus, on discovering the numerous hazard issues for bosom illness on the grounds that in Taiwan, women, notably young women, has toughened bosom malignant growth [16, 17]. Thus, on building the finding model, a couple of varieties of DNA infections during this exploration area unit examined. These DNA infections are area unit herpes simplex (herpes simplex infection type-1), Epstein-Barr virus (Epstein-Barr infection), cytomegalovirus (cytomegalovirus), HPV (human papillomavirus), and HHV-8 (human hepesvirus-8). Supported searching outcomes, either or can accomplished the indistinguishable high exactness. The first purpose of the investigation was to accumulate the bioinformatics concerning the bosom malignant growth and DNA infections. Apart from SVM-based model, another variety of determination model known as LDA (Linear separate examination) was likewise developed during this exploration. After observing the correctness's of each SVM and LDA, the exactness of SVM was far better than that of LDA. Arrangement procedures were used for anticipating the treatment value of medicative services administrations that was distended with fast development systematically and was turning into a principle worry for everyone.

Utilized associate incorporated selection tree model describes the skin infections in grown up and kids. The principle paying attention to this exploration was to look at the consequences of five trials on the six noteworthy skin ailments. The principle purpose of this exploration was to create the simplest discerning model in medicine by utilizing the selection tree and consolidate this choice tree with the neural system order methods. Supporting wildcat outcome, it has been discovered that neural system has 92.62% exactitude in forecast of skin ailments [18].

It is estimated and related clever medicinal selection, showing emotion supportive network that is passionate about SAS programming for the finding of heat infections. Thus, on developing the projected framework, neural system strategy was chiefly utilized. During this exploration, tests were performed on the knowledge taken from Cleveland coronary health problem information. On this premise of trials, it has been discovered that neural systems have 89.01% exactitude [19].

It pours down the mental pimping information utilizing BBN, thus, on distinguishing the foremost noteworthy variables of mental sicknesses and their relationships by acting probe real information nonheritable from Lugoj Municipal Hospital. During this examination, it has been discovered that BBN assumes a big job in healthful basic leadership method, thus, on predicating the probability of a mental pimping on the premise known indications [20].

Building up an alternative shows emotion validating network utilizing BBN for higher breaking down dangers that were connected with well-being. With the help of utilizing BBN, thus, on building the portion reaction relationship, the human ill and [International Journal of pc Applications (0975–8887) Volume a hundred and twenty – No.15, Gregorian calendar month 2015 forty two] malignancy hazards attributable to express substance area unit of the many destinations of this exploration were foreseen.

A projected savvy framework supported hereditary facilitate vector machines (GVSM) for higher breaking down the center valve ill. This framework separates the many components and characterizes the sign no heritable from the ultrasound of heart valve. During this exploration, the projected framework was primarily used for the determination of the center valve maladies. During this examination, the projected framework was assessed in

215 examples. Supporting tests' consequence, it has been discovered that the projected framework was booming to differentiate physicist heart sounds [21, 22].

We applied ANN for locating the respiratory organ maladies. This examination work dissects the chest CAT (CT) and concentrates crucial respiratory organ tissue highlight to decrease the knowledge size from the chest CT and subsequently freed literary credits got to neural system as contribution to seek out the various sicknesses with relevancy respiratory organ [23].

The cooperative characterization approach for higher dissecting of the human services information is projected. The projected methodology was the joined methodology that incorporated the affiliation that governs even as grouping rules. This coordinated methodology was valuable for locating rules within the information and subsequently utilizing these tips to make a productive classifier. During this exploration, investigations of the knowledge of heart pimpings were performed, therefore, on discovering that exactitude related to classifiers was superior to accuracy of customary classifiers. Apart from this, the examination likewise created the standards, utilizing substances that are familiar classifier [24].

Foreseen PS streamlining SVM (PSO-SVM) model for the higher uninflect vascular heart fitness cord is to ensure the success individuals and additional people life. At some stage in this examination, PSO was acclimated with the set of parameters of SVM. This examination shows the extenuation of expected model by exploiting MIT-BIH graphical record information of later primers that were performed. Maintaining primer outcomes, it has been discovered that the exactitude of expected model was above the preciseness of false neural system last of heart fitness cordis [25].

A model victimization, Artificial Neural Network (ANN), for separating chest ailments was planned, and a close assessment of chest diseases was performed victimization multilayer, summarized slip, probabilistic neural frameworks [26].

DNA fix characteristics were thought by Chuang et al., who originate deals to higher run of the mill of oral risky improvement by choosing a lone regular compound polymorphisms (SNPs) dataset. The picked dataset had positive samples of oral risky headway's pimpings. Throughout this assessment, each live analysis was performed. Maintaining starter result, it has been found that the exhibition of holdout cross endorsing was past one issue of the extenuation of 10-overlay cross facilitation. With the exception of this current, it has been equally found that the accuracy of delineation was 64.2%.

Anticipated perceptive models by victimization differed rule primarily based on the foremost half classifiers for the upper early revelation of irresistible malady contamination. Throughout this investigation, the differed normal primarily based typically classifiers that were utilized within the anticipated models were determination tree, brutal set classifier, sincere Thomas Bayes, and known with classifier. Thence, on envisioning the first revelation of irresistible disorder illness, many classifiers were analyzed throughout this assessment. The classifiers were investigated altogether and what is additional in mixture during this manner, assumes their introduction. Bolstering starter consequences, it has been found that the preciseness of various classifiers was higher than the accuracy of single classifier [27].

It used alternative tree calculation, therefore, on describing the smoking practices among smokers by evaluating their mental pain, mental well-being standing, utilization of liquor, and data point factors. The characterization examination was directly supported by alternative tree calculation, therefore, on discovering the association between the traditional quantities of fag utilization each day.

It used K-NN and Linear Discriminate Analysis (LDA) for characterization of eternal infection, therefore, on producing early cautioning framework. This examination work used KNN to interrupt down the association between vessel upset associate degree cardiovascular disease and, therefore, the hazard variables of various never-ending ailments, therefore, on building an early cautioning framework to diminish the issue event of those sicknesses [28].

A General, 0.5 breed alternative tree classifier for ordering the action of pimping having never-ending malady is projected. They additionally improved this alternative tree model to rearrange varied exercises of pimpings in increasingly actual manner.

K-NN classifier for breaking down the pimpings experiencing coronary diseased health is used. The knowledge was gathered from UCI and trial was performed utilizing while not democratic or with democratic K-NN classifier, and it absolutely was discovered that K-NN accomplished higher preciseness while not democratic in analysis of heart maladies once contrasted with democratic K-NN [29].

An improved Fuzzy K-NN classifier for designation thyroid complaint is planned. Molecule Swarm optimization (PSO) was to boot used for indicating downy quality limitation and neighborhood size [30].

It talked concerning the classifier in therapeutic field to analyze the skin malady, utilizing substances KNN classifier. Johnson *et al.* planned a time period technique, therefore, on higher location of extortion submitted by pimpings even as by suppliers for human services insurance agencies. The planned system likewise helps in decreasing Brobdingnagian expenses for insurance agencies. The planned approach was comprised of various stages as well as hazard assurance organization. The hazard limit was set by utilizing mostly the selection tree–based strategy. The planned approach was contrasted and unaided and controlled neural system strategies. During correlation, it has been discovered that the planned procedure beats unaided and directed neural system strategies, therefore, on establishing the deceit. Except for this, planned approach assumes an interesting job in approving the legitimated cases by obtaining the information from protection guarantee structures.

It reviewed the affiliation between careful reviewing and human services prices therefore on assessing that the careful examination will presumably decrease the final expenses of medical clinics simply if, once, it focused on high-chance methodology like large intestine malignant growth process [31].

The investigated immature organism (ESC) quality marks significance, therefore, on assessing the endurance of prostate malignant growth (PCa) pimpings at the hour of their finding. Within the examination, AN mixture of 641 ESC quality indicators (ESCGPs) was recognized by utilizing small array informational indexes. For evaluating the endurance, a k-closest neighbor (K-NN) calculation was used to appraise the final endurance.

15.3.1   SVM in Regression

Planned Substances Support Vector Regression (WSVR) that used substance issue supported device reading for giving consistent checking to pimpings, thus, on providing them higher healthful services administrations. During this examination, supporting explorative outcome, it has been discovered that the planned methodology would be suggested to exactness than basic vector relapse [32].

Regression for the estimation of relative hazard for various ailments was calculated, as an example, Diabetes, Angina, stroke, and so forth.

A regression alternative tree calculation was planned, thus, on anticipating the number of medication days during a people. Planned calculation was created, utilizing broad medical coverage claims informational indexes. Taking a look at consequences showed that planned calculation was performed altogether once all is alleged in done people even as in sub-populaces, thus, on foreseeing future medication.

Rail for numerous learning techniques like LinearRegression, LeastMedSq, SMOreg, Multilayer Percepton, KStart, Tree M5P, and so on was utilized. Within the assessment, tests were finished mistreatment 10-wrinkle cross endorsement. Once examinations were done, it has been found that statistical regression and Tree M5P gave best consequences for the convincing utilization of medicative center resources, improved crisis facility situating, and better client relationship organizations [33].

15.3.2   SVM in Clustering

Clustering is characterized as unsupervised learning that happens by simply looking autonomous factors whereas directed learning breaking down each free and ward factors. It is distinctive in relevancy grouping that could be a managed learning strategy. It is no predefined categories. See able of this clarification, bunch may well be best utilized for investigations of AN wildcat nature, primarily if those examinations embody monumental live of data, but not particularly considered data (for example, mass of data created by microarray examination). The target of bunch is distinct, whereas objective of characterization is discerning. The basic trip of unsupervised learning technique suggests that bunch strategy is to form the teams from monumental information supported similitude live. The target of bunch is to seek out another arrangement of categories, the new gatherings square measure of enthusiasm for themselves, and their appraisal is inherent. So as assignments, a major piece of the analysis is extraneous. Bunch dealt out the knowledge focuses obsessed on the similitude live. Bunch bunches data occurrences into subsets in such the way that comparable cases square measure gathered, whereas numerous cases encompasses a place with numerous gatherings. Bunch approach is used to acknowledge likeness between data focuses. Each information focuses within an identical bunch square measure having a lot of outstanding likeness as distinction with the knowledge focuses encompasses a place with alternative cluster. Bunch of things is as old because the humans demand for portrayal of the outstanding qualities of men and queries and identifying them with a form. On these lines, it handles totally different logical orders: from arithmetic and measurements to science and hereditary qualities, all of that uses numerous terms to portray the topologies framed utilizing this examination. From organic "scientific classifications" to restorative "disorders" and hereditary "genotypes" to aggregation "bunch innovation"—the difficulty is indistinguishable: framing classifications of drugs and authorization folks to the proper gatherings within it. Following square measure, the various bunch calculations are utilized in meditative services.

15.3.3 Partition Clustering

The greatest range of facts that focuses within the datasets is "n". With the help of "n" data focuses, the foremost extreme conceivable range of "k" bunches is non-inheritable. Therefore, on the non-inheritable "k" bunches from "n" data focuses, partitional bunch strategy is used. During this technique, each "n" data focus is identified with one and solely "k" bunches, whereas each "k" team will be identified with over "n" data focuses. Partitional bunch calculations need a consumer to enter k (which is that the amount of bunches). For the foremost half, partitional calculations lawfully migrate articles to k teams. Partitional categories area unit is organized; however, they move objects; however, they choose a bunch center of mass (or delegate) among articles within a (deficient) cluster, and the way they live likenesses among things and cluster centroids. Before we have a tendency to get the teams, this system needs to characterize the desired range of bunch that we have a tendency to may have to get from datasets. Supporting similitudes among articles and bunch centroids, this system [International Journal of pc Applications (0975 – 8887) Volume, a hundred and twenty – No.15, Gregorian calendar month 2015 forty four] is parcelled into two categories. These area units are K-means and KMediods. One among the foremost documented calculations of this technique is K-implies. Specially, else, it haphazardly chooses k articles and, at the moment, disintegrates this stuff into k disjoint gatherings by iteratively moving articles addicted to the likeness between the centroids and items. In k-implies, a bunch centriod is mean estimation of articles within the bunch. The subsequent calculation is K-mediods. Therefore, on amassing the bunch, it utilized mediods [34]. Mediod is critical in light substance of the very fact that, within the information, it is that data purpose that is most midway found. Therefore, on improving the human services administrations known with open social welfare house, Lenert *et al.* use the utilization of k-implies bunch, and by utilizing the bunch strategy, Belciug *et al.* acknowledged the repeat of bosom malady. Escudero *et al.* utilized the concept of Bioprofile and K-implies bunch for early location of Alzheimer's disease malady. The many little bit of leeway of partitional bunch calculations is their rife bunch exactitude as contrasted and graded bunch calculations that's the consequence of their worldwide improvement procedure (i.e., the algorithmic movements of items). Another most popular location is that partitional calculations will modify huge informational indexes that graded calculations cannot (i.e., higher adaptability) and might all the earlier cluster data. Intrinsically, we will say that partitional calculation area unit additional eminent and expert than numerous levelled calculations. One noteworthy drawback to the use of partitional calculations is that their bunch consequences rely on the underlying cluster centroids somewhat on the grounds that the centroids area unit haphazardly chosen. When partitional calculations are run once, distinctive bunch consequence is that area unit is non-inheritable.

15.3.4 Hierarchical Clustering

So, on parcelling the data focuses, this strategy may be used in two approaches. Information focuses may be distributed in an exceedingly tree route called varied levelled path by utilizing either prime down or base up methodologies. Supporting parcelled method, this system may be delegated clustered and factious. The foremost extreme range of knowledge focuses may be "n". Varied information focuses among n information focuses could have similitude with each other. The first purpose of clustered methodology is to union such information focuses into a solitary gathering. Troubled methodology initially takes this single gathering and iteratively distributed it into littler gathering till and except if each information point identifies with one and just one bunch. There are three types of varied levelled clump calculations: initial one is single-connect, another is finished affiliation, and therefore, the last one is traditional affiliation. The single-interface clump calculation chooses the room try of articles from two gatherings and live the similitude between things as gathering likeness. The entire affiliation calculation ascertains the likeness between the foremost remote try of articles from two gatherings. The conventional affiliation calculation chooses all sets of things from two gatherings and midpoints each conceivable separation between articles. The foremost comparable two gatherings, those having the briefest separation, are consolidated beyond computing similitudes or separations between gatherings. Among the varied various levelled calculations, the conventional affiliation calculation offers the most effective preciseness abundant of the time. A most basic popular location of the employment of progressive clump calculations is that the illustration capability that shows what quantity things within the informational index are comparable one another. What is additional, with the usage of a dendrogram, specialists will sanely figure the number of teams. This can be a particular part of varied levelled calculations on the grounds that alternative clump calculations cannot provide this valuable part, notably once there is no further information accessible regarding the data itself [35].

15.3.5 Density-Based Clustering

Density-based mostly bunch techniques assume a major job in medical specialty analysis since they are fit to handle any bunch of subjective form. Exploring its progress demonstrates that this method may be fruitfully. Associates in nursing is advantageous therefore there is numerous examples from an exceptionally huge information. Aside from density-based mostly bunch strategy, partitional bunch and numerous levelled bunch techniques do not free the necessary examples from medical specialty photos information in light substance of the actual fact that these two ways square measure fit agitate simply the teams of circular form not the bunches of self-assertive form. To evacuate the problem of partitional bunch and numerous levelled bunch ways, density-based mostly bunch technique is developed. Supporting density circulation capability following square measure, the basic methodologies of density-based mostly clustering are DBSCAN, OPTICS, and DENCLUE. Celebi *et al.* utilized density-based mostly bunch approach, therefore, on getting the dear examples from Associate in Nursing exceptionally huge medical specialty photos information. These examples assume a major job, therefore, on deciding homogenized shading. Their square measure is totally different preferences of the density-based mostly bunch. Initial one is that in density-based mostly bunch approach sooner than time the amount of teams does not needed. Another is that, it will, while not a lot of a stretch, handle the teams of any discretionary form. Also, the last one is that it tends to be utilized viably and effectively even in loud circumstances. *Per se*, it is performed equally well in boisterous circumstances. One noteworthy hindrance of density-based mostly bunch is that, if there is a lot of selection in densities aboard data focuses, then it cannot have the choice to agitate such varieties in data focuses. Another inconvenience is that separation live is the essential issue that computes its outcome.

15.3.6   PSO in Clustering

Progressive K-implies leading riotous or clustered methodology for higher examining huge smaller scale exhibit data are utilitized. It had been accounted for that riotous numerous levelled Kmeans were higher than progressive and K-implies agglomeration on bunch quality even as on process speed. Apart from this, it had been to boot documented that riotous numerous levelled K-implies builds up a superior agglomeration calculation fulfilling scientist's interest [36].

Projecting the 0.5 and 0.5 progressive agglomeration methodology for breaking down microarray data during this exploration, the projected 0.5 and 0.5 agglomeration methodology joins base up even as top-down numerous levelled agglomeration ideas, thus, with success and proficiently uses the standard of the two ideas for dissecting smaller scale exhibit data. The projected methodology was supported a shared cluster. A shared bunch may be a gathering of focuses nearer to at least one another than to another focuses. The exploration exhibits the projected strategy on reproduced even as on real miniaturized scale cluster data.

The methodologies of characterization trees and agglomeration calculations, thus, on anticipating the expense of human services [37] by utilizing the dataset of 3 years gathered from the insurance agencies to play out the examination are utilized. Supporting examination, following outcomes were gotten during this exploration. Initial outcome demonstrates that, thus, on providing actual expectation of restorative expenses and talking to an unbelievable quality for forecast of human services prices, data mining ways provide higher exactitude. Another outcome demonstrates that, thus, on anticipating the longer term prices, example of past data was useful.

We've used the clustered numerous levelled agglomeration approach for gathering the pimpings as indicated by their length of stay within the clinic, thus, on providing higher use of [International Journal of laptop Applications (0975 – 8887) Volume one hundred twenty – No.15, June 2015 forty five] medical clinic assets and provides higher administrations to pimpings [38].

The standard articulation data with the help of another numerous levelled agglomeration approach utilizing hereditary calculation was compound. During this exploration, the principle spotlight was on recovery of protein-protein helpful associations from genomic data. During this examination, the projected calculation will predicate the utilitarian affiliations exactly by considering genomic data.

A 0.5 and 0.5 methodology for higher examination of the threat contaminations bolstered edifying characteristics is anticipated. The anticipated philosophy used the K-suggests agglomeration with correct assessment (ANOVA) for quality assurance and SVM to explain the damaging development diseases. Bolstered preliminaries that were performed on scaled down scale show information; it has been found that the truth of K-suggests agglomeration with the mix of verifiable assessment was higher [39].

A Probabilistic Subtyping Model (PSM) that was within the essential sorted out throughout this fashion on found subtypes of unbelievable, affordable infections misuse longitudinal clinical markers gathered in electronic welfare record (EHR) databases and pimping libraries was foreseen. Foretold model was a model for agglomeration time game organization of clinical markers natural from routine visits anon acknowledge undistributed pimping subgroups.

Conceivable that among varied levelled, partitional, and thickness primarily based usually agglomeration, the dynamic agglomeration was given successful utilization of facility resources and gave improved pimping plan edges in financial aid.

Partner degree adaptive Benford recursive principle within the applying space of stimulating administrations assurance claims was anticipated. The anticipated estimation was a mechanized examination philosophy that utilizes partner degree unaided learning approach during this manner on managing inadequate or missing information. This method was applied to the innovation of coercion and ill-usage within the therapeutic inclusion cases mistreatment dataset, real welfare inclusion information. The dataset was researched. At the purpose, once the preliminary assessment of dataset, it has been found that the anticipated estimation has out and out improved preciseness than the quality Benford Approach within the world of coercion and ill-usage in therapeutic inclusion claims. Except for this current, it has been besides found that the anticipated computation was not confined to, while not a doubt, recognized instances of coercion.

Utilized agglomeration system thus acknowledges the suspicious healthful services frauds from large databases. Within the examination, two agglomeration ways, SAS EM and CLUTO, were utilized to a large real medical coverage dataset. When examination, it has been discovered that SAS EM outflanks the CLUTO.

15.4 Conclusion

A full comprehension of the variables connected with prescription adherence in pimpings with HF is needed, thus compelling intercessions to enhance medication adherence is created. However, most investigations of prescription adherence in pimpings with HF have had varied constraints that diminish the availableness of their discoveries. One in all these confinements is that the inability to utilize variable investigation ways to excogitate medication adherence. This examination attended this issue by utilizing SVM in recognizing indicators of drugs adherence in pimpings. SVM demonstrating may be a promising order approach for recognizing folks with basic diseases, for instance, polygenic disease and pre-diabetes within the people. This system needs to be, in addition, investigated in alternative complicated ailments utilizing basic factors.

References

1. Airaghi, Muller, S., Marchetto, J., Koumoutsakos, P., Optimization algorithms based on a model of bacterial chemotaxis, in: *Proceedings of the 6th International Conference on Simulation of Adaptive Behavior: From Animals to Animats*, pp. 375–384, 2000.
2. Alfi, and Fateh, M.-M., Intelligent identification and control using improved fuzzy particle swarm optimization. *Expert Syst. Appl.*, 38, 10, 12312–12317, 2011.

3. Chen, Su, W.-C., Yang, Y.-L., Application of constrained multi-objective hybrid quantum particle swarm optimization for improving performance of an ironless permanent magnet linear motor. *Appl. Math. Inform. Sci.*, 8, 6, 3111–3120, 2014.

4. Cheng, Chen, M.-Y., Fleming, P.J., Improved multiobjective particle swarm optimization with preference strategy for optimal DG integration into the distribution system. *Neurocomputing*, 148, 23–29, 2015.

5. Chuang, Y., Tsai, S.-W., Yang, C.-H., Chaotic catfish particle swarm optimization for solving global numerical optimization problems. *Appl. Math. Comput.*, 217, 16, 6900–6916, 2011.

6. Dai, S., Wei, Y., Chen, J., Zhang, Y., Ding, J., Seismic wavelet estimation based on adaptive chaotic embedded particle swarm optimization algorithm, in: *Proceedings of the 5th International Symposium on Computational Intelligence and Design (ISCID '12)*, October, vol. 2, pp. 57–60, 2012.

7. Daneshyari, and Yen, G.G., Constrained multiple-swarm particle swarm optimization within a cultural framework. *IEEE Trans. Syst. Man Cybern. Part A:Syst. Hum.*, 42, 2, 475–490, 2012.

8. Das, Pattnaik, P.K., Padhy, S.K., Artificial Neural Network trained by Particle Swarm Optimization for non-linear channel equalization. *Expert Syst. Appl.*, 41, 7, 3491–3496, 2014.

9. Davoodi, Hagh, M.T., Zadeh, S.G., A hybrid improved quantum-behaved particle swarm optimization simplex method (IQPSOS) to solve power system load flow problems. *Appl. Soft Comput. J.*, 21, 171–179, 2014.

10. Duan, Wang, X., Shu, S., Jing, C., Chang, H., Thermodynamic design of Stirling engine using multi-objective particle swarm optimization algorithm. *Energ. Convers. Manage.*, 84, 88–96, 2014.

11. Jia, F., Tian, F.C., Fan, S., He, Q.H., Feng, J.W., Yang, S.X., A novel sensor array and classifier optimization method of electronic nose based on enhanced quantum-behaved particle swarm optimization. *Sens. Rev.*, 34, 3, 304–311, 2014.

12. Ganguly, Multi-objective planning for reactive power compensation of radial distribution networks with unified power quality conditioner allocation using particle swarm optimization. *IEEE Trans. Power Syst.*, 29, 4, 1801–1810, 2014.

13. Ghanei, Assareh, E., Biglari, M., Ghanbarzadeh, A., Noghrehabadi, A.R., Thermal-economic multi-objective optimization of shell and tube heat exchanger using particle swarm optimization (PSO). *Heat Mass Transfer*, 50, 10, 1375–1384, 2014.

14. Son, L. H., Optimizing Municipal Solid Waste collection using Chaotic Particle Swarm Optimization in GIS based environments: A case study at Danang City, Vietnam. *Expert Syst. Appl.*, 41, 18, 8062–8074, 2014.

15. Yang, H., Lin, Y.-D., Chuang, L.-Y., Chang, H.-W., Double-bottom chaotic map particle swarm optimization based on chi-square test to determine gene-gene interactions. *BioMed Res. Int.*, 2014, Article ID 172049, 10 pages, 2014.

16. Chang, H.-Y., Huang, C.-L., Huang, W.-C., Yeh, Y.-C., Y. Tsai, C.-, Hybridization strategies for continuous ant colony optimization and particle swarm optimization applied to data clustering. *Appl. Soft Comput. J.*, 13, 9, 3864–3872, 2013.

17. Hu, Jain, G., Zhang, P., Schmidt, C., Gomadam, P., Gorka, T., Data-driven method based on particle swarm optimization and k-nearest neighbor regression for estimating capacity of lithium-ion battery. *Appl. Energy*, 129, 49–55, 2014.

18. Huang, Huang, W.-C., Chang, H.-Y., Yeh, Y.-C., Tsai, C.-Y., Hybridization strategies for continuous ant colony optimization and particle swarm optimization applied to data clustering. *Appl. Soft Comput. J.*, 13, 9, 3864–3872, 2013.

19. Jiang, and Wang, N., Cooperative bare-bone particle swarm optimization for data clustering. *Soft Comput.*, 18, 6, 1079–1091, 2014.
20. Juang, T., Tung, S.-L., Chiu, H.-C., Adaptive fuzzy particle swarm optimization for global optimization of multimodal functions. *Inf. Sci.*, 181, 20, 4539–4549, 2011.
21. Kennedy, and Eberhart, R., Particle swarm optimization, in: *Proceedings of the IEEE International Conference on Neural Networks*, December, vol. 4, pp. 1942–1948, 1995.
22. Kennedy, Bare bones particle swarms, in: *Proceedings of the IEEE Swarm Intelligence Symposium (SIS '03)*, Indianapolis, Ind, USA, pp. 80–87, 2003.
23. Khan, and Engelbrecht, A.P., A fuzzy particle swarm optimization algorithm for computer communication network topology design. *Appl. Intell.*, 36, 1, 161–177, 2012.
24. Mattos, L.C., Barreto, G.A., Cavalcanti, F.R.P., An improved hybrid particle swarm optimization algorithm applied to economic modeling of radio resource allocation. *Electron. Commer. Res.*, 14, 1, 51–70, 2014.
25. Manju, A., Nigam, M. J., Applications of quantum inspired computational intelligence: A survey. *Artif. Intell. Rev.*, 42, 79–156, 2014. https://doi.org/10.1007/s10462-012-9330-6.
26. Li, S., Zhou, J., Kou, P., Xiao, J., A novel chaotic particle swarm optimization based fuzzy clustering algorithm. *Neurocomputing*, 83, 98–109, 2012.
27. Liu, Ding, G., Wang, B., Bare-bones particle swarm optimization with disruption operator. *Appl. Math. Comput.*, 238, 106–122, 2014.
28. Aijun, L., Yu, Y., et al., Improved Collaborative Particle Swarm Algorithm for Job Shop Scheduling Optimization, Advanced Science Letters, American Scientific Publishers, 4, pp. 2180–2183(4), June/July 2011.
29. Lu, Jan, J.C., Hung, S.L., Hung, G.H., Enhancing particle swarm optimization algorithm using two new strategies for optimizing design of truss structures. *Eng. Optim.*, 45, 10, 1251–1271, 2013.
30. Pluhacek, M., Senkerik, R., Zelinka, I., Particle swarm optimization algorithm driven by multi-chaotic number generator. *Soft Comput.*, 18, 4, 631–639, 2014.
31. Amiryousefi, M.R., Mohebbi, M., Khodaiyan, F., Ahsaee, M.G., Multi-objective optimization of deep-fat frying of ostrich meat plates using multi-objective particle swarm optimization (MOPSO). *J. Food Process. Preserv.*, 38, 4, 1472–1479, 2014.
32. Norouzzadeh, M.S., Ahmadzadeh, M.R., Palhang, M., LADPSO: Using fuzzy logic to conduct PSO algorithm. *Appl. Intell.*, 37, 2, 290–304, 2012.
33 Campos, M., Krohling, R.A., Enriquez, I., Bare bones particle swarm optimization with scale matrix adaptation. *IEEE Trans. Cybern.*, 44, 9, 1567–1578, 2014.
34. Muller, Airaghi, S., Marchetto, J., Koumoutsakos, P., Optimization algorithms based on a model of bacterial chemotaxis. *Proceedings of the 6th International Conference on Simulation of Adaptive Behavior: From Animals to Animats*, pp. 375–384, 2000.
35. Abdullah, N., Bakar, A.H.A., Rahim, N.A., Mokhlis, H., Illias, H.A., Jamian, J.J., Modified particle swarm optimization with time varying acceleration coefficients for economic load dispatch with generator constraints. *J. Electr. Eng. Technol.*, 9, 1, 15–26, 2014.
36. Zhang, E., Wu, Y., Chen, Q., A practical approach for solving multi-objective reliability redundancy allocation problems using extended bare-bones particle swarm optimization. *Reliab. Eng. Syst. Saf.*, Elsevier, 127(C), 65–76, 2014.
37. Le Hoang Son, Optimizing Municipal Solid Waste collection using Chaotic Particle Swarm Optimization in GIS based environments: A case study at Danang city, Vietnam. *Expert Syst. Appl.*, 41, 18, 8062–8074, 2014.

38. Perera, Sevillano, E., Arteaga, A., de Diego, A., Identification of intermediate debonding damage in FRP-plated RC beams based on multi-objective particle swarm optimization without updated baseline model. *Compos. Part B: Eng.*, 62, 205–217, 2014.
39. Robati, Barani, G., Nezam Abadi Pour, H., Fadaee, M.J., Anaraki, J.R., Balanced fuzzy particle swarm optimization. *Appl. Math. Modell.*, 36, 5, 2169–2177, 2012.

16

IoT-Based Healthcare System to Monitor the Sensor's Data of MWBAN

Rani Kumari[1*] and ParmaNand[2]

[1]*Department of Computer Science and Engineering, MM University, Mullana, Ambala, India*
[2]*Department of Computer Science and Engineering Sharda University, Greater Noida, India*

Abstract

Storing all the things in human brain is not easy. Some limits are present to do mentally and physically work by human. Therefore, to reduce this problem of human's body, some approaches of Internet of Things (IoT) as well as Artificial Intelligence are applied. The involvement of new techniques or ideas in healthcare system with AI and WBAN provides a great medium to transform digital information from one source to another. System lifetime is a standout among the most critical measurements in Wireless Body Area Networks (WBANs). In this paper, we propose a system for healthcare monitoring based on IoT which monitors the sensor's data/information to analyze the patient's condition in mobile WBAN (MWBAN), and for this implementation, a transfer determination conspire is proposed under the topology which define a heuristic approach to enhance the network lifetime. It indicates the IEEE 802.15.6 standard to expand the lifetime of WBANs through defining and taking care of an enhancement issue where hand-off choice of every hub goes under the advancement variable. For this approach, we consider the assorted qualities of the sensor hubs in WBANs, the enhancement issue takes vitality utilization rate as well as vitality contrast among sensor hubs into record to enhance the system lifetime execution. Since it is non-deterministic polynomial-hard (NP-hard) and unmanageable, a heuristic arrangement is then intended to quickly address the advancement. In this paper, we also explain the relation among AI and IoT and explain different operational principles of IoT in healthcare. Despite IoT provides different benefits to healthcare system, every new invention or technology has some challenges related to data security. We can say that organizing data in better way does not mean it is secure from cyber threats. Therefore, in this paper, some security issues are also described related to healthcare system.

Keywords: WBAN, network lifetime, energy consumption, artificial intelligence, IoT principles, heuristic solution, IEEE 802.15.6

Corresponding author: ranichoudhary.phd@gmail.com

Abhishek Kumar, Pramod Singh Rathore, Vicente Garrcia Diaz and Rashmi Agrawal (eds.) Swarm Intelligence Optimization: Algorithms and Applications, (309–324) © 2021 Scrivener Publishing LLC. ISBN 978-1-119-77874-5

16.1 Introduction

In modern scenario, the Internet of Things (IoT) is implemented in every place of our daily life for handing large amount of data which adds a great sense in working. The IoT functionality can be extended with the help of Artificial Intelligence (AI) techniques to make the things easy and useful for end users and customers. For every patient and family, healthcare system is very useful; therefore, finding any solution for this is equally important for everyone. Storing all the information in mind is not an easy work. Many limitations exist for performance of human mental and physical activity. So, going to the maximum capability of brain and other activities, these technologies like the AI and IoT are regaled. The involvement of new techniques or ideas in healthcare system with AI and Wireless Body Area Network (WBAN) provides a great medium to transform digital information from one source to another.

Smart homes, municipal infrastructure, marketing, supply chain, retailing, healthcare, manufacturing, education, and life sciences—the whole digital system, an IoT ecosystem of interconnected sensor devices, has been generated and is improving stronger with every passing day. Empowered with the concept of AI and concept of Machine Learning, between other things, IoT is used as a means of equipping people with assistance of intelligent. Eventually, it is taken in account over both major and minor processes in a number of companies. Healthcare system is no exception [1].

16.1.1 Combination of AI and IoT in Real Activities

It works with in both ways—IoT and AI need the dependency of each other. Since IoT is a new technology that interconnects the gazillions of smart sensing devices, it can have some imperfections. For instance, these criteria are accurate and speed of IoT data transformation are yet to be grown and an AI ecosystem not mimics the person's way of performing all related tasks while it is learning from what it have patterns itself from. Nowdays, the mechanism for self-upgradation of the new technologies is AI. We can speak in general definitions; AI has more data for IoT to adopt advantage of this technology. In other sense, it is applied in the AI software embedded within IoT sensing devices and augmenting fog or edge computing technique solutions to bring intelligence with IoT devices. As a result of this, smart devices generate a huge amount of rapidly analyzed sensing data which it cannot help but some fuel Machine Learning techniques increase the intelligence of the physical things [2].

So, IoT provides a number of services with AI. But, when we talk about the human body area network, we can imagine number of facilities and fast services for early detection of serious disease. So, there is also a major requirement of IoT services embedded with the healthcare system. Therefore, Remote Body Area Networks (WBANs) have, as of late, risen as a subfield improvement of Wireless Sensor Networks (WSNs) and a promising innovation in short-go correspondence territory to give numerous essential and helpful applications in various spaces, for example, fundamental sign checking, intuitive gaming, and telemedicine. When all is said and done, a WBAN comprises one organizer and an arrangement of sensor hubs that must be extremely basic, small, and innocuous to the human body. These sensor hubs are typically set in the garments or on the skin of a man, some even embedded into the body to screen some specific parameters about human body. In the meantime, the facilitator goes about as a sink which gathers all the data achieved by the sensors and conveys it to the client or the remote server for additionally handling [3].

Keeping in mind the end goal to give palatable administrations in applications, organize lifetime of WBANs should be highlighted as a vital parameter. As we are probably aware, sensor hubs conveyed in WBANs are limited in measure, which implies that they are generally provided by non-inexhaustible and vitality restricted batteries. When at least one gadget must be embedded or worn by a man, colossal anxiety is caused by the battery substitution/energizing, which, sometimes, may require surgery. Moreover, every hub in WBANs has its one of a kind capacity that cannot be then again executed by different hubs. When one sensor comes up short on control, WBANs would not perform well or even quit working. Subsequently, it is a need to draw out the lifetime of every sensor hub in WBANs to diminish the worry of successive renew the sensor battery or replace them, basically for those sensors firstly which may be exhausted The main host has efficient energy as compare to other active nodes [4].

16.2 Related Work

To expand arrange lifetime, there are, as of now, various steering conventions and hand-off determination calculation for WSNs in the writing. Yossef *et al.* proposed a vitality mindful steering calculation that uses a base number of bounces for transformation of information. By shifting the transmission separate, the connections among the hubs can be change and diverse system topologies can be acquired. A vitality adjusted vigorous plan in view of swarm knowledge that picks the following hub in view of hub's neighborhood data was recommended by Zhang and Shen. This strategy adjusts stack equally among the hubs and can accomplish longer lifetime. Again, one more approach proposed in diminishes the aggregate devoured vitality in view of two improvement goals, i.e., way determination and bit designation. Parcels with the ideal size are handed-off to the combination hub from sensor hubs in the best middle of the road bounces. A hand-off choice calculation was proposed to define a streamlining issue to augment client information rates and limit the aggregate transmission energy of the system [5].

In any case, porting these arrangements from WSNs to WBANs is dangerous because of the diverse system models and working conditions. In WSNs, number of hundreds and thousands of sensor-hubs cover substantial ranges, offering an extensive level of excess, and utilize multi-bounce interchanges. Actually, WBANs cover a range restricted to the people body and offer no excess, just including two jumps. Information must be gathered dependably under remarkable attributes, for example, visit differing transmission medium conditions and transmission control limitation that are not exhibited in WSNs. In other words, an effective hand-off choice calculation ought to be composed particularly for WBANs [6].

In the writing, the writers proposed some hand-off supported correspondence handle for WBANs to upgrade vitality proficiency. These works put an accentuation on the association between transmitter sensor and hand-off hub with the thought of connection foundation system and overhead expenses. Be that as it may, how to choose a reasonable transfer for a transmitter sensor is as yet not tended to in these works. Steering conventions were additionally considered in the writing to broaden WBAN lifetime in view of multi-jump topology. By the by, these works abuse the topology limitation in IEEE 802.15.6 [7].

Elias proposed a vitality mindful WBAN topology display, which enhances the number and the area of transfers to be sent by a whole number direct programming model to limit the aggregate vitality cost of the system. An Ultra Wide Band (UWB)–based WBAN transfer determination calculation was proposed. The proposed calculation uses a vitality proficient determination paradigm to make transfer choice for add up to control utilization minimization. Another helpful transmission procedure for UWB-based WBAN was proposed in utilizing single hand-off to enhance the system lifetime. In the paper, a vitality effectiveness streamlining issue is planned on two down to earth on-body transmission situations. Creators proposed an instrument for WBANs to delay arranged lifetime through figuring the system lifetime as a component of hub transmission mode, helpful hub, transmission power and schedule vacancy, and boosting the system lifetime subject to asset assignment imperatives, at that point acquiring an ideal joint transfer choice procedure.

The creators exhibited an amusement theoretic hand-off choice and power control technique to explore the issue of transfer choice and power control with nature of administration limitations in WBANs. The proposed strategy concentrated on vitality effectiveness, and its exhibitions are analyzed in different situations. Be that as it may, references just focus on the vitality utilization rate while choosing transfers without considering sensor hubs' different conditions like leftover vitality. At the point when lingering vitality of every hub is not the same, the lifetime improvement of these calculations will be debased [8].

16.3 Proposed System

As we all know, the AI and IoT provide vital range of services in approximately all fields like in information and communication, education, science, travelling, etc. Therefore, we propose a healthcare system based on both AI and IoT to monitor the patient's health. With these two concepts, we also integrate one more approach for sensing sensor's status which is planted in the body of patient, outside the body, or on patient's cloth. For this, firstly, we describe the use of AI and IoT in medical field.

16.3.1 AI and IoT in Medical Field

The operational efficiency of medical department will improve by adding the concept of AI and IoT together. AI tracks the record, analyze the things, optimize and train, automate all the things, and control, and these are the main functions of AI which performed with IoT devices [9]. By using these concepts of both technologies, we can cut the load of different departmental works of medical employees. When all the medical activities performed by system, so doctors or officers could give much more time to patients and having main focus only on the patient other than all documentation and report generation work. Therefore, the main focus of the AI system with IoT-based approach is given below:

- Reduction in waiting time for emergency room;
- Medical employees, patients, and stock/supply of drugs tracking;
- Management of major or serious disease;

- Medicines management;
- Global tracking of health.

1	2	3	4	5
Medical staff, patients, and inventory tracking	Chronic disease management	Drug management	Emergency room wait time reduction	Remote health control

16.3.2 IoT Features in Healthcare

In healthcare system, the use of IoT principles provides a vast variety of AI-based facilities to understand the different disease in patient. The appropriate method is to explain why we need AI-based healthcare system to diagnose serious disease in patient's body and application of this system [10].

16.3.2.1 Wearable Sensing Devices With Physical Interface for Real World

Basically, the services provided by the healthcare system are a client-based request which correlate with the physical world. Despite, the basic use of these services includes all physical interfaces of caregivers, patients, and the device, etc. These devices are interconnected like robotics that interacts with medicine with the real-world environment associated with the many real-world interfaces. Generating innovative real-world interface for different transformation techniques, like Bluetooth, Ultra switch bandwidth, Wi-Fi connection, limited to bound the level of the quality for interaction with devices, flow of better unique data between IoT robotics, and increase representation of services, follow up or track the people's status. The basic reason for this is that given an IoT-based technique, the real-world scenario with interface may develop a wireless connection for networks. The IoT sensor devices that stand with limited sensors will be a grouping of devices together such as in this to collect devices in an easy manner to connect with the Internet network architecture, to gather information, and to complete procedure for well-organized activities [11].

16.3.2.2 Input Through Organized Information to the Sensors

IoT technology provides wireless network for sensors architecture. As we have told earlier, these networks can successfully update all the information between the real world and digitize world. It prevents the performance of the information transformation among those two real worlds will become a mess with the main organized data flow. Input data is gathered with the sensor nodes or send this information and controlling organization for next future feedback. In this field, there may be some information mediums that include simultaneous processing with several sensor nodes information collection that can be implemented with optimized latency. With this fact which is the maximum number of information sources that can, basically, be very long, the information records will remain short and well-organized due to main edge of analysis but long dynamic of IoT-based devices that give us permission to deduct missing data from adjacent nodes with the filling of gaps [12].

16.3.2.3   Small Sensor Devices for Input and Output

In this, several limited requirements for the existing and small length of the real-world input-output devices are discussed. Therefore, these needs must be gathered for the environmental melodies and different conditions. In these conditions, the sensor devices are executes. Thus, with these conditions of human interaction which needs relatively a high input and output from sensor devices, real-world interfaces received information from IoT devices with these sensor devices and provided this information that reverts to other computer devices with the wired or wireless connections. Therefore, here, it is not a requirement, while in this technology, it is a rare possibility for storing the long period of sensors lifetime with the input-output sensors energy reduction. Assume that these devices with such information implemented in future and monitors and devices continuously measuring and monitoring biochemical data.

1	2	3	4	5
Devices with physical interfaces to/from the real world	Structured data input through sensors	Tiny input/output devices	Human-machine-environment system drivers	Real-time action and decision control

16.3.2.4   Interaction With Human Associated Devices

Eventually, all machines interact with the procedure of transforming information among different professional human interacted systems. Therefore, the IoT can be based on developing a much complicated interface between patient system and executing condition. With this medical system, the condition around the system is mainly focused on things that implement with the addition of real world and sociological parameters. The physical controlling system for the external conditions and parameters is the main critical thing for the medical field after operating condition of the IoT techniques [13].

IoT includes sensor devices; in these devices, most are wireless, and these devices are interlinked to short industries of sensor devices. While on the basis of these major parameters, here, there is no existence of this network connection. We experienced after this implementation that IoT-based systems are develop by the developers and persons that use this system in different fields as per user demand to measure persons physical and emotions and thoughts, etc. This model of information creates a data series by using different models. This information used by the system to generate a table of data on the basis of AI facts [14].

16.3.2.5   To Control Physical Activity and Decision

AI- and IoT-enabled systems have the important feature that is to control the activity and reaction on the current activity on the current place. It mainly focuses on the patient's activity, treatment by the doctor, and plans for the treatment. A main advanced approach is to manage data of patient. Physical examination can be performed when the collected data is symmetric. Thus, this is rare possibility that complicated evaluation and calculations can be done by a system for many sensor devices and streaming of information. This is a medical system which is depending upon the concept of AI which can deduct the bulk data or acti-vate device to manage information management [15].

16.3.3   Approach for Sensor's Status of Patient

As talked about sometime recently, a WBAN is altogether different from a WSN. In a WSN, organized lifetime is, for the most part, determined as the time term between the system introduction/restart to the moment that the last sensor or the larger part of sensor hubs pass on. Notwithstanding, in a WBAN, every sensor hub is fundamental because of its one of a kind capacity. The depletion of one sensor hub may prompt system disappointment. As a result [44–48], arranged lifetime of a WBAN in this paper is indicated as the time length between the introduction/restart of a WBAN to the moment that the principal sensor hub in the system depletes [16].

16.4   System Model

In this paper, we consider a WBAN with one organizer and one sensor hub on a human body as appeared in Figure 16.1. The organizer is put at the front side of stomach area while

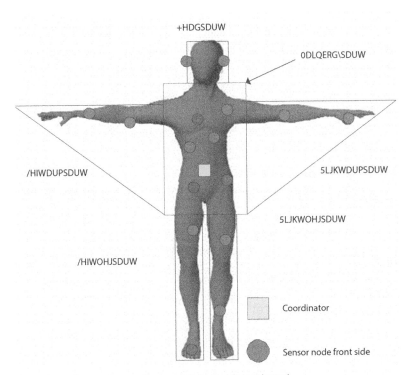

Figure 16.1 Network model.

the sensor hubs are conveyed in the diverse parts of the human body. Both direct transmission and helpful transmission are permitted in the system. The sensor hubs sent in the fundamental body part can be chosen as hand-off hubs on account of their shorter separation from the organizer. Transfer hubs ought not just transmit their own data to the facilitator, additionally hand-off the data from some different hubs when chosen as hand-off. What is more, hand-off hubs are permitted to utilize coordinated transmission just to agree to the IEEE 802.15.6 two-jump tree topology limitation. Just uplink information transmission from sensor hubs to the organizer is considered because of utilization situations like well-being checking where a large portion of the data transmitted are detected information. We accept that the facilitator knows the system topology and the separation between each match of hubs including itself.

A basic Time Division Multiple Access (TDMA) Media Access Control (MAC) is utilized in this model to manage multi-sensor transmission [17].

Note that this MAC is a typical utilized adaptation of reference point empowered superframe MAC indicated in IEEE 802.15.6. More particular, time is separated into superframes which have settled length [37–43]. A superframe has two sections: the dynamic part and the idle part. The dynamic part comprises of settled length schedule openings and every sensor hub has one orthogonal availability to send its detected information to the organizer without impact. On the off chance that a sensor hub is chosen as a transfer, additional schedule vacancies are given to it. The quantity of the additional schedule vacancies for a specific transfer is chosen by the quantity of handed-off sensors it has. Every sensor hub transmits the detected information to the recipients (either transfer or the facilitator) in its committed space, though hand-off hubs, if essential, tune in to their comparing sensor hubs for information gathering and transmit the handed-off information together with their own particular information to the organizer in their allotted openings. Amid the idle part, hubs go to rest mode. At the point when a WBAN sets up or re-begins, the availabilities portion will be made by the facilitator relying upon the transfer determination comes about. Typical sensor hubs are apportioned schedule openings first before hand-off hubs. In this paper, it is expected that all hubs have enough detected information to send amid their designated openings [18].

In MWBAN, main consumption of energy is on transformation of data and very high battery consumption in listening, controlling [27–36], and overlearning of network. As we have discussed in earlier part of this chapter, a TDMA algorithm is implanted for this. So, after implementing this algorithm, we have observed that no part of energy is consumed on abnormal activities. Therefore, the cost of energy for sensing the devices is very low so it may be ignored at time of comparison with the cost of transformation [19]. Consequently, we are mainly interested in consumption of energy on the transformation. In this chapter, we select the architecture of battery consumption in transformation that it can be used in different MWBAN models. The cost of energy consumption in transformation of data can be described with Eqs. (16.1) and (16.2):

$$E_T(v, s, n) = E_{Telec} \cdot v + E_{amp} \cdot v \cdot sn \qquad (16.1)$$

$$E_R(v) = E_{Relec} \cdot v \qquad (16.2)$$

This model receives n as cost of energy with the effect of variation in medium and d as distance represents the path among source and destination. E_T shows the energy of transmission, E_R shows the energy of receiver, E_{Telec} and E_{Relec} show the energy of the ratio to dissipate on execute circular sequence for the sending and receiving, respectively; E_{amp} shows energy of the sender amplifier. The main information and values for mentioned parameters can be dependent on the hardware. Parameter v also shows the number of bits in data send by the sender in transmission. n is the coefficient of pathloss that depend on the shadow effect.

While developing a connection in selection of relay, the value of energy cannot be the same.

These two main conditions must be considered for transmission:

1. A MWBAN connection should be created with sensors for multiple battery capacities.
2. A MWBAN recreates to restart the system while every sensor device has energy under varied consumption values.

The differences of vitality stockpiling of every hub in the system can bring evident impact on the execution of WBANs. Subsequently, when making transfer determination, the measure of vitality in every hub must be contemplated. As shown from the reasons expressed over, the vitality contrast among sensor hubs changes eccentrically. In this way, as per the Central Limit Theorem and the sign, we receive ordinary dissemination to speak to the vitality stockpiling state of every sensor hub. In the interim, we select a suitable upper bound and lower headed for the vitality stockpiling esteems to keep away from extraordinary vast or little arbitrary esteems in typical appropriation, which is difficult to show up in all actuality [20].

In rundown, the leftover vitality of the sensor node on the position of ith while we consider the optional transfer condition in this chapter considers for the simple appropriation which can be represent by the following:

$$Ei \sim N(\alpha, \Omega2), \quad \alpha - \Delta \leq Ei \leq \alpha + \Delta,$$

Here, α and Δ show standard parameters with the residual energy and highest energy deviation for main values for every sensor node. Here, $\Omega2$ abbreviates the energy difference unit among sensing devices. Highest values of $\Omega2$ represent the many residual equality for the sensing network [21].

16.4.1 Solution Based on Heuristic Iterative Method

The main basic concept of our proposed work may continuously improve lower period of life of sensor for the network architecture by activating the parameters of selection of relay for variables which accept binary values for the grid T, to improve the whole lifetime of network that is evaluated. The enhanced process for this approach is shown by Algorithm 16.1. All steps of the algorithm can be summarized in three large steps.

Calculate the minimum lifetime of each sensor device because the destination node wants to increase period of life. Perform the activity of selection of relay to increase period of life of destination node as per given prescribed situation for the device.

After comparing these increased period of life with earlier minimum value or select either the circulation must be terminated else not. When all these loops have ended, so these value for every digit parameter for selection of relay in grid M shows the conclude selection of relay solution with in sensing architecture [22].

Algorithm 16.1 Heuristic Iterative Algorithm

Step 1: We assume 1 sensor for the whole network and consider m number of nodes for relay.

Step 2: Node value is initialized by 1, and relay node value can be initialize by 1 to m, $T_{m,n} = 1$, $T_{m,n} = 0$,
$\forall m,n = 1, 2$ end with l, m/= n, constant = =0.

Step 3: for every m ∈ [1, 2]

Step 4: Compute period of life for sensor LT_i, with the help of Eqs. (16.1) & (16.2).

Step 5: for end

step 6: while constant = 0

do

Step 7: $k = \text{argmini}(LT_i)$
m∈[1,2]

Step 8: if $(n \le m)$ then

Step 9: else if (Rn == 0) then

Step 10: get constant = 0.

Step 11: else if

Step 12: $s = \text{argmaxi}(LT_i)$
$T_{m,n} = 1$

Step 13: Set Ts,k = 1, xk,m = 2, and $\forall i \in$ [1, 2], m/= s.

Step 14: end else if

Step 15: elseif $T_{m,n} == 0$ then

Step 16: considering the Node s is destination node,

Step 17: $s == \text{argmini}(d_{n,i})$,
m∈[1,2],m/=s

Step 18: now constant = 1.

Step 19: while

Step 20: $s = \text{argmini}(dn,i)$.
m∈[1,l],m/=n

Step 21: set = 1, Tn,i = 0, $\forall m \in$ [1, 2], m/= s.

Step 22: while end

Step 23: if

Step 24: $s = \text{argmaxi}(LTi)$
m∈[1,2]

Step 25: get Tn,s = 0, Tn,i = 1, $\forall m \in$ [1, 2], m/= s.

Step 26: if end
Step 27: for every m∈ [1, 2]
Step 28: Compute period of life LTi, with the help of Eqs. (16.1) & (16.2).
Step 29: for end
Step 30: LTmin = minimum{LTi|i∈ [1, 2]}
Step 31: store Lmin & compute and compare old result.
Step 32: if (LTmin != i++) then
Step 33: get constant = 1.
Step 34: while end

After the hand-off choice activity portrayed over, every one of the period of life for the system can be computed once. The base period of life between the majority for these devices/hubs should be stored and contrasted and past least esteems. In the event that the correlation demonstrates that the base esteem cannot increment any longer, the calculation will reach an end; generally, the cycle will keep on processing [23].

It ought to be seen that the calculation has a limited number of twofold factors and just two factors fluctuate their qualities in one emphasis. Consequently, aside from the uncommon conditions depicted by steps 9 and 10. The emphasis procedure portrayed with procedure one is at last united with a specific condition, in which some hand-off determination paired factors change in a circle mode. The normal estimation of circle measure is two, that is, transfer determination comes about are changed by the tenets indicated in Algorithm 16.1 between two diverse paired esteem blends for T with in circle state (bigger estimations for circle condition may likewise show up with the boundaries). The cycle should terminate with the meeting of the circle. The twofold esteem blends form T with in circles bigger than the period of life computed by Eq. (16.1) can be chosen like last after effects from the Algorithm 16.1. Some additional points of interest for boundary conditions mentioned in the proposed work with quick arrangement should be spoken to the following area.

Result Analysis

The time complexity evaluation of the HIS approach for their iterative method and for its respective looping status evaluation can be done before the computation of their lifetime performance of network. If we consider the theoretical point, it can say that the basic use of this simplified technique to evaluate the current simplified problem. So, the time complexity of HIS algorithm can be evaluated by $O(2n \times n)$. Therefore, if we talk about the proposed work of (HIS) heuristic iterative algorithm, the final time complexity of HIS can measure by $O(n \times n)$. In the opposite side, the experimental point of view shown in Table 16.1 demonstrates that the optimum cost of time can resolve the minimum problem with this simulation work of many sensor nodes in the sensing architecture, in which the cost of simulation is little bit high as compare to given HIS approach. With deeply manner, the period consumed in enumeration development gone quickly that varies in this improved amount of sensor devices. Therefore, the proposed algorithm grows little high and smoothed manner within a hundred nanoseconds. As shown in Table 16.1, the result of simulation of experimental evaluation for specified period complexity for simplification and the result of new technique is compared with previously exist approach's result [24].

Table 16.1 Time complexity of Heuristic Iterative Algorithm.

Node	Enumer.	Heuristic Iterative
5	0.003623s	0.000024s
10	0.065734s	0.000035s
15	0.623641s	0.000026s
20	8.301242s	0.000017s
25	216.373562s	0.000032s
30	5463.176524s	0.000023s

The hardware setup of system to implement this simulation is 10-GB RAM and i-7 CPU processor.

16.5 Challenges of Cyber Security in Healthcare With IoT

Besides, all the evident advantages which depend on the interfering of IoT that is elaborated, this proposed technique is also facing different challenges related to the secure transformation of data which is the main part of the existing medical system architecture. The main idea exists in external organized database; an unstructured data residing like electronic patient's information or different manuals are in maintaining much typical in arranging the data according to the old traditional approach. Thus, protection of data is the main point in all approaches. So, the proposed algorithm is the powerful algorithms that are more than efficient to contribute in most of the part to solve the given problem with data analysis. Therefore, collecting information and organization of data does not mean it is secure from cyber threats or hacking [25].

So, to implement the standards in respect of IoT, the main solution is the implementation of ecosystem. IoT wearable devices (sensing capability) or different IoT-enabled applications are generally developed to interact with personal or patient's disease related data prior they go to in malware. According to this proposed new innovative solution, the personal data regularity bodies say that the Health Insurance Portability and Accountability Act (HIPAA) can secure all medical data related to patient health transform one place to another for evaluation, these authorities provide basic protection of data from unwanted source of hackers for misuse of data would consider this misuse of data to send economical punishment of information. Solving many tough systems with AI-based IoT may not confirm creating advance certification of the involvement of new technologies in medical softwares. So, nowadays, it is also a main requirement that health controlling machines should be transformed with a secure and safety facility.

16.6   Conclusion

Many health care devices are connected to maintain the information about health and bring this information from the attached sensors. Consequently, some updation of information maintaining procedures is required. AI provides many benefits such as innovative techniques which are limited to develop highly smart conditions, so that they interact with human centric systems that must be much adaptive or, we can say, secure. In addition with IoT, some procedures to maintain medical health service provide each and every function in the real world. In this paper, a healthcare system is proposed by figuring a streamlining issue that considers both the vitality utilization rate and leftover vitality of every hub to augment the base lifetime of the hubs in the system. To sense the sensor data, HIS heuristic circular arrangement can be intended to quickly find the issue. These reenactment comes about to demonstrate that the heuristic arrangement fundamentally decreases the time many-sided quality with an exclusive 0.5% execution corruption when contrasted and the ideal estimations within the enhancement that shows the innovative plot can be reasonable with in a continuous frequently MWBAN framework. This assessment of execution for innovative things conspires on the clothes of patient's body-formed system. A MWABN system display indicated a standard of the networking that is IEEE 802.15.6 as for vitality distinction degree, arrange, and find the aggregate counting for the hubs, separately. It is represented by the recreation that comes about the innovative concepts for plot that dependably beats already present hand-off choice calculations as far as system lifetime of WBANs. Furthermore, the proposed hand-off determination calculation does not disregard the topology limitation of IEEE 802.15.6. Moreover, we make a short dialog on the most proficient method to execute our proposed plot in a genuine MWBAN framework to approve the attainability. Taking everything into account, HIS is a compelling and appropriate transfer choice strategy to sense the system result of MWBANs [26].

References

1. Braem, B., Latre, B., Moerman, I., Blondia, C., Reusens, E., Joseph, W., Martens, L., Demeester, P., The Need for Cooperation and Relaying in Short-Range High Path Loss Sensor Networks, in: *Proceedings of the International Conference on Sensor Technologies and Applications*, Valencia, Spain, pp. 566–571, 14–20 October 2007.
2. Cai, X., Yuan, J., Yuan, X., Zhu, W., Li, J., Li, C., Ullah, S., Energy-efficient Relay MAC with Dynamic Power Control in Wireless Body Area Networks. *KSII Trans. Internet Inf. Syst.*, 7, 1547–1568, 2013.
3. Chai, R., Wang, P., Huang, Z., Su, C., Network Lifetime Maximization Based Joint Resource Optimization for Wireless Body Area Networks, in: *Proceedings of the IEEE PIMRC 2014*, Washington, DC, USA, pp. 1088–1092, 2–5 September 2014.
4. Chen, M., Gonzalez, S., Vasilakos, A., Cao, H., Leung, V.C.M., Body area networks: A survey. *J. Mobile Netw. Appl.*, 16, 171–193, 2011.
5. Chih, S.L. and Po, J.C., Energy-efficient two-hop extension protocol for wireless body area networks. *IET Wirel. Sens. Syst.*, 1, 37–56, 2013.

6. Choudhary, R. and Kumar, S., Accurate and Efficient Crawling the Deep Web: Surfacing Hidden Value (Paper ID: 21041114). *Int. J. Comput. Sci. Inf. Secur. (IJCSIS)*, May issue, 9, 5, 149–153, 2011.

7. Choudhary, R. and Kumar, S., Modeling and Analyze the Deep Web: Surfacing Hidden Value (Paper ID: 19051113). *Int. J. Comput. Sci. Inf. Secur. (IJCSIS)*, June issue, 9, 6, 119–124, 2011.

8. Dae, Y.K., Wee, Y.K., Jin, S.C., Ben, L., EAR: An Environment-Adaptive Routing Algorithm for WBANs, in: *Proceedings of the IEEE ISMICT 2010*, Tainan, China, 27–29 October 2010.

9. Deepak, K.S. and Babu, A.V., Improving energy efficiency of incremental relay based cooperative communications in wireless body area networks. *Int. J. Commun. Syst.*, 1, 91–111, 2015.

10. Ding, J., Dutkiewicz, E., Huang, X., Fang, G., Energy efficient cooperative transmission in single-relay UWB based body area networks, in: *Proceedings of the IEEE ICC 2015*, London, UK, pp. 1559–1564, 8–12 June 2015.

11. Ding, J., Dutkiewicz, E., Huang, X., Fang, G., Energy-Efficient Cooperative Relay Selection for UWB Based Body Area Networks, in: *Proceedings of the IEEE ICUWB 2013*, Sydney, Australia, pp. 97–102, 15–18 September 2013.

12. Elias, J., Optimal design of energy-efficient and cost-effective Wireless Body Area Networks. *Ad Hoc Netw.*, 1, 560–574, 2014.

13. Elias, J. and Mehaoua, A., Energy-aware Topology Design for Wireless Body Area Networks, in: *Proceedings of the IEEE ICC 2012*, Ottawa, ON, Canada, pp. 3409–3413, 10–15 June 2012.

14. Fabio, D.F., Ilenia, T., Yu, G., 1 Hop or 2 Hops: Topology Analysis in Body Area Network, in: *Proceedings of the 2014 European Conference on Networks and Communications (EuCNC)*, Bologna, Italy, pp. 1–5 , 23–26 June 2014.

15. Fortino, G., Gravina, R., Raffaele, G., Philip, K., Roozbeh, J., Enabling Effective Programming and Flexible Management of Efficient Body Sensor Network Applications. *IEEE Trans. Hum. Mach. Syst.*, 1, 115–133, 2013.

16. George, S., Nikos, D., Rosario, S., Valeria, L., Fortino, G., Yiannis, A., Decentralized Time-Synchronized Channel Swapping for Ad Hoc Wireless Networks. *IEEE Trans. Veh. Technol.*, 10, 8538–8553, 2016.

17. Gomathi, C. and Santhiyakumari, N., OFSR: An Optimized Fuzzy Based Swarm Routing for Wireless Body Area Networks, in: *Proceedings of the IEEE SPIN 2016*, Noida, India, pp. 507–512, 11–12 February 2016.

18. Haibo, Z. and Hong, S., Balancing energy consumption to maximize network lifetime in data gathering sensor networks. *ACM Trans. Sens. Netw.*, 2, 1–25, 2009.

19. Hussein, M. and Francis, M.B., Optimal Relay Selection and Power Control With Quality-of-Service Provisioning in Wireless Body Area Networks. *IEEE Trans. Wirel. Commun.*, 8, 5497–5510, 2016.

20. IEEE Standard for Local and Metropolitan Area Networks Part 15.6: Wireless Body Area Networks, in: *IEEE Std. 802.15.6-2012*, IEEE, Piscataway, NJ, USA, pp. 1–271, 2012.

21. IshtaiqueulHuque, M.T., Munasinghe, K.S., Abolhasan, M., Jamalipour, A., EAR-BAN: Energy Efficient Adaptive Routing in Wireless Body Area Networks, in: *Proceedings of the IEEE ICSPCS 2013*, Carrara, Australia, 16–18 December 2013.

22. Iyengar, S., TempiaBonda, F., Gravina, R., Guerrieri, A., Fortino, G., Sangiovanni-Vincentelli, A.A., Framework for Creating Healthcare Monitoring Applications Using Wireless Body Sensor Networks, in: *Proceedings of the ICST 3rd International Conference on Body Area Networks*, Tempe, AZ, USA, 13–17 March 2008.

23. Khoa, T.P., Duy, H.N.N., Tho, L., Joint power allocation and relay selection in cooperative net-works, in: *Proceedings of the IEEE GLOBECOM 2009*, Honolulu, HI, USA, 30 November–4 December 2009, pp. 1–5.

24. Kumari, R. and Nand, P., An optimized routing algorithm for BAN by considering Hop-count, residual energy and link quality for route discovery. *IEEE Conference on Computing, Communication and Automation held on 5th-6th May 2017 at Galgotias University, Greater Noida (ICCCA 2017)*, https://doi.org/10.1109/CCAA.2017.8229884.

25. Kumari, R. and Nand, P., Implementation of Square-odd scanning technique in WBAN for energy conservation. *International Conference on Innovative Computing and Communications - Proceedings of ICICC 2019*, 21-22nd March 2019, Springer, (SCOPUS indexed).

26. Kumari, R. and Nand, P., Performance Analysis for MANETs using certain realistic mobil-ity models: NS-2. *Int. J. Sci. Res. Comput. Sci. Eng. (IJSRCSE)*, 6, 1, February 2018, (UGC approved and Thomson Reuters indexed Journal). https://doi.org/ 10.26438/ijsrcse/v6i1.7077 pp-70-77.

27. Kumari, R. and Nand, P., Performance Analysis of existing Routing Protocols. *Int. J. Sci. Res. Comput. Sci. Eng. (IJSRCSE)*, 5, 5, 47–50, October-2017. https://doi.org/10.26438/ijsrcse/v5i5.4750.

28. Kumari, R. and Nand, P., Performance Comparison of various Routing Protocols in WSN and WBAN. *IEEE Conference on Computing, Communication and Automation held on 29th-30th April 2016 at Galgotias University, Greater Noida (ICCCA 2016)*, https://doi.org/10.1109/CCAA.2016.7813814.

29. Kumari, R. and Nand, P., Recent Research onWireless Body Area Networks: A Survey. *Int. J. Sci. Res. Comput. Sci. Eng. Inf. Technol. (IJSRCSEIT)*, 3, 1, 492–503, January 2018.

30. Kumari, R. and Nand, P., Secure Communication using PFS in a distributed Environment. *On-line International Conferences on Ancient Mathematics and Science for Computing held on 24th-25th November 2017*.

31. Kumari, R. and Nand, P., Square-odd scanning for WBAN to reduce detection time. *Int. J. Innov. Technol. Explor. Eng.*, Volume-8, 8S2, 643–650, (SCOPUSindexed Journal), 2019.

32. Kumari, R. and Nand, P., Integration of Blockchain in medical healthcare system, in: *Blockchain Technology: A Revolution in IT*, Apple Academic Press CRC Group, USA, (SCOPUS Indexed), 2020.

33. Kumari, R. and Nand, P., Performance Analysis of existing MAC and routing protocols for WBAN. *IEEE sixth international Conference on system modeling and Advancement in system trends held on 29th - 30th December at TeerthankerMahaveer University, Moradabad (SMART-2017)*, 2020.

34. Kumari, R. and Nand, P., Integration of Blockchain in WBAN. *International Conference on Computing, Communication and Intelligent Systems held on 18th-19th October 2019 at Sharda University, Greater Noida*.

35. Kumari, R. and Nand, P., To improve the performance of routing protocol in mobile WBAN by optimizing the scheduling mechanism. *Int. J. Emerg. Res. Manage. Technol. (IJERMT)*, 6, 9, 86–92, September 2017.

36. Kumari, R. and Singhal, A., Energy Conservation in Wireless Sensor Network. *International Conference on Emerging Trends & development in science, management and Technology (ICETDSMT-2013)*.

37. Kumari, R. and Singh, S., Cloud Computing- An Overview of The Art. *International Conference on Technology and Innovative Advancement in Computing and Communication Engineering-2013 (TIACCE-2013)*.

38. Kumari, R. and Singh, S., Security threats and counter measures with Bluetooth devices. *International Conference on Emerging Trends & development in science, management and Technology (ICETDSMT-2013)*.

39. Liu, B., Yan, Z., Chen, C.W., Medium Access Control for Wireless Body Area Networks with QoS Provisioning and Energy Efficient Design. *IEEE Trans. Mob. Comput.*, 2, 422–434, 2017.

40. MoidSahndhu, M., Javaid, N., Imran, M., Guizani, M., Ali Khan, Z., Qasim, U., BEC: A Novel Routing Protocol for Balanced Energy Consumption in Wireless Body Area Networks, in: *Proceedings of the IEEE IWCMC 2015*, Dubrovnik, Croatia, 24–28 August 2015, pp. 653–658.

41. Raffaele, G., Parastoo, A., Hassan, G., Giancarlo, F., Multi-sensor fusion in body sensor networks: State-of-the-art and research challenges. *Inf. Fusion*, 5, 68–80, 2017.

42. Reusens, E., Joseph, W., Latre, B., Brae, B., Vermeeren, G., Tanghe, E., Martens, L., Moerman, I., Blondia, C., Characterization of On-Body Communication Channel and Energy Efficient Topology Design for Wireless Body Area Networks. *IEEE Trans. Inf. Technol. Biomed.*, 6, 933–945, 2009.

43. Riccardo, C., Flavia, M., Ramona, R., Chiara, B., Roberto, V.A., Survey on Wireless Body Area Networks: Technologies and Design Challenges. *IEEE Commun. Surv. Tutor.*, 3, 1635–1657, 2014.

44. Rui, P., Ding, J.C., Jaya, S.P., Yong, P.X., An Opportunistic Relay Protocol With Dynamic Scheduling in Wireless Body Area Sensor Network. *IEEE Sens. J.*, 7, 3743–3750, 2015.

45. Welsh, M., Exposing resource tradeoffs in region-based communication abstractions for sensor networks. *Comput. Commun. Rev.*, 1, 119–124, 2004.

46. Yasaman, K., Rashid, A., Ashfaq, K., Energy efficient decentralized detection based on bit-optimal multi-hop transmission in onedimensional wireless sensor networks, in: *Proceedings of the 2013 ITIP Wireless Days (WD)*, Valencia, Spain, 13–15 November 2013.

47. Youssef, M., Younis, M., Arisha, K.A., A constrained shortest-path energy-aware routing algorithm for wireless sensor networks, in: *Proceedings of the 2002 IEEE Wireless Communications and Networking Conference (WCNC2002)*, Orlando, FL, USA, 17–21 March 2002, pp. 794–799.

48. Zhang, R., Moungla, H., Mehaoua, A., An Energy-Efficient Leader Election Mechanism for Wireless Body Area Networks, in: *Proceedings of the IEEE GLOBECOM 2014*, Austin, TX, USA, pp. 2411–2416, 8–12 December 2014.

17

Effectiveness of Swarm Intelligence for Handling Fault-Tolerant Routing Problem in IoT

Arpit Kumar Sharma[1*], Kishan Kanhaiya[2] and Jaisika Talwar[3]

[1]Department of Computer and Communication Engineering, Manipal University Jaipur, India
[2]Netaji Subhas Institute of Technology, New Delhi, India
[3]Arya Institute of Engineering Technology and Management, Jaipur, India

Abstract

Swarm Intelligence Algorithms are most effective to handle the issues of routing problems in IoT. Swarm is optimization algorithm in depth so, here, the discussion about how can the drawbacks present in IoT can be compensated using Swarm Intelligence, which are described. The places where IoT is used, its benefits, as well as use of swarm in different fields are elaborated.

To improve the efficiency and reliability of the devices that are used in IoT, they should be free from fault. Many approaches and mathematical models are made so as to make the devices error free. Some of the algorithms are EARQ and SPSOA but the most widely used algorithm is IEIFTA (Improved Efficient and Intelligent Fault-Tolerance Algorithm). If any fault occurs, then IEIFTA can remove the fault at a fast rate as well as it improves the efficiency and any loss of the information. It is the fastest routing technique. The mutation of particle using multi-swarm technique is explained below including how the position and speed of the particle is updated if any clone occurs.

Keywords: Swarms, Swarm Intelligence, fault tolerance, Internet of Things

17.1 Introduction

Swarms are the groups of agents or any entities, and we use this type of intelligence in making the basics of Swarms Intelligence. In Swarm Intelligence, we will understand how an extremely complex task can be accomplished by a group of individuals [1]. Main applications based on the optimization of ants and bee colonies are also covered in this unit. To solve a set of problems, different algorithms as well as models are used. In the field like agriculture, robotics, medical, and biological, Swarm Intelligence is widely accepted [2]. Different methods are used to apply the Swarm Intelligence in the field of robotics (in Engineering). Nowadays, the problems based on IoT are also solved using swarms. All the drawbacks of IoT are compensated using Swarm Intelligence [3].

---

*Corresponding author: er.aks31@gmail.com

Abhishek Kumar, Pramod Singh Rathore, Vicente Garrcia Diaz and Rashmi Agrawal (eds.) Swarm Intelligence Optimization: Algorithms and Applications, (325–342) © 2021 Scrivener Publishing LLC. ISBN 978-1-119-77874-5

The devices used in IoT can suffer with different kinds of fault such as sensor faults, fault at nodes wiring, breakage in the devices, broken communication links, depletion of batteries, other environmental issues, impairment of some wires, etc. [4]. To predict the fault and to transfer the information successfully from sender to receiver, we need fault tolerance. So, in the cyber-physical system, for the communication process, faults become a critical issue, and hence, fault tolerance is required for a good communication procedure [5]. It is a very challenging process in cyber-physical system to provide fault tolerance routing with higher energy efficiency. IEIFTA (Improved Efficient and Intelligent Fault-Tolerance Algorithm) is the kind of algorithm that is used to remove the problem of fault tolerance by the use of network model using particles. By using this algorithm, fault tolerance based on IoT can be provided successfully by using lower amount of energy and with much efficiency and reliability [6].

17.1.1 Meaning of Swarm and Swarm Intelligence

Swarms are basically a group of insects or some entities and a class of some particular type of the animals that live together in harmony. These entities can be any organisms like algae or group of sarcopterygii and also Phytoplankton, and murmuring of birds. This class of entities that exhibit a similar pattern or a similar kind of behavior is referred to as "Swarm Behavior" [6]. A particular kind of purposeful work that these insects do is to reach at some meaningful results. Research is going on this type of behavior in medical and engineering field even by the biologists to take advantage of such type of intelligence [7].

Swarm Intelligence means to gain some intelligence by these independent entities. These insects follow some action and rules so that they get success. No one is the leader of their groups so they all work together by following those rules and coordinate with each other. They are their own self-guides which work by themselves without interrupting each other and even maintaining the distance among themselves so that they must not collide [8].

In short, making a problem from complex to simple in an easy way is called Swarm Intelligence. All the individuals should perform their task in a localized or redistributed manner. Swarm Intelligence includes swarm algorithm which are quick and are more effective in order to get a task accomplished. To solve the different problems, one of the best algorithms is the swarm fish algorithm which is basically used for the kinetic improvement [9].

More attainment of the algorithm in this intelligence makes the whole system much more desirable and effective [10].

Let us take the example of an ant that, too, moves in a line [11]. No one is the leader but they all work according to certain rules which are already planned [12]. If any one of them finds a prey, then they tell their mates about the prey with the help of trail lying [13]. Then, all of them according to their set of rules follow that trail so that they all can reach to their destination, implying that all of them can carry their prey with them together. For doing so, they all together, in a group, carry that prey with them, and this can be defined as the swarm behavior of ants (Figure 17.1) [14].

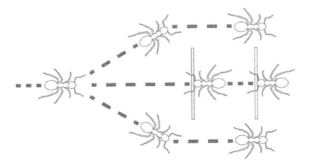

Figure 17.1 Swarm behavior of ants [2].

Many mathematical models have also been completed based on the swarm behavior, one of them being "Boids" developed by Craig Reynolds. Boids is a type of computer program which says that group of entities should be divided in three zones, basically:

1. The Repulsion Zone: In this zone, all the entities should maintain some distance with each other so that they all does not slam into each other.
2. The Alignment Zone: In this zone, all the entities must align themselves like we saw in the example of ants.
3. The Outermost Zone or the Attraction Zone: In this zone, the animal at the center or focus moves toward its neighbor.

Swarm robots are also in use so that we can improve the performance in different fields with the help of collection of robots. Different fields in which swarm robots can be used are medical, robotics, engineering, and even in the field of agriculture [15]. The benefits of using robots with Swarm Intelligence are that we can improve the efficiency of the work, their communication with each other can also be improved and even with the environment, sensing power can also be enhanced, performance and even compatibility with each other can be increased, and complexity can be reduced if they will work together. Even in fault tolerance, their flexibility can be improved.

17.1.2 Stability

Swarm intelligence is based on many principles such as quality, diversity, resilience, and stability. In the principle of stability of swarms, we must know that how different agnates of the group are moving, what is the distance between each of them, are they very close to each other or far away from each other? At what speed they are moving, i.e., what is their relative velocity? in order to judge all this, we must have some repulsive or attractive agents in the crew. But, still the research is going on as the stability of swarms is still a big problem. One-dimensional and two-dimensional structures of synchronized distributed controls are made, but for asynchronized distributed controls, stability is, again, a problem.

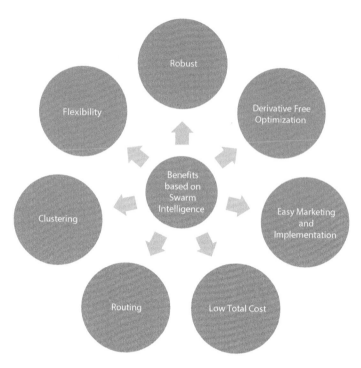

Figure 17.2 Benefits of Swarm Intelligence [1].

17.1.3 Technologies of Swarm

The concept of swarm is not new. Since 1980s, swarm technology is in use. It is just that some advancement in these technologies is taking place. Many near-field and far-field communication technologies are being used. Bluetooth technology is an example of near-field communication. Except Bluetooth, many other wireless technologies are also in use such as Wi-Fi, Zigbee, RFID, and LPWAN's (low-power wide-area networks). These are basically used in IoT on the concept of swarms. Many multisensory technologies that are widely in use nowadays are Raspberry Pi and Arduino [16].

Hardware is already a cultivated dais, we can say, but still the software is yet not cultivated. The software platform lacks in efficiency, and also, there is much loss of the data, and hence, it is also not reliable. So, we have to face many demands to fulfill the growing needs of people and eventually come to a point where we make a high rated proper platform which can run efficiently (Figure 17.2).

17.2 Applications of Swarm Intelligence

The most abundantly used algorithms in this type of the intelligence are described below [17].

17.2.1   Flight of Birds Elaborations

Birds are one of the best examples of Swarm Intelligence. When the birds move together in murmuration, then they can do their task much efficiently and even less energy is utilized by them. Lethargy of the birds is also reduced [18]. If we take the example of pelicans and note their motion, then we can see that all the pelican's move in unison. They all move together matching their steps one by one like they are dancing in the sky and it looks like they are choreographed in an enhanced way [19]. By moving in these groups, they can easily find their prey as they can communicate easily with each other, and also, they get the advantage of searching their stuff like food and silk, spider webs, and mud that are used to make their nest (Figure 17.3) [20].

17.2.2   Honey Bees Elaborations

Bees are also observed in colonies (group of bees) [20]. Bees divide their work in two groups. One colony is of engaged bees and other colony is of workless bees. They all do some different work which is employed to them. The group of engaged bees work by flying from one flower to another in search of nectar. When the engaged bees find a particular source of food, they inform all the remaining bees as well as to workless bees. They all find the shortest path or lane to reach their source. When they reach, they all are employed to collect the nectar from the flower. After all the bees complete their work, they all follow back the same path to the comb where they live (Figure 17.4).

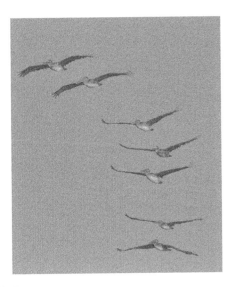

Figure 17.3 Flock of birds [20].

Figure 17.4 Colony of bees [6].

17.3 Swarm Intelligence in IoT

IoT is transforming the whole world and developing the technology so that our communication is based on a proper platform. Swarm Intelligence concept may be related to Cloud that is the technology which is used to transform the data, transfer the data from sender to receiver, and interpret the data. From all these things, we can even see in our android mobiles, personal computers, and iPhones too. They all do the same work. With the help of Cloud technology, we can even remove that thin layer between the real and imaginary world. IoT is applied to many areas such as for the security purpose, developing the nature, in arts, in different fields of science, for our safety purposes, in automation technologies, and even in robotics and other fields of engineering, etc.

Systems that are used in IoT are difficult to understand and confusing. They are even distributed to a small area and are much complex systems. But, as we have already learnt in Swarm Intelligence that systems are arranged in a systematic way and are decentralized so as to solve the hard and confusing problems of IoT, we can take the help of Swarm Intelligence. All the drawbacks of the IoT are stabilized by Swarm Intelligence. In many domains, SI has much advantages and even a good solution to the problems. So, by using the algorithms of SI, we can solve all the problems of IoT. In some of the applications, this process is also applied and this will provide us the path for our future thoughts (Figure 17.5).

Figure 17.5 Uses of IoT [19].

17.3.1   Applications

1. Data routing: Basically, SI is used in data routing for the purpose of conversation or the type of contact and connection. It is generally used for telecommunication procedure. So, we know that, for the communication, we firstly need a sender and receiver. Secondly, we need the information which is to be transferred from the sender to the receiver. But, to transfer the information, we have to store that information somewhere. The same process is followed in data routing. The sensors store all the information which is needed to be transferred.

    The AntNet algorithm is used in SI for proper routing of the data in a systematic way. In this AntNet algorithm, different agents are present which search for the particular path. Like we have seen in the examples of ants that they move by following a particular route in an alignment, so in data routing also, some ants move in front of the row and the other ants follow them. The ants which are ahead find their way to cloud and the ants which are following them store all the information in different stacks and carry it with themselves. Many of the IoT devices are also used in this process.

2. Cloud Computing: For storing large amounts of data, IoT is used [21]. Approximately, more than 1.2 Zettabyte of the data is to be handled for storing a large amount of the information. This large amount of the data is generated by IoT devices which are currently used in these processes. Storing such a large amount of data is a difficult process, and some amount of the data is also lost in this process. So, to prevent the loss of the data and to improve the overall effectiveness to carry the data, ACO is used. They process all the data very frequently without its loss and, in turn, give the best performance in a robust way. ACO is not like other IoT devices which work very slowly; it is a multitasking device. It can easily accept all the data from different devices and store all the data without any loss.

3. Connection of cars: the concept of connected cars is applied with the help of vehicle routing. For connection of different vehicles, IoT platforms are in use. With the help of this type of routing, the customers should be provided with different services. The running cost of the vehicles are reduced as "i" number of the customers should be provided to the service with "j" number of the cars that are in use. We can improve the performance also by utilizing the vehicle routing technology. These vehicles also generate a large amount of the data up to gigabytes so that they can use it for delivery purposes, in LDM, in healthcare, and carrying the people from one place to other, etc.

17.3.2   Human Beings vs. Swarm

There is full propagation of our language and our skills. From a simple letter to online elucidation, all the process of communication is now online through internet. Swarm has changed all this. From the past decades, step-by-step rise and even changes in functionality have developed the communication process to a much extent. Now, all the different functionalities are assembled and can even be found in a single device like mobile phones also.

Now, these smart phones contain a collection of the devices in a biological and innate way that we can relate from Swarm (which is also a group of entities or agents). Many types of barriers are also removed by a technology called unPad bestowed by a wireless research center called Berkeley. UnPad is also the collection of the devices which faced many challenges, but now, a full proof technology is there to work on. This technology is so advance that it can enable human to become much advanced and work faster than our five senses too (Figure 17.6).

17.3.3   Use of Swarms in Engineering

Robots are used based on the swarm approaches as well as techniques. Robots are set according to some guidelines so that they can work together in a group. Some of the mathematical

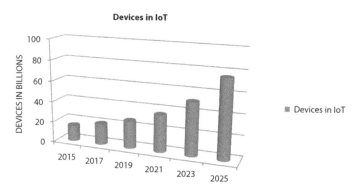

Figure 17.6 Number of devices use in near future representation by graph [12].

models are also made in engineering so as to meet the requirement of the swarm's related robots. Basically, swarms are used in Engineering so that a specific goal can be achieved using different approaches and algorithms based on swarms like ACO, etc. Kazadi is the one who is responsible for the formal research in this engineering in the year 2000 and gave some simple definitions about the Swarm Engineering. He also provided some different models so as to take the Swarm Engineering forward in the field.

Traditional schemes used in engineering are much complex and even not easy to solve, and different commands are given so as to solve a single problem. But, nowadays bottom-up schemes are in use in which the simple information leads to global acceptance and entities are ignored. Beni made an application based on robots in which the concept of cellular robotic system is used. In the system of cellular robots which are placed near to each other, they can communicate and pass the information further to accomplish different tasks. For solving simple problems, Brook put for this approach in which common robots are used which performs simple tasks.

Some advantages of using Swarm in Engineering are as follows:

1. Many of the robots are used in the group; hence, even if one of the robots fail to work, then other robots can work together to achieve the target, hence more reliable operation takes place.
2. Without any reprogramming, robots can be attached to the group or even removed from the group.
3. Design is simple; hence, less hardware is needed.
4. No leader is required in this process.

17.4   Innovations Based on Swarm Intelligence

For the process of getting the information from of any image or to improve a type of image, an approach called unmixing is used. For resolving some of the problem of mixing pixels, a model called LMM (Linear Mixing Model) is used. In this model, the linear members are arranged in a spectrum which is denoted by the equation:

$$x = v + Tc$$

where
x = the mixture of different elements.
v = the error in the model which are to be deleted.
$T = [t_1, t_2, t_3 \ldots\ldots\ldots\ldots t_p]$ also called the end member matrix.
$c = [c_1, c_2, c_3 \ldots\ldots\ldots\ldots\ldots c_p]$, $p*1$ order matrix in a non-negative coercion and subject to the sum of only one coercion.

Swarm Intelligence in preferred in these methods due to its self-organized structure. Now, the algorithm and certain approaches are also made on the ant example that we have already studied and also on different optimizations such as ACO and PSO (Particle Swarm Optimizations). These all algorithms are based on pixels using LMM.

According to a study, it is found that rather than ancient studies, the modern studies which include algorithms will give much profound results. Two approaches are given below:

1. Authentic approach based on pixels: We know that image is made up of small or tiny elements also known as pixels or picture elements. The combination of these picture elements should contain lowest amount of RMS error (Root Mean Square) so that an appropriate model can be made. Equation for its LMM is given as follows:

$$RMSE\left(\{x_i\}_{i=1}^n, \{m_j\}_{j=1}^p\right) = \frac{1}{n}\sum_{i=1}^n \sqrt{\frac{1}{B}\|x_i - \hat{x}_i\|_2^2}$$

where $\{x_i\}_{i=1}^n$ is the spectrum of picture elements; $\{n_i\}_{j=1}^p$ is the last element; $\hat{x}_i = \sum_{j=1}^p a_{ij} n_j$, i = 1, 2,........, r; here, $\hat{x}_i$ is the rth mixture of picture elements in LMM.

At the last, the conclusions can be drawn using PSO and ACO.

2. Merest approach based on volume: There are many drawbacks of approach based on pixels as due to RMS error; it does not confirm about the authentic pixels. Hence, to remove this, we must take into consideration the small amount of volume also so the equation for merest approach based on volume's equation will be like:

$$F(T) = RMSE\left(\{xi\}_{i=1}^n, T\right) + \mu V(T)$$

Here,

V (T) is the last element.

μ is the coefficient of penalty.

The term $RMSE\left(\{x_i\}_{i=1}^n, T\right)$ is the error.

ABC is a type of approach that is based on volume.

17.4.1   Fault Tolerance in IoT

We know that many different devices such as smart phone, speakers, sensors, robots, plugs and switches, universal remotes, etc., are used in IoT. But, this device can suffer with any type of faults like breakage between different wires, a type of processor fault, damage of some crucial parts of devices, and even the loss of data due to this type of faults. So, to protect your data from such type of faults, we need to be concerned about fault tolerance, and hence, its routing becomes important task to be done for cyber-security.

A different approach is used to tolerate different types of faults, which is known as IEIFTA which is widely used and can be improved also to remove all the types of fault that occur and even boost the efficiency by utilizing only a little amount of power (Figure 17.7).

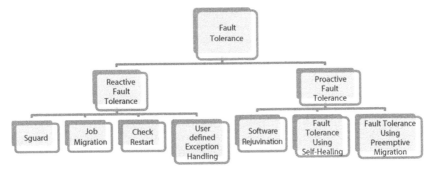

Figure 17.7 Type of fault tolerance and its characteristics [15].

17.5   Energy-Based Model

We know that energy get exhausted if it is carried to large distances; hence, if the distance is short than energy can be carried easily without any losses [15]. Equation for the amount of the energy which is engrossed in receiving the data of around 1 bit is given by:

$$E_R(j, d) = E_{CIRCUIT} * j$$

The equation for the energy which is engrossed in passing on the data of 1 bit up to d distance:

$$E_T(j,d) = \begin{cases} E_{CIRCUIT} * j + \varepsilon_{fs} * j * d^2, & d < d_0 \\ E_{CIRCUIT} * j + \varepsilon_{ma} * j * d^4, & d \geq d_0 \end{cases}$$

where
$E_{CIRCUIT}$ is the energy which is engrossed from the sender to accepting circuit.
Constant is the d_0 which depends upon the surroundings.
ε_{ma} is multiple debilitation models.
ε_{fs} is free space model amplifier energy engrossed.

17.5.1   Basic Approach of Fault Tolerance With Its Network Architecture

Some sensors and actuators are present in the networking architecture of the IoT. These sensors transfer the received data into useful information. The work of the actuators is to manage the phenomenal condition so that data is not lost and information can be received easily. All the work has to be done in digital (0 and1) format; hence, the data is converted from analog to digital signals through Data Acquisition Systems (DSA). Then, this data goes for further processing to the edge systems for the analysis of the information (Figure 17.8).

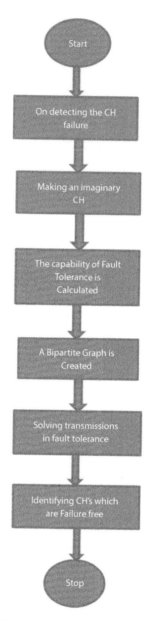

Figure 17.8 Network architecture of fault tolerance [15].

The nodes of the sensor commit to become a bundle which is known as Cluster Head (CH). But, in this bundle, the nodes are not evenly distributed, and hence, the energy of the bundle is more at one place and less at another. To remove this type of the error, we generally use a hierarchical model. Generally, three-level architecture is used which divide this bundle into different categories:

1. A common CH node;
2. Base Station Cluster (BSC) Head;
3. Base Station (BS);
4. Common Sensor Node (CS).

17.5.2   Problem of Fault Tolerance Using Different Algorithms

EARQ and SPSOA are the different approaches to solve the problem of fault tolerance but the most commonly used approach is IEIFTA (Figure 17.9). IEIFTA is majorly used because of its simplicity, efficiency, and reliability. All the critical conditions can be resolved using IEIFTA. There are not much losses and even information can be transferred easily to a long distance without any disturbance.

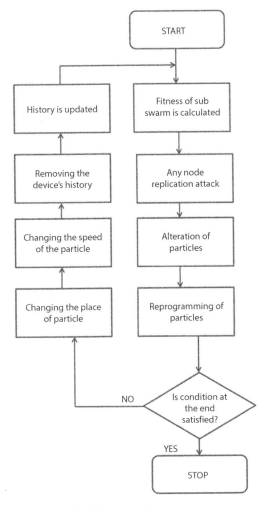

Figure 17.9 Flowchart representation of IEIFTA network [7].

The explanation of the flowchart can be given as follows (Figure 17.10):

1. START: Different targets are set in IEIFTA and λ are the number of particles in the swarm. In swarm, every particle includes λ/n number of particles.
   Here, n is the size of the population.
   A vector which is of D-dimension is also taken into account.
2. NEW FITNESS: calculation of fitness is done as follows:

$$NF[p_i(s,r)] = \frac{\sum_{n \in p_i(s,r)} energy(n)}{\xi_1 f_1 + \xi_2 f_2 + \xi_3 f_3 + 1}$$

Here,

NF = New fitness

f_1 is the distance between the edges of sub-tree vs. the distance between the
edges of path.

$$f_2 = \frac{by\ edges\ of\ the\ path\ the\ amount\ of\ the\ energy\ consumed}{by\ edges\ of\ the\ subtree\ the\ consumed\ amount\ of\ energy}$$

$\xi_1 + \xi_2 + \xi_3 = 1$. Here, ξ_3, ξ_2, ξ_1 is the distance coefficient's weight.

The more suitable path is achieved by higher fitness value.

3. NODE REPLICATION ATTACK:
   Particle's fitness α replication number
   We can get the number of replication or clone as follows:

$$N_C = \gamma N$$

where γ stands for the factor of clone.
N = amount of particles present.

4. Condition of termination (end)
   If the condition is satisfied, then the process will be stopped or rather it
   continues and changes the position, speed, as well as the history of particle;
   again, the same procedure is repeated [10]. The number of iterations that are
   used for the process to reach the end condition is given by $T_{ITERATION}$. Number
   of path increases if the condition is not satisfied.

5. Process of changing speed and position:
   The updated speed as well as position can be found using these equations:

$$x_{id}^{t+1} = x_{id}^{t} + V_{id}^{t+1}$$

$$V_{id}^{t+1} = \omega V_{id}^{t} C_1 U_1 \left(P_{gd}^{t} - x_{id}^{t} \right) + C_2 U_2 \left(P_{id}^{t} - x_{id}^{t} \right)$$

U_1, U_2 are the factors which are distributed in an unordered way lie among 0 to 1. ω is the weight of inertia. C_1 and C_2 = 1.5 are also called learning factors. As we have already talked about the ants, they also update their speed as well as position like given in the above equation [22].

6. Finally, fitness of the path:
    Depending upon the number of iterations, an optimal path is chosen and the same procedure again and again takes place.

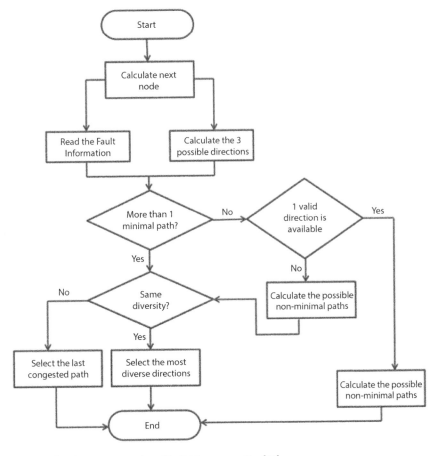

Figure 17.10 Flowchart representation of fault tolerance routing [22].

17.6   Conclusion

Nowadays, swarm and Swarm Intelligence have wide a application; hence, they are in frequent uses. Many of the complex problems can be solved using Swarm Intelligence. For making the process of IoT more efficient and reliable, we are using different algorithms such as ACO for the optimization process. Many of the applications based on IoT and Swarm Intelligence are also included. Fault tolerance, a process which is used to clear the entire fault in IoT devices, is elaborated with some algorithm such as IEIFTA which is promising of lowering the use of energy and to improve the quality of information which is to be carried from sender to receiver. In many of the different and critical condition, IEIFTA makes a favorable solution.

References

1. Zhang, B., Gao, L., Sun, X., Zhuang, L., Swarm intelligence: A reliable solution for extracting endmembers from hyperspectral imagery. *2015 7th Workshop on Hyperspectral Image and Signal Processing: Evolution in Remote Sensing (WHISPERS)*, Tokyo, pp. 1–4, 2015.
2. Zhu, Y.-f. and Tang, X.-m., Overview of swarm intelligence. *2010 International Conference on Computer Application and System Modeling (ICCASM 2010)*, Taiyuan, pp. V9-400-V9-403, 2010.
3. Willcox, G. and Rosenberg, L., Short Paper: Swarm Intelligence Amplifies the IQ of Collaborating Teams. *2019 Second International Conference on Artificial Intelligence for Industries (AI4I)*, Laguna Hills, CA, USA, pp. 111–114, 2019.
4. Wang, P., Huang, S., Zhu, Z., Swarm Intelligence Algorithms for Circles Packing Problem with Equilibrium Constraints. *2013 12th International Symposium on Distributed Computing and Applications to Business, Engineering & Science, Kingston upon Thames*, Surrey, UK, pp. 55–60, 2013.
5. Rosenberg, L., Lungren, M., Halabi, S., Willcox, G., Baltaxe, D., Lyons, M., Artificial Swarm Intelligence employed to Amplify Diagnostic Accuracy in Radiology. *2018 IEEE 9th Annual Information Technology, Electronics and Mobile Communication Conference (IEMCON)*, Vancouver, BC, pp. 1186–1191, 2018.
6. Rosenberg, L., Baltaxe, D., Pescetelli, N., Crowds vs swarms, a comparison of intelligence. *2016 Swarm/Human Blended Intelligence Workshop (SHBI)*, Cleveland, OH, pp. 1–4, 2016.
7. Ritthipakdee, A. and Thammano, A., Primate swarm algorithm for continuous optimization problems. *2017 18th IEEE/ACIS International Conference on Software Engineering, Artificial Intelligence, Networking and Parallel/Distributed Computing (SNPD)*, Kanazawa, pp. 11–15, 2017.
8. Rabaey, J.M., The human intranet — Where swarms and humans meet. *2015 Design, Automation & Test in Europe Conference & Exhibition (DATE)*, Grenoble, pp. 637–640, 2015.
9. Liu, W., Han, Y., Qin, Y., Huangfu, W., Ren, Y., Dong, J., Quaternion-Based Particle Swarm Optimization to Improve Cellular IoT Network Coverage. *2019 IEEE 19th International Conference on Communication Technology (ICCT)*, Xi'an, China, pp. 330–335, 2019.
10. Kirschenbaum, M. and Palmer, D.W., Perceptualization of particle swarm optimization. *2015 Swarm/Human Blended Intelligence Workshop (SHBI)*, Cleveland, OH, pp. 1–5, 2015.
11. Hardin, C.T. and Usher, J.S., Facility layout using swarm intelligence. *Proceedings 2005 IEEE Swarm Intelligence Symposium, 2005*, SIS 2005, Pasadena, CA, USA, pp. 424–427, 2005.

12. Chakraborty, T. and Datta, S.K., Application of swarm intelligence in Internet of Things. *2017 IEEE International Symposium on Consumer Electronics (ISCE)*, Kuala Lumpur, pp. 67–68, 2017.
13. Affijulla, S. and Chauhan, S., Swarm intelligence solution to large scale thermal power plant Load Dispatch. *2011 International Conference on Emerging Trends in Electrical and Computer Technology*, Nagercoil, pp. 196–199, 2011.
14. Li, T., Fong, S., Li, X., Lu, Z., Gandomi, A.H., Swarm Decision Table and Ensemble Search Methods in Fog Computing Environment: Case of Day-Ahead Prediction of Building Energy Demands Using IoT Sensors. *IEEE Internet Things J.*, 7, 3, 2321–2342, March 2020.
15. Luo, S., Cheng, L., Ren, B., Practical Swarm Optimization basedFault-Tolerance Algorithm for the Internet of Things. *KSII Trans. Internet Inf. Syst.*, 8, 3, 1178–1191, 2014.
16. Kordon, A., Swarm Intelligence: The Benefits of Swarms, Applying Computational Intelligence, chapter 06, pp. 145–174, Springer-Verlag Berlin Heidelberg 2010. 10.1007/978-3-540-69913-2_6.
17. Wanka, R., Swarm intelligence. *it – Inf. Technol.*, 61, 4, 157–158, 2019.
18. Raina, S., Swarm Intelligence, *Proceeding in RAMST National Conference Souvenir*, vol. 1, pp. 68–70, 2019.
19. Saggu, A., Yadav, P., Roopak, M., Applications of Swarm Intelligence. *IJCSMC*, 2, 5, 353–359, May 2013.
20. Ahmed, H. and Glasgow, J., "Swarm Intelligence: Concepts, Models and Applications," Queen's University, School of Computing Technical Reports At: Kingston, Canada Volume: Technical Report 2012-585.
21. Garnier, S., Gautrais, J., Theraulaz, G., The biological principles of swarm intelligence. *Swarm Intell.*, 1, 3–31, 2007.
22. Zedadraa, O., Guerrierib, A., Jouandeauc, N., Spezzanob, G., Seridia, H., Fortinodb, G., Swarm intelligence-based algorithms within IoT-based systems: A review. *J. Parallel Distrib. Comput.*, 122, 173–187, December 2018.

18

Smart Epilepsy Detection System Using Hybrid ANN-PSO Network

Jagriti Saini[1*] and Maitreyee Dutta[2]

[1]NITTTR Chandigarh, Chandigarh, India
[2]ICSE Department, NITTTR Chandigarh, Chandigarh, India

Abstract

Almost 65 million people are suffering from this disease throughout the world, and like many other neurological disorders, the most commonly used method for epilepsy detection is electroencephalogram. However, electroencephalogram signals are nonstationary and nonlinear in nature, so it becomes quite difficult for medical doctors to interpret details about the significant data. It is important to design a smart system by combining Internet of Things–based network with Artificial Intelligence to sense the disease conditions with more accuracy. In this work, an Artificial Neural Network–based design is proposed for automatic detection of epileptic signals from an electroencephalogram dataset obtained from Bonn University, Germany, which contains observations from the healthy and epileptic brain. The performance is further improved using swarm intelligence with Particle Swarm Optimization. Results of hybrid detection system were evaluated on the basis of four major parameters: classification accuracy (98.67%), specificity (98.7%), sensitivity (98.67%), and precision (98.7%).

Keywords: Epilepsy, electroencephalogram, mean square error, particle swarm optimization, Internet of Things, swarm intelligence, particle swarm intelligence, expert system

18.1 Introduction

The human brain is a highly complex system having rich spatiotemporal dynamics and millions of neurons. Epilepsy is a chronic neurological disease that affects 1% population in the whole world, leading to sudden unexpected electrical disturbances in the brain wiring. These seizures are generally marked with the temporary impairments of consciousness, memory, speech, perception, or motricity. The impact of seizure often varies from patient to patient with a variable frequency, duration, and level of impairment. These epileptic seizures are more common among children and adults. Studies reveal that, for most of the sufferers, these seizures may often go unnoticed, whereas in other cases, patients confuse them with other neurological events such as strokes. Out of the

[*]Corresponding author: jagritis1327@gmail.com

Abhishek Kumar, Pramod Singh Rathore, Vicente Garrcia Diaz and Rashmi Agrawal (eds.) Swarm Intelligence Optimization: Algorithms and Applications, (343–358) © 2021 Scrivener Publishing LLC. ISBN 978-1-119-77874-5

65 million epileptic patients throughout the world, 30% are not able to avail right treatment due to unpredictable causes of seizures, lack of information, or due to inappropriate diagnosis procedures [1]. An in-depth literature review is required to develop a deep understanding of epileptic seizures and detection techniques so that valuable diagnosis methods can be identified. An extensive review of already existing methods was already published by Jagriti S and Maitreyee [2]. This study was referred to improve the knowledge base for the proposed system. Among a wide range of imaging techniques available in the medical world for biosignal analysis, EEGs are considered as the most relevant options for analyzing sudden variations in brain activity due to epilepsy disease. The signal from the brain is acquired with the help of electrodes placed on the scalp, and it is read on a computer screen for a specific time duration. Now, as these recorded EEG signals are unstable, nonlinear, complex, and random in nature; therefore, neurologists may find it difficult to interpret the exact information about seizure activity [3]. Since visual inspection of EEG waveforms cannot provide valuable insights for seizure affected brain activity, it becomes essential to develop an automatic system for evaluating this complicated data. Several detection methods have been studied by researchers until now, and the list of most suitable detection procedures includes techniques such as Fourier Transforms [4], Wavelet Transforms [5, 20], Artificial Neural Network [6], Classifiers [7], and Optimization algorithms [8, 21]. Out of all these procedures, ANN is used for proposed study due to its ability to handle non-stationary data with higher efficiency. The ANN is learned by examples, so they are able to respond to seizure-oriented variations in EEG signals.

Most of the things in this technology-inspired world can be controlled using the Internet of Things (IoT). It has major applications in the medical health industry, including disease detection, diagnosis, and assisted living and control mechanisms. The electrode sensing environment for epilepsy disease detection can be also controlled using IoT for efficient data collection. It is possible to save the single channel as well as multi-channel EEG data on specific servers using IoT network. The data can be further accessed using advanced Artificial Intelligence (AI) algorithms to make decisions about disease detection and diagnosis. Furthermore, swarm intelligence provides efficient platform for optimizing the performance of the environment to ensure highly reliable results for disease detection.

The expert system is a common term used to represent an automatic disease detection system in the medical field. In this work, an expert system for epilepsy disease detection is presented. The design is completed with Feedforward Net–based ANN having three layers: an input layer, a hidden layer, and an output layer. The detection task is implemented on the EEG dataset collected from Bonn University, Germany, containing signals from healthy as well as the epileptic brain samples. The very first step for designing an automatic system for epilepsy disease detection is to extract essential features from input EEG data. The relevant set of features is used for training the neural network which learns the behavior of EEG signals obtained from the healthy and unhealthy brain signals. Network performance was further enhanced by designing a hybrid algorithm using smart intelligence. In this work, authors used Particle Swarm Optimization (PSO) to improve detection efficiency of the expert system. This overall design can be applied for real-time epilepsy detection using smart diagnosis approach.

18.2   Materials and Methods

In this work, the design of an expert system for epilepsy disease detection was completed with the help of features extracted from input EEG data. The Artificial Neural Network is used to implement the detection model.

18.2.1   Experimental Data

The experimental EEG database used for the proposed study was provided by the University of Bonn, Germany [9, 21]. This standard source of data contains EEG signals from the healthy brain and epileptic brain. These EEG signals are divided into five different data-sets named as S, N, F, O, and Z; each one of these sets possesses brainwave signals with 23.6-second duration, and 100 segments are present in each section. This experimental data was collected by adjusting sampling frequency to 173.6 Hz; hence, there are 4,097 samples in each set. Data obtained from healthy subjects is represented by set O and Z, where set O represents EEG signals obtained from a healthy patient with eyes open and set Z contains EEG signals of the subject with eyes closed. EEG signals obtained from the epileptic brain are represented by set S, N, and F with different recording conditions. Out of these three sets, dataset S contains EEG signals from the ictal state of the epileptic subject, whereas datasets N and F contain signal from inter-ictal states when electrodes are placed in differ-ent zones of the brain [10]. The proposed design is based on three datasets out of these five; the network is trained for signals carried by datasets F, S, and Z.

18.2.2   Data Pre-Processing

The spectral bandwidth of dataset under consideration ranges between 0.5 and 85 Hz; however, the medical professionals believe that EEG frequencies above 60-Hz frequency range contain noise 2014 and the valuable information lies only within the 0.5- to 60-Hz components. Thus, it is essential to perform filtration of EEG signal at the pre-processing stage so that a noise-free data can be utilized ahead for system expert system development. Considering this fact, the EEG signal filtration task was performed with the help of a de-noising filter having a cut of frequency equal to 60 Hz. There are two different techniques that can be applied at the pre-processing stage to obtain a significant signal component by discarding the noisy ones by either using Finite Impulse Response (FIR) filter and the second choice is Infinite Impulse Response (IIR) filter. The FIR filter is defined by its FIR to the input signal that means it settles to zero within the finite time duration. On the other side, an IIR filter may suffer signal dis-turbances because of internal feedbacks, so its response appears indefinite. The IIR filters are not useful for de-noising EEG dataset because the morphological effect cannot be tolerated for such sensitive medical data. Hence, FIR filter with hamming window technique was applied for de-noising F. S and Z datasets are used for the proposed study. The representation of a few samples of used EEG datasets is shown in Figure 18.1. This FIR low pass filter designed with a passband varying between 0 to 60 Hz, and the de-noising process was completed.

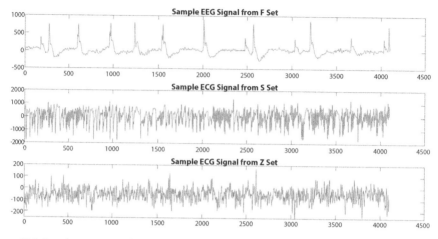

Figure 18.1 Sample EEG signals from dataset under consideration.

18.2.3 Feature Extraction

The performance of prediction model depends on two major considerations; the first one is defined as per features extracted from input EEG signals and the second major role is played by the technique used for the analysis of extracted features. The careful extraction of features helps to reduce losses present in the input EEG signal, and it also helps to determine the number of resources that will be required for the development of an expert system for disease detection.

In the proposed system for epilepsy detection, 15 features are extracted from the three input datasets (F, S, and Z) collected from Bonn University, Germany. The nonlinear behavior of EEG signals is highlighted using a combination of time domain and frequency domain features. In the list of extracted features, Mean, Mode, Standard Deviation, Entropy, Skewness, Energy, Coefficient of Variation, Kurtosis, Variance, and Zero Crossing Rate represent time-domain features of signal strength, whereas Min Amplitude, Max Amplitude, Median, Mean Power, and Signal-to-Noise Ratio are frequency domain features. The mathematical expressions for these features are listed in Table 18.1.

18.2.4 Relevance of Extracted Features

It is quite essential to pick an optimized set of features for analysis to improve the classification accuracy for complex EEG signal. Hence, the relevance of extracted 15 features was evaluated with the help of the Kruskal-Wallis Test. For each group of extracted features from input dataset (F, S, and Z), results of this test were available in the form of Chi-Square value and Significance Parameter (p). It has been observed that high Chi-Square value is mapped with low significance value (p). In order to define the relevance of a feature with reference to the input signal, significance parameter p was desired to be less than 0.05 ($p < 0.05$); hence, features that have Significance value greater than 0.05 were excluded from analysis. Results of the Kruskal-Wallis Test are shown in fourth column of Table 18.1.

Table 18.1 Statistical features obtained from raw data.

Sr. no.	Time domain features	Mathematical modeling	Chi-square value obtained from Kruskal-Wallis Test	p (Significance) obtained from Kruskal-Wallis Test
1.	Mode	$\text{Mode} = L + \dfrac{f_1 - f_0}{(2f_1 - f_0 - f_2)} * h$	55.9	7.26825e-13
2.	Mean	$\text{Mean} = \displaystyle\sum_{i=1}^{n} x/N$	16.73	0.0002
3.	Standard Deviation	$S_x = \sqrt{\dfrac{\sum_{i=1}^{n}(x_i - \overline{x})^2}{n-1}}$	263.1	7.39677e-58
4.	Energy	$E(n) = \dfrac{1}{N}\displaystyle\sum_{n=1}^{N} x(n)^2$	109.94	1.33636e-24
5.	Kurtosis	$\text{Kurt} = \displaystyle\sum \dfrac{(x-\mu)^4}{\sigma^4} - 3$	4.31	0.1159
6.	Skewness	$\text{Skewness} = E\left[\left(\dfrac{x-\mu}{\sigma^3}\right)^3\right]$	0.26	0.8798
7.	Entropy	$En(n) = \displaystyle\sum_{k=n}^{n+N} p(k)\log_2 p(k)$	96.65	1.02902e-21

(Continued)

Table 18.1 Statistical features obtained from raw data. (*Continued*)

Sr. no.	Time domain features	Mathematical modeling	Chi-square value obtained from Kruskal-Wallis Test	p (significance) obtained from Kruskal-Wallis Test
8.	Variance	$\text{Variance}(\sigma^2) = \dfrac{\sum_{i=1}^{n}(x_i - \mu)^2}{N}$	118.58	1.77685e-26
9.	Zero-Crossing Rate (ZCR)	$ZCR = \dfrac{1}{T-1}\displaystyle\sum_{t=1}^{T-1} 1_{R_{<0}}(s_t s_{t-1})$	51.75	5.79538e-12
10.	Coefficient of Variation	$C_v = \sigma/\mu$	42.7	5.33397e-10
Sr. No.	Frequency domain features	Mathematical modelling	Chi-square value obtained from Kruskal-Wallis Test	p (significance) obtained from Kruskal-Wallis Test
1.	Min Amplitude	Min (x)	108.35	2.95859e-24
2.	Max Amplitude	Max (x)	134.11	7.57289e-30
3.	Median	$\text{Median} = 1 + h\left(\dfrac{\frac{n}{f}}{2} - c\right)$	20.01	4.51951e-05
4.	Mean Power	Mean Power = mean (x^2)	109.89	1.3737e-24
5.	SNR	$SNR = \mu/\sigma$	74.41	6.95822e-17

As shown in Table 18.1, significance value of Kurtosis and Skewness was greater than 0.05; thus, both these features were excluded from further analysis. The Artificial Neural Network–based classification system was developed on the basis of the remaining 13 features only. They can ensure better accuracy due to higher relevance [11].

18.3   Proposed Epilepsy Detection System

In order to train the network with the input dataset, first of all, the essential features from raw data are extracted. These features were already discussed in previous sections. Further, the relevance of these features with respect to considered EEG dataset was obtained. Ultimately, 13 features were used for the final implementation of Epilepsy Disease Detection System. As already discussed, EEG waveforms use to be complex in nature, so the features extracted from the raw dataset were distributed in a wide range. Neural Network cannot process data with such highly variable values to the desired accuracy, so all features were normalized to a range between −1 and +1. As 13 unique features were already extracted from all 300 signals based upon time domain and frequency domain parameters, so at this stage, all obtained features were normalized using the mathematical formula of Min-Max Approach. The idea is to fit them in a standard range of −1 and 1.

$$Feature_{norm} = \frac{Feature_{value} - Min_{value}}{(Max_{value} - Min_{value})} \tag{18.1}$$

In Eq. (18.1), $Feature_{norm}$ is the normalized value of the selected feature. $Feature_{value}$, Min_{value}, and Max_{value} represent actual value, minimum, and maximum value of parameter under consideration, respectively.

Feedforward ANN is used to design the proposed classification model for epilepsy disease. As this algorithm is influenced by biological patterns, it can provide more valuable results for classification problems. These networks are designed using three different layers; the first one is input layer that picks up input data from external world, second one is the hidden layer, and the last part of the network is output layer. Note that all these layers have a direct connection to the previous layers. For example, the hidden layer is connected to input layer, and output layer takes data from hidden layer neurons. However, strengths of these layers depend upon the weights assigned to them by user. In order to design proposed model for epilepsy detection, authors have processed 13 features at input stage. These features work like inputs at first layer of the network that is why input layer consists of 13 neurons. The major target of this classification model is to divide the available dataset into three different classes. These classes are healthy, inter-ictal, and ictal epileptic datasets. Hence, the output layer of the model consists of three classes. The network optimization is achieved by varying number of neurons at the hidden layer. The network has been trainedusing feedforward neural network while updating the neurons at hidden layer to achieve best results. After several observations, the best accuracy was achieved with 3, 7, and 31 neurons in the hidden layer. As number of hidden layer neurons have direct relation to the speed of the network, soonly, three neurons were added for final evaluation. The proposed System Architecture for Epilepsy disease detection is shown in Figure 18.2.

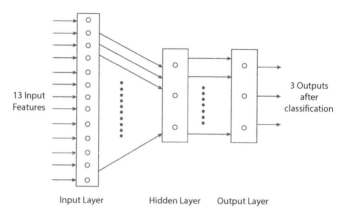

Input Layer   Hidden Layer   Output Layer

Figure 18.2 Proposed ANN model for epilepsy detection.

To enhance the efficiency and effectiveness of the classification accuracy of this expert system, the dataset was divided into three parts: the training set, the testing set, and the validation set. From available 300 samples, 70% of data was kept for training, 15% was used for testing, and rest 15% was used for validation.

18.4 Experimental Results of ANN-Based System

In order to design the proposed Computer-Aided Diagnosis System for epilepsy disease detection, implementation of the Artificial Neural Network was carried with 13 input neurons, 3 hidden layer neurons, and 3 output layer neurons. The normalized features were applied at input terminal and targets were created to define the expected output of the proposed network. MATLAB software was used to train the system with all set parameters, and it provided a network with the structure as shown in Figure 18.3.

Performance of this network was analyzed on the basis of the confusion matrix. The resultant confusion matrix obtained after above feedforward net–based training is shown in Figure 18.4.

Results of proposed work are evaluated in terms of four different parameters; they are accuracy, precision, sensitivity, and specificity. Below, we have highlighted mathematical formulas for each.

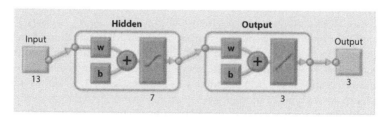

Figure 18.3 ANN structure obtained using feedforward net training.

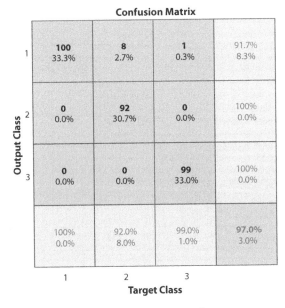

Figure 18.4 Confusion matrix obtained after ANN training on 300 datasets.

$$\text{Accuracy = Sum of correct Classifications / Total Number of Classifications} \quad (18.2)$$

$$\text{Precision = TP / (TP + FP)} \quad (18.3)$$

$$\text{Sensitivity = TP / (TP + FN)} \quad (18.4)$$

$$\text{Specificity = TN / (TN + FP)} \quad (18.5)$$

In above equations, TP = True Positive Predictions, FP = False Positive Predictions, FN = False Negative Predictions, and TN = True Negative Predictions.

Numerical values calculated from this confusion matrix are shown in Table 18.2.

Overall Precision = 97.00%

Overall Sensitivity = 97.23%

Overall Specificity = 97.00%

Overall Accuracy of Proposed Work = 97.0%

18.5   MSE Reduction Using Optimization Techniques

Medical applications deal with highly sensitive data, and one cannot allow errors to affect system performance because it has a direct relation with human life. EEG signals contain complex waveforms, and even for medical experts, they appear difficult to be analyzed. In order to use a CAD system for epilepsy detection in the practicalenvironment, it is desired

Table 18.2 Parameters calculated from the confusion matrix.

Parameter	Formula	Obtained value
Precision for Class A (F Set)	$TP_A / (TP_A + FP_A)$	100%
Precision for Class B (S Set)	$TP_B / (TP_B + FP_B)$	92.0%
Precision for Class C (Z Set)	$TP_C / (TP_C + FP_C)$	99.0%
Sensitivity for Class A (F Set)	$TP_A / (TP_A + FN_A)$	91.7%
Sensitivity for Class B (S Set)	$TP_B / (TP_B + FN_B)$	100%
Sensitivity for Class C (Z Set)	$TP_C / (TP_C + FN_C)$	100%
Specificity for Class A (F Set)	$TN_A / (TN_A + FP_A)$	100%
Specificity for Class B (S Set)	$TN_B / (TN_B + FP_B)$	92.0%
Specificity for Class C (Z Set)	$TN_C / (TN_C + FP_C)$	99.0%

to develop a system that has minimum or negligible chances of error. Although the proposed neural network-based system has already achieved 97.0% accuracy still, there are few chances to improve it further using optimization techniques. In order to improve network performance, three optimization techniques: PSO [12], Genetic Algorithm (GA) [13], and Simulated Annealing (SA) [14, 19] have been applied. They work for the reduction of Mean Square Error obtained from Neural Network–based training.

Performance of these techniques was tested for a variable set of hidden layer neurons of Feedforward Network. The results obtained from these tests are presented in Table 18.3.

Table 18.3 Effect of PSO, GA, and SA on MSE of ANN.

Neurons in hidden layer	MSE obtained from feedforward neural network	Impact of PSO on MSE	Impact of GA on MSE	Impact of SA on MSE
3	6.844e-04	**6.621e-04**	6.700e-04	6.844e-04
7	8.354e-04	**5.979e-04**	8.355e-04	8.355e-04
9	4.089e-04	4.047e-04	**3.637e-04**	4.091e-04
15	1.57e-03	**1.50e-03**	1.56e-03	1.57e-03
20	5.27e-03	**5.15e-03**	5.21e-03	5.32e-03
31	1.31e-03	1.30e-03	1.30e-03	1.31e-03
40	2.34e-03	2.32e-03	**2.30e-03**	2.34e-03
51	2.20e-03	**2.01e-03**	2.16e-03	2.20e-03
62	3.20e-03	**3.11e-03**	3.19e-03	3.20e-03

The table represents optimized values of MSE in comparison to the original values obtained from Artificial Neural Network. The obtained result of SA shows poor performance as compared to all three optimization techniques. On the other side, GA was able to reduce MSE with better performance as compared to SA. Further, the PSO was able to show the best performance among all three techniques. There were few cases when GA was able to reduce MSE value below optimization obtained from PSO but at an average performance of PSO was rated better for different settings of hidden layer neurons.

Due to very minute variations on a compact scale, the performance appears comparatively equal for all techniques, but the deep analysis reveals that PSO delivers minimum value for MSE for most of the cases. Table 18.3 reflects the performance of all optimization techniques and rates PSO as the best option for MSE optimization because it can lead to effective reduction with all settings of hidden layer neurons. The reason behind is that PSO is capable enough to handle multidimensional problem spaces in a much efficient manner with its advanced algorithm. This technique can further help to develop a hybrid system for disease detection while ensuring higher accuracy.

18.6   Hybrid ANN-PSO System for Epilepsy Detection

PSO is widely known as a heuristic optimization algorithm that is controlled by population initialization. This method was first proposed in 1995 by Kennedy and Eberhart. It is basically inspired by the social behavior of the large group of birds flying together to find food. This Swarm Intelligence–based algorithm shares many similarities with other evolutionary computation methods such as GA. The optimization algorithm is initialized using random solutions for population, and it keeps on searching for optima by simply updating generations after each iteration [15].

The algorithm initialization is performed with the help of a random group of particles that are responsible for finding an optimal solution in the search space. After every iteration, the particles are updated based on two parameters: pBest and gBest where first one represents personal best solution for the individual particle, whereas second one defines global best solution achieved by any particle in the population (swarm).

The standard equation for PSO is given as follows:

$$v[] = v[] + c1 * rand() * (pbest[] - present[]) + c2 * rand() * (gbest[] - present[]) \tag{18.6}$$

$$present[] = present[] + v[] \tag{18.7}$$

Here, v[] is defined as particle velocity, present [] is current solution (particle), pbest and gbest are already defined, rand() represents a random number, whereas c1 and c2 are learning factors, usually declared as c1 = c2 = 2.

This evolutionary computation algorithm based on Swarm Intelligence can be applied to neural network by considering three different attributes: network connection weights, network learning algorithms, and network architecture (network topology and network transfer function). In this book chapter, authors have designed a hybrid ANN + PSO system by using optimization algorithm at weight update stage of ANN. The main goal was to improve accuracy of the expert system and to ensure stable results for real-time implementation of the proposed system. The confusion matrix available after applying Swarm Intelligence algorithm is shown in Figure 18.5.

As observed from the confusion matrix, the hybrid ANN + PSO–based epilepsy detection system provides higher accuracy as compared to the basic ANN-based epilepsy detection system designed above. The performance of this hybrid expert system for disease detection can be observed in terms of precision, sensitivity, specificity, and accuracy values given below:

Precision of the hybrid ANN + PSO system = 98.67%
Sensitivity of the hybrid ANN + PSO system = 98.7%
Specificity of the hybrid ANN + PSO system = 98.67%
Accuracy of the hybrid ANN + PSO system = 98.7%

Results obtained from the new system prove that a hybrid system can provide more reliable performance for monitoring, classification, and real-time implementation of the expert system [16]. The performance of this hybrid system is also observed to be stable because the PSO is applied to the weight update stage and it helps to fix the weights of the system to optimized value. With this, it is possible to obtain set accuracy even after every test conducted on the proposed expert system [17, 18].

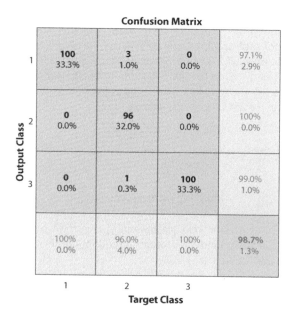

Figure 18.5 Confusion matrix of hybrid ANN + PSO epilepsy detection system.

18.7   Conclusion

The EEG dataset of the epileptic brain is quite difficult to be analyzed due to the wide variation in signal waveforms obtained from the human brain. Although several detection systems have been already developed, the requirement was to design a system that can deliver higher accuracy and can ensure an error-free outcome for disease detection. The computer-aided diagnosis system for epilepsy disease takes EEG data from theepileptic patient and healthy person as input and then classification task is performed on the basis of 13 extracted features that are proven to be most relevant to dataset under consideration. These highly relevant time and frequency domain feature help in the highly accurate detection and classification of disease-affected and healthy EEG signals. As results indicate, the relevant set of features can easily enhance the performance of the network to classify input dataset, and further appropriate selection of hidden layer neurons delivered a practically implementable solution for disease detection.

As epileptic patient uses to live in seizure oriented and seizure-free intervals, so the EEG signals for the current study were taken from both ictal and interictal portions. Both these datasets helped proposed network to work upon deep variations in electrochemical signals of epileptic patients. Generally, EEG signals captured from epileptic brain use to contain complicated structure that is difficult to be analyzed without a digital tool. In order to rate these minute variations in captured data with more accuracy, the relevance of all 13 features was tested using the Kruskal-Wallis test in MATLAB software. The updated feature-based input dataset provided quality performance for disease detection system. The results are analyzed on the basis of sensitivity, specificity, precision, and accuracy. The neurons in hidden layer were updated several times to obtain higher accuracy, and the best results were obtained when three neurons were set at hidden layer. Further, PSO, GA, and SA optimization techniques were utilized to optimize Mean Square Error of the proposed system so that a practically useful system can be obtained.

The proposed swarm intelligence–based smart computer–aided diagnosis system provides 98.7% accuracy for detection of EEG signals that are collected from the healthy as well as an epileptic patient. The proposed hybrid system provides considerable accuracy so that system can be implemented in practical applications associated with the medical world. It is possible to combine this advanced expert system with the IoT sensor network to design a fully automatic machine for medical health world. The combination of IoT and Swarm Intelligence can provide a solid solution for patient monitoring system that can be installed at hospital and care centers as well. These automatic epilepsy monitoring and detection systems can help neurologists to take adequate decisions for treatment before it is too late. At the same time, the caregivers can ensure continues updates about the disease condition and any possible deterioration in patient health. The performance of the network can be further increased by using classifiers-based techniques.

References

1. Asha, A.S., Sudalaiman, C., Devanand, P., Elizabeth, T.T., Sudhamony, S., Automated seizure detection from multichannel EEG signals using support vector machine and artificial neural networks. *Proceedings of International MultiConference on Automation, computing, communication, control and compressed sensing (iMac4s)*, IEEE Publishers, Kottayam, Kerala, India, 2013.
2. Avneet, K. and Supreet, K., Spike-based epilepsy detection algorithm from an EEG signal. *Int. J. Sci. Res.*, 5, 75–78, 2016.
3. Gamze, C.D., Ozdemir, C., Mehmet, B.C., The detection of Normal and Epileptic EEG Signals using ANN Methods withMatlab based GUI. *Int. J. Comput. Appl.*, 114, 45–50, 2015.
4. Inger, L., Simulated Annealing: practice versus theory. *J. Math. Comput. Model.*, 18, 29–57, 1993.
5. Jagriti, S. and Maitreyee, D., An extensive review on development of EEG-based computer-aided diagnosis systems for epilepsy detection. *Netw.: Comput. Neural Syst.*, 28, 1, 1–27, 2017a.
6. Jagriti, S. and Maitreyee, D., Epilepsy disease detection using artificial neural network and performance improvement using PSO and GA. *Int. J. Electr. Electron. Data Commun.*, 5, 9, 18–21, 2017b.
7. Jagriti, S. and Maitreyee, D., Epilepsy disease detection using artificial neural network and MSE Optimization with GA. *Int. J. Innov. Res. Sci. Eng. Technol.*, 6, 7, 13977–13981, 2017c.
8. Kshirsagar, P. and Akojwar, S., Optimization of BPNN parameters using PSO for EEG signals. *Adv. Intell. Syst. Res.*, 137, 385–394, 2016.
9. Meenakshi, R., Singh, K., Singh, A.K., Frequency analysis of healthy and epileptic seizure in EEG using fast Fourier transform. *Int. J. Eng. Res. Gen. Sci.*, 2, 683–69, 2014.
10. Meenakshi, S. and Sunil, V.B., Design and development of prediction model to detect seizure activity utilizing higher order statistical features of EEG signals. *Res. J. Pharm. Biol. Chem. Sci.*, 5, 3, 1129–1145, 2014.
11. Mijanur, M.R. and Tania, A.S., An Implementation for Combining Neural Networks and Genetic Algorithms. *Int. J. Comput. Sci. Technol.*, 6, 3, 218–222, 2015.
12. Mousavi, S.R., Niknazar, M., Vosoughi, V.B., Epileptic seizure detection using AR model on EEG signals. *Proceedings of Cairo International Biomedical Engineering Conference (CIBEC)*, IEEE Publishers, Cairo, Egypt, 2008.
13. Nesibe, Y., Gulay, T., Cihan, K., Epilepsy diagnosis using artificial neural network learned by PSO. *Turk. J. Electr. Eng. Comput. Sci.*, 23, 421–432, 2015.
14. Pradipta, D.K., Ayeskanta, M., Mohit, P.R., Epilepsy disorder detection from EEG signal. *Int. J. Intell. Comput. Appl. Sci.*, 1, 1, 41–49, 2013.
15. Saadat, N. and Hossein, P., A novel real-time patient specific seizure diagnosis algorithm based on analysis of EEG and ECG signals using spectral and spatial features and improved particle swarm optimization classifier. *ACM J. Comput. Biol. Med.*, 42, 8, 848–856, 2012.
16. Sema, A., Gulay, T., Hakan, I., EEG Signals Classification Using Hybrid Structure of ANN and PSO. *Int. J. Future Comput. Commun.*, 1, 170–172, 2012.
17. Shubhashree, S. and Mukta, D., Prediction of Epileptic Seizure: A Review. *IOSR J. Comput. Eng.*, 18, 2, 28–30, 2016.
18. Sobri, K. and Rahmi, M.C., Classifying epilepsy disease using artificial neural networks and genetic algorithm. *J. Med. Syst.*, 35, 489–498, 2011.
19. Vasios, C.E., Matsopoulos, G.K., Nikita, K.S., Uzunoglu, N., Classification of event-related potentials using multivariate autoregressive modelling combined with simulated annealing. *J. Autom. Control University of Belgrade*, 13, 1, 7–11, 2003.

20. Vivek, N.P. and Danial, G., A Neural-Network-Based Detection of Epilepsy. *J. Prog. Neurosurg. Neurol. Neurosci.*, 26, 55–60, 2013.
21. Yoedong, S. and Pietro, L., A new approach for epileptic seizure detection: sample entropy based feature extraction and extreme learning machine. *J. Biomed. Sci. Eng.*, 3, 556–567, 2010.
22. Zainab, H., Yanquing, Z., Hamid, Z.S., Semi-automatic epilepsy spike detection from EEG signal using Genetic Algorithm and Wavelet Transform. *Proceedings of International Conference on Bioinformatics and Biomedicine Workshops (BIBMW)*, Georgia, USA, IEEE Publishers, 2011.

Index

Printed and bound by CPI Group (UK) Ltd, Croydon, CR0 4YY